ISBN 978-1-5281-1619-0
PIBN 10906541

This book is a reproduction of an important historical work. Forgotten Books uses
state-of-the-art technology to digitally reconstruct the work, preserving the original format
whilst repairing imperfections present in the aged copy. In rare cases, an imperfection in
the original, such as a blemish or missing page, may be replicated in our edition. We do,
however, repair the vast majority of imperfections successfully; any imperfections that
remain are intentionally left to preserve the state of such historical works.

1 MONTH OF
FREE
READING

at
www.ForgottenBooks.com

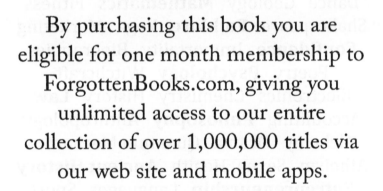

By purchasing this book you are eligible for one month membership to ForgottenBooks.com, giving you unlimited access to our entire collection of over 1,000,000 titles via our web site and mobile apps.

To claim your free month visit:
www.forgottenbooks.com/free906541

English
Français
Deutsche
Italiano
Español
Português

www.forgottenbooks.com

Mythology Photography **Fiction**
Fishing Christianity **Art** Cooking
Essays Buddhism Freemasonry
Medicine **Biology** Music **Ancient**
Egypt Evolution Carpentry Physics
Dance Geology **Mathematics** Fitness
Shakespeare **Folklore** Yoga Marketing
Confidence Immortality Biographies
Poetry **Psychology** Witchcraft
Electronics Chemistry History **Law**
Accounting **Philosophy** Anthropology
Alchemy Drama Quantum Mechanics
Atheism Sexual Health **Ancient History**
Entrepreneurship Languages Sport
Paleontology Needlework Islam
Metaphysics Investment Archaeology
Parenting Statistics Criminology
Motivational

U. S. FOREST SERVICE

Pacific North West Research Note

FOREST AND RANGE EXPERIMENT STATION · U.S. DEPARTMENT OF AGRICULTURE · PORTLAND, OREGON

PNW-1   January 1963

A CASE HISTORY OF A MUD AND ROCK SLIDE

ON AN EXPERIMENTAL WATERSHED

by

R. L. Fredriksen

On December 19, 1961, almost 3,000 feet of creekbed in experimental watershed 3 on the H. J. Andrews Experimental Forest near Blue River, Oreg., was scoured to bedrock by a tumbling, churning mass of mud, rocks, and logs. Five thousand cubic yards of this debris accumulated in two log jams in the main channel. Another 100 cubic yards of sand, silt, and gravel were washed on downstream and almost filled a small catchment basin which had collected only 57 cubic yards since 1956.

Slides like this are not uncommon in the forested mountains of western Oregon and Washington, but seldom does one occur on an experimental watershed where it can be measured. While there were no witnesses, it is possible to reconstruct what happened with some certainty. Three elements were involved: (1) a steep and unstable soil mantle evidenced by characteristic slump topography, (2) a logging road constructed across the watershed in 1959 but allowed to lie idle until logging began in 1962, and (3) a sequence of snow and rainstorms which thoroughly wet the soil.

During the early morning hours of December 19, several inches of wet snow fell on a modest snowpack remaining from previous storms. Rain followed and, together with melting snow, evidently wet the soil to a level not reached since road construction. Shortly before the storm peaked, about 30 cubic yards of material below a short section of the logging road slumped into a tributary of the main creek. This material

Figure 1.--Debris dam left in the stream channel by the slide.

Figure 2.--Stream channel scoured to bedrock by the slide (looking downstream).

created a short-lived dam which, when breached, triggered a massive flow of mud, rock, and logs. More debris was picked up as the flow moved down the channel, plucking whole down trees from the side slopes of the drainage. For almost 3,000 feet, the channel was scoured to bedrock leaving behind isolated gravel deposits, small log jams, and two large debris dams (figs. 1 and 2). About 1 acre of mineral soil was exposed along the margin of the stream channel.

The accompanying chart traces some of the events occurring during the storm. As a result of rain on snow, streamflow rose rapidly to about 37 cubic feet per second (c.f.s.). At this stage, a surge of water, carrying silt, sand, and gravel, passed through the gage where streamflow is measured. The stream reached a peak discharge of over 50 c.f.s. and then settled down to some minor fluctuations, probably associated with the shifting and settling of the debris dams.

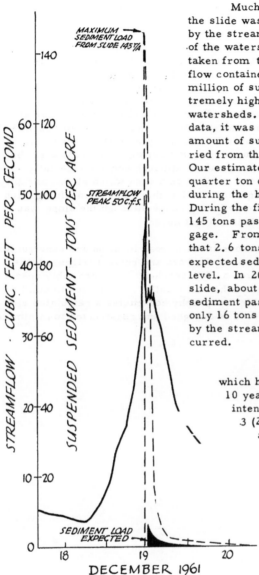

STREAMFLOW · CUBIC FEET PER SECOND

SUSPENDED SEDIMENT – TONS PER ACRE

MAXIMUM SEDIMENT LOAD FROM SLIDE 145 T/A

STREAMFLOW PEAK 50 c.f.s.

SEDIMENT LOAD EXPECTED

18   19   20

DECEMBER 1961

Much of the soil loosened by the slide was carried in suspension by the stream and moved rapidly out of the watershed. Samples of water taken from the stream near peak flow contained over 6,000 parts per million of suspended sediment-- extremely high for these forested watersheds. From these and other data, it was possible to estimate the amount of suspended sediment carried from the watershed each hour. Our estimate showed that about one-quarter ton of sediment was lost during the hour before the slide. During the first hour after the slide, 145 tons passed through the stream gage. From past records we know that 2.6 tons per hour would be the expected sediment load at this water level. In 20 hours following the slide, about 260 tons of suspended sediment passed the gaging station; only 16 tons would have been carried by the stream had the slide not occurred.

This is the only slide which has occurred in the past 10 years during which we have intensively studied watershed 3 (250 acres) along with two adjacent watersheds (149 and 237 acres). There is, however, abundant evidence of old slides in deep deposits of colluvium near the mouth of the streams. The presence of old log jams indicates that slides, such as the one described, have been a natural occurrence in these watersheds during the last few decades.

The true cause of this slide is not known. From evidence on the ground, there is little doubt about the instability of the area. It is reasonable to assume that a natural slide might have occurred even without the presence of the roadbed. The unstable condition of the ground at the head of this tributary was recognized during road reconnaissance, and a location was chosen to avoid the more active slump areas. In both design and construction, roads were "full benched," and soil removed was pushed several hundred feet to make a fill at the head of the creek. No soil was deliberately side cast over the slope on which the slide originated, although some accidentally spilled over the edge of the roadbed on a bank which sloped abruptly to the creekbed. A culvert installed at this point for draining ditch water may have been a contributing cause although the slope was protected in part with a half-culvert apron.

In spite of precautions taken in road location and construction, it appears that the presence of the road and culvert triggered this mass soil movement. Even a "full benched" road inevitably upsets the balance of forces within the soil mantle. A decision to build a road in an area of unstable topography constitutes a calculated risk no matter how well the road is designed and constructed to minimize damage.

U. S. FOREST SERVICE

Pacific
North
West
Research Note

FOREST AND RANGE EXPERIMENT STATION · U.S. DEPARTMENT OF AGRICULTURE · PORTLAND, OREGON

PNW-2   May 1963

BOARD-FOOT TREE VOLUME EQUATIONS

FOR

ELECTRONIC COMPUTERS

by

Floyd A. Johnson

Now that electronic computers are taking over the job of processing timber cruise data, tree volume tables are being replaced by equations.

Tables can be used in electronic data processing, but they are unwieldy and they often consume too much of a computer's capacity.

Of the six equations presented in this report, two (equations 3 and 6) have been used for several years by three Federal agencies in the Pacific Northwest (Forest Service, Bureau of Land Management, Bureau of Indian Affairs) for their extensive, allowable cut surveys. Equations 1, 2, 4, and 5, which are all based on the International rule, were developed very recently for use by these agencies.

The six equations offered here are for the benefit of any other agency that might find them useful and also for the benefit of anyone interested in allowable cuts as estimated for public forests.

These equations cover all coniferous species in the Pacific Northwest. They are based on Bruce's[1] adaptation of Behre's[2] expression for tree taper. Bruce[1] invented the basic procedure for developing the equations, but he published only one of them (equation 3A below). His concern was obviously with volume tables rather than with volume equations.

Attention is directed to the verbal sections of three publications by Bruce and Girard.[3] Underlying assumptions and fundamental details of procedure for developing the equations are given in these sections. Additional details of procedure appropriate to each equation are given in the final section of this report.

All six equations require the same three tree measurements: diameter at breast height, Girard 16-foot form class, and total height from stump to tip.

The following key will assist in selecting an appropriate equation.

---

[1] Bruce, Donald, and Girard, James W. Tables for estimating board foot volume of trees scaled in 16 foot logs based on diameter form class and total height. 46 pp. Portland, Oreg.: Mason, Bruce & Girard. [n. d.]

[2] Behre, C. Edward. Form-class taper curves and volume tables and their application. Jour. Agr. Res. 35: 673-744, illus. 1927.

[3] Girard, James W., and Bruce, Donald. Tables for estimating board foot volume of trees in 16 foot logs. 44 pp., illus. Portland, Oreg.: Mason, Bruce & Girard. [n. d.]

Girard, James W., and Bruce, Donald. Tables for estimating board foot volume of trees in 32 foot logs. 40 pp., illus. Portland, Oreg.: Mason, Bruce & Girard. [n. d.]

See also footnote 1.

Key to the Equations

Specification	Equation number					
	1	2	3	4	5	6
International 1/8-inch log rule	X			X		
International 1/4-inch log rule		X			X	
Formula Scribner rule[4]			X			X
Top diameter, 5 inches	X	X				
Top diameter, one-half of the diameter at top of first 16-foot log but not less than 8 inches			X	X	X	X
16-foot scaling length for logs	X	X	X	X	X	
32-foot scaling length for logs						X
0.3-foot trim allowance per log	X	X	X	X	X	
0.6-foot trim allowance per log						X

---

[4] Staebler, George R. The formula Scribner log rule. U.S. Forest Serv. Pac. NW. Forest & Range Expt. Sta. Res. Note 78, 6 pp. 1952.

Special attention is directed to equation 6. The 16-foot form class is used for this equation even though the scaling length for logs is 32 feet.

Glossary of Symbols

d_i = diameter inside bark in inches at the top of the ith log in a tree

d_u = diameter inside bark in inches at the upper limit of merchantability (i.e., at the top of the top log)

d_o = diameter outside bark in inches at breast height (4.5 feet)

G = Girard form class (d_1/d_o)

H = total height of tree in feet from stump to tip

N = number of 16-foot logs in a tree

D_i = d_i/d_1 = diameter at top of the ith 16-foot log divided by diameter at top of first log

D_u = d_u/d_1

L_i = distance from tip of tree to top of ith 16-foot log divided by the distance from tip to top of first log

L_u = distance from tip of tree to top of top log divided by the distance from tip to top of first log

k = log position (i.e., $k = 2$ indicates second log from bottom and $k = N$ indicates the top log)

v_i = volume of ith log as calculated under the specifications of a particular equation

V_j = volume of a tree as calculated under the specifications of the jth equation

f = Bruce's factor for calculating tree volumes based on total height when d_1 is less than 16 inches

a_1, a_2, b_1, b_2, c_2, a_3, b_3, and c_3 = constants

-4-

Equation 1

$$V_1 = 0.0363(Gd_o)^2 + 1.0955(Gd_o) - 2.0259$$
$$+ \left[0.02437(Gd_o)^2 - 0.0574(Gd_o) - 0.1306\right] H$$

Unit of measure---------------------------- Board foot
Log rule------------------------------------ International
                                              1/8-inch
Top diameter (d_u) ---------------------- 5.0 inches
Stump height------------------------------- Local practice
Trim allowance per log -------------------- 0.3 foot
Scaling length of logs -------------------- 16 feet

Equation 2

$$V_2 = 0.0328(Gd_o)^2 + 0.9912(Gd_o) - 1.8330$$
$$+ \left[0.02205(Gd_o)^2 - 0.0519(Gd_o) - 0.1182\right] H$$

Unit of measure --------------------------- Board foot
Log rule------------------------------------ International
                                              1/4-inch
Top diameter (d_u) ---------------------- 5.0 inches
Stump height ------------------------------ Local practice
Trim allowance per log -------------------- 0.3 foot
Scaling length of logs -------------------- 16 feet

Equations 3A and 3B

$Gd_o \geq 16$

$$V_{3A} = \left[0.02032(Gd_o)^2 - 0.0637(Gd_o) - 0.1625\right] (H \div 8)$$

$Gd_o < 16$

$$V_{3B} = 30 + \left[0.01610(Gd_o)^2 + 0.1118(Gd_o) - 1.8893\right] H$$

Unit of measure--------------------------- Board foot
Log rule---------------------------------- Scribner formula
Top diameter (d_u) ---------------------- 50 percent of
                                              d_1, but not less
                                              than 8.0 inches

Equations 3A and 3B (continued)

      Stump height --------------------------- Local practice
      Trim allowance per log ------------------ 0.3 foot
      Scaling length of logs -------------------- 16 feet

Equations 4A and 4B

$Gd_o \geq 16.00$ inches

$$V_{4A} = \left[0.02264(Gd_o)^2 - 0.0484(Gd_o) - 0.0552\right](H+8)$$

$Gd_o < 16.00$ inches

$$V_{4B} = 38 + \left[0.01596(Gd_o)^2 + 0.2239(Gd_o) - 2.6898\right]H$$

Unit of measure -------------------------- Board foot
Log rule ------------------------------------ International
                                               1/8-inch
Top diameter (d_u) ----------------------- 50 percent of
                                         d_1, but not less
                                         than 8.0 inches
Stump height --------------------------- Local practice
Trim allowance per log -------------------- 0.3 foot
Scaling length of logs -------------------- 16 feet

Equations 5A and 5B

$Gd_o \geq 16.00$ inches

$$V_{5A} = \left[0.02048(Gd_o)^2 - 0.0438(Gd_o) - 0.0499\right](H+8)$$

$Gd_o < 16.00$ inches

$$V_{5B} = 34 + \left[0.01444(Gd_o)^2 + 0.2026(Gd_o) - 2.4336\right]H$$

Unit of measure -------------------------- Board foot
Log rule ------------------------------------ International
                                               1/4-inch
Top diameter (d_u) ----------------------- 50 percent of
                                         d_1, but not less
                                         than 8.0 inches
Stump height --------------------------- Local practice
Trim allowance per log ------------------ 0.3 foot
Scaling length of logs ------------------- 16 feet

Equations 6A, 6B, and 6C

$Gd_o \geq 14.4$

$$V_{6A} = -0.2541(Gd_o)^2 + 0.2894(Gd_o) - 1.3600$$
$$+ \left[0.02064(Gd_o)^2 - 0.0643(Gd_o) - 0.1624 \right] H$$

$13.5 \leq Gd_o < 14.4$

$$V_{6B} = -50 + \left[0.02064(Gd_o)^2 - 0.0643(Gd_o) - 0.1624 \right] H$$

$Gd_o < 13.5$

$$V_{6C} = -15.3180(Gd_o) + 156.8560$$
$$+ \left[0.5214(Gd_o) - 4.3340 \right] H$$

Unit of measure ------------------------------ Board foot
Log rule -- Scribner formula
Top d. i. b. (d_u) --------------------------- 50 percent of
 d_1, but not less
 than 8.0 inches
Stump height ---------------------------------- Local practice
Trim allowance per log --------------------- 0.6 foot
Scaling length of logs ---------------------- 32 feet

Procedure Used in Developing the Equations

Equation 1

Step 1. --For a hypothetical tree with particular values
for d_1 and N, 16-foot scaling diameters for each log in
the tree were calculated by:

$$d_i = d_1 D_i \qquad (1)$$

where

$$D_i = \frac{L_i}{0.49 L_i + 0.51} \qquad (2)$$

$$L_i = \frac{H - (16.3)k}{H - 16.3} \qquad (3)$$

$$L_u = \frac{H - (16.3)N}{H - 16.3} \text{ ----------------- (5)}$$

$$H = \frac{(N - L_u)16.3}{1 - L_u} \text{ ---------------- (6)}$$

$$L_u = \frac{D_u(0.51)}{1 - D_u(0.49)} \text{ ---------------- (7)}$$

$$D_u = \frac{d_u}{d_1} \text{ ---------------------- (8)}$$

$$d_u = 5 \text{ ----------------------- (9)}$$

Step 2. -- For each scaling diameter calculated in step 1, log volume according to the International 1/8-inch rule was calculated by:

$$v_i = 0.88d_1{}^2 - 1.52d_i - 1.36$$

Step 3. -- Volumes for all logs in the hypothetical tree were then added.

Step 4. -- Steps 1, 2, and 3 were repeated for several hypothetical trees, all of which had the same d_1, but with N different for each tree.

Step 5. --Constants a_1 and b_1 for the relationship $V_1 = a_1 + b_1 H$ were calculated using the several tree volumes from step 4. Note that N can be converted to H from (6). There was no residual variation in the relationship V on H.

Step 6. -- Steps 1 through 5 were repeated for several different values of d_1.

Step 7. -- Constants a_2, b_2, and c_2 were calculated for the following curvilinear relationship of b_1 on d_1:

$$b_1 = a_2 + b_2 d_1 + c_2 d_1{}^2$$

Step 8. -- Constants a_3, b_3, and c_3 were calculated for this curvilinear relationship of a_1 on d_1:

$$a_1 = a_3 + b_3 d_1 + c_3 d_1{}^2$$

Step 9. --Results of steps 7 and 8 led directly to equation 1:

$$V_1 = a_3 + b_3 d_1 + c_3 d_1{}^2 + \left[a_2 + b_2 d_1 + c_2 d_1{}^2 \right] H$$

Equation 2

Each constant in the V_1 equation was simply multiplied by 0.904762 which is the factor for converting volume by the International 1/8-inch rule to volume by the International 1/4-inch rule.

Equation 3A

This equation has already been presented in the Bruce-Girard green book,[5] and the procedure used in its development has been described on pages 41-46 of that publication.

Equation 3B

Equation 3A is applicable only when the diameter at the limit of merchantability is 50 percent of d_1. However,

[5] See footnote 1.

when a minimum 8-inch top merchantability limit is
imposed, equation 3A will not be appropriate. This
will be true whenever d_1 is less than 16 inches.

Bruce[6] described the procedure for the case where d_1
is less than 16 inches (pages 45-46 in his green book),
but he gave no equation. Instead, he gave a table of
factors which, when multiplied by H, would give tree
volume less 30 board feet.

These factors could be used directly in electronic
computers. However, since an equation may be preferred, constants for a second degree curve were
found for the relation between Bruce's factors and d_1.
Thus:

$$f = a + bd_1 + cd_1^2$$

where f = Bruce's factor

and since

$$V_{3B} = fH + 30$$

$$V_{3B} = \left[a + bd_1 + cd_1^2 \right] H + 30$$

Equation 4A

Specifications for tree volumes under equation 4A are
identical with specifications for equation 3A with the
one exception that the International 1/8-inch rule was
used for 4A while the formula Scribner rule was used
for 3A.

[6] See footnote 1.

For the International 1/8-inch rule:

$$v_i = 0.88d_i^2 - 1.52d_i - 1.36$$

and for the formula Scribner rule:

$$v_1 = 0.79d_i^2 - 2d_i - 4$$

Constants for equation 4A were found by applying ratios of corresponding constants in the log rules to constants in equation 3A. Thus   :

$$0.02264 = 0.02032\left(\frac{0.88}{0.79}\right)$$

$$0.0484 = 0.0637\left(\frac{1.52}{2}\right)$$

$$0.0552 = 0.1625\left(\frac{1.36}{4}\right)$$

Equation 4B

The procedure used for equation 4B was identical to the procedure used for equation 1 with these exceptions:

1. $D_u = 8/d_1$

2. Calculations were limited to values of d_1 less than 16.

3. Values for a_1 (steps 5 and 8 under Procedure for Equation 1) were all so close to 38 that 38 could safely be substituted for the first three terms in equation 1.

Equations 5A and 5B

Constants in equations 4A and 4B were simply multiplied by 0.904762 to give corresponding constants for 5A and 5B.

-11-

The procedure used for equation 1 was also used for equation 6A. The exceptions in this case were:

1. $D_u = \dfrac{d_u}{d_1} = 0.5$

2. Scaling diameters for 32-foot logs instead of for 16-foot logs were found in step 1. (Note that d_1 in this case was still taken as diameter at the top of the first 16-foot log even though logs were scaled in 32-foot lengths.)

3. Although equation 6A was developed for the case where d_1 was 16 inches or greater, it was found that by applying it down to $d_1 = 14.4$, a better transition to equation 6B was effected.

Equation 6B

Equation 6A was originally extended down to $d_1 = 13.5$, but it was found that if the sum of the first three terms of 6A were taken as (-50) for all cases where $13.5 \le d_1 < 14.4$, a better transition was effected between 6A and 6C.

Equation 6C

The general procedure used for equation 1 was also used here with these exceptions:

1. $D_u = 8/d_1$

2. Scaling diameters for 32-foot logs instead of for 16-foot logs were found in step 1. (Note that d_1 is still the diameter at the top of the first 16-foot log and that the 16-foot form class is implied.)

3. Linear instead of curvilinear relationships
    were found for b_1 on d_1 and for a_1 on d_1 in
    steps 7 and 8. Thus the c_2 and c_3 constants
    were not needed. In this restricted range of
    d_1's (i.e., 8.0 inches to 13.5 inches), there
    was no evidence of curvilinearity.

U. S. FOREST SERVICE

Pacific **N**orth **W**est · Research Note

FOREST AND RANGE EXPERIMENT STATION · U.S. DEPARTMENT OF AGRICULTURE · PORTLAND, OREGON

PNW-3   June 1963

DISPERSAL OF LODGEPOLE PINE SEED INTO CLEAR-CUT PATCHES

by

Walter G. Dahms

In 1959, a study was begun to learn more about lodgepole pine (Pinus contorta) seed production and dissemination in south-central Oregon. This research note reports the first 4 years of record on frequency of seed crops, time of seedfall, and distance and direction of seed dispersal into clear-cut patches.

Production and dissemination of lodgepole pine seed from a timber edge are matters of very real interest in the Pacific Northwest because most lodgepole pine cones in this region open and shed their seed promptly following ripening.[1] Seed for natural reproduction of clear-cut areas must, therefore, come largely from surrounding timber edges. This seed supply situation contrasts sharply with that of lodge-pole pine in the Rocky Mountain region where several years' production

---

[1] Critchfield, William B. Geographic variation in Pinus contorta. Maria Moors Cabot Found. Pub. 3, 118 pp., illus. 1957.

Mowat, Edwin L. No serotinous cones on central Oregon lodgepole pine. Jour. Forestry 58: 118-119. 1960.

Trappe, James M., and Harris, Robert W. Lodgepole pine in the Blue Mountains of northeastern Oregon. Pac. NW. Forest & Range Expt. Sta. Res. Paper 30, 22 pp., illus. 1958.

is usually held in sealed, or serotinous, cones and where unburned slash usually contains a good supply of seed. [2/]

STUDY METHODS

Study areas consist of two recent clear cuttings on the Winema National Forest, not far from the southeast corner of Crater Lake National Park. One of the areas is 70 acres in size, the other 25. Both are surrounded by uncut lodgepole pine timber.

Seed production and dissemination are sampled by placing seed traps under the timber and at regular intervals from timber edge out into the clear cuttings.

During the first year (1959), main efforts were given to development of exploratory information on variation of seed catch among traps approximately 2 by 3 feet in size. Only 16 traps were used, but the 1959 findings provided a basis for final study design as well as a good relative measure of size of the 1959 seed crop.

Starting with the 1960 seed crop, 80 traps of the 2 by 3-foot size have been used. Traps are placed in groups of 20 according to the arrangement and relation to timber edge shown in figure 1. Each group is oriented to either an east, west, north, or south timber edge and extends into the clear cutting a distance of 462 feet at right angles to timber edge.

Seeds are collected from traps each year on about October 1 and November 1 and once again during the following summer. In 1961, however, early snow prevented the November 1 collection. Seed soundness is determined by a cutting test.

SIZE AND FREQUENCY OF SEED CROPS

Under undisturbed lodgepole pine timber, fall of sound seeds per acre ranged from a low of 14,000 for the 1961 crop to a high of

---

[2/] Critchfield, footnote 1.

Tackle, David. Silvics of lodgepole pine. Intermountain Forest & Range Expt. Sta. Misc. Pub. 19, 24 pp., illus. 1959.

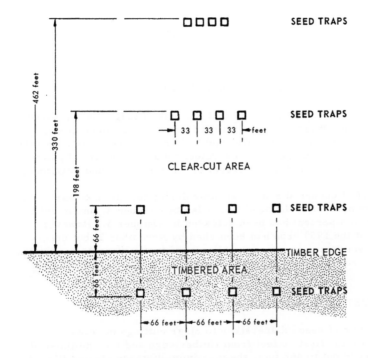

Figure 1.--Arrangement of seed traps in relation
to a timber edge.

well over half a million for the 1962 crop. Total fall for 1962 is not yet known, but a cumulative count through the November 1 collection reached 572,400 sound seeds per acre. For the 1959 and 1960 crops, total catch per acre was 178,200 and 230.400 sound seeds, respectively. Thus far, moderate-to-good seed crops were produced in each of 3 years, while an almost complete failure occurred in the 4th year.

TIME OF SEEDFALL

Limited evidence suggests that the bulk of lodgepole pine seed in south-central Oregon is usually shed from cones by November 1 and in some cases may be mostly shed by early October. Thus in 1960, 75 percent of the seed had fallen by October 4 and 97 percent by October 31. Similarly in 1961, 88 percent of the seed was shed by October 9.

Seedfall occurred somewhat later during the other 2 years. In 1959 only 39 percent of the seed had fallen by October 4, and in 1962 not more than 8 percent had been released by October 3. However, 89 percent of the 1959 crop had been shed by November 3; but observations not yet complete may possibly reveal that a sizeable proportion of the 1962 crop was shed after November 1, the last seed collection date.

DISTANCE AND DIRECTION OF SEED DISPERSAL

Number of seeds dispersed into clear cuttings decreased sharply within the first 66 feet from timber edge and then diminished more gradually out to 462 feet, the maximum distance studied (fig. 2). This finding was consistent for timber edges on all sides of clear cuttings (north, south, east, and west) and for all 3 years in which seed dispersal was studied. In terms of average annual seedfall for the 1960-62 period number of seeds decreased from 272,300 per acre within the timber to 17,200 seeds at 66 feet from timber edge, to 2,450 seeds at 198 feet. and to only 540 seeds at a distance of 462 feet.

Although pattern of dispersal was similar for all timber edges, the most seeds were dispersed along the west boundary of the clear cutting and the fewest along the south boundary (fig. 2) These differences were significant[3] for he 1962 seed crop and also for the

---

[3] Chi square test at odds of 99 out of 100.

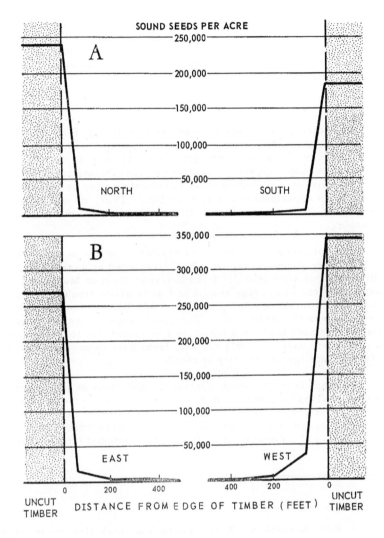

Figure 2.--Average annual seed catch for the period 1960-62,
inclusive, by distance and direction from trap to seed source.
A , North and south timber edges; B, east and west timber edges.

-5-

average seed crop produced over the 3-year period 1960-62. Differences among timber edges were nonsignificant for the 1960 seed crop, however, and the 1961 seed crop was too small to provide data for a meaningful analysis.

DISCUSSION

Periodicity, and volume of seed crops cannot be fully evaluated in a period as short as 4 years. However, evidence from the present study on frequency of seed crops agrees closely with Mowat's[4] conclusion for lodgepole pine in central Oregon: "Many trees bore persistent cones in such numbers as to indicate a crop nearly every year, but with occasional years of scarcity." Thus, we can be fairly confident that the present estimate of three seed crops in 4 years is reasonable.

The only seed production data available for comparison comes from the Rocky Mountain Region. Boe[5] reported an average of 17,500 seeds per acre annually from a 4-year study in Montana. Bates[6] reported an average annual per-acre production of 72,922 seeds from a 10-year Wyoming study and 320,053 seeds from a concurrent 10-year Colorado study. The great range among these widely scattered locations leads to a tentative conclusion that lodgepole pine seed production varies greatly not only from year to year but also with site factors and age and density of stand.

Findings from the south-central Oregon study on pattern of seed dispersal from a timber edge are very similar to those reported by other investigators Boe,[7] for example, reported that number of seeds dispersed into a clear-cut area from surrounding timber fell off sharply at a distance of 66 feet He concluded further that

---

[4] See footnote 1.

[5] Boe, Kenneth N. Regeneration and slash disposal in lodgepole pine clear cuttings. Northwest Sci. 30: 1-11, illus. 1956.

[6] Bates, C. G. The production, extraction, and germination of lodgepole pine seed. U.S. Dept. Agr. Tech. Bul. 191, 92 pp., illus. 1930.

[7] See footnote 5.

number of seeds disseminated more than 198 feet "is inadequate and undependable for reproducing a stand." Munger's observations of old burns in central Oregon led to similar conclusions.[8] He reported that a full stand of reproduction usually extended about 200 feet from seed source and a fair number of seedlings extended another 500 feet.

CONCLUSIONS

In south-central Oregon, good crops of lodgepole pine seed are produced in most years. Because seeds in this general area are not stored in serotinous cones, however, natural regeneration of clear cuttings depends largely upon seeds dispersed from surrounding timber. Number of seeds dispersed into clear cuttings falls off very rapidly as distance from a timber border increases and reaches a very low level at distances beyond 200 feet. Consequently, foresters should restrict the width of clear-cut strips, patches, or blocks to about 400 feet if they plan to provide an ample seed supply for prompt natural regeneration.

The south-central Oregon study provides considerable evidence that most of the current year's crop of seed is shed by November 1 and in some cases by early October. Seed-catch records also indicate that seed dispersal from a western timber edge of a clear cutting is above average, while that from a southern timber edge is below average. Additional years of record will be needed to confirm or disprove both of these hypotheses.

----

[8] Munger, Thornton T. The encroachment of lodgepole pine on western yellow pine on the east slopes of the Cascade Mountains in Oregon. U.S. Dept. Agr., Forest Service. (Typed manuscript on file at Bend Silviculture Laboratory.) 1908.

U. S. FOREST SERVICE

Pacific North West Research Note

FOREST AND RANGE EXPERIMENT STATION · U.S.DEPARTMENT OF AGRICULTURE · PORTLAND, OREGON

PNW-4   June 1963

RELATION BETWEEN MOISTURE CONTENT OF FINE FUELS

AND RELATIVE HUMIDITY

By

Harold K. Steen

Measurements indicate a relation between diurnal curves of relative humidity and moisture content of some important fuels of Oregon and Washington. Some of these measurements were made in early years of forest fire research in this region.[1] [2] The data in this note were collected at intervals throughout 4 days (in September 1938) at the Wind River Experimental Forest near Carson, Wash. The relations presented here will be of interest when the new National Fire Danger Rating System is used in the Pacific Northwest. This system bases its estimate of fine-fuel moisture content on relative humidity measurements.

Experience has shown that forest fires burn more readily as fuel moisture decreases. Relation of moisture content to relative humidity has been used for years in forest fire control. This note illustrates how that relation affected moisture content of fine fuels on several days in one locality in the Pacific Northwest.

---

[1] Hofmann, J. V., and Osborne, Wm. B., Jr. Relative humidity and forest fires. U.S. Forest Serv., 16 pp. [unnumbered], illus. 1923.

[2] Simson, A. Gael. Relative humidity and short-period fluctuations in the moisture content of certain forest fuels. Monthly Weather Rev. 58(9): 373-374. 1930.

METHOD OF STUDY

Relative humidity and the moisture content of more than 100 samples of fine fuels were simultaneously measured. Measurements began in early morning and continued until late evening. The fuels were: (1) fine screenings of reddish rotten wood from the decayed surface of Douglas-fir (Pseudotsuga menziesii) logs; (2) duff (screened through a 1/4-inch mesh), with no covering of twig litter, from an overmature stand of Douglas-fir and western hemlock (Tsuga heterophylla); (3) dead needles from the top layer of ponderosa pine (Pinus ponderosa) litter; (4) dead cheatgrass (Bromus tectorum) from the previous growing season; and (5) dead western bracken (Pteridium aquilinum var. pubescens) from the previous growing season. These are common fuels in the Pacific Northwest.

The rotten wood and duff were spread in shallow metal pans. The cheatgrass, pine needles, and bracken were spread on trays. During the test period, the fuels were exposed on the ground in a sunny location.

Moisture content of only the very top layer of these fuels was measured by the ovendry weight method. During the tests, a hygrothermograph (in a white wooden shelter on the ground) recorded both temperature and relative humidity within 20 feet of the fuels (fig. 1).

Figure 1.--Rotten wood and duff in the pans. Ponderosa pine needles on the screen. A hygrothermograph in a wooden shelter at the upper left.

RESULTS

Relative humidity and moisture contents of fine fuels are compared in figures 2 and 3. The patterns of moisture content and humidity are similar. Even the sudden change in humidity at 1330 hours (caused by passing clouds) on September 9 was accompanied by a like change in fuel moisture. Although the trend of fuel moisture closely followed humidity, the fuel moisture that accompanied a given humidity varied. This variation was greatest when the humidity was falling or rising. The relation between relative humidity and fuel moisture is more consistent in the afternoon than in the morning

Since fine fuels have a great surface area compared with their volume, such quick responses to changes in atmospheric moisture could be expected. Bracken usually had the highest moisture content. During midday, cheatgrass (the most responsive) and rotten wood had the lowest moisture content. Pine needles and duff showed less response to humidity change. Excluding bracken, whenever the humidity was below 50 percent, fine-fuel moisture was nearly always less than 10 percent. When the humidity was about 30 percent, fine-fuel moisture was about 5 percent.

DISCUSSION

At many locations in Oregon and Washington, diurnal changes in humidity, similar to those in figures 2 and 3, will probably be accompanied by fuel-moisture trends similar to those shown. It is likely that heavy nighttime dew occurred at Wind River during the sampling period. Patterns of fuel moisture at stations where no dew forms will probably differ from those at Wind River (particularly in the morning hours) even though daytime relative humidity patterns are similar. Differences in temperature and amount of sunshine at various stations may cause somewhat different fuel moisture patterns for relative humidities like those shown in figures 2 and 3. Since humidity was measured only a few inches above the ground for these tests, relations between fuel moisture and humidity measured at 4 to 5 feet will be different.

Diurnal humidity changes consistently affected moisture content of the fine forest fuels tested. Moisture content of these fine fuels may be predicted when trends and values of relative humidity are similar to those in figures 2 and 3. Probability of ignition of such fuels from certain causes may be determined more objectively

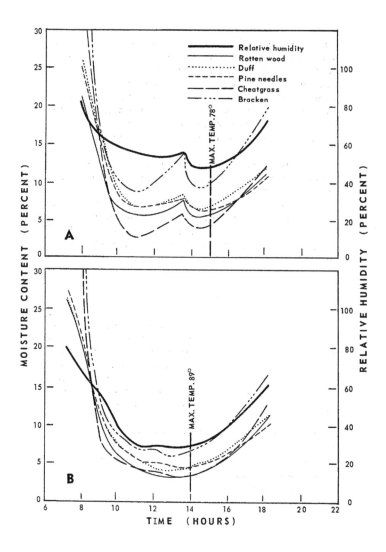

Figure 2.--Relation between relative humidity and the moisture content of some fine fuels on September 9 (A) and September 12 (B).

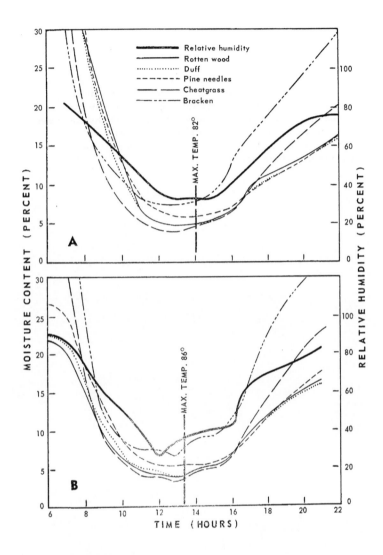

Figure 3. --Relation between relative humidity and the moisture content of some fine fuels on September 20 (A) and September 21 (B).

with the aid of the relations shown in this note. Exact estimates of moisture content of fine fuels depend not only on current humidity, but also on amount of moisture absorbed during the night and on solar radiation reaching the fuel. On the west slopes of the Cascade Range of southern Washington and in other localities with weather similar to the study area, the relations shown in this note can be used to estimate the moisture content of fine fuels.

U. S. FOREST SERVICE

Pacific North West Research Note

PNW

FOREST AND RANGE EXPERIMENT STATION · U.S. DEPARTMENT OF AGRICULTURE · PORTLAND, OREGON

PNW-5   July 1963

REPELLENTS REDUCE DEER BROWSING

PONDEROSA PINE SEEDLINGS

by

Richard S. Driscoll

Winter range for many central Oregon mule deer herds includes
the lower elevation areas of the ponderosa pine forests. Clear-cut
logging and broadcast slash burning during the 1920's and early 1930's
created reforestation problems in these areas. These timber management practices provided good conditions for natural regeneration of
deer browse and cover plants, including antelope bitterbrush (Purshia
tridentata), snowbrush ceanothus (Ceanothus velutinus), and pine
manzanita (Arctostaphylos parryana var. pinetorum). This inadvertant
improvement of habitat attracted deer and probably favored population
increases.

Repeated attempts have been made to reforest these areas with
ponderosa pine nursery stock. In many instances, complete failures
occurred. In other cases, survival was only mediocre. Deer browsing
during the fall, winter, and spring is a hazard affecting the success of
many plantations in addition to careless planting, harsh sites, mortality
due to rodents, insects, and disease, and unknown mortality causes
Browsed trees that do survive are deformed, and growth is retarded
(fig. 1).

Figure 1.--Repeated deer browsing of this 27-year-
old ponderosa pine has produced a stunted and
malformed tree.

Fencing and wire cages have been used to protect planted
seedlings from browsing. However, emphasis is now being placed
on the use of foliar chemical repellents[1] and systemic compounds.[2]

[1] Besser, Jerome F., and Welch, Jack F. Chemical
repellents for the control of mammal damage to plants. 24th No.
Amer. Wildl. Conf. Trans. 1959: 166-173.

[2] U.S. Bureau of Sport Fisheries and Wildlife. Wildlife
research progress--1961. Fish & Wildl. Serv. Cir. 146, 50 pp.
1962.

THE STUDY

The effectiveness of three chemical foliar repellents, ZAC (zinc dimethyldithiocarbamate cyclohexylamine complex), TMTD (tetramethylthiuram disulfide), and copper omadine (the copper salt of 1-hydroxy-2-pyridine thione), for reducing deer browsing on planted ponderosa pine seedlings was tested from 1958 to 1960 on a site IV that had been logged about 1933.[3] Each chemical, applied as a spray, was formulated as an aqueous suspension containing 10 percent of the active ingredient, 10 percent acrylic resin adhesive (Rhoplex AC-33), 0.2 percent Methocel (a thickening agent), and 0 6 percent Hexadecanol-ethanol (a defoaming agent).[4]

In April of 1958, sixty 2-0 ponderosa pine seedlings were handplanted with 8- by 8-foot spacing in each of 15 plots. The plots were separated into three groups of five plots each. All trees in one plot of each group were subjected to one of the following treatments: (1) spraying with ZAC, (2) spraying with TMTD, (3) spraying with copper omadine, (4) piling brush around seedlings, and (5) control with no spray and no brush piling.

Each seedling in the spray treatments was thoroughly wetted with the respective chemical formulation immediately after planting.

---

[3] A cooperative study with the Pacific Northwest Forest & Range Experiment Station, U.S. Bureau of Sport Fisheries and Wildlife, and the Deschutes National Forest. The Experiment Station designed the experiment, laid out the field plots, and provided statistical analyses of the data. Chemicals, formulations, and method of application were suggested and provided by the Denver Wildlife Research Center, Bureau of Sport Fisheries and Wildlife. The Deschutes National Forest furnished land, tree seedlings, and seedling planting.

[4] A ZAC formulation may be obtained commercially as Improved Z.I.P. A TMTD formulation is available as Selco TMTD-Rhoplex Rabbit and Deer Repellent Concentrate. TMTD may also be obtained as Arasan 75 or Arasan 42-S to which the adhesive, defoaming, and thickening agents must be added. No commercial supply of copper omadine is known. This does not constitute an endorsement of products by the Forest Service.

A hand-operated pressure tank sprayer was used. About 3 quarts of
solution were needed for the 180 trees in each repellent treatment.
At the same time, brush was piled around seedlings selected for
this treatment. Subsequent sprayings and brush rearrangements
were made in September 1958 and September 1959 to protect new
growth.

Starting in June 1958, observations were made at 4-month
intervals until June 1960. Each seedling was examined for evidence
of browsing. When dead or missing seedling spots were found, an
attempt was made to determine the cause of death.

RESULTS AND DISCUSSION

Effectiveness of the Treatments

None of the treatments prevented all browsing, but both
chemical and mechanical protection significantly reduced the amount
of browsing as compared with no protection (fig. 2). Also, all chemical sprays resulted in significantly fewer browsed seedlings as compared with mechanical protection. On the average, no chemical
formulation was superior to the others.

For the 2 years, 32 percent of the unprotected live seedlings
were browsed. This compares with only 18-percent browsing of the
mechanically protected seedlings and 10-, 7-, and 7-percent browsing
of seedlings sprayed with copper omadine, TMTD, and ZAC formulations, respectively. Less browsing might be expected on those

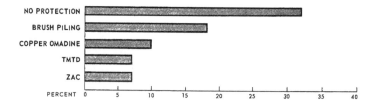

Figure 2.-- Percent of live ponderosa pine seedlings
browsed, June 1958 to June 1960.

-4-

trees protected by brush piling. However, high winds during the winter and spring blew the brush covering off some seedlings and exposed them to browsing.

Equally important to the general effectiveness of the various treatments is the protection each provided during various seasons. Figure 3 summarizes the intensity of browsing of live ponderosa pine seedlings, by treatment, during three seasonal periods.

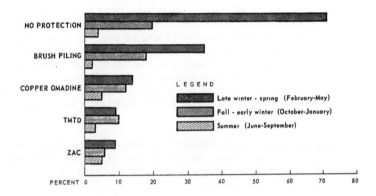

Figure 3.--Seasonal browsing intensity of live ponderosa pine seedlings, June 1958 to June 1960.

The period when most browsing occurred, when protection was most necessary, was in the late winter-spring season from February through May. Deer browsed 71 percent of the unprotected live seedlings during this season as compared with 20 percent in the fall-early winter season (October-January) and only 4 percent in the summer (June-September). This late winter-spring season corresponds to the time when winter deer forage produced the preceding year becomes scarce and spring growth has not reached a maximum.

All of the protective treatments significantly reduced the amount of browsing during the late winter-spring period as compared with the control. Only 35 percent of the brush-covered seedlings were browsed. However, the brush-covering treatment was not as effective as any of the three chemical sprays. Only 14, 9, and 9 percent of the live seedlings were browsed in the copper omadine, TMTD, and ZAC treatments, respectively. The differences in the amount of protection afforded by the chemical formulations were not significant during this season.

ZAC appeared to be the most effective protectant during the fall—early winter season (October-January). Only 6 percent of the live seedlings treated with this formulation were browsed. This amount is significantly less than the 18 and 20 percent browsed in the brush-covered and control plots but is essentially no different from the 10- and 12-percent browsing in the TMTD and copper omadine plots. However, TMTD and copper omadine did not provide appreciably more protection than the brush cover, and none of these three treatments resulted in a significant reduction in browsing as compared with no protection.

Browsing of seedlings during the summer (June-September) appears to be inconsequential. Only 4 percent of the live seedlings in the control plots were browsed. During this season, desirable forage for deer is usually ample.

On the basis of this study, deer browsing on planted ponderosa pine seedlings can be reduced either by spraying with 10-percent formulations of ZAC, TMTD, or copper omadine or protecting each seedling with brush. The ZAC formulation appears to be the most effective treatment since it provides more overall protection during the critical time of the year, fall through winter. The operation is not a one-shot procedure, however. Even though the additives used (adhesive, thickening, and defoaming agents) weather well,[5] the seedlings must be sprayed each year to protect new growth. The spraying should be done in the fall, after current growth is complete, to insure total coverage of all new plant material and maximum available protection during subsequent severe weather conditions and deer concentrations. The number of years spray treatments must be carried out was not determined.

---

[5] Besser, Jerome F. Special report--effectiveness of repellent treatments for protection of trees from animal damage (1956-57). U.S. Bur. Sport Fisheries & Wildl. Wildl. Res. Lab., Denver, Colo., 19 pp. (mimeo.) (n.d.)

Mortality

Approximately 48-percent mortality (434 seedlings) occurred among the test seedlings. This loss was not due to toxic action of the chemical formulations.[6]

Mortality by causes other than recognizable animal damage accounted for 75 percent of the total loss (table 1). Most of these seedlings died during the summer (39 percent of total mortality) and death could be attributed to combinations of low soil moisture and high soil surface temperature conditions, possible competition from existing vegetation, or mortality by unknown causes. Death of some of these seedlings was caused by poor planting. Evidence of this was noted when dead seedlings were excavated. In many instances, root ends were either upturned or the entire root system was tightly compacted. Planting-tool damage to the roots was another cause of death of many seedlings.

Table 1.--Mortality analysis of 434 dead ponderosa pine seedlings 2 years after planting

(In percent)

Season	Mortality caused by deer	Mortality caused by gophers	Mortality by other causes[1]	Total mortality
Summer (June-Sept.)	--	5	39	44
Fall--early winter (Oct.-Jan.)		7	25	33
Late winter--spring (Feb.-May)		12	11	23
Total		24	75	100

[1] Mortality by other causes includes poor planting (roots upturned, compacted, or damaged by planting tool), drought, high soil temperatures, possible competition from existing vegetation and unknown factors.

[6] See footnote 5.

Gophers had killed 24 percent of all dead trees. Half of these, 12 percent of the total number of dead trees, were killed during the late winter--spring season. The rest of the gopher kills occurred in about equal numbers during the summer and fall--early winter seasons.

Only 1 percent of the total number of dead trees could have been killed by deer. In all cases, mortality by this cause occurred during the summer, and the seedlings affected had been heavily browsed during the late winter--spring season. Death by deer may have been secondary and associated with other causes since many other heavily browsed seedlings survived.

SUMMARY

Deer browsing of ponderosa pine seedlings can be reduced by spraying with 10-percent solutions of either zinc dimethyldithiocarb-amate cyclohexylamine complex (ZAC), tetramethylthiuram disulfide (TMTD), or copper omadine, each mixed with 10 percent acrylic resin adhesive (Rhoplex AC-33), 0.2 percent Methocel (a thickening agent), and 0.6 percent Hexadecanol-ethanol (a defoaming agent). Covering with brush also reduces browsing. ZAC provides the most effective protection on a year-round basis.

The spray treatment must be applied each year to provide protection to yearly growth. This should be done in the fall after current growth is completed and before deer concentrate in plantation areas. The number of years spray treatments must be carried out was not determined

Seedling mortality was high (48 percent) during the 2-year study period. Death by causes other than recognizable animal damage accounted for most of the loss. Seasonal mortality was greatest during the summer.

U. S. FOREST SERVICE

Pacific North West

Research Note

FOREST AND RANGE EXPERIMENT STATION · U.S. DEPARTMENT OF AGRICULTURE · PORTLAND, OREGON

PNW-6   September 1963

SEASONING AND SURFACING DEGRADE IN KILN-DRYING

WESTERN HEMLOCK IN WESTERN WASHINGTON

by

Douglas L. Hunt

The potential lumber yield and value of saw logs can be appreciably affected by losses of volume and grade during sawing, seasoning, and surfacing.

There are relatively few reported studies of degrade losses, and it is assumed that most lumber manufacturers have to estimate the seasoning and machining losses that occur in their operations. Results obtained in one study cannot be used to predict losses that would occur in processing timber from a different area or in manufacturing at a different plant. Nevertheless, the recent findings, reported here, of one company do indicate where serious losses can occur.

In 1962 this study, involving more than 175,000 board feet of lumber, was made on the Olympic Peninsula in Washington to determine the degrade (loss in volume and value) of western hemlock cut, kiln-dried, and surfaced in accordance with usual industry practices. The degrade measured included (1) the reduction in grade due to seasoning, surfacing, and manufacturing defects and (2) the loss in volume due to culling and trimming of surfaced dry lumber. Degrade is expressed both as a percentage of the rough green lumber input and as a loss in value per thousand board feet of lumber.

STUDY PROCEDURE

All lumber was first carefully graded, marked, and tallied in the rough green condition at the sawmill to establish its potential grade[1] and value. It was kiln-dried under the usual production schedules of the mill, then surfaced, transported to the yard, and carefully regraded. Pieces that had been misgraded, because of difficulty in discerning all characteristics in the rough green condition, were eliminated and the original tally corrected accordingly. The difference between the potential grade and volume of rough green lumber (corrected input) and the final grade and volume of surfaced dry lumber (output) is recorded as degrade.

Grading in both the rough green and surfaced dry condition was done by the same Pacific Lumber Inspection Bureau grader. Lumber was graded under Standard Grading and Dressing Rules Number 15 of the West Coast Lumber Inspection Bureau.

All Dimension stock was dried in relatively new end-loaded, steam-heated, internal fan, double-track kilns with automatic temperature and humidity controls. A typical company schedule for drying the Dimension is shown in table 1. No conditioning or equalizing treatments were used to relieve casehardening stresses. Planer feed speeds ranged from 475 feet per minute for 2 by 10's to 625 feet per minute for 2 by 4's.

Shake was included in this study as a seasoning defect, although it was omitted in a previous degrade study of western hemlock in western Oregon.[2] Shake was treated as a seasoning defect because the company had only recently installed dry kilns and was interested in learning the degrade experienced in changing from a surfaced green shipping basis to a surfaced dry. Whether shake is a true seasoning defect or not, its inclusion provides sawmill operators with some indication of the losses that can occur in drying a species containing shake.

---

[1] Potential grade is the surfaced dry grade of lumber one could expect to obtain from the green lumber if no defects resulted from sawing, seasoning, or surfacing.

[2] Knauss, A. C., and Clarke, E. H. Seasoning and surfacing degrade in kiln-drying western hemlock in western Oregon. U.S. Forest Serv. Pac. NW. Forest & Range Expt. Sta. Res. Note 207, 11 pp. 1961.

Table 1.--Typical kiln-drying schedule for western hemlock;

1962 study in western Washington

Thickness and grade	Time from start of drying	Temperature		Equilibrium moisture content
		Dry bulb	Wet bulb	
	Hours	---- Degrees F. -----		Percent
2-inch Dimension	0	155	145	11.7
	20	160	145	9.4
	38	165	145	7.9
	54	170	142	6.2
	62	175	142	5.5
	70	180	142	4.6
	94	out		

RESULTS AND DISCUSSION

Grade Recovery

The rough green lumber inputs and the surfaced dry lumber outputs are shown by amount and grade in tables 2 and 3. The proportion of lumber that remained ongrade, the proportion that changed in grade, and the volume loss in cull and trim are shown for each grade-thickness item.

Seasoning, Surfacing, and Manufacturing Degrade

The types of seasoning, surfacing, and manufacturing defects that occurred in the study lumber and the proportion of degrade caused by each are shown in table 4. The degrade shown by this study for 1-inch Finish may not be representative of industry experience in general, since this mill was cutting primarily for 2-inch Dimension. The 1-inch Finish was developed from side-cut lumber or by resawing and re-edging 2-inch material. After kiln-drying, the thickness of Dimension lumber was insufficient to permit satisfactory planing of the resawn 1-inch boards, and the degrade was substantially greater than it would be at a mill sawing for 1-inch Finish. At this mill, the emphasis was on efficient sawing of 2-inch Dimension, and the small volume of 1-inch Finish that was developed was sold locally in a surfaced green condition without degrade.

Loss in value per thousand board feet (using average prices for the Douglas-fir region) occasioned by each seasoning, surfacing, and manufacturing defect is shown in table 5. Although the values in table 5 should not be considered absolute, i.e., total loss for Construction 2 by 4's for any given time may never be exactly $6.01, they should be important and useful when considered as relative values. For instance, examination of the table should be helpful in determining areas in the manufacturing process that could be improved.

Each manufacturer should find it profitable to determine individually the major causes of degrade losses. Such information can be determined by two men--a grader and a tallyman--and will permit management to make decisions based on facts rather than estimates. Experiment Station staff members will be glad to assist interested operators in developing simplified degrade study procedures to fit their needs.

Table 2.--Grade recovery of western hemlock Finish lumber following kiln-drying and surfacing; 1962 study in western Washington

Thickness and grade	Rough green lumber input		Grade recovery of surfaced dry lumber as percent of input							
	Width	Corrected volume tested	C and better	D	Construc-tion	Standard	Utility	Economy	Cull and trim loss	Total degrade
	Inches	Board feet	Percent							
1-inch Finish:										
C and Better	4	914	42.6	21.4	--	18.0	16.5	0.3	1.2	57.4
	6	1,958	48.4	8.0	6.6	25.4	9.4	.5	1.7	51.6
	8	2,451	52.4	6.5	4.9	22.9	8.9	2.0	2.4	47.6
D	4	59	--	69.4	--	15.3	15.3	--	--	30.6
	6	196	--	68.4	--	20.4	6.2	2.0	3.0	31.6
	8	474	--	68.4	2.7	19.4	7.6	--	1.9	31.6

Table 3.--Grade recovery of western hemlock Dimension lumber following kiln-drying and surfacing; 1962 study in western Washington

Rough green lumber input			Grade recovery of surfaced dry lumber as percent of input						
Thickness and grade	Width	Corrected volume tested	Select Structural	Construction	Standard	Utility	Economy	Cull and trim loss	Total degrade
	Inches	Board feet	Percent						
2-inch Dimension:									
Select structural	4	6,768	75.9	0.7	6.3	14.8	1.6	0.7	24.1
	6	7,012	74.8	1.4	10.6	11.0	.6	1.6	25.2
	8	10,125	83.3	2.1	5.5	8.2	.8	.7	17.3
	10	4,951	71.8	5.9	13.6	6.5	--	2.2	28.2
Construction	4	9,520	--	78.1	4.6	14.5	1.9	.9	21.9
	6	15,248	--	78.6	7.7	11.9	.6	1.2	21.4
	8	7,761	--	77.5	2.6	16.6	2.3	1.0	22.5
	10	16,980	--	80.6	8.3	9.2	.3	1.6	19.4
Standard	4	6,753	--	--	83.8	13.7	2.0	.5	16.2
	6	7,414	--	--	80.9	17.4	.8	.9	19.1
	8	7,718	--	--	81.8	16.6	.9	.7	18.2
	10	6,974	--	--	86.1	12.5	.4	1.0	13.9
Utility	4	12,398	--	--	--	92.9	6.7	.4	7.1
	6	7,378	--	--	--	94.5	5.2	.3	5.5
	8	15,332	--	--	--	89.8	10.0	.2	10.2
	10	6,404	--	--	--	93.3	6.4	.3	6.7
Economy	4-10	21,707	--	--	--	--	99.6	.4	.4

Table 4.--Seasoning, surfacing, and manufacturing degrade in kiln-dried western hemlock lumber;
1962 study in western Washington

Rough green lumber input			Proportion of input degraded during processing, by cause																		Total degrade
Thickness and grade	Width (Inches)	Corrected volume tested (Board feet)	Seasoning and surfacing defects (Percent)													Manufacturing defects (Percent)					
			Warp	Season check	End check	Planer split	Machine burn	Planer gouge	Torn grain	Stain	Knot-holes	Broken knots	Shake	Cull and trim loss	Total	Thin	Narrow	Mechanical damage	Cull and trim loss	Total	(Percent)
1-inch Finish:																					
C & Better	4	914	2.6	0	0	0.6	0	0	7.6	0.6	0	0	0	0.1	11.5	19.3	23.4	2.1	1.1	45.9	57.4
	6	1,958	2.6	1.7	0	1.0	0	0	2.1	0	0	0	0	1.0	8.4	14.4	26.6	1.4	.8	43.2	51.6
	8	2,451	2.1	1.3	0	2.5	0	0	3.1	0	0	0	0	1.3	10.3	9.5	24.2	2.5	1.1	37.3	47.6
D	4	59	0	0	0	0	0	0	0	0	0	0	0	0	0	30.6	0	0	0	30.6	30.6
	6	196	0	2.0	0	0	0	0	0	0	0	0	0	1.5	3.5	12.8	13.8	0	1.5	28.1	31.6
	8	474	1.9	0	0	.6	0	0	0	0	0	0	0	1.9	5.4	8.9	17.3	0	0	26.2	31.6
2-inch Dimension																					
Select structural	4	6,768	2.5	6.4	0	0	0	0	0	0	0.2	0.3	3.4	.4	13.2	4.7	4.7	1.1	.4	10.9	24.1
	6	7,012	2.0	10.7	0.3	0	0	0	0	0	.2	.2	3.1	1.0	17.5	3.6	1.4	2.1	.6	7.7	25.2
	8	10,125	0	9.8	.6	0	0	0	0	0	0	.2	2.3	.4	13.3	1.1	1.5	1.1	.3	4.0	17.3
	10	4,951	0	12.6	.5	0	0	0	0	0	0	.5	.5	1.2	15.3	4.4	4.9	2.6	1.0	12.9	28.2
Construction	4	9,520	5.2	2.4	0	0	0	0	0	0	1.1	.1	1.8	.4	11.0	5.3	3.2	1.9	.5	10.9	21.9
	6	15,248	2.7	5.2	.1	0	0	0	0	0	1.4	1.3	3.4	1.0	15.1	3.4	1.2	1.5	.2	6.3	21.4
	8	7,761	.3	12.7	.3	0	0	0	0	0	.3	0	2.4	.7	16.7	1.0	2.4	2.1	.3	5.8	22.5
	10	16,980	0	11.0	.1	0	0	0	0	0	1.1	0	1.0	1.3	14.5	3.6	.7	.2	.4	4.9	19.4
Standard	4	6,753	2.0	2.9	0	0	0	0	0	0	1.4	.2	3.4	.3	10.2	2.6	2.9	.3	.2	6.0	16.2
	6	7,414	3.2	5.7	.2	0	0	0	0	0	2.2	.8	2.1	.5	15.1	1.5	1.1	1.0	.4	4.0	19.1
	8	7,718	0	8.3	.4	0	0	0	0	0	1.6	2.9	1.4	.6	15.2	.6	1.2	1.2	.1	3.0	18.2
	10	6,974	.5	6.3	0	0	0	0	0	0	2.6	0	1.5	.6	11.5	.8	.4	.8	.4	2.4	13.9
Utility	4	12,398	1.0	.6	0	0	0	0	0	0	.1	0	4.1	.2	6.0	.7	.7	0	.1	1.1	7.1
	6	7,378	0	.7	.3	0	0	0	0	0	0	0	3.6	.2	4.8	0	0	.5	.2	.7	5.5
	8	15,332	.1	3.6	.7	0	0	0	0	0	.3	.1	5.0	.1	9.5	.4	.4	.2	.1	.7	10.2
	10	6,404	0	.4	.7	0	0	0	0	0	0	0	4.5	.1	5.7	0	0	.4	.1	1.0	6.7
Economy	4-10	21,707	0	0	0	0	0	0	0	0	0	0	0	.3	.3	0	0	0	.1	.1	.4

Table 5.--Loss in value of kiln-dried western hemlock lumber due to seasoning, surfacing, and manufacturing degrade.

1962 study in western Washington

Thickness and grade	Width (Inches)	Corrected volume tested (Bd. ft.)	1962 lumber prices (Dollars per M bd. ft.)	Seasoning and surfacing defects (Dollars per M bd. ft.)													Manufacturing defects (Dollars per M bd. ft.)					Total loss in value (Dollars per M bd. ft.)
				Warp	Season check	End check	Planer split	Planer gouge	Machine burn	Torn grain	Stain	Knot-holes	Broken knots	Shake	Cull and trim	Total	Thin	Narrow	Mechan-ical damage	Cull and trim	Total	
1-inch Finish:																						
C & Better	4	914	130.67	1.11	0	0	0.46	0	0	2.53	0.16	0	0	0	0.13	4 39	12.44	14 61	1 13	1.44	29.62	34.01
	6	1,958	130.67	1.77	1.17	0	.63	0	0	.74	0	0	0	0	1.30	5 61	10.22	17.05	36	1.04	28.67	34.28
	8	2,451	130.67	1.95	.86	0	2.28	0	0	.80	0	0	0	0	1.70	7 45	7.05	16 49	.72	1 44	25.70	33.15
D	4	59	104.69	0	0	0	0	0	0	0	0	0	0	0	0	0	12.99	0	0	0	12.99	12.99
	6	196	104.69	0	.83	0	0	0	0	0	0	0	0	0	1.57	2 40	6.54	6.65	0	1.57	14.76	17.16
	8	474	104.69	.79	0	0	.98	0	0	0	0	0	0	0	1.99	3 76	4.78	7.12	0	0	11.90	15.66
2-inch Dimension:																						
Select structural	4	6,768	83.10	.93	2.44	0	0	0	0	0	0	0.02	0.04	1.43	.33	5 19	1.52	1.60	.28	.33	3.73	8.92
	6	7,012	83.10	.70	3.25	0.10	0	0	0	0	0	.02	.02	1.33	.84	6 26	.94	.26	.42	.50	2.12	8.38
	8	10,125	83.10	0	3.00	.16	0	0	0	0	0	0	.02	1.08	.25	4 51	.32	.30	.23	.25	2.10	5.61
	10	4,951	83.10	0	3.19	.06	0	0	0	0	0	0	.06	.10	1.00	4 41	.78	1.12	.75	.08	2.73	7.14
Construction	4	9,520	71.05	1.47	.78	0	0	0	0	0	0	.15	0	.59	.21	3 21	1.15	.69	.60	.36	2.80	6.01
	6	15,248	71.05	.77	1.11	.03	0	0	0	0	0	.19	.15	1.04	.71	4 00	.55	.15	.22	1.06	1.06	5.06
	8	7,761	71.05	.08	3.57	.08	0	0	0	0	0	.05	0	1.03	.50	5 31	.16	.55	.47	.21	1.39	6.70
	10	16,980	71.05	0	2.26	.03	0	0	0	0	0	.11	0	.26	.92	3 58	.51	.11	.06	.28	.96	4.54
Standard	4	6,753	63.00	.45	.57	0	0	0	0	0	0	.28	.04	.91	.19	2 44	.57	.67	.13	.13	1.50	3.94
	6	7,414	63.00	.65	1.13	.04	0	0	0	0	0	.44	.16	.59	.32	3 33	.30	.24	.24	.25	1.03	4.36
	8	7,718	63.00	0	1.73	.08	0	0	0	0	0	.32	.64	.35	.38	3 50	.12	.22	.24	.06	.64	4.14
	10	6,974	63.00	.10	1.34	0	0	0	0	0	0	.51	0	.30	.38	2 63	.16	.08	.16	.25	.65	3.28
Utility	4	12,398	43.20	.23	.14	0	0	0	0	0	0	.02	0	.93	.09	1 41	.07	.16	0	.04	.27	1.68
	6	7,378	43.20	0	.16	.07	0	0	0	0	0	0	0	.82	.09	1.14	0	0	.11	.09	.20	1.34
	8	15,332	43.20	.02	.82	.07	0	0	0	0	0	.07	0	1.14	.04	2.18	0	.09	.05	.04	.18	2 36
	10	6,404	43.20	0	.09	.16	0	0	0	0	0	0	.02	1.02	.04	1 31	.11	0	.09	.04	.24	1.55
Economy	4-10	21,707	20.43	0	0	0	0	0	0	0	0	0	0	1.31		1 31	?	0	0	.33	.33	1.64

U. S. FOREST SERVICE

Pacific North West Research Note

FOREST AND RANGE EXPERIMENT STATION · U.S.DEPARTMENT OF AGRICULTURE · PORTLAND, OREGON

PNW-7   October 1963

COMPOUNDS LEACHED FROM WESTERN REDCEDAR SHINGLE TOW

FOUND TOXIC TO DOUGLAS-FIR SEEDLINGS

By

Kenneth W. Krueger

Shingle tow, the stringy byproduct from the manufacture of western redcedar shingles, has been used for many years as packing material around roots of forest tree seedlings. Ready availability, good moisture-holding capacity, and a tendency to retard mold development have made it popular in western nurseries (2). However, information from recent literature and preliminary test results indicate that compounds contained in shingle tow may be damaging to seedlings under some conditions.

LITERATURE SURVEY

Pathologists have credited decay resistance of western redcedar heartwood to presence of two groups of compounds, thujaplicins and polyhydric phenols (8, 10). Concentrations as low as 10 to 20 parts per million of thujaplicins strongly inhibit spore germination and growth of fungi (8, 9). In addition, thujaplicins produce detrimental effects on bacteria and on both warm- and cold-blooded animals (11, 4). Although only about one two-hundredth as toxic as the thujaplicins, polyphenols occur in heartwood at 20 to 100 times greater concentration (3). While concentration varies widely between and within trees, by weight thujaplicins average about 5,000 p.p.m. and polyphenols 100,000 p.p.m. of ovendry western redcedar wood (7).

A probable explanation for the wide-range toxicity of thujaplicins has recently been provided. Most living organisms derive a
major portion of their energy via a process known as oxidative
phosphorylation. Thujaplicins in concentrations of approximately 16
to 160 p.p.m. inhibit this energy-capturing system; at still lower
concentrations, they "uncouple" the system or "throw it out of gear"
(5). In either case, "usable" energy available to the organism is
lowered, and synthetic processes such as root regeneration may be
impaired.

While the effect of thujaplicins or polyphenols of western redcedar on green plants has not been reported in the literature, shingle
tow or cedar sawdust has commonly been leached with water prior to
horticultural use. Leaching does remove toxic compounds. In one
small study[1] with outplanted ponderosa pine, only 33 percent of
seedlings whose roots had been immersed for 3 hours in the solution
from a shingle tow "soaking tank" survived the first growing season,
compared to 90 percent survival for untreated seedlings. Because
very low concentrations of these compounds affect respiration (5),
the need for effective leaching is evident.

EXPLORATORY EXPERIMENTS

The first study was made to determine whether thujaplicins
and polyphenols of western redcedar were toxic to 2-month-old
Douglas-fir seedlings that had been grown in a greenhouse. About
one-fourth of the seedlings were dormant at time of treatment.

Hot water extracts of fresh cedar sawdust were separated into
a polyphenol- and a thujaplicin-containing fraction on the basis of the
latter's solubility in n-hexane (6). The hexane fraction was evaporated
to dryness and the residual redissolved in water. Concentration of
the thujaplicin and the polyphenol solution was then determined (1, 6),
and a set of four or five dilutions was made from each solution.

Groups of 15 seedlings were then randomly assigned for 2-,
26-, or 74-hour treatments in each dilution. Roots of each group of

---

[1] Tarrant, R. F., Isaac, L. A., and Mowat, E. L. Unpublished progress report on Deschutes 1950 test on ponderosa pine field
planting. February 7, 1951. On file Pac. NW. Forest & Range Expt.
Sta., Portland, Oreg.

seedlings were immersed at room temperature in the assigned aerated solution for the designated time. Following treatment, trees of each group were individually potted in lightly fertilized vermiculite; all trees treated with the same chemical fraction were randomly arranged on a greenhouse bench and grown for 75 days under 16 hours of illumination per day.

Most seedlings whose roots were immersed for 74 hours in a 160-p.p.m. solution of thujaplicins or 1,000-p.p.m. solution of polyphenols died after treatment (table 1). Some seedlings died from shorter immersion at the same concentrations or from immersion at lower concentrations for 74 hours. Both dormant and nondormant seedlings were killed, the latter somewhat more rapidly.

Table 1.--Number of Douglas-fir seedlings dead 75 days

after treatment, by concentration of solution

and hours of immersion[1]

Solution	Concentration	2 hours	26 hours	74 hours
	P.p.m.	------------- Number ---------------		
Thujaplicins	0	1	0	0
	1.6	0	0	0
	16	0	0	3
	160	2	1	13
Polyphenols	0	0	1	0
	1	0	0	1
	10	0	0	2
	100	0	0	2
	1,000	0	7	13

[1] Fifteen seedlings were used for each combination of concentration and period of immersion.

Since the polyphenols of western redcedar are largely uncharacterized, the second study was limited to the effects of thujaplicins on dormant 2-0 Douglas-firs. Seedlings were lifted from a transplant bed in early March and their roots immersed in a 65-p. p. m. thujaplicin solution for 48 hours. They were then replanted in the same way as for the greenhouse study and placed in a controlled environment chamber where they burst their buds in about 30 days. Sixty days after planting, 13 of 18 treated seedlings were dead whereas all water-treated controls were healthy. Actually, only one of the five living seedlings appeared healthy enough to survive in the field and its new needles were much shorter than those of untreated seedlings.

How do these thujaplicin concentrations compare with those found in shingle tow placed around seedling roots? The following concentrations were found in samples of shingle tow as used at three different nurseries (duplicate analyses; dry weight basis):

Nursery	Collection	Concentration (p. p. m.)
No. 1	August	<10
No. 1	November	<10
No. 1	December	18, 18
No. 2	March	15, 20
No. 3	August	100, 110

DISCUSSION

Although the techniques used in the laboratory studies do not fully duplicate field practice, they appear to have direct applicability. Seedling survival tests under greenhouse or growth chamber environment are less severe than under field conditions. Hence, mortality resulting in these studies is probably the minimum that one might expect. Under severe field conditions, lower, nonfatal but debilitating concentrations might also indirectly cause seedling deaths. For example, death might be attributed to drought whereas the primary cause could have been weakening of the seedling by an introduced

toxin. Such weakening seems plausible, since previous investigators
have observed retarded root growth while seedlings were stored in
shingle tow (2).

Analytical values obtained by laboratory extraction methods
may not reflect exactly the potential effect of extractives on roots in
contact with the moist surface of shingle tow in use. Differences
likely arise from variations in existing temperatures, in degree of
root contact with the packing material, in length of exposure, and in
moisture content of the shingle tow. Technical difficulties have thus
far prevented direct determination of concentrations available to
seedling roots from the packing material, but preliminary results
from a variety of laboratory tests indicate that potential toxic or lethal
levels may sometimes exist.

Evidence now available clearly shows that high concentrations
of thujaplicins are damaging to Douglas-fir seedlings. Further work
is needed to fully determine the effects of low concentrations. Until
a critical evaluation is available from work now in progress, it would
seem advisable to substitute some other packing material for shingle
tow.

LITERATURE CITED

(1) Association Official Agricultural Chemists.
      1960. Official methods of analysis. 9th Ed., 832 pp., illus.
      Washington, D. C.

(2) Deffenbacher, Forrest W., and Wright, Ernest.
      1954. Refrigerated storage of conifer seedlings in the Pacific
      Northwest. Jour. Forestry 52: 936-938.

(3) Gardner, J. A. F., and Barton, G. M.
      1958. The extraneous components of western red cedar.
      Forest Prod. Jour. 8(6): 189-192, illus.

(4) Halliday, John E.
      1959. A pharmacological study of gamma-thujaplicin. Jour.
      Amer. Pharm. Assoc., Sci. Ed. 48(12): 722-726.

(5) Lyr, Horst.
   1961. Die Wirkungsweise toxischer Kernholz-Inhaltstoffe
           (Thujaplicine and Pinosylvine) auf den Stoffwechsel
           von Mikroorganismen. Flora 150: 227-242.

(6) MacLean, Harold, and Gardner, J. A. F.
   1956. Analytical method for thujaplicins. Anal. Chem. 28(4):
           509-512.

(7) MacLean, H., and Gardner, J. A. F.
   1956. Distribution of fungicidal extractives (thujaplicin and
           water-soluble phenols) in western red cedar
           heartwood. Forest Prod. Jour. 6(12): 510-516.

(8) Rennerfelt, Erik.
   1948. Investigations of thujaplicin, a fungicidal substance in
           the heartwood of Thuja plicata D. Don. Physiologia
           Plant. 1: 245-254.

(9) _____ and Nacht, Gertrud.
   1955. The fungicidal activity of some constituents from
           heartwood of conifers. Svensk Bot. Tidskr. 49:
           419-432.

(10) Roff, J. W, and Atkinson, J. M.
   1954. Toxicity tests of a water soluble phenolic fraction
           (thujaplicin-free) of western red cedar. Canad.
           Jour. Bot. 32(1): 308-309.

(11) Southam, Chester M.
   1946. Antibiotic activity of western red cedar heartwood.
           Soc. Expt. Biol. Med. Proc. 61(4): 391-396.

Pacific
North
West

Research No

FOREST AND RANGE EXPERIMENT STATION · U.S. DEPARTMENT OF AGRICULTURE · PORTLAN

PNW-8   November 1963

THIRTEEN YEARS OF THINNING IN A
DOUGLAS-FIR WOODLAND

By

Norman P. Worthington

The impressive, integrated forest products industries and large forest ownerships of the Douglas-fir region are well known. Sometimes overlooked are the 53,000 owners of woodlands of under 100 acres, the average holding being 35 acres. These small tracts, totaling 1,900,000 acres, are growing timber at rates far below their potential.[1]

To secure localized information helpful to these owners, a 40-acre tract on the McCleary Experimental Forest[2] in Grays Harbor County, Wash., has been managed for the past 13 years to demonstrate that an annual income can be produced from thinnings, and, at the same time, the potential growth of the land can be maintained or even increased.

This 57-year-old stand, which became established after repeated burns of the area, is about two-thirds Douglas-fir, interspersed with western redcedar, western hemlock, and red alder. The soil, derived from a basalt cap, is Olympic loam. Site quality is II for Douglas-fir. Elevations range from 270 to 440 feet. Annual precipitation averages 60 inches, 14 inches falling during the April-to-September period, and average frost-free growing season is 184 days.

---

[1]U.S. Forest Service. Timber Resources for America's Future. U.S. Dept. Agr. Forest Resource Rpt. 14, pp. 552-553. 1958.

[2]A privately owned tract of forest land maintained through a cooperative lease agreement with Simpson Timber Co., Shelton, Wash.

MANAGEMENT APPLIED

The tract, which is closely adjacent to and on one side of a county road, was divided into five compartments of about 8 acres each to simplify scheduling of thinning operations. One compartment was thinned each year so that the entire tract was cut over every 5 years. Three compartments have been thinned three times; the others, twice. The first cutting was made in 1949; thus, the 1961 harvest marked a 13-year thinning record.

Annual sales were made to a small local sawmill during the summer and early fall for a negotiated total price, derived from a marked tree scale. Logging was done in conjunction with other sales on the Experimental Forest by a 2- to 3-man crew using in most instances small crawler tractors and forklift loaders for skidding and loading. Minimum supervision was required since the contractors were experienced in thinning work.

Prior to cutting, a cruise was made of the three or four 1/5-acre sample plots in each compartment to determine growth over the previous 5 years. The average cutting has amounted to 55 percent of current increment, 45 percent being left to supplement growing stock.

Timber marked in the first 5-year cycle consisted of branchy open-grown dominant and badly misshapen trees plus those that were either dead or dying. Each operation was a crown thinning that removed trees averaging 16.5 inches d.b.h. from a stand averaging 14.0 inches. In the second and third cycles, trees were marked primarily to improve spacing and to salvage mortality. These operations, more nearly low thinnings, removed trees averaging 13.9 inches d.b.h. from a stand averaging 15.5 inches. Minimum tree diameters marked were 10 and 12 inches at breast height for conifers and alder, respectively.

In 13 years, the average diameter of trees over 10 inches has increased from 14.0 inches d.b.h. to 16.2 inches. Proportion of volume represented by trees under 16 inches d.b.h. has declined while that of trees over 16 inches has increased (fig. 1). In an even-aged stand cutting subdominant trees, of course, favors the better dominants and codominants. Volume removed in a single thinning averaged 4,446 board feet per acre for the first few years and 2,989 board feet per acre for the 13-year period.

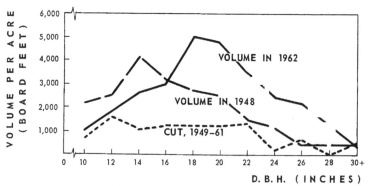

Figure 1. — Board-foot volume per acre by tree size classes.

INCREMENT

In 1948, volume for all species on the tract was 853,040 board feet, Scribner rule.[3] By 1962 it had increased to 1,121,560 board feet. This increase of 268,520 board feet added to the 328,358 board feet removed in cuttings indicates a total growth of 596,878 board feet (table 1). Thus, increment amounted to 1,067 board feet per acre annually over the 14-year period. Net annual board-foot increment for Douglas-fir has been 4.3 percent, based on an average of starting and ending inventories. However, for residual trees remaining in 1962, a 6.2-percent rate was being realized.

Table 1. — Volume and increment record, 1948-62

Item	40 acres	Per acre	Per acre per year
	M Bd. ft.	Bd. ft.	Bd. ft.
Starting inventory (1948)[1]	853	21,326	--
Ending inventory (1962)[1]	1,122	28,039	--
Increase	269	6,713	480
Thinnings[2]	305	7,641	546
Salvaged mortality[2]	23	568	41
Increment	597	14,925	1,067

[1] From sixteen 1/5-acre plots.

[2] From actual sales.

COSTS AND RETURNS

Coniferous timber, comprising 85 percent of the total cut, was made into saw logs and veneer logs. Alder was utilized as saw logs and pulpwood. Total stumpage sales for the 13 year period brought $3,383.54, or $6.51 per acre annually. Stumpage averaged $11.13 per M board feet for Douglas-fir, $5.43 for alder, or $10.30 for both. Fixed private ownership expenses were $320.88. Direct management expenses such as yield taxes, roads, marking, and sale administration were $1,494.10. Average for all costs was $3.48 per acre annually (table 2). Thus, net annual cash return from operation of the tract has been $3.03 per acre. Added to this amount should be the increase in growing stock, worth at present prices ($15.00 per M board feet) $4,027.80, or $7.20 per acre per year, so that total net return has been $10.23 annually. A compound interest rate of 5.7 percent annually has been realized on the 1948 value of the growing-stock volume.[4]

[3] All trees 10 inches d.b.h. or larger to an 8-inch minimum top.
[4] No allowance for costs of land acquisition, which undervalues the forest investment to a small degree.

Table 2. — Management and thinning costs, 1949-61 (inclusive)

Type of expenses	Total cost[1]	Annual cost per acre	Cost per M bd. ft.
	---------------------------Dollars---------------------------		
Fixed ownership:			
General administration	249.08	0.48	0.76
Fire patrol	45.80	.09	.14
Ad valorem taxes	26.00	.05	.08
Total	320.88	.62	.98
Direct management & thinning:			
Sale administration	418.26	.80	1.27
Road depreciation	406.72	.78	1.24
Marking	328.77	.63	1.00
Yield taxes	241.15	.46	.73
Road maintenance	99.20	.19	.30
Total	1,494.10	2.86	4.54
Grand total	1,814.98	3.48	5.52

[1] Labor costs including 15 percent overhead averaged $2.33½ per hour, plus allowance for a car. Road deprecia-tion was for a 1,500-foot road prorated over 328 M board feet of sales plus 1,122 M board feet of ending inventory. All other costs per M board feet are based on thinning sale volume alone.

Value of salvaged mortality has averaged 46 percent of road depreciation and maintenance costs for the 13-year period. Mortality salvaged in stands over 40 years old can in many cases finance the total cost of road construction and maintenance.

Although this study was designed as an annual operation, making cuttings every year may not be the most practical or economical. Operations ranging over the entire area at 3- to 6-year intervals may, in some instances, be more suitable to the circumstances. Less fre-quent cuts could materially reduce sale administration and tree-marking expenses and thus increase net returns. Furthermore, intermittent cutting could enable the owner to take advan-tage of favorable markets, although it would reduce mortality salvage slightly.

This study illustrates that the modern woodland can represent a valuable investment, that annual returns during the period of growth and development can be had through skillful management, and finally, that the cost of such management would be more than repaid by salvage of values that otherwise would be wasted and by the assurance of better and con-tinuing future values.

U. S. FOREST SERVICE

Pacific North West Research Note

FOREST AND RANGE EXPERIMENT STATION · U.S. DEPARTMENT OF AGRICULTURE · PORTLAND, OREG.

PNW-9   December 1963

DOMINANT PONDEROSA PINES DO RESPOND TO THINNING

by

James W. Barrett

In 1953, a study was established in a pole-sized stand of ponderosa pine (Pinus ponderosa) to determine the growth response of dominants released from all lower crown class tree competition.[1] This research note presents the results measured 6 years after thinning and discusses their significance and application.

Forest trees in a dominant position appear to have much greater access to light, nutrients, and moisture than do associated lower crown class trees. While it seems logical that such dominants in an unthinned stand would grow at near capacity, this study showed that dominant ponderosa pine poles respond markedly to complete removal of all adjacent subordinate trees. Thus, stands having a good distribution of dominant trees need not be bypassed culturally because of the belief that they are growing as rapidly as possible. Such stands may be treated to further accelerate growth of the fastest growing trees to help attain desired size classes at an earlier age.

EXPERIMENTAL AREA

The study is located on the Pringle Falls Experimental Forest in central Oregon. The stand, situated on a south-facing slope, was 65 years old at the time of plot establishment in 1953. Heights of

---

[1] Establishment of this study and collection of much of the field data was by Walter G. Dahms.

scattered old-growth trees proximate to the study area indicated a site index of 78, although heights of pole-size trees indicated a site index of only 60.[2] No significant mortality had taken place in the stand for a number of years. Tree density for age 65 was considerably greater than shown in tables for normal stands,[3] but such overstocked stands are common in central Oregon.

Soil in the study area is the Lapine series, a Regosol developed in dacite pumice from the prehistoric Mount Mazama eruption. The pumice layer, averaging about 33 inches deep, covers a much older, fine-textured, sandy loam residual soil containing cinders and basalt. Average annual precipitation is about 24 inches.

THE STUDY

Each of the ten 1/10-acre plots, established on a 300-acre segment of the 65-year-old stand, was carefully selected to minimize variation in stand structure. Dominant trees on the 10 plots were number tagged. Treatment consisted of removing all subordinate trees on each of five randomly selected plots, while the remaining five plots were left unthinned to serve as controls.

Measurement data recorded at beginning and end of the 6-year period consisted of diameter, total height, and height to green crown. These measurements were made on all released dominants on the five thinned plots and on comparable tagged dominants on the five unthinned plots. Cubic-foot volume of tagged trees was computed, using a formula derived from stem measurements made on standing trees. This approach to volume computation gave more confidence to volume increment comparisons between treatments than use of a standard volume table.

STAND FEATURES

Before treatment, both thinned and unthinned stands were similar in cubic volume, basal area, and height, although some difference in average diameter and number of trees existed (table 1).

---

[2] Meyer, Walter H. Yield of even-aged stands of ponderosa pine. U. S. Dept. Agr. Tech. Bul. 630, 60 pp., illus. 1938.

[3] See footnote 2.

Very little ground vegetation was evident at the time of thinning (fig. 1). An occasional plant of antelope bitterbrush (Purshia tridentata), snowbrush ceanothus (Ceanothus velutinus), and pine manzanita (Arctostaphylos parryana var. pinetorum) was found.

Dominant trees constituted only about 9 percent of the number before treatment but accounted for approximately one-third of the total stand basal area (table 1). On the average, cubic-foot volume of dominant trees was about 10 percent greater on the unthinned plots than on the thinned plots. Spacing between dominant trees averaged 17 feet. Treatment contrast is readily seen in figures 1, 2, and 3.

Table 1.--Average characteristics of thinned and unthinned stands at age 65 and 6 years later (per acre)[1]

Stand	Stand age	Number of trees	Average d.b.h.	Average height	Basal area	Volume[2]
	Years		Inches	Feet	Sq.ft.	Cu.ft.
Thinned:						
Total stand (before thinning)	65	1,874	4.12	32	173.2	2,537
Dominant trees (residual stand)	65	156	7.57	42	48.1	774
Dominant trees	71	156	8.57	47	61.6	1,079
Unthinned:						
Total stand	65	1,504	4.54	33	169.1	2,434
Total stand	71	1,408	5.09	--	--	--
Dominant trees	65	154	7.93	43	52.8	855
Dominant trees	71	154	8.45	48	60.0	1,056

[1] Average of five thinned and five unthinned plots, each one-tenth acre in size.

[2] Volume of entire stem, inside bark.

-3-

Figure 1.--Typical stand condition before thinning. Plot supported 172 square feet of basal area per acre.

Figure 2.--Same stand (fig. 1) immediately after thinning. Plot has 44 square feet of basal area. Dead limbs have been pruned from all remaining trees.

Figure 3.--Same stand (figs. 1 and 2) 6 years after thinning, showing the decomposition of thinning slash.

GROWTH RESPONSE

Diameter

Dominant tree diameter increment in the thinned stand was twice that of comparable trees in the unthinned stand for the 6-year period (fig. 4). On the average, response was essentially the same for all diameters observed. In terms of yearly increment, thinned trees grew 0.165 inch compared with 0.087 inch for unreleased trees. Increment cores from released trees indicate that a very small portion of the response to thinning occurred during the first 2 years. Most of this rather surprising increment, therefore, occurred during the latter part of the observation period. Future increments could be substantially greater than for the period reported here.

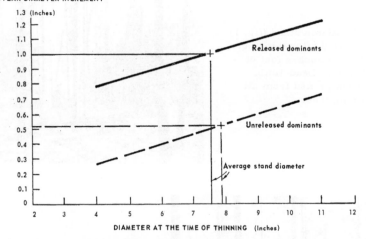

Figure 4.--Average 6-year diameter growth of dominant ponderosa pine in relation to initial diameter.

Figure 1.--Typical stand condition before thinning. Plot supported 172 square feet of basal area per acre.

Figure 2.--Same stand (fig. 1) immediately after thinning. Plot has 44 square feet of basal area. Dead limbs have been pruned from all remaining trees.

Figure 3.--Same stand (figs. 1 and 2) 6 years after thinning, showing the decomposition of thinning slash.

GROWTH RESPONSE

Diameter

Dominant tree diameter increment in the thinned stand was
twice that of comparable trees in the unthinned stand for the 6-year
period (fig. 4). On the average, response was essentially the same
for all diameters observed. In terms of yearly increment, thinned
trees grew 0.165 inch compared with 0.087 inch for unreleased trees.
Increment cores from released trees indicate that a very small portion of the response to thinning occurred during the first 2 years.
Most of this rather surprising increment, therefore, occurred during
the latter part of the observation period. Future increments could be
substantially greater than for the period reported here.

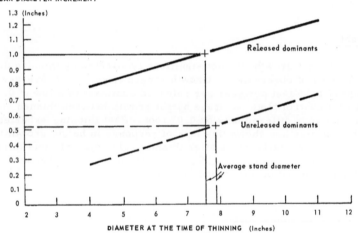

Figure 4.--Average 6-year diameter growth of dominant
ponderosa pine in relation to initial diameter.

The growth-retarding influence of lower crown class trees on diameter of dominants can be substantiated further by measurements taken in an adjacent comparable, thinned stand.[4] Diameter growth of dominant trees of the adjacent stand averaged 0.123 inch annually in contrast to 0.165 inch for the dominant trees of the study reported here. This growth comparison was made using equal numbers of trees from each stand. However, the adjacent stand had sufficient numbers of subordinate crown class trees to constitute an overall spacing of 9 by 9 feet compared with the 17- by 17-foot spacing of the dominant trees of the study plots where all subordinate crown class trees were removed. This indicates that even the moderate numbers of subordinate trees of the 9- by 9-foot spacing reduced growth of dominant trees.

A similar response has been recognized in dominant Douglas-fir poles where only two or three adjacent competing trees are removed.[5]

Height

Height growth was not significantly affected by thinning during the 6 years of observation. Growth ranged from a plot average height of 1 15 feet per year per released dominant to a low of 0.68 foot on a control plot. Average height growth between thinned and un-thinned stands differed only by 0.07 foot. Past thinning experience in this species has shown this lack of response in height growth to be expected in the early years after thinning. , In adjacent plots thinned to 9- by 9-foot spacing, height growth response did not become evident until the end of the second 5-year period of observation.[6]

---

[4] Barrett, J. W. and Mowat, E. L. Fourth progress report on ponderosa pine thinned plots 14-18, Pringle Falls Experimental Forest. Unpublished typewritten report. Pac. NW. Forest & Range Expt. Sta.

[5] Reukema, Donald L. Response of individual Douglas-fir trees to release. U.S. Forest Serv. Pac. NW. Forest & Range Expt. Sta. Res. Note 208, 4 pp., illus. 1961

[6] See footnote 4.

Volume

Volume increment of the five thinned plots averaged 50.7
cubic feet per acre per year. Dominant trees in the unthinned stand
produced only an average, of 33.5 cubic feet per acre per year. The
difference of 17.2 cubic feet between thinned and unthinned stands is
significant at the 5-percent level of probability. The yearly production rate of 50.7 cubic feet per acre in the thinned stand has
already reached 65 percent of full production as determined from
adjacent fully stocked stands.

Regression showing individual tree volume increment (fig. 5)
indicates that even the very largest trees of superior dominance are
capable of response.

CROWN CHANGE

Very few of the lowest limbs on released trees died, but
more than 2.5 feet (measured along the bole) of lower crown died on

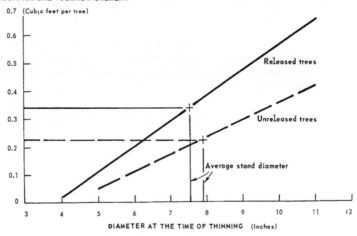

Figure 5. --Average annual cubic-foot volume increment per
dominant tree in relation to initial diameter.

unreleased dominants. Height to green limbs on dominants of the unthinned stand increased from 19.2 to 21.8 feet in 6 years. On released trees height to green limbs increased only 0.3 foot.

Lumber grade recovery might be significantly affected by this trend. During the early commercial harvests, the quality advantage might be in favor of the thinned stand because tight, green knots are preferred to loose, dead knots. Later, however, as trees approach maturity, persistence of green limbs could reduce accretion of high-quality, clear wood. Artificial pruning of lower limbs, dead or alive, would minimize the problem.

CONCLUSIONS

In this experiment dominant ponderosa pine poles responded to thinning. During the first 6 years after thinning, dominant tree response to release was in diameter increment with no clear-cut stimulus to height growth. Response to release based on width of growth rings was about the same for all size classes from 4 to 12 inches d.b.h. Cubic volume, of course, accumulated at a greater rate on released trees.

Lower crown on released trees remained live longer than on dominant trees in the natural, unthinned stands. Without pruning, this trend could lead to significant lumber grade differences between thinned and unthinned stands.

Release of dominant trees to wide spacing may help to maintain or stimulate the flow of wood to market by accelerating attainment of tree size classes which might be lacking in the existing stand structure.

FOREST AND RANGE EXPERIMENT STATION · U.S. DEPARTMENT OF AGRICULTURE · PORTLAND, OREGON

PNW-10   January 1964

SOME CHARACTERISTICS OF A SAMPLE OF LOGGING

RESIDUE IN EASTERN OREGON

by

Thomas C. Adams

A 1958 study of logging utilization in eastern Oregon found that board-foot logging residue amounted to 1.02 percent of the volume removed from the area.[1] The data of this study have been analyzed to determine classification of logging residue by species, size, and type of defect.

The study was conducted on seven logging operations chosen at random from operations of all mills in eastern Oregon. Although this was not a large sample, it gives at least a rough indication of the kind and amount of residue associated with current logging methods, which are considered as basically the same today as at the time of study. Six of the seven sample logging operations were in old-growth ponderosa pine types, with associated species of Douglas-fir, white fir, and western larch. The seventh fell in an upper-slope type containing Engelmann spruce, lodgepole pine, and subalpine fir, from which all merchantable sawtimber trees were cut. This was relatively small-sized timber on private land and had much of the character of a young-growth stand.

---

[1] Minore, D., and Gedney, D. R. Logging utilization in eastern Oregon. Office report on file, Pac. NW. Forest & Range Expt. Sta. U.S. Forest Serv., Portland, Oreg. February 1960.

Cutting in the ponderosa pine types was under what may generally be described as the sanitation-salvage method, where cutting the older, poorly formed, decadent, or high-risk trees removes 10 to 30 percent of the stand volume in the initial cut.

Board-Foot Residue

The measured board-foot residue included all pieces from the merchantable bole that were at least 8 inches in diameter, inside bark, by 8 feet in length. Most operators do not take pieces as small as 8 inches by 8 feet. Utilization standards on east-side National Forest sales include a minimum diameter of 8 inches, a minimum length of 10 feet, a minimum net volume of 30 board feet, and a requirement that all pieces be at least one-half sound (white fir) or one-third sound (pine and other species).

Most of the board-foot residue was in pieces below these National Forest standards. Distribution of board-foot residue, according to factors affecting merchantability, is as follows:

	Percent of number of pieces
Volume 30 board feet or less	54.0
Length under 10 feet	40.5
Dead at time of cutting	18.9
Excessive knots	16.2
Center rot	10.8
Sap rot	8.1
Crook	2.7
Pitch shake	2.7
Split or break	2.7
Other undesirable characteristics	5.4
Free of defect	5.4

Many logs had two or more undesirable characteristics (fig. 1). Only
8.1 percent was less than 40 percent
sound.

Figure 1.--Ponderosa pine log
left due to crook, multiple
breaks, large knots, and
heart rot.

Some pieces, even though sound, were from tops of older
trees and much poorer in quality than the same size of material from
younger, more vigorous trees (figs. 2 and 3). This was due chiefly
to the presence of large knots or knot clusters. The few pieces free
of defect averaged 50 board feet in volume and appeared to have been
simply overlooked in skidding.

◀ Figure 2.--Douglas-fir top,
left as logging residue.
This piece could have been
bucked 2 to 4 feet farther
up the bole. Bucker prob-
ably misjudged point of 8-
inch minimum top, d.i.b.

Figure 3.--Ponderosa pine top, ◀
rot-free but unsuited to utilization due to large knots and
hidden break.

Cubic-Foot Residue

Cubic-foot residue included all pieces 4 inches by 4 feet and larger (including all the material classified as board-foot residue). Total cubic-foot residue was 4.24 percent of the cubic volume removed from the area. Four-foot and longer pieces scaling 1 cubic foot or more, and at least 60 percent sound, amounted 3.82 percent of volume removed. Similar pieces 8 feet or longer amounted to 2.80 percent of volume removed. Much of the cubic-foot residue was composed of rough crooked pieces, broken chunks, or older knotty tops.

Species composition of the cubic-foot residue was as follows:

	Percent of volume
Ponderosa pine	63.3
Douglas-fir	15.0
White fir	7.6
Lodgepole pine	7.4
Western larch	2.9
Engelmann spruce	1.9
Subalpine fir	1.9
Total	100.0

Prospects for Utilization

Cut per acre was not measured, but if a cut of 10,000 board feet per acre is assumed, for example, estimated net board-foot residue would be only 102 board feet per acre, and total cubic-foot residue would be 63.7 cubic feet per acre. Due to these low volumes per acre, small size, and the various kinds of defect, there is very little prospect for early economic utilization of such material. Pieces now unmerchantable because of defect are likely to remain so. Pieces considered unmerchantable because of small size, by today's standards for lumber manufacture, fall into two groups: (1) rough tops of older trees and (2) small, vigorous trees of mixed species left in clear-cutting the upper-slope types (fig. 4). Material of this second group, together with thinnings, offers a prospect for increased utilization as pulpwood or as small stud logs. Material of the first group is likely to remain uneconomic for utilization, in the light of existing markets and alternative raw material sources.

Figure 4.--Upper-slope type in Blue Mountains. Area
was clearcut for saw logs. Sound logging residue
and residual trees suitable for utilization as
pulpwood.

U. S. FOREST SERVICE

Pacific
North
West

Research Note

FOREST AND RANGE EXPERIMENT STATION · U.S. DEPARTMENT OF AGRICULTURE · PORTLAND, OREGON

PNW-11   February 1964

SUPPLEMENTAL TREATMENTS TO AID PLANTED DOUGLAS-FIR

IN DENSE BRACKEN FERN

by

Edward J. Dimock II

Why do some forest lands restock quickly and well after timber cutting but others do not? Answers have been slow in coming--partly because of empiricism in research, partly because of the problem's general complexity   A part of the general problem concerns the poor survival of planted Douglas-fir (Pseudotsuga menziesii var. menziesii) on cutovers densely infested with western bracken fern (Pteridium aquilinum pubescens). Though there is some evidence that bracken can serve as an effective "nurse" cover to Douglas-fir,[1] a generalization about bracken's protection of natural or planted seedlings would be misleading under certain conditions. On sites where bracken grows to 6 feet in height, as in Washington's coastal zones, growth and survival of planted trees is effectively reduced,[2] and natural regeneration is virtually eliminated.

To survive, an individual conifer seedling must successfully compete for light, nutrients, and moisture as well as withstand the annual smothering effect of the matted, dead fern fronds. Also,

---

[1] McCulloch, W. F. The role of bracken fern in Douglas-fir regeneration. Ecology 23: 484-485. 1942.

[2] Worthington, Norman P. A comparison of conifers planted on the Hemlock Experimental Forest. U.S. Forest Serv. Pac. NW. Forest & Range Expt. Sta. Res. Note 111, 5 pp. 1955.

because areas of dense bracken fern form highly favorable habitats for wildlife, browsing and clipping by various mammals may seriously curtail growth--and ultimately survival--of young conifers.[3]

THE STUDY

A planting site under dense bracken fern cover was selected on the Hemlock Experimental Forest[4] near Hoquiam, Wash. The area was logged about 1900, and repeated subsequent fires presumably stimulated bracken growth and eliminated most conifer regeneration. Surrounding conifer stands now contain western hemlock (Tsuga heterophylla), either pure or in mixture with Douglas-fir and western redcedar (Thuja plicata), ranging in age from 45 to 60 years.

Objectives. -- The purpose of study was to assess the value of a fertilizer application and of two mechanical fern-suppression methods, used in conjunction with planting Douglas-fir on the above site. The fertilizer used was a pelletized, slow-release type.[5] The two mechanical treatments were use of paper overlays and periodic cutting of bracken, both applied around individual seedlings.

Experimental design. --Six treatments were tested in a randomized block design:

1. Seedlings unfertilized, control
2. Seedlings unfertilized, building paper overlay
3. Seedlings unfertilized, bracken periodically cut
4. Seedlings fertilized, control
5. Seedlings fertilized, building paper overlay
6. Seedlings fertilized, bracken periodically cut

A row of 25 seedlings was used per treatment, and treatments were randomized within each block. The three adjacent replications required the planting of 450 seedlings (18 rows of 25 per row) at an 8- by 8-foot spacing.

---

[3] Staebler, George R., Lauterbach, Paul, and Moore, A. W. Effect of animal damage on a young coniferous plantation in southwest Washington. Jour. Forestry 52: 730-733. 1954.

[4] Maintained in cooperation with St. Regis Paper Co.

[5] Austin, R. C., and Strand, R. F. The use of slowly soluble fertilizers in forest planting in the Pacific Northwest. Jour. Forestry 58: 619-627, illus. 1960.

Treatments.--Seedlings used for the test were standard 2-0 Douglas-fir stock that had been raised at the Capitol Forest Nursery of the Washington State Department of Natural Resources from seed gathered near Quinault, Wash. Seedlings were planted during April 10 to 18, 1957.

Fertilizer was applied at time of planting by dropping one nitrogen-phosphorus fertilizer pellet[6] into each planting hole. Placement of a pellet just below the roots of a seedling required only slight additional effort to normal slit-planting routine. A small amount of soil was allowed to cover each pellet to reduce possible "burning" of seedling roots.

For the paper treatment, double thickness kraft paper, with an asphalt sticker between the paper layers, was placed on the ground surrounding each seedling. Overlays measured 2 by 3 feet with a 1-inch hole in the center to accommodate the seedling. Installation required some scalping of dead bracken fronds and other brush to insure a close contact between ground and paper. Available loose dirt, wood chunks, or other debris were used to hold down corners of each overlay. Scalping and paper-laying were moderately time consuming.

Periodic bracken cutting treatment was preceded at time of planting by scalping all dead fronds, brush, and roots down to mineral soil for a radius of 30 inches around each seedling. Done with a planting hoe, scalping was the most laborious treatment supplemental to normal planting. Developing fern fronds, were then cut back by hand sickle as they reached a height between 2 and 3 feet. Cuttings were in May, June, and July of each growing season for 3 years, and each cutting required about 3 man-hours.

Since considerable animal damage was anticipated at the outset, some means of protecting the seedlings was needed to reduce the confounding of test results. All seedlings had been sprayed in the nursery with ZAC repellent before outplanting, and later control was

_____

[6] Individual pellets weighed 15 grams with 11.25 grams of N source and 3.75 grams of P source. Source compounds were urea-formaldehyde and phosphoric acid. Pellets for the study were supplied by Crown Zellerbach Corp.

attempted by annually spraying each seedling with a contact repellent--primarily to discourage clipping by snowshoe rabbits (Lepus americanus washingtonii Baird). Spraying was carried out during late summer or early fall coincident with each annual examination.[7]

Since paper overlays proved ineffective during the first few growing seasons, all seedlings thus treated were given a supplementary chemical treatment on July 29, 1960, to reduce bracken competition and to assess the effect of an experimental phytocide spray on planted Douglas-fir seedlings. The chemical[8] was applied in 8-foot strips on the six rows previously treated with paper overlays. Solution strength was 8 pounds acid equivalent of active ingredient per 100 gallons of water. Spraying was done with a backpack pump can when bracken fronds were at nearly full development. An application rate of 50 gallons solution per acre was approximated.

RESULTS

No treatment especially enhanced total height growth or survival of planted Douglas-fir seedlings (table 1). Mechanical bracken suppression with paper overlays, followed by chemical suppression 3 years later, significantly reduced both total seedling height growth and survival. However, this reduction was slight, and stocking currently remains at acceptable levels.

----

[7] Harry Hartwell, formerly of the U.S. Fish and Wildlife Service and now Wildlife Biologist, Department of Natural Resources, State of Washington, assisted in all annual plantation measurements and repellent spraying operations. Sprays used were: 1957 (in nursery), 10 percent ZAC (Zinc dimethyldithiocarbamate cyclohexylamine complex); 1957, 10 percent ZAC; 1958, 10 percent ZAC; 1959, 10 percent ZAC plus TMTD (Tetramethylthiuram disulfide); 1960, 10 percent TMTD; 1961, 10 percent TMTD; 1962, 10 percent TMTD.

[8] The chemical was supplied by John H. Kirch of Amchem Products, Inc. Designated as ACP M-251, the formulation contained 4 pounds per gallon of butoxy ethanol ester of 4-chloro-phenoxy acetic acid.

Table 1.--Condition of Douglas-fir seedlings in 1962

Treatment	Average total height	Survival	Average annual incidence of animal damage[1]		
			Rabbits	Deer	Both
	Inches	Percent	-------- Percent ---------		
Unfertilized:					
Control	17.9	79	23	5	28
Paper overlay	12.6	63	20	6	26
Bracken cutting	19.1	84	35	13	48
Fertilized:					
Control	18.7	85	25	4	29
Paper overlay	14.3	72	23	7	30
Bracken cutting	20.3	88	41	12	53

[1] Animal damage included only removal of the upper portion of the terminal shoot--either through clipping by hares or browsing by deer. Browsing or clipping of lateral shoots was ignored.

A notable incidental result was the comparatively high level of clipping by rabbits[9] and browsing by black-tailed deer (Dama hemionus columbiana (Richardson))[10] of seedlings that had been released from bracken competition by periodic frond cutting.

Fertilizer. -- Pelletized fertilizer gave little stimulus to Douglas-fir seedling growth or survival, and no burning effects were noted. Treatment means indicate that the fertilized seedlings were somewhat taller in all years (table 2) and survived slightly better after 1959 (table 3). However, these differences when tested at the 5-percent level of probability failed to show significance.

[9] Mountain beaver (Aplodontia rufa rufa (Rafinesque)) frequented the experimental site and may have caused some of the damage attributed to rabbits.

[10] Wapiti (Cervus canadensis roosevelti Merriam) may also have caused some of the browsing damage recorded.

Table 2.--Average total height of Douglas-fir seedlings

Treatment	1957	1958	1959	1960	1961	1962
			--------------- Inches ---------------				
Unfertilized:						
Control	4.3	4.8	7.9	11.6	17.3	17.9
Paper overlay[1]/	4.2	4.4	7.1	10.0	11.7	12.6
Bracken cutting	4.3	4.2	7.4	10.6	15.7	19.1
Fertilized:						
Control	5.0	5.7	8.9	11.9	16.8	18.7
Paper overlay[1]/	4.3	4.9	8.2	11.3	13.9	14.3
Bracken cutting	4.7	4.6	8.0	11.7	18.0	20.3

[1]/ Effects of phytocide spray superimposed from 1960 through 1962.

Table 3.--Survival of Douglas-fir seedlings

Treatment	1957	1958	1959	1960	1961	1962
			--------------- Percent ---------------				
Unfertilized:						
Control	97	95	85	81	80	79
Paper overlay[1]/	97	88	76	71	68	63
Bracken cutting	99	93	87	85	84	84
Fertilized:						
Control	97	91	89	85	85	85
Paper overlay[1]/	100	93	84	76	73	72
Bracken cutting	100	93	91	89	88	88

[1]/ Effects of phytocide spray superimposed from 1960 through 1962.

Paper overlays. -- The failure of paper overlays to achieve desired objectives was obvious within the first few months of the 1957 growing season. The paper was ineffective in either suppressing bracken or protecting seedlings. Vigorous bracken shoots penetrated the paper in most instances or grew up around its edge and partially lifted the overlay from the ground. In a few cases, the lifted paper blocked sunlight and killed the seedling. Furthermore, a number of papers were dislodged or penetrated by the hooves of deer. However, no significantly adverse effects from the paper overlays occurred during the first three growing seasons, at the end of which time the paper had almost completely disintegrated.

The spraying with phytocide in 1960 had some measurable consequences. All fronds within each application zone were killed back the first season after spraying. Evidently, a considerable quantity of chemical also reached the underlying rhizomes, since frond growth was severely curtailed in 1961 and moderately suppressed in 1962. This result seems particularly important since the treated zones were narrow (8 feet) and surrounded by healthy plants that could be expected to hasten regrowth of the treated bracken.

Nearly all seedlings within the sprayed zones were adversely affected by chemical treatment. Needle browning was common, as was a peculiar fusing of needles on some growing shoots. Increased mortality of seedlings within the sprayed zones was significant (5-percent level) by 1962 (table 3). Total height was reduced--the differences being highly significant (1-percent level) in 1961 and significant (5-percent level) in 1962.

Bracken cutting. -- This treatment is of interest--more because of its effect on animal damage to seedlings than its influence on growth or survival. During the 1957 season, rabbits clipped terminal shoots on 72 percent of all planted Douglas-fir seedlings. Moreover, the damage to seedlings exposed by bracken cutting (85 percent) differed with high significance (1-percent level) from that to the controls (66 percent). Though this trend seemed to persist (table 4) in ensuing years, it was not again significant (1-percent level) until 1960. During that year, browsing by deer was recorded for the first time. Both browsing and clipping damage on the bracken cutting treatments differed with high significance (1-percent level) from that on controls during 1961. However, only browsing damage remained significant (1-percent level) in 1962. Retarded growth of fern fronds, though ameliorating, was still evident 3 years after

Table 2.--Average total height of Douglas-fr seedlings

Treatment	1957	1958	1959	1960	1961	1962
			Inches			
Unfertilized:						
Control	4.3	4.8	7.9	11.(	17.3	17.9
Paper overlay[1]	4.2	4.4	7.1	10.(	11.7	12.6
Bracken cutting	4.3	4.2	7.4	10.	15.7	19.1
Fertilized:						
Control	5.0	5.7	8.9	11.	16.8	18.7
Paper overlay[1]	4.3	4.9	8.2	11.	13.9	14.3
Bracken cutting	4.7	4.6	8.0	11/	18.0	20.3

[1] Effects of phytocide spray superimposd from 1960 through 1962.

Table 3.--Survival of Douglas-fir sedlings

Treatment	1957	1958	1959	190	1961	1962
			Percer			
Unfertilized:						
Control	97	95	85	1	80	79
Paper overlay[1]	97	88	76	1	68	63
Bracken cutting	99	93	87	5	84	84
Fertilized:						
Control	97	91	89	35	85	85
Paper overlay[1]	100	93	84	76	73	72
Bracken cutting	100	93	91	39	88	88

[1] Effects of phytocide spray superimpsed from 1960 through 1962.

Paper overlays. -- The failure of paper overlays to achieve desired objectives was obvious within the first few months of the 1957 growing season. The paper was ineffective in either suppressing bracken or protecting seedlings. Vigorous bracken shoots penetrated the paper in most instances or grew up around its edge and partially lifted the overlay from the ground. In a few cases, the lifted paper blocked sunlight and killed the seedling. Furthermore, a number of papers were dislodged or penetrated by the hooves of deer. However, no significantly adverse effects from the paper overlays occurred during the first three growing seasons, at the end of which time the paper had almost completely disintegrated.

The spraying with phytocide in 1960 had some measurable consequences. All fronds within each application zone were killed back the first season after spraying. Evidently, a considerable quantity of chemical also reached the underlying rhizomes, since frond growth was severely curtailed in 1961 and moderately suppressed in 1962. This result seems particularly important since the treated zones were narrow 8 feet) and surrounded by healthy plants that could be expected to hasten regrowth of the treated bracken.

Nearly all seedlings within the sprayed zones were adversely affected by chemical treatment. Needle browning was common, as was a peculiar fusion of needles on some growing shoots. Increased mortality of seedlings within the sprayed zones was significant (5-percent level) by 1962 (table 3). Total height was reduced--the differences being highly significant (1-percent level) in 1961 and significant (5-percent level) in 1962.

Bracken cutting. -- This treatment is of interest--more because of its effect or animal damage to seedlings than its influence on growth or survival. During the 1957 season, rabbits clipped terminal shoots on 7 percent of all planted Douglas-fir seedlings. Moreover, the damage to seedlings exposed by bracken cutting (85 percent) differed with high significance (1-percent level) from that to the controls (66 percent). Though this trend seemed to persist (table 4) in ensuing years. it was not again significant (1-percent level) until 1960. During that year, browsing by deer was recorded for the first time. Both browsing and clipping damage on the bracken cutting treatments differed with high significance (1-percent level) from that on controls during 1961. However, only browsing damage remained significant 1-percent level) in 1962. Retarded growth of fern fronds, though ameliorating, was still evident 3 years after

-7-

periodic cutting had ceased. Curiously, clipping by rabbits in 1962, though moderate throughout all treatments, was significantly greater (1-percent level) on fertilized than on unfertilized seedlings.

Table 4.--Annual incidence of animal damage to terminal shoots

of Douglas-fir seedlings

Type of damage and treatment	1957	1958	1959	1960	1961	1962	Annual average 1957-62
Percent							
Clipping (rabbits):							
Unfertilized:							
Control	68	48	5	7	3	8	23
Paper overlay	57	35	11	8	1	9	20
Bracken cutting	79	41	7	55	17	15	35
Fertilized:							
Control	65	37	1	19	4	23	25
Paper overlay	72	32	9	9	3	13	23
Bracken cutting	91	51	3	67	13	20	41
Browsing (deer):							
Unfertilized:							
Control	0	0	0	1	1	25	5
Paper overlay	0	0	0	0	3	29	6
Bracken cutting	0	0	0	11	16	49	13
Fertilized:							
Control	0	0	0	0	3	21	4
Paper overlay	0	0	0	1	3	36	7
Bracken cutting	0	0	0	5	12	57	12

DISCUSSION AND CONCLUSIONS

Seedling survival was surprisingly high despite very heavy bracken competition. Even in the unfertilized control treatment, 79 percent of the seedlings survived after 6 years. Exceptionally good first-year survival (averaging 98 percent for all treatments) probably contributed greatly to this performance record. In an earlier planting study in the same general area, only 50 percent of the seedlings survived after 6 years.

Seedling height on all treatments, averaging 17.2 inches 6 years after planting, remained low. Both these results--high survival and poor height growth--undoubtedly tended to obscure treatment effects.

Contrary to general opinion, which holds that most animal damage occurs during the late fall, winter, and early spring months, the bulk of browsing and clipping damage appeared to have occurred during the summer. Fresh clipping by rabbits was common in nearly all years in the late summer. Browsing, on the other hand, seemed to be concentrated around late June or early July, when terminal shoots were nearing full growth but still succulent. A similar pattern of summer damage was recorded on 100 unsprayed seedlings planted adjacent to the study. Since spraying with contact repellent was done only at examination time, spray applications were, for the most part, ineffective in protecting seasonal shoot growth.

A definite change from clipping by rabbits in the early years of the study toward browsing by deer in later years (table 5) was apparent. This change seemed logical since small seedlings growing under dense cover would probably be less attractive to deer or wapiti than larger ones. The seedlings appeared equally attractive to rabbits and deer in 1961 but more attractive to deer in 1962.

The more frequent browsing and clipping damage to seedlings released by periodic fern cutting was undoubtedly due to increased seedling exposure. The harmful effects of increased animal damage in this treatment, however, appeared to be offset by the benefits of release from bracken competition since final heights and survival did not differ significantly from the controls.

Of greatest import was the extremely slow growth of Douglas-fir seedlings under all treatments. Seedlings averaged only about 17 inches in total height 5 years after planting, or 7 years from seed.

Several more years will be necessary for the seedlings to outstrip bracken and show reduced susceptibility to animal damage. On forest lands of high site quality, such long regeneration periods are excessively costly in time and expense. Measures more effective than those tested are needed to supplement planting in regenerating Douglas-fir under dense bracken cover.

MORE NATURAL REGENERATION BY CONTROLLING
SEED-EATING RODENTS

by

William I. Stein

One way to increase seedling yield from a seed crop is to reduce depredation by seed-eating rodents. At least three methods or combinations thereof might be used to minimize such depredations: (1) reduce small mammal population with poison bait, (2) condition rodents with repellent-treated seed to leave natural seed fall alone, and (3) prepare sites to minimize habitat suitability for rodents. All three approaches still have major limitations and have not been fully evaluated. This note details one successful attempt to protect natural seed fall by reducing rodent population with poison bait.

STUDY AREAS

The study was conducted on two adjacent areas less than one-fourth mile apart in sec. 31, T. 29 S., R. 1 E., Willamette meridian, South Umpqua River drainage, Umpqua National Forest. The areas lie on Acker Divide, a major landform rising east of Tiller, Oreg., between the South Umpqua River and a main tributary to the south, Jackson Creek. Locally, the smaller of the two areas has been called Junction Springs unit 2; the larger, unit 3.

Both areas have comparable elevations ranging from about 3,100 to 3,300 feet. Easy topography on each area includes gentle-to-moderate slopes on several aspects, minor ravines and knolls, and limited low spots of poorly drained soil. Unit 2 is 16.1 acres in size and slopes mainly to the south and southwest. Unit 3 totals 21.8 acres, sloping mainly to the south.

In early 1953, both areas were tractor-logged as part of a timber sale. All merchantable Douglas-fir, grand fir, and incense-cedar were harvested, but all ponderosa and sugar pine were left as seed trees. Residual stand components were as follows:

	Number per acre	Average d.b.h. (Inches)
Unit 2:		
Ponderosa pine	5.1	40.1
Sugar pine	1.9	43.4
Both species	7.0	41.0
Unit 3:		
Ponderosa pine	5.7	33.3
Sugar pine	1.1	39.1
Both species	6.8	34.3

The seed trees varied substantially in size and distribution (fig. 1). D.b.h. of ponderosa pine on unit 2 ranged from 19 to 65 inches, for sugar pine from 17 to 62. For unit 3, comparable values were 13 to 59 inches for ponderosa pine, 13 to 65 for sugar pine. Practically all ponderosa pines were mature, old-growth trees, but the smaller sugar pines were generally immature.

Logging slash was burned on September 2, 1953, after the first soaking rains. Slash was burned early to avoid destruction of seed from the maturing medium cone crop. A successful, relatively complete slash burn was obtained with only partial scorching of a few tree crowns and lower trunks.

RODENT CONTROL

Rodent population on each area was sampled beginning September 9. Fifty large snap traps with modified triggers were selectively placed at about half-chain intervals in two or more lines through each area. Traps were baited with peanut butter and rolled oats. For 3 days they were serviced daily and reset as necessary.

Figure 1.--All pines were left on the areas for seed trees:
A, Long, limb-free boles on unit 2 are partially obscured
by saplings killed in the slash fire; B, smaller trees
were clustered toward the top of the knoll on unit 3.

Results in 150 trap-nights revealed presence of a moderate number of rodents (table 1). Nine mice were caught on each area. There was evidence in sprung traps that several more deer mice escaped. as did one rabbit on unit 3. Not all molesting of traps was by rodents; several were sprung by grasshoppers. and undoubtedly insects removed bait at others.

Table 1.--**Daily trapping results for each**

area before treatment

Trap condition	Unit 2			Unit 3		
	Sept. 10	Sept. 11	Sept. 12	Sept. 10	Sept. 11	Sept. 12
	Number					
Unmolested	41	41	43	34	36	42
Bait eaten, not sprung	2	5	2	12	4	5
Sprung, empty	3	3	1	2	4	2
Deer mouse caught[1]	4	1	2	2	6	1
Red-backed mouse caught[2]	0	0	2	0	0	0
Total	50	50	50	50	50	50

[1] Deer mouse, *Peromyscus maniculatus*.

[2] Western red-backed mouse, *Clethrionomys occidentalis*.

On unit 2, natural seed fall was protected from rodent consumption with the same successful baiting techniques used in a direct seeding trial the previous year (Stein 1957). These techniques called for an initial baiting to reduce or eliminate resident rodents, followed by one or more rebaitings as rodent activity renewed on the protected area. Renewed activity was detectable by presence of newly hulled seeds from natural seed fall. and by loss of sugar pine seeds placed periodically in acceptance spots located systematically through the unit. Natural seed fall was not protected on unit 3.

Wheat treated with sodium fluoroacetate (1080) was distributed on unit 2 for the first time on September 17. The bait was uniformly distributed in sheltered spots averaging less than 50 feet apart through· out the area and extending about a chain into surrounding uncut timber

In late November. some pine seeds on unit 2 were eaten by rodents. On December 17, the cutover area only was uniformly rebaited in spots, using thallium-sulfate-treated oats,

Poisoned bait was distributed on unit 2 for the third time on April 15, 1954. In this application, wheat treated with 1080 was broadcast within the cutover This baiting followed proof of seed removal by rodents as evidenced by substantial depredation of sugar pine seeds in acceptance spots placed April 14 and checked after one night's exposure. Rodent pressure on this seed was heavier on unit 3 than on unit 2, with seeds taken from 31 percent of the spots on unit 3 compared with 22 percent on unit 2. Repeat of seed exposure in acceptance spots the following night showed an even greater difference in depredation between the unprotected and protected units, 46 and 24 percent, respectively. Some seeds were eaten at the acceptance spot, but most were carried off.

SEED FALL

Ten 2. by 3-foot seed traps were placed in each area on September 10 and 11, 1953. Traps were located about 2 chains apart, distributed to achieve the most representative coverage possible for each area. Seed was collected on October 9 and December 17, 1953 and April 16, 1954.

Seed fall on the protected and unprotected area did not differ significantly. Total fall on protected unit 2 numbered 100,098

(S. E. ± 11,573) seeds per acre; on unit 3, seeds per acre numbered
96,307 (S. E. ± 30.731). A majority of seeds on both areas was
ponderosa pine

	Unit 2		Unit 3	
	(Number)	(Percent)	(Number)	(Percent)
Ponderosa pine ·	78,107	78.0	84,174	87.4
Sugar pine	19,716	19.7	7,583	7.9
Douglas-fir	2,275	2.3	4,550	4.7
Total	100,098	100.0	96,307	100.0

In 1953, most seed fell between October 9 and December 17 (table 2).
Ponderosa pine seed fall was slightly later than sugar pine. Douglas-
fir produced too few seeds to reveal any trend.

Table 2.--Cumulative total seed fall in the two study areas,

by species and dates

Date	: Ponderosa : pine :	: Sugar : pine :	: Douglas- : fir :	: : :	Total seed fall per acre
	----- Percent of yearly total[1] -----				Number
Unit 2:					
Oct. 9, 1953	1.0	15.4	0		3,792
Dec. 17, 1953	76.7	100.0	100.0		81,899
Apr. 16, 1954	100.0	100.0	100.0		100,098
Unit 3:					
Oct. 9, 1953	0	20.0	0		1,517
Dec. 17, 1953	71.2	80.0	16.7		66,732
Apr. 16, 1954	100.0	100.0	100.0		96,307

[1] Not precisely a yearly total since traps were not exposed for
the entire year. However, for practical purposes it is a yearly total
since any seed falling after mid-April had little chance of germinating
in 1954.

Four-fifths of sugar pine seeds caught in the traps and two-thirds of ponderosa pine were sound (table 3). Few Douglas-fir seeds were sound, and the few western hemlock and grand fir seeds found in the traps were so abortive-appearing they were not included in the seed count. Seed soundness was estimated by cutting test from a pooled lot comprising all seeds caught in the seed traps.

Table 3.---Number of seeds caught and percent sound

Species	Seed fall period						Total	
	To Oct. 9		Oct. 9 to Dec. 17		Dec. 17 to Apr. 16			
	No.	Pct	No.	Pct.	No.	Pct.	No.	Pct.
Ponderosa pine	1	100.0	157	73.9	56	53.6	214	68.7
Sugar pine	6	33.3	28	89.3	2	100.0	36	80.6
Douglas-fir	0	--	4	25.0	5	0	9	11.1

GERMINATION

In spring 1954, lines of milacre plots were spaced 2 chains apart, north and south across each area. Plots were located at 1-chain intervals within each line, totaling 59 for unit 2 and 72 for unit 3. All seedlings that germinated on the plots in 1954 were counted, and those found alive were marked with wire pins for later reexaminations.

Nearly four times as many seedlings were found on protected unit 2 as on unprotected unit 3 (table 4). A statistical comparison between plots sampled revealed chances were better than 99 out of 100 that seed germination on the two areas was different.[1] Ponderosa pine seedlings were by far the most numerous, 93 and 83 percent, respectively, for unit 2 and unit 3.

---

[1] Data were handled by analysis of variance to test the hypothesis that populations of seedlings on the two areas did not differ. Since place and treatment variations are confounded, statistical comparisons do not permit expression of results as treatment differences.

Table 4.--Seedling production per acre on the two study areas

Species	:	Protected unit 2	:	Unprotected unit 3	
	Number	Percent	Number	Percent
Ponderosa pine	4,169	92.8	1,000	82.8
Sugar pine	288	6.4	167	13.8
Douglas-fir	34	.8	42	3.4
Total	4,491	100.0	1,209	100.0

Seedling return as percent of total seed fall differed by species:

Species	Unit 2	Unit 3
Ponderosa pine	5.3	1.2
Sugar pine	1.5	2.2
Douglas-fir	1.5	.9

The protective value of poisoning to save natural seed fall seems substantiated by relative returns of ponderosa pine, the species present in greatest abundance on both protected unit 2 and unprotected unit 3. Percent returns for sugar pine and Douglas-fir do not show similar results. Infrequent and spotty germination of these two species on both areas raises doubt that valid conclusions could be drawn about the degree of protection afforded sugar pine or Douglas-fir by baiting.

DISCUSSION

In most respects, the two study areas were very similar, yet seedling production was markedly different. Topographically, these areas were as nearly comparable in elevation, exposure, slope, and microrelief as can be found in this terrain. Harvesting and slash burning methods were identical on both areas; quantity of seed fall was similar but differed somewhat in composition. Rodent pressure prior to seed fall was also comparable. A single major dissimilarity distinguished the two areas--one received poison to control rodents, the other did not. Though not subject to rigid statistical comparison because of confounding effects between treatment and area, a nearly fourfold difference in total germination seems most reasonably explained as the product of the protective treatment applied.

This logical conclusion is further supported by limited evidence from acceptance spots exposed in April 1954. Removal of sugar pine seeds on the first night showed a difference in rodent activity between protected unit 2 and unprotected unit 3--22 and 31 percent of spots disturbed, respectively. Following bait distribution the second day, overnight seed loss showed an even greater difference--24 and 46 percent for units 2 and 3, respectively. These data provide evidence of differences in rodent pressure on the two areas following three successive bait applications. This difference was not evidenced before bait was distributed.

Evidence from several investigations (Hooven 1953, 1955; Stein 1955, 1957) has shown that initial rodent populations are not always completely eliminated following distribution of poison bait. Furthermore, rapid reinvasion of even large areas may also occur (Hooven 1953; Spencer 1951; Spencer 1954). The net aim, then, of a series of baitings on a protected area is to keep the rodent population reduced, thus increasing amount of seed available for germination.

Distributing poison bait to reduce rodent populations and thus gain a greater seedling yield from a seed crop has been tried repeatedly. Partial evaluation of many such efforts gave the impression that some gain in seedling germination had been obtained. However, in most such trials, comparability of seed fall, of rodent population, or of environmental conditions between control and protected areas remained in doubt. Without such comparability, there was always some hesitation to conclude, unequivocally, that seedling gain was the product of rodent population reduction by poison bait. The present study and one by Krauch (1945) on Douglas-fir regeneration in the Southwest appear to demonstrate clearly that substantially more natural regeneration may be obtained by reducing rodent populations by one or more applications of poison bait.

LITERATURE CITED

Hooven, Edward F.
   1953. Some experiments in baiting forest lands for the control
         of small seed eating mammals. Oreg. State Bd. For.
         Res. Bul. 8, 70 pp., illus.

_____ 1955. Midsummer baiting to control seed-eating mammals.
         Oreg. State Bd. For. Res. Note 22, 4 pp.

Krauch, Hermann
   1945. Influence of rodents on natural regeneration of Douglasfir
         in the Southwest. Jour. Forestry 43: 585-589.

Spencer, Donald A. (comp.)
   1951. Investigations in rodent control to advance reforestation
         by direct seeding. Progress report--spring 1951.
         U.S. Fish & Wildlife Serv., Wildlife Res. Lab.,
         Denver, Colo., 32 pp., illus.

_____ 1954. Rodents and direct seeding. Jour. Forestry 52: 824-826.

Stein, William I.
   1955. Some lessons in artificial regeneration from southwestern
         Oregon. Northwest Sci. 29: 10-22, illus.

_____ 1957. A successful direct seeding of sugar pine. U.S. Forest
         Serv. Pac. NW. Forest & Range Expt. Sta. Res.
         Paper 25, 19 pp., illus.

U. S. FOREST SERVICE

P acific
N orth
W est

FOREST AND RANGE EXPERIMENT STATION · U.S. DEPARTMENT OF AGRICULTURE · PORTLAND, OREGON

PNW-13   May 1964

A COMPARISON OF HIGH-LEAD YARDING PRODUCTION RATES IN WINDTHROWN AND STANDING TIMBER

by Virgil W. Binkley

A severe windstorm struck western Oregon and Washington on October 12, 1962, and blew down or damaged an estimated 17 billion board feet of timber along a 400-mile path.[1] Forest-land owners and public forest agencies immediately began a major salvage program, aimed at harvesting as much as possible of this blowdown before May 1964 to prevent a potential insect outbreak of bark beetles and to accomplish salvage before decay. This provided an opportunity to study production rates (output per man-hour and output per machine-hour) of felling and bucking and yarding in windthrown timber as compared with corresponding rates in standing timber. Results of this study should be helpful in determining production rates elsewhere, during the present salvage program and in the future.

This study was conducted in the Fall Creek drainage of the Cascade Head Experimental Forest, near Otis, Oreg., where approximately 1.5 million board feet of blowdown occurred. The predominantly 115-year-old windthrown stand in this drainage was adjacent to an intact stand of nearly the same age class, stocking, slope gradient, and aspect. Purpose of the study was to compare conventional high-lead yarding production rates in the two stands.

PROCEDURE

Two adjacent high-lead settings were laid out, with one in the standing green timber area and the other in the blowdown area (figs. 1 and 2). Volumes logged, machine-hours, and man-hours were recorded separately for each area. Comparative felling and bucking production rates were recorded over each complete area.

Figure 1.--Blowdown study area at Cascade Head Experimental Forest before harvest. In this study, the standing green timber area indicated at left and blowdown area at right were both logged by the conventional high-lead method for comparison of logging production rates.

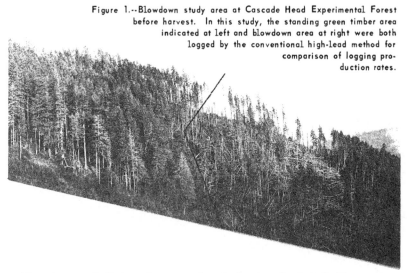

[1] Revised estimate by Northwest Pest Action Council See also· Orr, P W Windthrown timber survey in the Pacific Northwest, 1962. U S Forest Serv Pacific Northwest Region, 22 pp , illus 1963

Figure 2.--Same view as figure 1, with high-lead yarding completed on standing green timber study area (left) and trees felled on the blowdown area (right). Note the tree-length logs in the lower right of the photo. High-lead spar used to yard the blowdown area was not rigged when this photo was taken.

Data on log count, machine-hours, and man-hours were recorded by the logging crews for each complete area during actual yarding operations. Log volume was obtained at a highway scaling station in the usual manner by the Columbia River Log Scaling and Grading Bureau.

The same felling and bucking crew was used in both areas. Felling and bucking in the standing timber area was carried out in the conventional manner, felling trees and then bucking them into suitable log lengths. For safety reasons, however, bucking in the blowdown area consisted of bucking only at stump and top or in multiple log lengths.

High-lead yarding was accomplished in a normal manner on the standing green timber area. Yarding on the blowdown area was by the same high-lead yarder and crew, with the addition of a high-lead swing to the landing used to yard the standing timber area. This was a hot swing and is considered to have had no effect on the production because yarding was not held up by the swing operation (see fig. 3). Logs were yarded in tree length or multiple log lengths from the blowdown area, and were bucked into logs at the final landing by the chaser and second loader between turns and in slack periods prior to loading.

Yarding production data were collected over the entire standing green timber area, but over only that segment of the blowdown area having terrain features similar to that of the standing green timber area (fig 3).

A 130-horsepower, triple-drum yarding machine and an eight-man high-lead crew were used to yard both areas. Yarding crew consisted of a foreman (hooker), yarder engineer, chaser (unhooker at the landing), signalman, rigging slinger (foreman of rigging crew) and three choker setters.

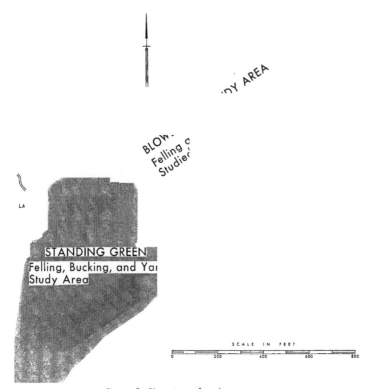

Figure 3 --Plan view of study areas

4

RESULTS

Felling and Bucking

Gross log production per man-hour of felling and bucking was 27 percent greater in the blowdown area than in the standing green timber area (table 1) This was due chiefly to the difference in method of bucking as described above Since the remaining bucking of wind-thrown timber was carried out at the landing by members of the yarding crew during otherwise slack time, this subsequent bucking time was not included in the calculation of man-hours related to output. This procedure may not be justified, however, under other conditions Without the available slack time at the final landing, the man-hours for bucking at the landing would have to be included in the total man-hours bucking time, and any delays to yarder, loader, or trucks would have to be accounted for or avoided.

Table 1.--Felling and bucking data from yarding study,

Cascade Head Experimental Forest, 1963

Item	Total standing green timber area	Total blowdown area
Gross log volume . . . . bd. ft.[1]	711,530	1,300,170
Net log volume . . . . bd. ft.[1]	607,000	1,045,670
Total logs . . . . number	3,323	5,132
Average gross log volume . . . . . . bd. ft.	214	253
Average net log volume . . . . . . bd. ft.	182	204
Area of setting . . . . acres	11.29	22.08
Gross log volume per acre . . . . . . bd. ft.	63,023	58,884
Log defect . . . . percent	14.7	19.6
Felling and bucking time . . . . . . man-hours[2]	528	760
Gross log volume per man-hour . . . . bd. ft.	1,348	1,711
Net log volume per man-hour . . . . . bd. ft.	1,150	1,376

[1] Volumes scaled by Columbia River Scaling and Grading Bureau at highway scaling station

[2] Time was kept by two 2-man felling crews, each man equipped with powersaw

Defect was greater in logs from the blowdown area than in logs from the standing green timber area. On a gross log basis, log production per man-hour (felling and bucking) was 27 percent greater in the blowdown area

Yarding

Average external yarding distance, as calculated from the area traverse, was 722 feet for the standing green timber area and 963 feet for the blowdown area. Converting these externals to average yarding distance by the factor 0.707 gives 510 feet for the standing green timber area and 680 feet for the blowdown area.[2]

Gross yarding production per hour on the standing green timber area was 4,906 board feet, on the blowdown area it was 4,067 board feet (table 2). This 21-percent apparent difference in favor of the standing timber area can be made more meaningful by taking into account the difference in average yarding distance and volume per turn in the two areas and their effect on production. Equations for the relationships between production time and yarding distance, slope, volume per turn, and crew size were developed by Tennas, Ruth, and Berntsen from a controlled study using a similar triple-drum yarder on the Cascade Head Experimental Forest in 1954.[3]

Table 2.--High-lead yarding data from yarding study,

Cascade Head Experimental Forest, 1963

Item		Total standing green timber area	Blowdown yarding study area[1]
Machine time[2]	hours	145	203.8
Gross log volume	bd. ft.	711,530	829,140
Net log volume	bd. ft.	607,000	684,280
Gross log volume per yarder hour[2]	hours	4,906	4,067
Delay time[3]	hours	8.5	28.9
Breakdown time	hours	21.5	11.0
Rig-up and take-down time	hours	200.5	398
Turns	number	1,482	1,166
Logs per turn	number	2.24	3.14
Gross log volume per turn	bd. ft.	480	711
Turns per hour	number	10.22	5.72
Average yarding distance (slope distance)[4]	feet	510	680
Average slope	percent	48	55

[1]Comparative area as shown in figures 1, 2, and 3.

[2]Excludes breakdown and delay time, includes delays less than 10 minutes.

[3]Delay time kept by logging crew for all delays of 10 minutes or greater.

[4]Average yarding distance is external slope distance times factor of 0 707 Average external slope distance of standing green timber area was 722 feet, average external slope distance of blowdown area was 963 feet.

[2]Matthews, Donald M Cost control in the logging industry. 374 pp, illus. New York: McGraw-Hill Book Co 1942

[3]Tennas, M E, Ruth, Robert H, and Berntsen, Carl M An analysis of production and costs in high-lead yarding U S Forest Serv Pac NW Forest & Range Expt Sta Res. Paper 11, 37 pp., illus. 1955

These equations are as follows, in which Y = time in hundredths of minutes:

Inhaul $\quad Y_i = 34.76 + 0.167D + 0.000265D^2 + 0.0000485DV + 0.00072VS$

Haulback $\quad Y_{hb} = 16.99 + 0.089D$

Hooking $\quad Y_c = 271.6 + 0.195D - 49.25C$

Unhooking $\quad Y_u = 43.08 + 8.60N$

Calculation of average turn time for the two areas, and corresponding production per hour, is as follows:

		Standing green timber area		Blowdown area	
Slope distance (D)	=	510	feet	680	feet
Slope (S)		48	percent	55	percent
Turn volume (V)	=	480	board feet	711	board feet
Number of logs (N)	=	2.24	logs	3.14	logs
Choker setters (C)	=	4	men	4	men
Inhaul time (Y_i)	=	2.17	minutes	3.22	minutes
Haulback time (Y_{hb})	=	0.62	minute	0.78	minute
Hooking time (Y_c)	=	1.74	minutes	2.07	minutes
Unhooking time (Y_u)	=	0.62	minute	0.70	minute
Total time per turn		5.15	minutes	6.77	minutes
Turns per hour		11.65	turns	8.86	turns
Output per hour		5,592	board feet	6,299	board feet

Actual yarding output per hour was 4,906 board feet in the standing green timber area, or 12.27 percent less than output calculated by formula (table 3). Had the conditions been the same on the blowdown area, expected output should likewise have been 12.27 percent less than calculated output, or 5,526 board feet (table 3). However, actual production in the blowdown area was only 4,067 board feet, or 26 percent less than would be expected on the same ground without blowdown. The major part of this difference can be attributed to yarding problems associated with the blowdown.

Table 3.--Comparative yarding production, from yarding study,

Cascade Head Experimental Forest, 1963

Area	Output per hour		
	Calculated by formula	Actual production	Expected production
	- - - - - - - Board feet - - - - - - -		
Standing green timber	5,592	4,906	[1]4,906
Blowdown	6,299	4,067	[2]5,526

[1] The 4,906 board feet per hour is used as a base for expected or the actual production in standing timber by this machine and crew

[2] Developed using the ratio $\frac{5,592}{6,299} = \frac{4,906}{x}$, or x = 5,526

CONCLUDING REMARKS

Results of this comparative study indicate that felling and bucking in windthrown timber does not decrease production per man-hour when accomplished in the manner described in this report. In fact, production per man-hour was 27 percent greater in the blowdown area than in a comparable area of standing green timber. This reduction in felling and bucking time can be attributed to the reduced work involved in tree-length bucking. No doubt felling and bucking production in the standing green timber area could have also been increased by tree-length or multiple-log-length bucking.

Yarding output per hour was 26 percent less in the blowdown area, as compared with the output that would be expected for similar conditions without the blowdown. This is largely accounted for by the additional minor delays and hangups in yarding through the additional slash, high stumps, and root wads in the blowdown area (fig. 4).

Under suitable conditions, tree-length yarding in high-lead operations can reduce felling and bucking time, and should be able to increase yarding production by reducing number of pieces handled and by increasing average turn volumes. Bucking on the landing not only occupies slack time, characteristic of high-lead yarding, but also allows for supervised bucking so that the maximum log grade recovery can be realized.

Future studies are needed to develop operational techniques for tree-length yarding in conventional high-lead operations and to determine what increases in production can be anticipated.

Figure 4.--**A**, Standing green timber area with yarding nearly completed. Timber was felled along the contour resulting in a lay of the logs at 90° to the lead of the spar tree. **B**, Blowdown area with yarding completed. High stumps in this area are caused by the righting of root wads during yarding. Most of the windthrown timber was lying at 90° to the lead of the spar tree.

9

U. S. FOREST SERVICE

Pacific **N**orth **W**est *Research Note*

FOREST AND RANGE EXPERIMENT STATION · U.S. DEPARTMENT OF AGRICULTURE · PORTLAND, OREGON

PNW-14   June 1964

LITTER FALL IN A YOUNG DOUGLAS-FIR STAND

AS INFLUENCED BY THINNING

by

Donald L. Reukema

Litter fall plays a fundamental role in soil formation ~~and fertility~~ fertility and thus has a basic influence on forest productivity. To determine amount and timing of litter fall and how these factors are influenced by thinning, a study was begun in 1950 on Voight Creek Experimental Forest,[1] in western Washington. Resulting information is of considerable scientific interest and provides background data for studies, now underway, of nutrient cycling in forest stands. Results of an analysis made at the end of the first 6 years were reported by Dimock in 1958.[2]

STUDY AREA

The area sampled ranges in elevation from 920 to 1,140 feet. The land slopes generally to the north and west. Soils are developed on Pleistocene glacial material and have gravelly sandy loam and sandy clay loam textures. The nearest weather station[3] receives an average annual precipitation of 46 inches, of which 15 inches fall during the period April to September. Average annual temperature is 50.4° F.; the April-to-September average is 58.0° F.

---

[1] Maintained by the Pacific Northwest Forest and Range Experiment Station in cooperation with St. Regis Paper Co.

[2] Dimock, Edward J. II. Litter fall in a young stand of Douglas-fir. Northwest Sci. 32: 19-29, illus. 1958.

[3] Buckley, Wash., elevation 685 feet.

The present forest stand became established about 1912, following cutting and repeated burns. Douglas-fir accounts for about 80 percent of the cubic volume and is dominant except in moist areas, where red alder, bigleaf maple, and black cottonwood occur. There is a scattering of western hemlock, western redcedar, and bitter cherry throughout the stand.

DESIGN OF STUDY

The Experimental Forest is devoted primarily to study of various commercial thinning regimes. Thinnings were begun in the fall of 1948, when the stand was 37 years old, to compare four treatments: (1) heavy thinning at 9-year intervals; (2) medium thinning at 6-year intervals; (3) light thinning at 3-year intervals; and (4) no thinning. Thinnings have tended to be from below, but most large, limby dominants have been removed and many codominants have been cut to free crowns of adjacent trees.

The litter-fall study has been conducted on one replication (four 17-1/2-acre compartments) of the thinning experiment. Average site index in each thinned stand is 145 feet, and in the unthinned stand, 120 feet. Basal areas before initial treatment averaged about 155 square feet per acre in the unthinned and heavily thinned stands and 180 square feet in the lightly and moderately thinned stands. Initial heavy, medium, and light thinnings reduced basal areas to about 100, 140, and 150 square feet per acre, respectively.[4] Subsequent thinnings altered the relative standings of the four treatments as illustrated in figure 1. Average basal areas on the lightly, moderately, and heavily thinned stands have been 86, 84, and 67 percent, respectively, of the basal area on the unthinned stand.

Litter fall is sampled by 40 systematically spaced traps--10 in each treatment compartment. The trap tops, measuring 2 by 3 feet, allow transmittal of seed and coniferous foliage to the interior and intercept heavier debris, such as branches, twigs, and hardwood leaves.[5] Seed and litter are collected five times a year on a schedule

---

[4] Based on fifteen 1/5-acre plots per treatment.

[5] Material larger than about three-fourths inch in diameter (other than cones) has not been collected.

designed to sample seed dissemination effectively: August 22, October 1, October 21, December 10, and April 9.[6] Collected litter is
ovendried and weighed.

BASAL AREA
IN PERCENT OF UNTHINNED STAND

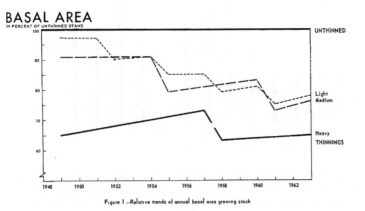

Figure 1 --Relative trends of annual basal area growing stock

RESULTS

Analyses of variance showed differences between treatments,
years, and collection periods to be highly significant. Treatment X
year interaction was nonsignificant, but treatment X period and
period X year interactions were significant.

Annual and Seasonal Variations

Variations in amount of annual litter fall have been considerable, the maximum being more than three times the minimum (fig. 2).
Total material falling in 1954 was greatest up to that time, but has
been exceeded in all subsequent years. Peaks occurred in 1955 due
to abnormal November cold,[7] in 1958[8] because of heavy winds, and
in 1960 due to an accumulation of wet, heavy snow.

---

[6] Actual collection dates have deviated slightly. This paper
is concerned only with the litter fall aspect of the study.

[7] Duffield, J. W. Damage to western Washington forests
from November 1955 cold wave. U.S. Forest Serv. Pac. NW. Forest
& Range Expt. Sta. Res. Note 129, 8 pp., illus. 1956.

[8] Data for April 9 to October 21 are missing, but a peak rate
of litter fall occurred between October 21 and December 10, 1958.

ANNUAL LITTER FALL

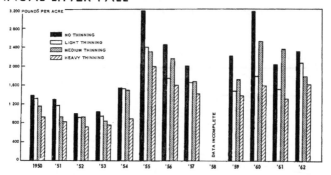

Figure 2 --Amount of annual litter fall, by year and treatment

Rate of litter fall generally reached a maximum in October and a minimum about April (fig. 3). However, in 1955, 1958, and 1960, abnormal weather conditions noted above resulted in greater rates of fall in November than in October; the cold wave of November 1955 was followed by excessive litter fall until October of the following year. In general, about half of the total litter fell in October and November. Average daily fall for the first 3 weeks in October was 16 pounds per acre, whereas during the 8-1/2-month period, December 10 through August 22, the average was only 2.4 pounds per acre.

Effect of Treatment

Over the 13-year period sampled, [9] the unthinned stand produced the most litter, averaging 1,974 pounds per acre. Treated stands averaged 1,666, 1,555, and 1,262 pounds per acre for medium, light, and heavy thinnings, respectively. All differences between treatment averages are significant, except that between medium and light thinnings.

On the average, litter fall was approximately proportional to basal area--about 85 percent of unthinned on lightly and moderately thinned plots and 65 percent on heavily thinned. Variation in basal

---

[9] Annual averages are based on 12 years, since the 1958 data are incomplete.

-4-

DAILY LITTER FALL

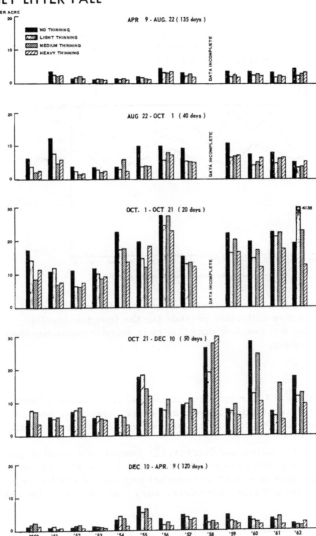

Figure 3 –-Seasonal rates of daily litter fall, by year and treatment

area followed a definite trend, influenced by growth and cutting (fig. 1), whereas year-to-year fluctuations in relative litter fall overshadowed any general trend that might exist (fig. 4).

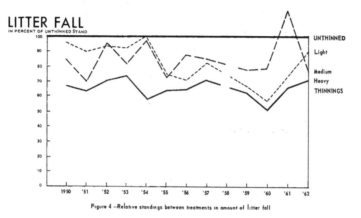

Figure 4 —Relative standings between treatments in amount of litter fall

The slight variation in proportion of total litter fall deposited during each of the five collection periods for the four treatments (fig. 3) is probably due more to differences in stand composition than to effects of treatment.

Discussion

Composition of litter reaching the forest floor under a Douglas-fir stand is varied, consisting of needles, twigs, branches, buds, cones, bark, and leaves and fruits of hardwoods and lesser vegetation.

According to Harlow and Harrar,[10] Douglas-fir needles generally persist for 8 years or more; Mathews[11] indicated 3-1/2 to 5-1/2 years. Lengths of shoots and number and size of needles depend in part upon climate and may, therefore, vary considerably from year

[10] Harlow, W. H., and Harrar, E. S. Textbook of dendrology. Ed. 3, 555 pp., illus. New York: McGraw-Hill Book Co., Inc. 1950.

[11] Mathews, J. D. Some applications of genetics and physiology in thinning. Forestry 36(2): 172-180. 1963.

to year. In a nearby stand, thinning that greatly stimulated stemwood production had virtually no effect on amount of annual branch elongation. If we assume that thinning also had no effect on number and size of needles per unit twig length, then a thinned stand, with fewer trees, would have less total foliage than an unthinned stand.

Both live and dead twigs are shed as a result of snow and wind and whipping action within interlaced crowns. Loss of live twigs would, of course, result in loss of young needles.

Hardwoods and lesser vegetation add considerably to total litter fall. Their growth tends to be stimulated by thinning; thus, the proportion of such litter to the total is higher in thinned stands.

The actual thinning operation brings much litter to the ground in the form of tops of harvested trees and branches stripped from residual trees. Unfortunately, litter from this source is not adequately sampled in this study since trees were felled away from the traps to prevent damage to them. However, any such litter that did fall on the traps was collected. Thus, our sample is primarily of normal fall from the residual stand, but it does contain a small part of the thinning debris.

Sources of peak amounts of litter fall are easily explained; the general trend is not. It was noted immediately following the 1955 cold wave that defoliation was heavy and needles remaining on the trees browned. Amount of litter collected was more than normal into October of the following year. When crowns were examined in 1958, very few needles more than 3 years old were present. All of this indicates that the freeze resulted in loss of many needles that normally would have been shed over the ensuing years. It would seem that litter fall should have tended to diminish after 1956; instead, it consistently remained higher than in any year prior to 1955.

There are some factors that tend to offset this excessive loss of needles. Probably most important is the considerable sprouting from dormant buds during the years immediately following the freeze. However, in light of needle longevity mentioned earlier, this would not be expected to start contributing to litter fall before 1959 at the earliest.

SUMMARY AND CONCLUSIONS

A 13-year record from a young Douglas-fir stand illustrates how amount and timing of litter fall are affected by thinning treatment and climatic variations.

During the 13-year period, maximum annual litter fall was more than three times the minimum, as a result of climatic conditions. Average litter fall in the unthinned stand was 1,974 pounds per acre per year. Rate of fall was at a minimum about April and usually reached a maximum in October. Generally, about one-half of the total fell during October and November.

On the average, litter fall over this 13-year period was nearly proportional to basal area. Thus, thinning reduced amount of litter fall. There were only minor variations between treatments in the proportion of total litter deposited during each of five seasonal collection periods.

Results are discussed in light of factors influencing litter fall.

FOREST AND RANGE EXPERIMENT STATION · U.S.DEPARTMENT OF AGRICULTURE · PORTLAND,

PNW-15   September 1964

DOUGLAS' SQUIRRELS CUT PACIFIC SILVER FIR CONES

IN THE WASHINGTON CASCADES

by

Jerry F. Franklin

The Douglas' squirrel *(Tamiasciurus douglasii douglasii)* cuts the cones from Pacific silver fir *(Abies amabilis)* trees, directly affecting both present and future seed crops of this species. This conclusion is based upon observations of the Douglas' squirrel in the Washington Cascade Range during September 1962. Red squirrels *(Tamiasciurus hudsonicus)* and tassel-eared squirrels *(Sciurus aberti aberti)* have been known for some time to adversely affect cone crops of ponderosa pine *(Pinus ponderosa)* by cutting off mature cones and small branches,[1] but this type of damage has not previously been reported for any western true firs. Cone cutting by the Douglas' squirrel was observed in two localities on the eastern slopes of the Cascade Range--Crystal Springs Campground near Snoqualmie Pass and Rainy Creek near Lake Wenatchee.

----

[1] Adams, Lowell. Pine squirrels reduce future crops of ponderosa pine cones. Jour. Forestry 53: 35, illus. 1955.
    Lawrence, William H., Kverno, Nelson B., and Hartwell, Harry D. Guide to wildlife feeding injuries on conifers in the Pacific Northwest. West. Forestry & Conserv. Assoc., 44 pp., illus. 1961.
    Pearson, G. A. Management of ponderosa pine in the southwest. U.S. Dept. Agr. Monog. 6, 218 pp., illus. 1950.
    Squillace, A. E. Effect of squirrels on the supply of ponderosa pine seed. U.S. Forest Serv. North. Rocky Mtn. Forest & Range Expt. Sta. Res. Note 131, 4 pp. 1953.

Cones were collected from the ground soon after they were cut, and most cones were found attached to twigs up to 9-1/2 inches long:

	At Crystal Springs (45 cones examined)	At Rainy Creek (73 cones examined)
	(Percent)	(Percent)
Cones with complete twigs, including branch tips	76	81
Cones with section of twig but without tip	13	16
Cones without portion of twig	11	3
	100	100

Because mature Pacific silver fir cones are closely attached to their twigs, the squirrels can probably cut supporting twigs more easily than cone pedicels. Observations in other areas indicate squirrels often trim the cones from the twigs on the ground before storing. Unfortunately, many of these cone-bearing twigs bear female buds which could produce next year's cones. These buds are readily identifiable since they are on the upper side of the twig and are much larger than vegetative buds (fig. 1). Of the cut twigs collected, about one-third of those with cones attached also bore one or more female buds:

	Twigs with female buds	
	(Number)	(Percent)
Crystal Springs	12	35
Rainy Creek	16	27
	28	30

Apparently, squirrels' cutting of Pacific silver fir cones can reduce cone production in both the current and succeeding years. Since Pacific silver fir is not prolific, cone production being generally confined to the uppermost branches, any twig cutting in this portion of the crown may have an especially significant effect on the next year's cone crop.

The importance of these observations cannot be appraised objectively, of course, until information is available on the extent to which squirrels cut Pacific silver fir cones over broad areas. In general, rodents are believed to prefer seeds of associated species.[2]

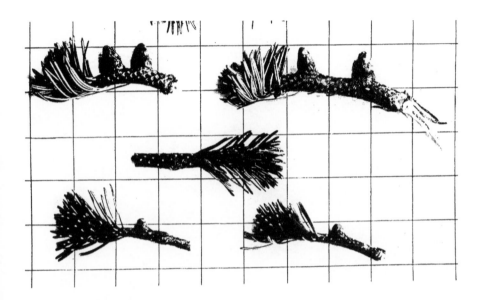

Figure 1.--Female buds of Pacific silver fir, illustrating their readily identifiable character. Buds on the two upper twigs have begun to swell prior to bud burst. One-inch grid on background.

[2] Abbott, Herschel G. Tree seed preferences of mice and voles in the Northeast. Jour. Forestry 60: 97-99. 1962.

Dick, James. A direct seeding of Pacific silver fir. Weyerhaeuser Co. Forestry Res. Note 33, 4 pp. 1960.

LIGHT THINNING OF DOUGLAS-FIR DOES NOT STIMULATE R[...]

by

Norman P. Worthington and Charles F. Heebne[...]

Figure 1.--
    stand wi
    understo

'igure 2.--Unthinned area with
    its numerous subdominant trees
    and reduced sunlight.

During the summer of 1961, a study was made of natural regeneration occurring in thinned and unthinned stands (figs. 1 and 2) of 70-year-old site II Douglas-fir on the McCleary Experimental Forest in Grays Harbor County, Wash.[1] Major soil type is Olympic loam, a residual soil derived from a basalt cap overlying marine strata deposits. Annual precipitation amounts to 59 inches, of which 14 inches fall from April through September.

Between 1949 and 1961, an area of 115 acres was lightly thinned on a 5-year cutting cycle. All of the area was covered at least twice, and slightly more than half of the area three times, by 13 annual thinnings. Thinnings removed 75 percent of the board-foot increment, or an average of 25 percent of the approximately 60,000 board feet per acre of initial volume. In 1961, the area thinned three times contained approximately 195 square feet of basal area and 40,000 board feet per acre, compared with 210 square feet and 50,000 board feet on the area thinned twice and 250 square feet and 70,000 board feet on the unthinned area.

THE STUDY

Regeneration, ground-cover vegetation, and light intensity were measured to investigate relationships between these factors and thinning. Data were gathered from 15 systematically spaced forest inventory locations, 10 in thinned and 5 in unthinned stands. A total of 60 annular 4-milacre plots, patterned after Neebe and Boyce,[2] were established around these locations, 4 sample plots (1 in each cardinal direction) being placed 50 feet from each location center. Stocking of conifers and alder was determined on each plot. Estimation of vegetative ground cover, by a modification of Daubenmire's canopy cover method,[3] was made on the northeastern milacre quadrant of each plot. Canopy coverage of plant species other than trees was estimated for aboveground strata below 1½ and 4½ feet. Due to overlapping of crowns, coverage estimates often exceeded 100 percent. Four light-

---

[1] McCleary Experimental Forest is maintained jointly by the Pacific Northwest Forest & Range Experiment Station and Simpson Timber Co.

[2] Neebe, David J., and Boyce, Stephen G. A rapid method of establishing permanent sample plots. Jour. Forestry 57: 507, illus. 1959.

[3] Daubenmire, R. A canopy-coverage method of vegetational analysis. Northwest Sci. 33: 43-64, illus. 1959.

RESULTS

Light Intensity

Light measured at ground level averaged 2.9 percent (range 0.5 to 8.6) of full sunlight under the unthinned stand and 4.9 percent (range 2.0 to 10.6) under the thinned. At $3\frac{1}{2}$ feet above ground, after-thinning light intensity was 23.8 percent (range 5.6 to 33.0) of full sunlight, nearly three times that under the unthinned stand. Ground level light differences were not statistically significant; however, differences $3\frac{1}{2}$ feet above ground were significant at the 1-percent level.

Stocking

Total stocking[6] of Douglas-fir seedlings was 30 percent in the thinned area and 15 percent in the unthinned (table 1). Analysis by age classes, however, presents a somewhat different picture. Stocking with Douglas-fir seedlings from 3 to 6 years old was 15 percent in the unthinned area and only 8 percent in the thinned area--statistically nonsignificant. The remaining stocked plots in the thinned stand had only 1- and 2-year-old seedlings. Many of these, even though on exposed mineral soil favorable to germination, would not be expected to survive. In this younger age class, stocking differed significantly (at the 5-percent level) between thinned and unthinned stands.

Hemlock, cedar, and alder stocking showed nonsignificant differences between thinned and unthinned areas.

----

[4] Dore, W. G. A simple chemical light-meter. Ecology 39: 151-152, illus. 1958.

[5] Rediske, J. H., Nicholson, D. C., and Staebler, G. R. Anthracene technique for evaluating canopy density following application of herbicides. Forest Sci. 9: 339-343, illus. 1963.

[6] Based on percent of 1/250-acre annular plots having at least one seedling; thus 30 percent stocking means a minimum of 75 well-spaced seedlings per acre, as compared with 250 well-spaced seedlings for 100-percent stocking.

Table 1.--Regeneration stocking, McCleary Experimental Forest[1]

Species	Thinned plots	Unthinned plots
	----------Percent----------	
Douglas-fir:		
3- to 6-year-old seedlings	8	15
1- to 2-year-old seedlings	22	0
All-age seedlings	30	15
Hemlock	20	15
Cedar	15	10
Any conifer	45	30
Alder	22	5

[1] Stocking measured as percent of 1/250-acre annular plots having at least one seedling.

GROUND COVER

Ground cover vegetation under the thinned stand greatly exceeded that under the unthinned at both the 1½- and 4½-foot estimation levels:

	Percent of area covered	
	Under 1½ feet	Under 4½ feet
After two thinnings	49	107
After three thinnings	55	92
Unthinned	36	57

There was no significant difference in density of understory vegetation between plots thinned twice and those with three thinnings.

DISCUSSION

Establishment of Douglas-fir and associated tree species is not occurring under the light, frequent thinning regime used at McCleary.

-4-

Apparently, the thinning did stimulate Douglas-fir germination but not survival. Light conditions have not been altered sufficiently to encourage seedling growth and development in thinned areas. Vegetative cover less than 4½ feet high was significantly denser on thinned areas and was probably a hindrance in securing adequate regeneration.

Studies are needed in stands opened more severely than at McCleary to clarify the influence of light and ground cover on natural regeneration and establishment of seedlings. More exhaustive studies should be made on environmental effects of stand modification through cutting. Particularly pertinent are the light requirements of thrifty Douglas-fir seedlings and the degree to which natural regeneration may be limited by vegetative ground cover.

U. S. FOREST SERVICE

Pacific North West Research Note

FOREST AND RANGE EXPERIMENT STATION · U.S.DEPARTMENT OF AGRICULTURE · PORTLAND, OREGON

PNW-17   September 1964

A MEASURE OF WIND-CAUSED FUELS

by

Harold K. Steen

A major windstorm hits the Pacific Northwest every decade or so. Enormous amounts of timber are blown down by these winds, and the resulting problems of salvage, insects, and fire hazard are well known to foresters. But what of the problems in forest areas where no blowdown occurs but where the wind creates significant quantities of ground fuel in the form of tops and branches? Methods of measuring blowdown (whole trees) are well defined and the effects of blowdown on fire problems have been estimated, but blow-off (tops and branches only) has received much less attention. Protection agencies recognize this increase in blowoff fuel, but their methods of measuring it are not well defined and tend to overestimate the amount. A practicable method of measuring increases in wind-caused fuel would be useful to these agencies. Ideally, data such as N acres covered with X amounts of fuel distributed in manner Y should be recorded.

Measurement System Tested

An especially severe windstorm hit the Pacific Northwest on October 12, 1962, emphasizing the need for a reliable wind-caused fuel sampling system. Ten months after the October 12 storm, 4-milacre circular plots were established at 1-chain intervals in a stand of 60- to 70-year-old Douglas-fir in northwest Oregon. The 4-milacre plot size was chosen for its convenience. An estimate of the proportion of ground covered by branches and tops was made on each milacre quadrant. The proportion of ground covered was recorded in units of one-fifths of the total quadrant area (table 1); for example, 40-percent cover was recorded as two-fifths.

In this stand, about 43 percent of the ground was covered with tops and branches. Vertical dimensions of the fuel were not considered in this sample. With a larger sample, fuel continuity could have been determined by plotting the samples on a map, much the same way a type map is constructed.

The merits of this system of measuring blowoff are that it is both easy to teach and to use in the field. No precise measurements are needed

in the field work; interplot distances can be paced, the plot size is
small enough to be easily estimated, and the one-fifths covered by fuel
are readily determined. With a little practice, a qualified man can
collect field data almost as fast as he can walk. The office analysis
of the data is uncomplicated and the overall reliability of the method
ought to be similar to other systematic sampling techniques.

Table 1.--Field tally of proportion of ground covered by blowoff fuel

(In one-fifths of milacre quadrant)

Plot	Milacre quadrants				Average number of one-fifths by milacre quadrants	Percent cover of 4-milacre plot
	1	2	3	4		
1	1	0	0	1	0.50	10
2	2	3	2	4	2.75	55
3	2	0	1	1	1.00	20
4	1	0	0	1	.50	10
5	1	1	4	1	1.75	35
6	4	2	2	2	2.50	50
7	3	3	1	2	2.25	45
8	1	5	5	4	3.75	75
9	4	3	2	0	2.25	45
10	1	2	1	3	1.75	35
11	3	2	0	0	1.25	25
12	2	2	4	2	2.50	50
13	5	5	5	5	5.00	100
14	2	2	2	3	2.25	45
15	1	2	3	4	2.50	50
16	4	3	2	1	2.50	50
17	0	1	3	1	1.25	25
Total	--	--	--	--	36.25	725
Average	--	--	--	--	[1]/2.13	42.6

[1]/ $\underline{2.13}$ x 100 = 42.6-percent cover.

The disadvantages of this system are apparent, as are those of any similar or comparable system. The estimator has to decide what is blowoff fuel and what is not. Bias will be difficult to avoid since the areas with blowoff will have to be arbitrarily separated from areas with too little blowoff to be of significant hazard.

General Observations

The field test of this method yielded some unexpected information. It seemed logical that areas adjacent to heavy blowdown would have had numerous tops and branches broken off; however, this was generally not the case. Blowoff in old-growth timber was slight; usually, the whole tree went down or nothing. This was most apparent along the edges of blowdown where trees 3 feet in diameter were twisted and broken, while a few feet away in the standing timber no sign of broken branches or tops appeared.

The 50- to 100-year-age stands, or those about 50 to 125 feet in height, seemed to be highly susceptible to blowoff. Usually, no blowoff occurred in stands under 50 years, and stands older than 100 years behaved much as did old growth. Within 1 year after the storm, all of the needles had dropped off the branches, greatly decreasing fire hazard. Fine twigs and larger limbs covered the ground to a depth of 6 inches in some locations (fig. 1). There were some concentrations of fuel whose depths could be measured in terms of feet (fig. 2). The small number of these heavier concentrations probably would not significantly increase the overall rate of spread of a ground fire. Figure 3 illustrates the general appearance of blowoff near the edge of a stand in the 50- to 100-year age class.

Figure 1.--Blowoff of fine twigs and branches 6 inches deep beneath Douglas-fir in the 50- to 100-year age class.

described more damage in thinned than unthinned stands, while the other report showed more damage in the unthinned. This may indicate that factors other than spacing of the trees have more influence on wind damage.

Summary

Following high winds, damage in the form of tops and branches on the ground commonly occurs in 50- to 100-year-old stands but is not often found in very young stands or in old growth. A method of measuring this blowoff, utilizing an estimate of the proportion of the ground covered by wind-caused fuel, shows promise.

Figure 2.--A heavy concentration of blowoff branches and tops 1-1/2 feet deep beneath Douglas-fir in the 50- to 100-year age class.

Figure 3.--Blowoff on the forest floor near the edge of a Douglas-fir stand in the 50- to 100-year age class.

FOREST AND RANGE EXPERIMENT STATION · U.S. DEPARTMENT OF AGRICULTURE · PORTLAND, OREGON

TESTING PARTIAL ATMOSPHERIC FUMIGATION FOR ERADICATING EUROPEAN
PINE SHOOT MOTH ON BALED AND BAGGED PINE SEEDLINGS

by

V. M. Carolin and W. K. Coulter

SUMMARY

Partial atmospheric fumigation with methyl bromide was tested as a
means of eradicating European pine shoot moth on baled and bagged ponderosa pine seedlings. Preliminary results show that, with overwintering
larvae, treatment periods can be reduced at least 30 percent, as compared
with conventional atmospheric fumigation, and still result in 100-percent
shoot moth control. Judging from larval mortality, both baled and bagged
seedlings can be effectively treated by partial atmospheric fumigation
during the dormant period with minor damage resulting.

INTRODUCTION

Studies in the Seattle, Wash., area during 1960-61 showed atmospheric
fumigation with methyl bromide to be effective in eradicating European
pine shoot moth on ornamental pines growing in the ground or in containers.
Inexpensive, portable fumigation chambers were developed and standard fumigation procedures were devised whereby 100-percent kill of the shoot moth
can be obtained under widely varying out-of-door conditions. These standard procedures were incorporated in shoot moth quarantines of the Federal
Government and of several Western States.

In 1961-62, the fumigation method was tested on ponderosa pine planting stock, chiefly for phytotoxicity, in a forest nursery of the Washington
Department of Natural Resources. Seedlings in beds were fumigated in mid-
winter. Seedlings in bales, held up to 3 months in cold storage, were
treated monthly from December until April. Outplanted seedlings from the

fumigated bales showed little damage, but this was not conclusive because penetration of the methyl bromide into the bales may not have been
adequate for complete kill of the shoot moth. Larvae of the moth were
not introduced into the bales, since the test nursery was in a shoot
moth-free zone. In general, the method of outdoor treatment was not
entirely satisfactory for baled stock because of the limited capacity
of the portable chambers and the difficulty of controlling temperatures
within prescribed limits at this time of year.

A method of packaging conifer planting stock, devised by Duffield
and Eide,[1] is likely to replace baling. The new method has advantages
in shipping and handling, but its adaptability to fumigation has not
been explored. A 3-ply multiwall kraft bag is used. The inner wall is
a 10-pound polyethylene laminate on 50-pound kraft paper and the outer
wall, 50-pound, wet-strength kraft. Bunches of 50 seedlings each are
placed in the large bags alternately, with roots of one bunch lining up
with tops of another bunch. Rotted wood chips or peat may be placed on
the roots, but this is not necessary. Bag tops are sealed by wrapping
and tying or folding and stapling.

Partial atmospheric fumigation, also called vacuum fumigation, was
suggested by J. R. Fisher[2] as a possible means of treating both baled
and bagged stock. This method, which requires large permanent chambers
properly equipped, is said to result in gas penetration superior to that
of atmospheric fumigation. By treating in large quantities, this method
promises cost savings in comparison with treatment in portable chambers.
However, there is a possibility that fumigation by partial vacuum would
increase the risk of damage to the trees. The method is used by Federal
Plant Quarantine offices at some ports of entry, and recommendations for
treatment time at a given chamber temperature are quite similar to those
derived in the Seattle tests. At ports of entry, survival of plants is
considered secondary to the destruction of noxious insects present.

A cooperative study by the Pacific Northwest Forest and Range Experiment Station, Portland, Oreg., and the Dow Chemical Co., Seattle, Wash.,
was initiated in the spring of 1963 to explore the capabilities of vacuum
fumigation.[3] Station personnel planned the experiment, obtained a supply of shoot moth infested twigs for testing purposes, made records durin

---

[1] Duffield, J. W., and Eide, R. P. Polyethylene bag packaging of
conifer planting stock in the Pacific Northwest. Jour. Forestry 57(8):
578-79. 1959.

[2] Entomologist, Research and Development, The Dow Chemical Co.,
Seattle, Wash.

[3] Memorandum of Understanding for Forest Insect Research, dated
March 14, 1963.

the testing, provided for examination of treated material, and inter-preted the results. The Dow Chemical representative arranged for the use and operation of fumigation chambers, obtained the desired number of packages of ponderosa pine seedlings through the Washington Department of Natural Resources, provided the fumigant, and insured that fumigation instructions were followed by the commercial operator. The Ruddy Fumigant Co. in Seattle, Wash., provided the chambers for the tests and operated the equipment.

OBJECTIVES

This study was to compare the efficiency of partial atmospheric fumigation with that of atmospheric fumigation in obtaining 100-percent control of the shoot moth when seedlings were dormant and larvae inactive. Specific objectives were to determine for partial atmospheric fumigation whether:

1. Complete control can be obtained in shorter treating time than with standard atmospheric fumigation.
2. Complete control can be obtained both in baled and packaged pines.
3. Damage to trees differs in comparison with atmospheric fumigation.

METHODS

Partial atmospheric fumigation is accomplished by creating a partial vacuum, introducing the gas, and then releasing the vacuum. A 15-inch (approximately 50 percent) vacuum was used in these tests. With the chambers used, 7 to 8 minutes were required to obtain the desired vacuum, 2 to 3 minutes to introduce the gas, and about 5 minutes to release the vacuum. Treatment time was construed to start after release of the vacuum and to end at the beginning of gas evacuation.

The actual fumigation was done on March 14 and 15, a relatively cool period, in an unheated warehouse. Chamber temperatures ranged from 42° to 50° F., except for a brief period during and immediately after gas introduction. Temperatures were depressed when the vacuum was drawn but rose when the vacuum was released. Starting temperatures after release of the vacuum were usually about 6° above original chamber temperatures, but return to original chamber temperatures took place within 5 to 10 minutes.

Gas concentration was 4 pounds per 1,000 cubic feet. The large, cylindrical, metal chambers, relics of Prohibition days, were of 1,800-cubic-foot capacity, so that 7.2 pounds of actual fumigant were used in each chamber. Gas was circulated by means of one fan placed on the floor toward the rear of the chamber near the gas inlet.

Five test runs, each consisting of two chambers, were made. Runs were designated as A to E. In four runs, partial atmospheric fumigation was used in both chambers. Treatment time in one chamber in each run was "standard," as derived from tables of temperature and time prepared for atmospheric fumigation in previous studies. Treatment time in the second chamber was reduced; percent reductions from calculated standard treatment time by test run were: A-20, B-22½, C-25, and E-30. In the remaining test run (D), atmospheric fumigation was used in one chamber and partial atmospheric fumigation in the other; treatment time was standard according to tables for atmospheric fumigation and identical for the two chambers.

The pine material used in each test run was packaged in four different ways:

1. Standard bale with 1,000 2-0 ponderosa pine seedlings.
2. Large kraft bag with 1,000 2-0 ponderosa pine seedlings.
3. Small kraft bag with 100 2-0 ponderosa pine seedlings.
4. Control group of infested twigs of Scotch, mugho, or Monterey pine, anchored in sand in clay pots.

Packages in categories 1, 2, and 3 were "salted" with infested bud clusters from twigs collected at 13 points on Mercer Island, Wash., on March 13. Bud clusters on a short section of twig were systematically placed in different positions in the bales and bags. Numbers of bud clusters used for each kind of bundle were: (1) standard bale, 40; (2) large bag, 40; (3) small bag, 10; and (4) control twigs, 27 to 35.

Location and tree species from which infested bud clusters were collected were replicated by category of package in the two chambers used in a test run. This was done to equalize any differences in natural mortality associated with tree source. Table 1 shows the distribution of the infested samples within the test material.

Percent larval mortality was used as index of fumigation success. After each test run, fumigated bales and bags were opened and all bud clusters removed. These bud clusters and infested twigs from the clay pots were placed in separate polyethylene bags according to test run, chamber number, and category of package. During the next two weeks, all bud clusters were opened under a binocular microscope and the condition of each larva was recorded as living or dead.

Incidence of damage to the seedlings was sampled by taking 10 fumigated trees from each bale and each large bag and planting them on the property of J. R. Fisher. The planting site was previously rototilled five times to a 6-inch depth until grass was completely removed. Trees were planted on March 17 in rows of 10 trees running north and south, and 20 rows running east and west, totaling 200 trees. Tree survival was recorded in detailed examinations on August 6, 1963, and April 13, 1964.

Table 1. <u>Distribution of infested bud clusters among packages</u>

<u>of pine material fumigated in five test runs, 1963</u>

Test run and treatment time and package category	Pine species	Collection point	Bud clusters per chamber
A, chamber 1 (standard) and chamber 2 (reduced 20 percent):			Number
Bale	Mugho	1	25
Bale	"	2	15
Large bag	"	3	20
Large bag		4	20
Small bag		5	10
Twigs		5	10
Twigs		6	20
B, chamber 1 (reduced 22½ percent) and chamber 2 (standard):			
Bale	Mugho	5	40
Large bag	"	5	25
Large bag	"	7	15
Small bag	Scotch	8	10
Twigs	"	8	27
C, chamber 1 (standard) and chamber 2 (reduced 25 percent):			
Bale	Mugho	9	40
Large bag	"	9	40
Small bag	"	5	10
Twigs	Scotch	10	35
D, chamber 1 (standard) and chamber 2 (standard):[1/]			
Bale	Scotch	10	40
Large bag	"	10	40
Small bag	"	11	10
Twigs		11	30
E, chamber 1 (standard) and chamber 2 (reduced 30 percent):			
Bale	Mugho	5	5
Bale	"	9	15
Bale	Scotch	10	20
Large bag	"	11	15
Large bag	Mugho	12	25
Small bag	"	9	2-3
Small bag	Scotch	10	8-7
Twigs	"	10	18
Twigs	Monterey	13	12

[1/] Conventional atmospheric fumigation was used in chamber 1, partial atmospheric fumigation in chamber 2. Treatment times were identical.

RESULTS

The relatively low chamber temperatures resulted in lengthy treatment periods, up to 3 hours and 31 minutes for standard treatments. Reductions in treatment time ranged up to 59 minutes for a 30-percent time reduction. Results by test run and chamber are summarized in Table 2.

Complete kill of all European pine shoot moth larvae was obtained in all test runs, regardless of reduction in treatment time, and with all types of packages. A total of 905 dead larvae was found (table 3).

Analysis of tree damage was confounded by mortality caused by the dumping of weed killer in the planting area 2 years previously. However, since not more than five trees from any bale or bag were in the contaminated area, conclusions were drawn from the remaining trees. Damage was defined as death of seedlings or failure to produce current growth. With partial atmospheric fumigation at standard treatment time, no difference in damage between baled and bagged seedlings was evident. On August 6, average survival was 91 and 93 percent, respectively. At reduced treatment time, average survival of baled and bagged seedlings was 87 and 100 percent, respectively. The 20 trees treated with standard atmospheric fumigation showed no damage. On April 13, examination showed essentially no change in the area uncontaminated with weed killer, with three more trees showing damage and one recovering from damage. In the contaminated area, many damaged trees were missing and four additional trees showed damage.

CONCLUSIONS

The test resulted in the following general conclusions:

1. With overwintering larvae, treatment periods using partial atmospheric fumigation can be reduced at least 30 percent, as compared with conventional atmospheric fumigation, and still result in 100-percent control of shoot moth larvae. Minimum effective treatment periods remain to be determined.

2. Judging from larval mortality, both baled or bagged pine seedlings can be effectively treated by partial atmospheric fumigation.

3. Tree damage resulting from partial atmospheric fumigation during the dormant period is minor. Damage to trees in bags, with little protection to roots, is no greater and probably less than damage to baled trees.

-6-

Table 2.--Summary of shoot moth survival and seedling damage resulting from partial

atmospheric fumigation, Seattle, Wash., March 14-15, 1963

Test run	Treatment time	Fumigation exposure			Shoot moth larvae		Trees planted[1]	
		Duration		Temperature range	Total	Surviving	Total	Undamaged
		Hrs.	Min.	Degrees F.	Number		Number	
A, chamber 1	Standard	3	24	46-48	93	0	20	16
A, chamber 2	Reduced 20 percent	2	43	46-48	122	0	20	19
B, chamber 2	Standard	3	12	48-50	108	0	18	17
B, chamber 1	Reduced 22½ percent	2	29	48-50	116	0	10	7
C, chamber 1	Standard	3	14	48-50	97	0	10	9
C, chamber 2	Reduced 25 percent	2	29	48-50	90	0	14	14
D, chamber 2	Standard	3	31	44-45	54	0	20	19
D, chamber 1	Standard[2]	3	31	44-45	63	0	20	20
E, chamber 1	Standard	3	15	47-53	83	0	20	19
E, chamber 2	Reduced 30 percent	2	16	47-53	79	0	20	19
--	--	--	--	--	905	0	172	159

1/ Excluding trees planted in area contaminated with weed killer.
2/ This was the only treatment in which conventional atmospheric fumigation was used.

Table 3.--<u>Larvae found in packaged material, by test run</u>

<u>and treatment time, 1963</u>[1]/

Packaged material	Test runs									
	A1	A2	B1	B2	C1	C2	D1	D2	E1	E2
1,000-tree bales	25	34	39	45	33	30	12	14	26	30
1,000-tree bags	28	30	47	33	26	26	19	14	21	22
100-tree bags	8	14	8	6	14	20	4	3	6	5
Infested twigs	32	44	22	24	24	14	28	23	30	22
Total	93	122	116	108	97	90	63	54	83	79

[1]/ Number "1" designates standard treatment time.

REFERENCES

Carolin, V. M., and Coulter, W. K.
  1963. Eradicating European pine shoot moth in commercial nurseries
         with methyl bromide. U.S. Forest Serv. Res. Paper PNW-1,
         11 pp., illus.

Carolin, V. M., Klein, W. H., and Thompson, R. M.
  1962. Eradicating European pine shoot moth on ornamental pines
         with methyl bromide. U.S. Forest Serv. Pac. NW. Forest
         & Range Expt. Sta. Res. Paper 47, 16 pp., illus.

Klein, W. H., and Thompson, R. M.
  1962. Procedures and equipment for fumigating European pine shoot
         moth on ornamental pines. U.S. Forest Serv. Pac. NW.
         Forest & Range Expt. Sta. Res. Paper 50, 25 pp., illus.

U. S. FOREST SERVICE

Pacific North West Research Note

FOREST AND RANGE EXPERIMENT STATION · U.S. DEPARTMENT OF AGRICULTURE · PORTLAND, OREGON

PNW-19   December 1964

GRADES FOR INLAND DOUGLAS-FIR SAW LOGS

IN STANDING TREES

by

Paul H. Lane

INTRODUCTION

An improved system for grading inland Douglas-fir saw logs in standing trees has been developed by the Station as part of the U.S. Forest Service log and tree grade research program. This research note presents the grading specifications and a summary statement of their interpretation and application. A more complete publication is being prepared to explain how these grades were developed and illustrate how they estimate lumber grade yield and segregate logs into value classes.

The Station is currently investigating tree grades for inland Douglas-fir--a system for evaluating the entire tree in contrast with grading fixed segments or logs in the stem. This research is nearing completion and may provide timber cruisers with choice of using tree grades or log grades for estimating the quality of standing inland Douglas-fir sawtimber. For this reason, the log grades described in this paper have been adopted for Forest Service use on an interim basis.

THE GRADING SPECIFICATIONS

Grade 1

> Branches and
> branch stubs: Any number, live or dead, less than 1 inch in
>   diameter permitted.
>
> Scars: None permitted.

<u>Grade 2</u>

Branches and
branch stubs: Live: Any number 3 inches or less in diameter
                    permitted.

                Dead: Any number 2 inches or less in diameter
                    permitted.

Scars: None permitted (see exception).

Sweep and
crook: Cruise volume deduction must not exceed 20 per-
                cent of gross volume (see exception).

<u>Exception</u>:   Any log meeting Grade 1 specifications for
                branches and stubs may have any number of
                scars and may also have sweep and crook in
                excess of 20 percent.

<u>Grade 3</u>

Includes all logs not qualifying for Grades 1 and 2 that are
at least 6 inches in diameter, 8 feet long, and estimated to
have at least one-third of their gross cruise volume in sound
wood suitable for manufacturing standard lumber.

INTERPRETATION OF THE SPECIFICATIONS

<u>Log Length</u>

These grades are primarily for application to logs in nominal 16-
foot lengths as cruised in standing trees. The actual cruised log
lengths may vary slightly from 16 feet because of estimated stump
height, trimming allowance, top diameter limit, and cruising methods
for handling forked stems, broken tops, or other tree characteristics.
Appropriate regional or local cruising instructions should be followed
in establishing the nominal 16-foot grading lengths.

If segments other than 16 feet are graded, e.g., top logs, the
grading specifications will be applied without any adjustment for
length. The minimum length to be considered for grading is 8 feet.

<u>Log Diameter</u>

Log diameter is an inherent part of the grading system and is not
considered in establishing the grade of a log. In application, it is
handled by developing the log grade performance data by log diameter
classes.

Minimum diameter considered for grading will be 6 inches, estimated top d.i.b.

Merchantability Standards

Only logs from live trees will be graded. Logs must have an estimated one-third or more of their gross cruise volume in sound wood that is judged to be suitable for manufacturing standard lumber, as defined by the Western Wood Products Association. Logs that are estimated to have less than one-third of their gross cruise volume in sound wood are considered Cull and will not be further graded.

Grading Characteristics

Grading is based solely on surface characteristics of the log that are visible as it stands in a tree. Each log is to be graded on its own characteristics, without considering the characteristics of other logs in the tree. Consider all of the log surface as cruised, including any trimming allowance. Three general types of visible characteristics determine the grade of a log: (1) branches or branch stubs, (2) scars, and (3) sweep or crook. Other log characteristics are disregarded in determining log grade.

Branches and Branch Stubs

The most important factor in determining grade is the size and type of branches and/or branch stubs. The grading specifications for branches and branch stubs include branches broken off at the log surface and holes from which limbs have broken out. Overgrown branches ("indicators") are not considered.

The two classes of branches and branch stubs considered are live and dead. A live branch (or live stub) is one to which the bark still adheres and is expected to result in an intergrown or tight, sound knot in lumber. A dead branch or branch stub is one that has been dead for several years and is without bark. It is expected to result in an encased or loose, unsound knot in lumber.

When branch clusters are present, the branch and branch stub specifications will be applied to the largest branch (or stub) in the cluster.

The diameter of a branch or branch stub is the estimated outside diameter adjacent to, but outside of, any branch collar present at the juncture of the branch and tree stem.

Scars

The degrading scars referred to in the specifications are timber defects commonly described as fire scars, cat faces, seams, frost cracks, lightning scars, rotten holes, mechanical damage, and other such injuries. Such scars in inland Douglas-fir are most common in the butt log but may extend into, or originate in, the upper portion of the bole. All scars are considered degrading if they are overgrown. Partially overgrown scars will also be considered degrading if the underlying wood is judged to be decayed, excessively pitchy, or severely checked to the extent that lumber recovery is affected. Fresh scars or injuries that are judged to be superficial with respect to lumber recovery will be disregarded. The grader must decide if scars of recent origin are super- ficial--if old and partially overgrown, they are almost always degrading.

Sweep and Crook

Any sweep or crook that results in a cruising volume deduction in amounts described in the specifications will be considered.

APPLICATION OF THE GRADES

In applying these grades to logs in standing trees, the suggested procedure is to first determine the branch size and type (live or dead) category. For most inland Douglas-fir trees, it can easily be deter- mined if any visible limbs or stubs are less than 1 inch (potentially Grade 1) or, if they are larger, whether the dead limbs exceed 2 inches and the live ones exceed 3 inches. If there are no degrading scars, sweep, or crook, the grade is thus established; if these defects are present, the grade can be quickly determined by applying the appropriate specifications.

As explained previously, log diameter is an integral part of the grading system, and all performance data should be collected and applied on a diameter class basis.

SUMMARY OF THE
SAW LOG GRADES FOR INLAND DOUGLAS-FIR

The following is a pocket-size summary of the grading specifications for quick field reference.

SUMMARY OF INLAND DOUGLAS-FIR SAW LOG GRADES[1]

Grade	Grading Specifications
1	Any number of live or dead branches or stubs, _less_ than 1 inch. No scars permitted. Volume deduction for sweep or crook not exceeding 10 percent.
2	Any number of _live_ branches or stubs, 3 inches or less. Any number of _dead_ branches or stubs, 2 inches or less. No scars permitted (see exception)[2] Volume deduction for sweep or crook not exceeding 20 percent (see exception)[2]
3	Any log not qualifying for Grade 1 or Grade 2 that is at least 8 feet long, 6 inches d.i.b., and one-third sound.

[1] Prepared by the Douglas-fir Log and Tree Grade Research Project, Pacific Northwest Forest and Range Experiment Station, Portland, Oregon.

[2] Any log meeting Grade 1 specifications for branches and stubs may have any number of scars and also sweep and crook in excess of 20 percent.

INTERPRETATION OF THE SPECIFICATIONS

Log length — Grades primarily for 16-foot logs as cruised—apply to other lengths without adjustment. Logs graded must be at least 8 feet long.

Log diameter — Do not consider in grading (except logs must be at least 6 inches top d.i.b.).

Merchantability — Grade only logs in live trees that are at least one-third sound.

Grade characteristics — Consider only branches or branch stubs, scars, or sweep and crook.

Branches — Estimate diameter outside bark and collar. In clusters consider largest branch or stub. Disregard "indicators."

Scars — Consider as degrading all overgrown fire scars, cat faces, seams, frost cracks, lightning scars, rotten holes, mechanical damage, etc. Consider partially overgrown scars degrading if judged to affect lumber recovery. Disregard fresh scars or injuries judged to be superficial.

Sweep or crook — Consider when cruising volume deduction is in amounts described in the specifications.

U. S. FOREST SERVICE

Pacific North West

Research Note

FOREST AND RANGE EXPERIMENT STATION · U.S. DEPARTMENT OF AGRICULTURE · PORTLAND, OREGON

PNW-20

January 1965

RUST CANKERS ---- A THREAT TO CENTRAL OREGON LODGEPOLE PINE?

by   Walter G. Dahms

Rust cankers on lodgepole pine were found to be both numerous and damaging during the course of a 1957-58 Oregon yield study.[1] Out of 1,644 felled trees, 733, or 44.6 percent, had one or more cankers on the bole. Incidence of rust was highest on the largest trees.

This tally of rust-infected trees was made as an incidental part of the yield study. Therefore, kinds of cankers were not recorded separately and samples were selected strictly on the basis of the yield study requirements. However, the large number of cankers found indicates their importance.

Damage caused includes outright killing of some infected trees, top killing (everything above the canker), and weakening the stem at the point of the canker. Thus, because of cankers, windbreak is increased and number of trees that can qualify for such relatively high-value products as poles or saw logs is reduced.

Western gall rust (fig. 1), caused by Peridermium harknessii,[2] was by far the most common kind of rust found. A diamond-shaped canker (fig. 2), caused by Cronartium stalactiforme,[3] was encountered much less frequently. The difference was large and easily observable without a tally.

Trees examined were those felled for growth measurement purposes as a part of the previously mentioned yield study. Sampling objectives of the yield study were twofold:

1. To obtain a good geographical representation of lodgepole pine stands as they occur on pumice soils in central and south-central Oregon.

2. To sample, for each 10-year age span from 30 to 120 years, 10 stands representing the widest possible range in site quality.

---

[1] Dahms, Walter G. Gross and net yield tables for lodgepole pine. Pac. NW. Forest & Range Expt. Sta. U S. Forest Serv. Res. Paper PNW-8, 14 pp., illus. 1964.

[2] Peterson, Roger S. Western gall rust cankers in lodgepole pine. Jour. Forestry 59: 194-196, illus. 1961.

[3] Mielke, James L. The rust fungus (Cronartium stalactiforme) in lodgepole pine. Jour. Forestry 54: 518-521, illus. 1956.

Figure 1.--Western gall rust canker caused by _Peridermium harknessii._

Plot locations were further limited to pure, even-aged stands with densities high enough to fully occupy the site but not so high that height growth of the tallest trees would be retarded. No plots were selected that suffered substantial mortality during the preceding 10 years. These stocking and mortality limitations could have eliminated some heavily infected stands.

Trees on a given plot were selected for felling strictly on the basis of diameter. The 10 largest trees were selected on all but 3 of the 89 plots used. Smaller trees were chosen in proportion to the number in each diameter class. Actual selections were made in a strictly mechanical manner from a diameter listing of trees without reference to any other tree characteristic.

Plots were one-tenth acre in size for stands younger than 50 years and one-fifth acre in older stands. Thus, largest trees were selected at the rate of 50 or 100 per acre, depending upon plot size.

Figure 2.--A, Portion of a canker caused by _Cronartium stalactiforme._ Bark has sloughed off completely on the left and is alive only on the extreme right. The complete canker extends up on the bole several feet above d.b.h. and downward almost to the ground. _B_, This type of canker has a distinctive diamond shape.

2

Percent of rust-infected felled trees on individual plots ranged from 0 to 94 percent. All rust frequencies within this range were well represented. There was no correlation between stand age and percent of rust-infected trees.

Of 883 trees selected as largest on their respective plots, 437, or 49.5 percent, were cankered (fig. 3). Of 761 trees not selected as largest, only 296, or 38.9 percent, were cankered. This difference in percentage of rust-infected trees between largest and other trees was highly significant statistically.. It means that rust attacks occur more frequently on the larger, more vigorous trees than on the smaller, less vigorous ones.

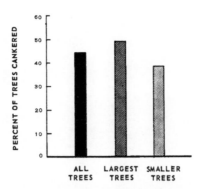

Figure 3.--Percentage of trees with cankers by tree-size class. Note: "Largest trees" are the 10 largest per plot; "smaller trees," all other trees.

FOREST AND RANGE EXPERIMENT STATION · U.S. DEPARTMENT OF AGRICULTURE · PORTLAND, OREGON

PNW-21   April 1965

AN EXPLORATORY STUDY OF CONE MATURITY IN NOBLE FIR[1/]

by

Jerry F. Franklin

Poor seed quality is often a problem in artificial regeneration of true firs (*Abies* sp.). Much true fir seed is sterile or blighted, and viability of sound seed is highly variable. Broadcast seedings require large amounts of seed, and nursery yields of seedlings from a given quantity of seed are variable. Reasons suggested for this poor quality relate to pollination, maturation, collection, processing, and storage of cones and seed.

The relationship of yield of viable noble fir *(Abies procera)* seed to (1) time of cone collection, (2) treatment of cones after collection, and (3) specific gravity and moisture content of cones at the time of collection was explored in this study.

TECHNIQUE

The major portion of this study was conducted in 1961 with cones collected from five mature trees located near the summit of Marys Peak, a 4,097-foot mountain in the Oregon Coast Ranges. Cones on each tree were mapped and numbered, and treatments were assigned to individual cones at random. Cones with external indicators of insect infestation were not used. Collections took place at 2-week intervals beginning August 22 and ending October 3. Natural seedfall occurred between October 8 and 18. Four cones on each tree were wired to prevent shattering and were collected on October 31.

[1/] The use of facilities and equipment of the Oregon State University Forest Research Laboratory and the U.S. Department of Agriculture Seed Cleaning Research Laboratory and the cooperation of the Oregon State Seed Testing Laboratory are gratefully acknowledged. The author also acknowledges the aid from Dr. J. H. Rediske of Weyerhaeuser Co., who supplied a manuscript copy of his paper on seed maturity in noble fir.

On each date, except October 31, five groups of four cones were collected from each tree and treated respectively as follows:

1. Spread out to dry in a garage loft; seed extracted on October 13.

2. Packed in paper wadding and stored dry in boxes for 2 weeks before seed extraction.

3. Packed in paper wadding and stored dry in boxes for 6 weeks before seed extraction.

4. Packed in moist peat moss and stored in boxes for 2 weeks before seed extraction.

5. Packed in moist peat moss and stored in boxes for 6 weeks before seed extraction.

Treatment 1 will hereafter be referred to as the "standard" treatment, because it approximates commercial handling. In treatments 2 through 5, each box contained only the four cones from a single tree. Boxes were kept in a room with a constant temperature of 40° F. and 70-percent relative humidity.

On each collection date, an additional group of four cones from each tree was gathered for specific gravity and moisture content determinations. They were kept in closed plastic sacks during transport. Specific gravity was determined by a water immersion technique. Weight was measured to the nearest gram, volume to the nearest cubic centimeter.

Seed was extracted and dewinged by hand, then cleaned in a pneumatic separator to eliminate empty and aborted seeds. Constant checks insured that less than 5 percent of sound seed was lost. The Oregon State Seed Testing Laboratory tested germination of four 100-seed lots drawn randomly from each tree-treatment-collection date combination. Seeds were stratified for 4 weeks at 5° C. and then tested with light for 21 days at temperatures of 20° C. at night and 30° C. during the day. Only seeds germinating normally were included in the germination percentages.

A smaller experiment was carried out on noble fir cones collected at about a 4,000-foot elevation on Red Mountain, a 4,977-foot peak on the crest of the Cascade Range in southern Washington. Eight cones were collected from each of five trees on four collection dates (September 1, 11, and 20 and October 3). Half were used for specific gravity determinations; the remainder were stored in the loft only 2 weeks before seed extraction. Snow prevented gathering those cones that had been wired for collection after the time of natural seedfall. Noble fir seedfall in this area occurred between October 9 and 25 in 1961.

Germination

Seed from cones collected in late August and early September, more than 1 month prior to natural seedfall (October 8 through 18), showed surprisingly high germination percentages, considering the earliness of collection (table 1). Although there is a slight upward trend from the first to the last collection (fig. 1), a regression analysis failed to reveal a significant correlation between germination

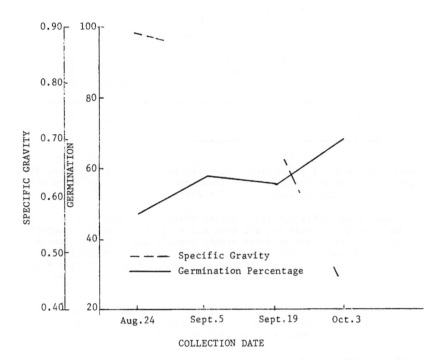

Figure 1.--Relation between specific gravity of freshly
          picked cones and germination percentages of
          seed extracted from cones receiving the stand-
          ard treatment (Marys Peak collections).

Table 1.--Noble fir seed germination percentages by trees and

collection dates, Marys Peak, Oreg., from cones given

the standard treatment (each figure represents a

mean of tests run on four 100-seed lots)

Tree	Collection date				
	Aug. 24	Sept. 5	Sept. 19	Oct. 3	Oct. 31
1	20.00	35.50	37.50	44.75	48.50
2	0	.75	31.50	4.25	27.00
3	62.50	80.50	73.00	79.00	68.75
4	63.00	75.50	59.50	72.75	68.25
5	42.00	42.25	48.50	78.50	60.00
Average (excluding tree 2)	46.85	58.40	54.65	68.65	61.20

percent and date of collection. However, an analysis of variance did indicate the existence of highly significant[2] differences in germination percentages between collection dates.

Seed from individual trees varied widely in maturity at different collection dates (table 1); the tree and collection date interaction in the analysis of variance was highly significant. Seed collected from trees 1 and 5 (prior to natural seedfall) showed a regular increase in germination as collection date advanced, whereas seed from trees 3 and 4 showed no general trend but fluctuated between 60- and 80-percent germination.

Large differences in viability of seed were found to exist between different trees, when comparisons were made of the highest germination values obtained from each (table 1). Of seed from the

---

[2]

In this note, "highly significant" is used in the statistical sense and means differences were shown to exist at the 1-percent level of probability. Analyses of variance on Marys Peak data were conducted twice--with and without the inclusion of data from tree 2--but the results of the tests were the same in all cases.

last collection date, germination percentages range from 27.00 to
68.75 percent, with three trees showing percentages above 60 percent.[3]
Differences in germination percent between trees were highly significant.

Results of Red Mountain germination tests were essentially the
same as those of the Marys Peak tests (table 1) with a single exception.
Germination percentages, averaged for all trees for each collection date,
were 39.80, 43.50, 56.00, and 24.28, progressing from September 1 to
October 3. Data from four of the five trees sampled showed this marked
reduction in germination of seed from the last collection date. Differences in germination of Red Mountain seed (1) from individual trees,
(2) on various collection dates, and (3) the interaction between trees
and collection date were highly significant. Germination percent was
not correlated with collection date, however.

The effects of the Marys Peak after-ripening treatments were generally deleterious (table 2). Dry storage was the least damaging with
small differences between 2- and 6-week storage times. Moist storage
was the most damaging, 6-week storage notably more so than 2-week
storage. Differences in germination percent between after-ripening
treatments were highly significant.

The analysis of variance indicated effects of after-ripening treatments varied with trees and with collection dates (highly significant
interaction terms).

Specific Gravity and Moisture Content

As collection date advanced, specific gravity of freshly picked
cones from Marys Peak declined steadily from a high of 0.89 on August
24 to 0.43 on October 3 (table 3). Regression analysis of specific
gravity on collection date revealed a highly significant correlation

---

[3] In the writer's opinion, cones from tree 2 were not comparable
to those from the remaining trees. When the study trees were selected,
cones on tree 2 appeared normal. Marked differences appeared at the
time of the first collection, however, including: cones were of low
specific gravity compared with the other trees; cones were spongy
rather than hard or firm; seed was of very low quality, much of it
empty or containing shriveled embryos; and cones had a high percentage
of insect infestation. Furthermore, when placed in either dry or moist
storage, cones from tree 2 developed an unusual mold for conifer cones,
tentatively identified as *Cephalothecium roseum* by James W. Edgren of
the Pacific Northwest Forest and Range Experiment Station.

Table 2.--Noble fir seed germination percentages, by after-ripening
treatments of cones collected from Marys Peak, Oreg. (data
from all trees, except tree 2, combined)

Treatment	Collection date				Average
	Aug. 24	Sept. 5	Sept. 19	Oct. 3	
Standard (loft storage until October 13)	46.85	58.40	54.65	68.65	57.14
Dry storage, 2 weeks	49.81	48.25	29.31	62.94	47.58
Dry storage, 6 weeks	36.25	47.81	30.81	54.38	42.31
Wet storage, 2 weeks	38.12	39.75	27.25	47.06	38.04
Wet storage, 6 weeks	24.38	22.44	25.50	47.00	29.83

Table 3.--Specific gravity of freshly picked noble fir
cones collected on Marys Peak, Oreg., figures
being average values for four cones

Tree	Collection date			
	Aug. 24	Sept. 5	Sept. 19	Oct. 3
1	0.90	0.88	0.65	0.43
2	.75	.82	.69	.51
3	.88	.84	.66	.49
4	.87	.86	.76	.42
5	.89	.86	.71	.39
Average (excluding tree 2)	.89	.86	.70	.43

(correlation coefficient r = 0.93), indicating most variability in specific gravity can be accounted for by collection date. Except for tree 2, there was relatively little tree-to-tree variation in specific gravity. The moisture content data had trends similar to those obtained for specific gravity. Specific gravity did not reflect fluctuations observed in germination percent (fig. 1), and regression analysis showed there was no correlation between germination percent and specific gravity.

Data for specific gravity and moisture content from the Red Mountain noble fir cones corroborated the results of the Marys Peak portion of the study.

DISCUSSION

Collection Date

Viability of noble fir seed collected in late August and early September was higher than expected. Cones collected from Marys Peak on August 24, 6 weeks prior to seed dissemination, produced seed that germinated nearly three-fourths as well as the seed collected on October 3. For the first three collections, the increase in germination as collection date advanced was more marked in the Red Mountain data.

An important reason for these results relates to the time span covered by the study. If collections had begun in July, a much greater increase in germination percentage of Marys Peak seed would undoubtedly have occurred, and a significant correlation between germination percent and collection date would be expected. For example, Pfister[4] studied maturity of grand fir seed beginning in late July 1961, and found a highly significant increase in germination with collection date. However, it is noteworthy that the germination percent of grand fir seed in Pfister's study continued to increase right up to the time of seed dispersal, whereas germinability of noble fir seed leveled off as time of dissemination approached.

A second important reason why a more dramatic increase in germination in relation to collection date did not occur may pertain to storage of the seed in cones following collection. Rediske and Nicholson[5] found noble fir seed required a maturation period in the

---

[4] Pfister, Robert Dean. Effects of artificial cone ripening techniques and determination of seed maturity in grand fir (*Abies grandis* Lindl.). M.S. thesis on file Oreg. State Univ., 48 pp., illus. 1964.

[5] Rediske, J. H., and Nicholson, David C. Maturation of noble fir seed--a biochemical study. 14 pp. 1962. (Submitted for publication as a Weyerhaeuser Forestry Paper.)

cone following collection, during which there was a movement of organic substances from the cone into the seed. They felt seed maturity was associated with a calendar date and, therefore, the earlier cones were collected the longer seed would have to remain in the cone before it fully matured. This may be why seed collected from Marys Peak in August and early September had high viability. None was extracted from cones until October 13; seed was allowed to after-ripen in cones for periods proportional to the earliness of collection. The stronger upward trend of germination of seed from Red Mountain (for the first three collection dates) could be the partial result of processing these cones after only 2 weeks' storage so that the leveling effect of maturation in the cone was not realized.

The depression in germination of seed obtained from Marys Peak trees 3 and 4 on September 19 or the major reduction in germinability of seed collected on Red Mountain at the last collection cannot be explained from available data. These cones were handled in the same manner as the others. Pfister (see footnote 4) encountered a similar decrease in average germination in a late August collection of grand fir seed.

After-Ripening Treatments

Artificial ripening procedures have been found useful in improving germination of early collected Douglas-fir seed (Silen 1958).[6] Pfister (see footnote 4) studied the effects of a variety of after-ripening treatments on germination of grand fir seed and found all, except storage of cones in wet peat moss, improved germination. Rediske and Nicholson (see footnote 5) noted no adverse effects of noble fir cone storage in open 3-gallon cans left in the shade. However, the storage treatments used in this study obviously were not favorable to the maturation of noble fir seed during after-ripening.

The dry-storage treatments in this study would be expected to have resulted in germination the same as, or slightly better than, the loft-storage or standard treatment in which cones were exposed to temperature and humidity fluctuations. In fact, the germination was usually below, sometimes far below, that obtained in the standard treatment. This was evidently the result of mold, developing in some of the boxes as a result of constant environmental conditions and absence of air circulation. In many cases, insect-infested cones developed intensive mold which spread to other cones in the same box. Extensive mold, in combination with anerobic storage conditions, was probably also responsible for the even poorer germination of seed from cones stored in moist peat moss.

---

[6] Names and dates in parentheses refer to Literature Cited, pp. 11-12.

After-ripening procedures for improving germination of early collected noble fir seed should be developed. Rediske and Nicholson (see footnote 5) feel that moisture is a requirement for after-ripening of noble fir seed in the cones and that drying out of cones for seed extraction is sufficient to stop the after-ripening process. Pfister (see footnote 4) found a shaded outdoor exclosure provided the best conditions for after-ripening grand fir cones. Ideal conditions will involve a balance between the moist situation favorable for after-ripening and the dryness needed to discourage fungal growth. In any case, cones should not be stored in tightly closed containers, which prevent air circulation, nor tightly packed during after-ripening. Insect-infested cones, which serve as foci for fungal infection, should be removed when possible.

Variation Between Trees

Variations between trees at different dates reflected differences between trees in both timing of seed maturation and viability of seed produced (table 1). On Marys Peak, cones on trees 4 and 5 were obviously more mature by August 24 than were cones on trees 1 and 3, as shown by the increase in germination percentages from later collections. Time of cone maturation commonly varies between trees in the same vicinity in many species (Ching 1960, Fowells 1949, Rediske and Nicholson (see footnote 5), and others).

Erratic germinative behavior of seed from Marys Peak tree 2 may have been related to self-pollination or poor coordination between the receptivity of the female strobili and pollen flight. The many shriveled embryos suggest the former; the many empty seed suggest the latter. Recent work by Mergen and Lester (1961) suggests irregularities in the division of reproductive cells (meiosis) might also have been operative in causing these defective seeds.

Although no quantitative data were taken, observations indicate infestation of cones by insects varied greatly from tree to tree. The high percentage of infested cones on Marys Peak tree 2 has already been noted. Cones on some trees, such as Marys Peak 3 and 4, escaped infestation almost entirely.

Specific Gravity

A survey of the literature reveals specific gravity is the most widely used measure of cone maturity. Specific gravity indices have been developed for a large number of pines (Eliason and Hill 1954, Fowells 1949, McLemore 1954, Maki 1940) and several spruces (Cram 1956, Cram and Worden 1957) and could be developed for Douglas-fir (Ching and Ching 1962). Pfister (see footnote 4) studied several different characteristics of grand fir seed and cones and concluded specific gravity was the best indicator of maturity. Other measures of cone maturity, such as color (Crossley 1953, Pfister (see footnote 4)) or characteristics

of the seed embryo or endosperm (Pfister, footnote 4), have been less
successful. Excellent indices of maturity, based upon biochemical
analyses of extracted seed, have been developed for Douglas-fir (Rediske
1961) and noble fir (Rediske and Nicholson, footnote 5), but these require laboratory facilities and trained technicians.

In this study, specific gravity and moisture content show strong
relationships to date of collection. Specific gravity and moisture
content were not correlated with germination percent in this study,
however, and failed to reflect fluctuations in germination encountered
for individual trees or major anomalies such as the large reduction in
germination occurring in the last Red Mountain collection. As mentioned
earlier, failure to obtain a correlation is probably due to the late date
at which collections were begun. The time span covered by the study was
evidently beyond the period of rapid change for most trees. During the
period of time represented, specific gravity was not a valid criterion
for determining appropriate times for cone collection. However, since
good germination was usually obtained from seed collected as early as
late August, an index of cone maturity would have been of little importance in commercial collection over the time span covered by this study
in 1962--the seed not having been extracted immediately after collection.

There was some indication that a specific gravity of about 0.90
is critical, however. The two trees showing the greatest percentage
increase in germination after the first collection date--Marys Peak
tree 1, 20.00 to 48.50 percent, and Red Mountain tree 2, 13.00 to
70.00 percent--had cones with specific gravities of 0.903 and 0.959,
respectively, at the time of the first collection. The remaining trees
had cones with specific gravities below 0.90 and did not show as marked
an increase in germination for later collections. This specific gravity
may indicate the earliest collection time possible if a reasonable percentage of the maximum potential germination of the seed is to be obtained, even when cones are stored for several weeks after collection.
It is noteworthy that Pfister (footnote 4) tentatively suggested use
of a specific gravity of 0.90 as an index for determining when collection of grand fir cones should begin.

Conclusion

This study indicates that early collection of noble fir cones, per
se, is not necessarily the most important cause of poor seed germination.
Poor germination may also result from the treatment of cones after collection and the extraction, cleaning, and storage of seed; or, more
likely, from a cumulative effect of these factors, including early
collection.

Much research needs to be done on maturity indices and seed quality
for western true firs. The relationship between specific gravity and
germination of noble fir seed should be studied beginning in late July
and the proposed critical specific gravity of 0.90 carefully evaluated.

Other important true firs such as Pacific silver fir and subalpine fir
should be studied. An adequate method of after-ripening cones needs
to be developed.

SUMMARY

A study was made of the relationship of seed germination to date
of collection, after-ripening treatment, and specific gravity of noble
fir cones collected in the Oregon Coast Ranges and Washington Cascade
Range. Noble fir seed, obtained from cones collected 6 weeks prior to
natural seedfall and allowed to after-ripen in the cones, germinated
about three-fourths as well as seed from later collections.

Both dry and moist after-ripening treatments of cones, carried
out in this study, were generally deleterious in their effect on seed
germination when compared with a standard treatment of open storage in
a garage loft. Molding was a major problem.

Specific gravity and moisture content of freshly picked cones were
closely related to time of collection but did not reflect fluctuations
noted in seed germination. Lack of relation between specific gravity
and seed germination is probably due to the late date at which collections were begun. However, it is tentatively recommended that cones
not be collected until they have attained a specific gravity of 0.90.

Major differences existed in the highest germination values of
seed obtained from different study trees. Furthermore, cones on different trees matured at different times and responded differently to the
after-ripening treatments.

LITERATURE CITED

Ching, Te May.
    1960. Seed production from individual cones of grand fir
        (Abies grandis Lindl.). Jour. Forestry 58: 959-961.

_____ and Ching, Kim K.
    1962. Physical and physiological changes in maturing Douglas-
        fir cones and seed. Forest Sci. 8: 21-31, illus.

Cram, W. H.
    1956. Maturity of Colorado spruce cones. Forest Sci. 2: 26-30.

_____ and Worden, H. A.
    1957. Maturity of white spruce cones and seed. Forest Sci. 3:
        263-269.

Crossley, D. I.
    1953.   Seed maturity in white spruce. Canad. Dept. Resources
            & Devlpmt. Forestry Br., Forest Res. Div. Silvic. Res.
            Note 104, 16 pp., illus.

Eliason, E. J., and Hill, Joseph.
    1954.   Specific gravity as a test for cone ripeness with red
            pine. Tree Planters' Notes 17: 1-4.

Fowells, H. A.
    1949.   An index of ripeness for sugar pine seed. U.S. Forest
            Serv. Calif. Forest & Range Expt. Sta. Res. Note 64,
            5 pp., illus.

McLemore, B. F.
    1959.   Cone maturity affects germination of longleaf pine seed.
            Jour. Forestry 57: 648-650.

Maki, T. E.
    1940.   Significance and applicability of seed maturity indices
            for ponderosa pine. Jour. Forestry 38: 55-60, illus.

Mergen, Francois, and Lester, Donald T.
    1961.   Microsporogenesis in *Abies*. Silvae Genetica 10: 146-156,
            illus.

Rediske, J. H.
    1961.   Maturation of Douglas-fir seed--a biochemical study.
            Forest Sci. 7: 204-213, illus.

Silen, Roy R.
    1958.   Artificial ripening of Douglas-fir cones. Jour. Forestry
            56: 410-413, illus.

U. S. FOREST SERVICE

Pacific North West

Research Note

FOREST AND RANGE EXPERIMENT STATION · U.S.DEPARTMENT OF AGRICULTURE · PORTLAND, OREGON

PNW-22   May 1965

ECONOMIC EVALUATION
of Potential European Pine Shoot Moth Damage
in the Ponderosa Pine Region

BY DONALD F. FLORA

SUMMARY

An examination is made of the regional economic impact that might occur if the European pine shoot moth were to move from its present area of containment in western Washington and British Columbia into the ponderosa pine region of the United States. Analysis is limited to the ponderosa pine type.

Various assumptions are made as to rate of spread of the insect and its survival in destructive numbers at low winter temperatures. Effects on timber harvest and timber-related employment are considered for both the invasion period and the long run, where the long run is a period far enough in the future that access development has been completed and all stands have passed through a period of susceptibility agewise. Results are summarized in table 1.

Over the long run, after long-term development programs have been accomplished, it is estimated that from 4 to nearly 23 million acres of the ponderosa pine type could be affected seriously by the European pine shoot moth. This wide range of possible effects is due to the variation between assumptions as to the temperature and frequency required to kill or inhibit the moth. The corresponding longrun impacts of this infestation include the possible loss of from 651 million to 4,375 million board feet of allowable timber cut per year and the loss of from 11,000, to nearly 74,000 jobs per year.

Table 1.--Summary of effects of potential European pine shoot moth invasion
in the ponderosa pine region

Item	Infested area remaining, low and medium sites[1]	Average curtailment of allowable cut per year[2]	Number of jobs lost[2]	Annual payroll loss[2]	Annual stumpage receipts foregone[2]
	Thousand acres	Million board feet		Million dollars	Million dollars
20-year invasion period:					
−20° F.[3]	3,410	400	6,800	25.6	9.1
−15° F.[4]	760	100	1,800	6.6	2.5
50-year invasion period:					
−20° F.[3]	5,900	700	11,700	44.4	15.8
−15° F.[4]	1,450	200	3,600	13.4	5.0
Long run:					
−20° F.[3]	22,670	4,375	73,900	279.9	38.7
−15° F.[4]	3,921	651	11,000	41.6	7.3

[1] For invasion periods, reference is to the end of the period.

[2] Effects are assumed constant during the periods indicated. This follows from an assumption that ultimate growth impact is reflected throughout the period by reduction of the allowable cut.

[3] Assumes a temperature of −20° F., occurring five times every 20 years, will limit or kill the moth.

[4] An alternative assumption that −15° F., occurring four times every 20 years, will limit or kill the moth.

INTRODUCTION

This report is an estimate of the regional economic impact that might occur if the European pine shoot moth were to move from its present area of containment in western Washington and British Columbia into the ponderosa pine region of the United States.

Since its introduction in 1914, the European pine shoot moth has been a serious attacker of two- and three-needle pines in the Eastern and Central States. It has been especially destructive in forest plantations, as it inhibits growth by boring into and killing buds and developing shoots.

For several years, the insect has been found on nursery stock and on ornamental plantings in the Northwest, notably in Seattle but also at scattered points around Puget Sound and in the Willamette Valley. Efforts to prevent spread of the insect have included uniform plant quarantines among the Western States, designation of a containment area in the State of Washington, and eradication of infested trees found outside the containment area. Owners of infested plants have understood the problem and have worked closely with the Federal and State control personnel. More than $250,000 has been spent on surveys, eradication, and research in the Northwest. None theless, the insect has invaded lodgepole pine stands near Shelton, Wash., and has been found on a native ponderosa pine near Summerland, British Columbia. An infestation on ornamentals in Spokane, Wash., in the pine region, appears to have been eradicated.

Concern with the possibility of ultimate escape of the shoot moth into ponderosa pine stands in eastern Washington or Oregon, and thence throughout the West, led the Northwest Forest Pest Action Council in 1964 to undertake an assessment of the outcome of such an escape. This report is one product of that inquiry. Because western pine forests have not been exposed to damage by this insect, assumptions must be made about shoot moth behavior in the pine region and its biologic effect on host trees. The biologic underpinnings of this report are based on experience with this insect in plantations in Eastern and Central United States and Canada and expert opinion provided by researchers in these regions.

The dollar and employment impact figures given here are oriented to local affected communities. Largely ignored are secondary and substitution effects that may make the shoot moth problem appear quite different when viewed in a national or broad social context.

ACREAGE IMPACT

The shoot moth's possible occupation of the ponderosa pine region has been divided into three phases. During the first phase, here called the invasion period, the insect is assumed to move outward from one or more initial spot infestations, by means of flight or transportation of infested nursery stock, until the entire region is occupied. On the assumption that stands over 40 years of age would not be damaged economically by insect attack, the second period is recognized, during which merchantable stands in the West are harvested and reproduction becomes susceptible, agewise, to attack. It is assumed that public agencies' long-term, access development policies will be realized during the second period. A third phase, the long run, follows the second period. This analysis is concerned with the invasion period and the long run.

In the Lake States, it has been shown (6)[1] that the shoot moth's effect on red pine growth varies chiefly with site quality. Trees growing at a rate of 15 inches or more a year, both before and after establishment, are not seriously damaged. Trees that grow less than 15 inches before establishment but more than 15 inches after establishment will tend to recover from shoot moth attack. Trees growing less than 15 inches a year both before and after establishment will be perennially susceptible to damage by the shoot moth.

From the foregoing, it is assumed that the impact of the European pine shoot moth in the West on low sites will be to completely eliminate the net growth of ponderosa pine; on middle sites it is assumed that, although survival would not be strongly affected, the insects' destruction of terminal buds would lead to a degree of forking and crooking that would materially affect merchantable values. The ponderosa pine region was arbitrarily divided into low, medium, and high site classes: below site index 70, between site index 70 and 100, and above site index 100.

It appears that the shoot moth is not an important damaging agent in that part of the Lake States in which minimum temperatures commonly reach 20° below zero (10). The upper half of table 2 relates this limiting temperature to the ponderosa pine forest. On the assumption that a temperature of -20°F., occurring five times in 20 years, is required to kill or limit the spread of the moth, about 4.8 million acres of low-site area would be protected. At the same time, a balance of some 10.9 million acres of ponderosa pine forest would not be protected because it lies outside that temperature zone.

The lower half of table 2 presents estimates of area which would be protected under an alternative assumption: that a temperature of -15°F., occurring four times in 20 years, would kill or limit the spread of the moth. If this assumption holds, then all of the low-site areas of ponderosa pine forest, for example, would be protected. This comparison of these two assumptions illustrates the key nature of temperature as a limit on shoot moth populations and underscores the need for additional research to provide additional biological information useful for planning control programs.

---

[1] Italic numbers in parenthesis refer to Literature Cited, p. 13.

Table 2.-- Estimated acres of ponderosa pine forest type susceptible to European pine shoot moth invasion, by temperature zone, region, and site class

Limiting temperature and region	Temperature limits moth [1]			Temperature not limiting		
	High site	Medium site	Low site	High site	Medium site	Low site
If −20° F. occurs five times in 20 years:	- - - - - - - - - - - - - - - - - - Thousands of acres - - - - - - - - - - - - - - - -					
Pacific Northwest (2)	--			891	7,851	3,300
California (14)	--	--	--	617	1,884	1,037
Rocky Mountain States [2]	56	3,268	4,838	17	2,024	6,577
Total	56	3,268	4,838	1,525	11,759	10,914
If −15° F. occurs four times in 20 years:						
Pacific Northwest	891	7,851	3,300	--	--	--
California	--	--	--	617	1,884	1,037
Rocky Mountain States	73	5,292	11,415	--	--	--
Total	964	13,143	14,715	617	1,884	1,037

[1] Based on Kincer (9), figures 7, 8, and 9.

[2] Sources: (1, 3, 4, 7, 8, 14, 15, 16).

Table 3.-- Estimated acreage of ponderosa pine type of an age to be susceptible to European pine shoot moth invasion and expected annual increase in acreage susceptible[1]
(In acres)

Low and medium sites, ponderosa pine type	Pacific Northwest	California	Rocky Mountain States	Total
Now less than 40 years old:				
Outside −20° zone	440,000	300,000	1,010,000	1,750,000
Outside −15° zone	0	300,000	0	300,000
Increase, acres per year:				
Outside −20° zone	35,000	23,000	25,000	83,000
Outside −15° zone	0	23,000	0	23,000

[1] The acreage of restockable burns is not included.

However, there is evidence that pine stands cease to be susceptible to shoot moth attack after attaining an age of about 40 years. Thus, not until the long run are the total acreages cited in the foregoing tables being damaged. Until then, some stands will be within infested areas but protected by their ages. The initial acreage that is susceptible, by being both young and infested, and the expected rate of increase in affected acreage through harvesting, are indicated by regions in table 3.

VOLUME IMPACT

Distinction will be made between shoot moth impact during the invasion period and during the long run. Analysis of the invasion period is based on stand structure and access as it is expected to develop during the next 20 to 50 years. Longrun estimates are founded on a more or less regulated, even-aged forest with negligible problems of access. The longrun assumptions are consistent with present public forest management objectives.

Most of the shoot moth impact is expected to fall on public lands, where the current allowable cut is based on long-term growth expectations. Thus, it is reasonable to assume that, following escape of the moth to the pine region, allowable cut would be adjusted throughout the West, even though the insect had not yet arrived in some areas. The method used here of revising the allowable cut is a generalization of that employed in Region 6, U.S. Forest Service, in which the allowable cut is based on the average of current and prospective growth.

Although the allowable cut is normally computed separately for each working circle, a single calculation is made here for the entire affected area. Because allowable cut during the invasion period is the average of two numbers, only one of which is affected by the insect, an ultimate reduction of growth by 100 percent leads to a reduction in allowable cut of 50 percent during the invasion period. In the long run, of course, allowable cut drops to zero in the affected areas if no merchantable growth is expected.

Growth estimated for uninfested medium sites is 425 and 187 board feet per acre per year for managed and unmanaged stands, respectively. It is assumed that half of medium sites would be placed under intensive management in the long run; the average growth rate on medium sites is then 306 board feet per acre per year.

It was assumed that no low sites would receive intensive silvicultural treatment. A growth rate of 71 board feet per acre per year was assigned to low sites. Table 4 summarizes, by site and length of invasion period, acreage occupied and annual growth not realized at the end of the invasion period. Also shown is the reduction of allowable cut during the invasion period.

Estimates of shoot moth impact in the long run are based on assumptions that infested stands would otherwise be managed for timber production and that all low and medium sites have been susceptible at some time; i.e., their age has been less than 40 years at some time after arrival of the shoot moth. Impact on timber production in the long run on low and medium sites is shown in table 5.

6

Table 4.--Estimated total area infested, annual growth not realized, and annual curtailment on allowable cut in event of European pine shoot moth attack on ponderosa pine, by length of invasion period and temperature criterion

Minimum temperature criterion	Invasion period	Area infested at end of period			Annual growth reduction, end of period			Annual reduction of allowable cut during invasion period
		Low site	Medium site	Total	Low site	Medium site	Total	
	Years	M acres	M acres	M acres	MM bd.ft.	MM bd.ft.	MM bd.ft.	MM bd.ft.
−20° F.	20	1,030	2,380	3,410	73	728	801	400
	50	1,780	4,120	5,900	126	1,261	1,387	694
−15° F.	20	100	660	760	7	202	209	104
	50	100	1,350	1,450	7	413	420	210

Table 5.--Estimated total annual increment not realized in long run in event of European pine shoot moth attack on ponderosa pine, by site class and temperature zone

Sites	Annual increment lost, long run	
	Outside −20° F. zone	Outside −15° F. zone
	- - - - - - - - - Million board feet - - - - - - - - -	
Low	775	74
Medium	3,600	577
Total	4,375	651

High sites, assumed to be unaffected by the shoot moth, are also assumed to be managed intensively in the long run. A mean annual increment of about 670 board feet per acre per year has been estimated for high sites. It follows that, for the long run, total mean annual growth in the ponderosa pine region is estimated to be about 6.8 billion board feet if infestation does not occur. This is almost 80 percent more than United States production of ponderosa pine in 1962. This figure is consistent with the 40-year, medium-level demand projections for lumber and plywood developed in the Timber Resource Review, which suggests more than a doubling of demand for these products.

The likelihood of replacing ponderosa pine with other species has not been discussed. This is a distinct possibility in areas where species associated with ponderosa pine are not themselves susceptible to shoot moth attack. Although failure to analyze species replacement opportunities gives the apparent impact an upward bias, this tends to be offset by omission of impact figures for lodgepole pine.

There is apparently no reasonable means of controlling widespread European pine shoot moth infestations. Therefore, it is important to assess the feasibility of correcting the damage done to the tree by the moth, thereby reducing the impact. One means of doing this is by pruning to remove insect-caused forks.

Talerico and Heikkenen (11) explored this method and found that an average of 11 percent of the trees had acquired noncorrectible forks in the preceding 4 years of infestation in red pine plantations attacked by the pine shoot moth. On the normal and correctible trees, an average of 1.4 forks were formed per tree in the 4 years and at the rate of 3.5 forks per tree per decade. If forking were to occur at this rate on the ponderosa pine, it would produce a degree of crooking that would be unacceptable to the log markets. It follows that, on medium sites, the saw log resource would be lost in the event of shoot moth attack unless pruning to correct forking of crop trees were undertaken.

To assess the relative economic merits of pruning versus forsaking saw log production on middle sites, it was necessary to employ a compound interest formula which would compare costs and returns at a common point in time. Both costs and returns were compounded at a 4 percent interest rate to the end of the pine rotation. It was assumed that no other management costs would be affected by a pruning decision.

Experience with pruning dwarfmistletoe infections from ponderosa pine suggests that forking could be corrected on medium sites at a cost of 2 cents per fork.[2] It was assumed that pruning would be done at 10-year intervals beginning at age 10. It appears that pruning would not be necessary beyond age 40. The compounded value of pruning cost per tree is:

3.5 forks per decade X 2 cents per fork =7 cents per decade
Compounded to age 110 at 4 percent:

Pruning at age 10 =$3.54
Pruning at age 20 = 2.39
Pruning at age 30 = 1.61
Pruning at age 40 = 1.09
————
Total $8.63 per tree

---

[2] Costs for pruning dwarfmistletoe infections from ponderosa pine have been studied recently as part of a broad study of dwarfmistletoe control. These results are found in a report in preparation for publication by D.F. Flora, " Economic Guidelines for Ponderosa Pine Dwarfmistletoe Control. "

If it is assumed that a crop tree has 300 board feet when harvested at age 110, that mortality of crop trees is negligible during the rotation, and that a crop tree is worth $15 per thousand board feet as stumpage, then its value when harvested is $4.50. This compares with the cost of $8.63 per tree for pruning, thus implying that pruning is generally not economic for reducing the impact of widespread European pine shoot moth infestation.

EMPLOYMENT IMPACT

The employment impact of the shoot moth will not be abrupt like a sudden natural catastrophe such as a hurricane. Rather, society should have time to ameliorate its losses by shifting and retraining the labor supply. Estimated here, however, is the employment reduction attributable to shoot moth infestation, without an offsetting estimate of reemployment.

Hair (5) uses a productivity estimate for logging in the West of 59.1 cubic feet per year, moved from the stump to local points of delivery, per man employed in timber harvesting. By use of employment and output figures from the same source, a productivity of 41.3 cubic feet of logs per year per man employed in sawmills in the West was obtained. An arbitrary board-foot/cubic-foot ratio of 5.5 was applied to the estimated shoot moth growth impact.

The ratio of "service" to "basic" employment in counties of Washington and Oregon known to be primarily dependent upon sawmilling was studied. Census data (12, table 85) was used. Such ratios, though commonly cited, are sensitive to arbitrary distinctions between basic and nonbasic industries. Basic industries were defined to include manufacturing, logging, agriculture, mining, forestry, and fishing. Nonbasic or service industries include retail and wholesale trade, transportation, utilities, finance, and government. A basic-service ratio of 1:1.26 was derived. This ratio understates the amount of nonlocal wholesaling, transportation, and equipment manufacture and servicing that would be affected by decline of a portion of the forest industry, but an adequate quantitative measure would be difficult to obtain.

An estimate of employment that potentially might be displaced from the ponderosa pine region by shoot moth invasion is given in table 6. It should be noted that the long-run employment figures shown in table 6 represent the difference between anticipated employment under an 80-percent increase in forest output in the West and expected employment under shoot moth infestation. Hence, nearly half of the employment impact in the long run applies to industry expansion foregone rather than present industry displaced.

9

Table 6...-Potential employment displacement from the ponderosa pine region
by European pine shoot moth invasion, by temperature zone and
period of time

Temperature criterion	Average number of workers affected		
	During 20-year invasion period	During 50-year invasion period	Long run
- - - - - - - - - - - - - - - - - -		Persons - - - - - - - - - - - - -	
−20° F.	6,800	11,700	73,900
−15° F.	1,800	3,600	11,000

PAYROLL LOSS

Average income per worker in logging and sawmilling was estimated by dividing total payroll for all employers in these pursuits in the Mountain and Pacific States by the number of loggers and sawmill workers in the same States (13, table 2). The resulting average annual income was about $4,650.

Income per worker in the service sector could not be obtained directly. Instead, it was estimated by subtracting total income of forest workers from total income of all workers in selected forest-oriented counties (12, table 86) and dividing the result by the number of nonforest workers. Estimated average annual income in the service area thus obtained was about $3,100. This figure unfortunately includes some basic workers; however, their number is small in the counties chosen. These incomes were applied to the aforementioned employment figures to estimate payroll loss in table 7.

Table 7.--Potential annual payroll loss in ponderosa pine region
of European pine shoot moth invasion, by temperature
zone and period of time

Temperature criterion	Average annual payroll loss		
	During 20-year invasion period	During 50-year invasion period	Long run
- - - - - - - - - - - - - - -		Million dollars - - - - - - - - - - - - -	
−20° F.	25.6	44.4	279.9
−15° F.	6.6	13.4	41.6

Because the shoot moth attacks only young trees, it is not anticipated that moth invasion would have important effect on local stumpage prices during either a 20- or 50-year invasion. It is supposed that, in the long run under the -20° F. criterion, volume damaged by the shoot moth would be about 5 percent of United States saw log-veneer log consumption, assuming that prices of these products remain generally constant. Assuming an inelastic demand for stumpage and recognizing opportunities to import wood products and develop substitute materials, a longrun price increase of 2 percent is theorized for the -20° F. criterion. Approximately constant stumpage prices are assumed for all other time period-temperature criteria. Stumpage value assumptions follow:

Site	Stumpage value per M board feet (Dollars)
Medium	12
Low	5

There are certain costs associated with the sale of stumpage. If shoot moth infestation reduces the volume of stumpage sold, such costs diminish. Since the costs are largely payments for labor, their reduction represents a loss to those who would receive them. Because it is difficult to identify their level, stumpage-related labor costs have not been subtracted from stumpage values nor included as payroll impact. Presumably, their inclusion as stumpage impact exactly offsets their omission from salary impact.

As with employment, a measurement of the dollar value of timber production foregone by the method used here is rather like taking a bucket of water from a lake. A real void is created, but it is immediately obscured by a countervailing displacement of water nearby. Water closest to the void is displaced farthest. Our problem is to estimate the average displacement throughout the lake and how much the lake level drops, with only the size of our bucket as a guide.

The average annual amounts of stumpage payment reduction expected under different combinations of temperature limitation and invasion period are estimated in table 8.

Table 8.--Average annual total stumpage payment increase in ponderosa pine region of European pine shoot moth invasion, by temperature zone and period of time

Temperature criterion	Average annual total stumpage payment increase		
	During 20-year invasion period	During 50-year invasion period	Long run
		Million dollars	
−20° F.	9.1	15.8	38.7
−15° F.	2.5	5.0	7.3

CONCLUSIONS

The potential impact of infestation of the ponderosa pine forests of Western North America by the European pine shoot moth is imposingly large even by the most conservative measures. Such impacts add up to a cumulative disaster over time.

We can also conclude that sensitivity of the European pine shoot moth to low temperatures is a very important determinant of economic impact.

However, the question persists: How much can we justifiably spend to control this insect? At the present time we cannot answer this question. More research is needed on the biology of the shoot moth. More research is needed to determine effective and feasible control measures for widespread infestations. When it becomes possible to predict the effectiveness of alternative control measures (both natural and man induced) at alternative levels of cost, it will be possible to judge whether control would be worthwhile economically in view of the economic values saved through control.

LITERATURE CITED

(1) Andrews, Stuart R., and Daniels, John P.
    1960.   A survey of dwarf mistletoes in Arizona and New Mexico. Rocky Mountain Forest & Range Expt. Sta. Sta. Paper 49, 17 pp., illus.

(2) Cowlin, R.W., Briegleb, P.A., and Moravets, F.L.
    1942.   Forest resources of the ponderosa pine region of Washington and Oregon. U.S. Dept. Agr. Misc. Pub. 490, 99 pp., illus.

(3) Cummings, L.J., and Kemp, Paul D.
    1940.   Forest increment in north Idaho. North. Rocky Mountain Forest & Range Expt. Sta. Forest Survey Release 18, 74 pp., illus.

(4) Finch, Thomas L.
    1951.   How fast is timber growing in eastern Montana? North. Rocky Mountain Forest & Range Expt. Sta. Res. Note 88, 7 pp.

(5) Hair, Dwight.
    1963.   The economic importance of timber in the United States. U.S. Dept. Agr. Misc. Pub. 941, 91 pp., illus.

(6) Heikkenen, Herman J., and Miller, William E.
    1960.   European pine shoot moth damage as related to red pine growth. Lake States Forest Expt. Sta. Sta. Paper 83, 12 pp., illus.

(7) Kemp, Paul D.
    1943.   Highlights of the forest situation in western Montana. North. Rocky Mountain Forest & Range Expt. Sta. Forest Survey Statis. Serv. 14, 19 pp. (unnumbered), illus.

(8) _____ and Dickerman, M.B.
    1950.   Montana forest resource and industry statistics. North. Rocky Mountain Forest & Range Expt. Sta. Sta. Paper 25, 48 pp., illus.

(9) Kincer, Joseph B.
    1928.   Atlas of American agriculture. Pt. 2, Climate. Sect. B, Temperature, sunshine, and wind. U.S. Dept. Agr. Bur. Agr. Econ., 34 pp., illus.

(10) Pointing, P.J.
    1963.   The biology and behavior of the European pine shoot moth *Rhyacionia buoliana* (Schiff.) in southern Ontario. Pt. 2, Egg, larva, and pupa. Canad. Entomol. 95: 844-863, illus.

(11) Talerico, R.L., and Heikkenen, H.J.
        1962. Stem injury to young red pine by the European pine shoot moth. Jour.
               Forestry 60: 403-406, illus.

(12) U.S. Bureau of the Census.
        1960. Census of population: 1960. General social and economic character-
               istics. Oregon, pp. 81-168; Washington, pp. 21-86.

(13) _____
        1961. Census of manufactures: 1958. V.2, Industry statistics, Pts. 1 and 2,
               various pagings.

(14) U.S. Forest Service.
        1954. Forest statistics for California. Calif. Forest & Range Expt. Sta.
               Forest Survey Release 25, 66 pp., illus.

(15) _____
        1958. Timber resources for America's future. Forest Resource Rpt. 14,
               713 pp., illus.

(16) Wilson, Alvin K.
        1962. Timber resources of Idaho. Intermountain Forest & Range Expt. Sta.
               Forest Survey Release 3, 42 pp., illus.

14

FOREST AND RANGE EXPERIMENT STATION · U.S. DEPARTMENT OF AGRICULTURE · PORTLAND, OREGON

PNW-23   May 1965

SNOW ACCUMULATION AND MELT IN STRIP CUTTINGS ON THE

WEST SLOPES OF THE OREGON CASCADES

by

Jack Rothacher

SUMMARY

First-year results from snow measurements in 2-chain-wide, east-west, clearcut strips show greater accumulation but more rapid melt of snow. At the time of maximum accumulation in March 1964, water content of snow in the clearcut strip was 35 percent greater than that under the undisturbed forest. By June 15, only 3 of 36 plots in the open were snow covered in contrast to 26 of 36 plots snow covered under the undisturbed forest.

In recent years, timber harvesting in Oregon has been extended to the upper edge of the commercial timber zone and even into the subalpine zone on the west slopes of the Cascade Range. Moderately heavy snowpacks, common to these areas, present some possibilities for cutting practices to aid in better distribution of streamflow through delay of snowmelt runoff.

Because of our maritime climate, characterized by wet winters and dry summers, streamflow from drainages on the west slopes of the Oregon Cascades is poorly distributed throughout the year. Minimum flows occur during mid to late summer when water is most in demand by downstream users. Anderson[1] and others intensively studied the hydrology of California's snow zone and have made a number of suggestions for managing snow zone forests for specific objectives. It is our purpose to determine the applicability of some of their recommendations for strip cutting to delay snowmelt under Oregon climatic conditions.

---

[1] Anderson, Henry W. Managing California's snow zone lands for water. U.S. Forest Serv. Res. Paper PSW-6, 28 pp., illus. 1963.

The cutting pattern used in this experiment is essentially the first stage of Anderson's "wall and step" cut. Six 2-chain-wide strips, 15 chains long and oriented in an east-west direction, were cut in a uniform mountain hemlock-true fir forest at approximately 4,500-foot elevation near Willamette Pass, Oreg. Cut strips were separated by a 10-chain leave strip.

Records from weather stations a few miles east (Weather Bureau No. 6251 and Cooperative Snow Survey Station at Cascade Summit) show an average annual precipitation of 59 inches and a water content of 36.4 inches in the snow at time of maximum accumulation near the end of March. The March 1964 water content at Cascade Summit was 37.4.

Topography is gentle with south to southwest aspect. The undisturbed forest is moderately dense with little understory vegetation (figs. 2 and 3). Mountain hemlock made up 61 percent of the volume removed from the cut strips; noble and Shasta fir, 29 percent; other true firs, 7 percent; white pine, 2 percent; and Douglas-fir, the remaining 1 percent. An average of 24,000 board feet per acre was harvested from the six strips. Dominant and codominant trees ranged from 85 to 135 feet in height, averaging about 105 feet.

METHODS

Three sample plots were randomly chosen on each of two north-south transects across each clearcut strip. Transects were also randomly located with the restriction that they be at least 5 chains from the ends of the strips. The transects were extended either north or south into the 10-chain uncut area between strips. Sample plots within the forest were taken at 3.00, 3.75, and 4.50 chains from the edge of the cut strip to place them well within the undisturbed forest and beyond the transition zone.

Snow depth and water content were measured monthly at each sample plot, beginning January 14, 1964. At the height of the snowmelt period, an intermediate sampling was made on May 28. Observations were also made on June 8 and July 4. Snow was measured at points approximately 5 feet from the sample stake at the end of 45° radii starting at NNE. and proceeding clockwise. This procedure prevented repeat sampling in the same spot and permitted sampling the variety of conditions caused by random spacing of trees of all sizes near the plot center. All sampling was done by personnel from the Oakridge Ranger Station, Willamette National Forest, using standard procedures for measuring snow with a snow tube as practiced in Federal and State cooperative snow surveys.[2]

---

[2] Soil Conservation Service. Snow-survey sampling guide, U.S. Dept. Agr., Agr. Handb. 169, 37 pp., illus. 1959.

The cycle of accumulation and melt of the snowpack clearly shows that snow depth and water content[3] were greater in the open strips until early May (fig. 1). However, because of the higher rate of snowmelt in the open, snow disappeared first from the cut strips. By May 28, 11 of the 36 plots in the open were bare; by June 8, 23 were bare. At the last measurement date, June 15, only three plots in the open had snow--two measured 1.0 inch deep, the other 8.5 inches (average water content for the 36 plots in the open was 0.29 inch). By contrast, the average depth of all 36 plots within the forest on June 15 was 8.8 inches (water content 4.5 inches). At this time, 10 of the forest plots were bare; the other 26 had snow depths ranging from 2.5 to 24 inches. June 8 photographs (figs. 3 and 4c) show the contrast between the undisturbed forest and the cut strip. Photo for figure 4c was taken with the camera aimed along the north edge of strip 3; that for figure 3 was taken with the camera rotated 180° to show conditions under the forest. The bare ground in the foreground connects with the bare area in the cut strip.

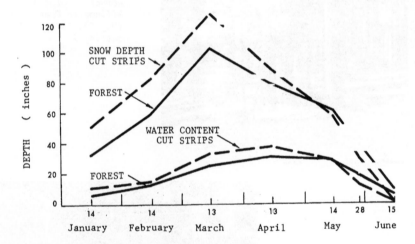

Figure 1.--Accumulation and melt of snowpack,
Willamette Pass, Oreg., 1964.

---

[3] Water content measurements for February 14, 1964, were subject to error due to hard ice layers, especially in cut strips.

When observed on July 4, no sample plots, either in the open or under the forest, had snow remaining. A search of the clearcut strips revealed only one small spot of snow of a few square yards in the southwest corner of strip 3 and another small patch half in, half out of the cut strip near the center of the south edge of plot 4. Under the forest, there were innumerable small patches of snow in sheltered spots.

Snow depth under the forest, measured from 3 to 4-1/2 chains from the edge, showed no trend with distance from the clearcut strip. This indicates that our forest measurements are far enough from the cutting to be fairly representative of the uncut forest. No samples were taken, this first year, in the transition zones on each side of the cut strips.

Figure 2.--Undisturbed forest, northwest corner of plot 3, Willamette Pass, Oreg. (May 29, 1963, before cutting.)

Figure 3.--Undisturbed area west of plot 3, Willamette Pass, Oreg., June 8, 1964.

A, *May 18*

B, *May 27*

Figure 4.--*Progress of snowmelt, spring of 1964. Northwest corner of plot 3, Willamette Pass, Oreg.*

C, *June 8*

Anderson has found that only about half the difference in snow accumulation associated with cut strips is found in the strip itself, the other half being in the adjacent forest. Although snow patches found at the time of the last observation in July were generally far from the edges of the cut strips, this transition zone should be sampled in future studies.

Average snow depth and its water content under the forest and in the open is shown in figure 1. At the time of maximum accumulation in March, snow depth was 23 percent greater in the open than under the forest; water content was 35 percent greater. Density of the snow was at this time higher in the open than under the forest, 0.26 and 0.24 cubic inch of water per cubic inch of snow, respectively. At the time snow was rapidly disappearing, density had increased to over 0.5 inch.

Progress of snowmelt within the cut strips is shown by figure 4. Snow melted first along the north edge of the strip where solar radiation was least interrupted by tree crowns of the uncut forest.

In the open strips, snow depth decreased with distance from the south edge of the timber both during the period of accumulation (January through March) and the period of snowmelt (April through June). This trend in snow depth during the accumulation period probably resulted from both greater deposition in the lee of the south timber edge (prevailing winds from southwest) and greater melt along the north timber edge during warm periods. The decrease of snow depth from north to south across the strips was further accentuated during the melt period. Timber shading the south edge of the strip slowed snowmelt and the north timber edge reflected infrared radiation speeding snowmelt.

For our range in slope and aspect, Anderson has recommended strips one-half to one tree height in width. The strips as cut are a little over one tree height in width. The progress of snowmelt within the strips indicates that shade from adjacent timber to the south might have been more effective in delaying snowmelt if we had limited width of the strip to 1 to 1-1/2 chains rather than the 2-chain width used. However, under conditions observed throughout the area this first year of measurement, there is no indication that snow would persist longer, in any practical width strip, than it would under shade of the forest.

DISCUSSION

Although first-year results are admittedly preliminary, we do find that our results are similar to those found by Anderson and others who have studied snow accumulation and melt. With this reassurance, we might speculate about the implication to management of our forests within the snow zone.

1. Although we have no comparison of evaporation and condensation rates from snow surfaces in the open and under the forest, we

can be reasonably sure that more water will be obtained from
the cut strips than the uncut. The accumulation of snow water
is greater (33.3 inches in open, 24.7 inches under forest) and
transpiration is practically eliminated. Recent studies by
Ziemer[4] indicate that under similar conditions in California
almost 7 inches less water was used during the summer in a
clearcut strip than under the forest. Soil in the bare clearcut areas remains near field capacity throughout the summer.
Hydrologists now believe that slow drainage from these areas
of high soil moisture contribute to streamflow even during
late summer. Future measurements in this area will include
sampling of soil moisture in June and again in October before
snow falls.

2. Increased accumulation of snow on a soil which has remained
   high in water content may increase the possibility of a rapid
   rise in streamflow during flood-producing, rain-on-snow events.

3. The presence of late snow patches within the forest, where
   small openings are present but well shaded, gives some support
   to the idea that many of our high-elevation forests are naturally nearly ideal for maximum delay of snowmelt. Under conditions of this study, strip cutting resulted in decreased
   effectiveness of the forest for snow retention. Narrower
   strips and block or selective cutting might have been more
   effective.

4. Even though snow patches may persist longer under the forest,
   their time of disappearance coincides with the period of
   heaviest transpiration use by the forest cover and the start
   of soil moisture depletion. Meltwater from the lingering
   snow patches within the forest may not contribute materially
   to summer streamflow, but may be beneficial to tree growth.

5. Early melting of snow, exposing bare ground along the north
   edge of the cut strip, may extend the normally short growing
   season, favoring more rapid establishment and growth of
   regeneration.

---

[4] Ziemer, Robert W. Summer evapotranspiration trends as related
to time after logging of forest in Sierra Nevada. Jour. Geophys. Res.
69: 615-620. 1964.

CORRECTION OF AVERAGE YARDING DISTANCE FACTOR

FOR CIRCULAR SETTINGS

by

Hilton H. Lysons and Charles N. Mann

INTRODUCTION

In performing cost analysis of logging operations, a factor is commonly used to obtain the average yarding distance. The geometry which
the setting most closely approximates (rectangular, square, triangular,
or circular) determines the factor to be used. The distance from the
landing to the external edge of the setting is multiplied by this factor
to obtain an average yarding distance for the setting.

This note is concerned with settings which are roughly circles, with
the landing in the center, or those which approximate circular sectors
(pie-shaped areas), with the landing at the apex. The factor given by
Matthews (p. 82)[1] and Bureau of Land Management (Table 4 (9331.22B))[2]
is 0.707, but the analysis below shows that the factor should be 2/3
(0.667). A brief review of the literature has indicated that the 0.707
factor is in common usage, and no source could be found giving the 2/3
factor.

---

[1] Matthews, Donald Maxwell. Cost control in the logging industry.
374 pp., illus. New York and London: McGraw-Hill Book Co., Inc. 1942.

[2] U.S. Department of Interior Bureau of Land Management. Logging
costs; schedule 14 (9331.2). 1964.

ANALYSIS

The average yarding distance ($\bar{y}$) is equal to the total yarding distance (Y) for a particular setting divided by the total number of turns (T):

$$\bar{y} = \frac{Y}{T} \tag{1}$$

If we assume that the logs are evenly distributed over the setting (which is never the case but which is quite often close enough to allow the analysis), then the number of turns for a small area of the setting is the same as for any other small area of the same size in the setting. The total number of turns (T) equals the total setting area (A) multiplied by the turn density or log density (D):

$$T = AD \tag{2}$$

Now, consider a small area (ΔA) of the setting for which the yarding distance is constant. The total yarding distance for this small area is equal to the log density times the area (which is the number of turns in the small area) times the yarding distance (y). And for the entire setting, the total yarding distance is obtained by summing the distances for all areas:

$$Y = \Delta A_1 y_1 D + \Delta A_2 y_2 D + \Delta A_3 y_3 D + \ldots \tag{3}$$

In terms of integral calculus, this becomes,

$$Y = \int_A DydA \tag{4}$$

and, in general terms,

$$\bar{y} = \frac{\int_A ydA}{A} \tag{5}$$

this equation holds for any shape setting.

For a circular setting of radius R, using polar coordinates,

$$dA = 2\pi r dr$$

$$y = r$$

$$A = \pi R^2$$

$$\int_A y dA = \int_0^R 2\pi r^2 dr = \frac{2}{3}\pi R^3 \qquad (6)$$

and

$$\bar{y} = \frac{\frac{2}{3}\pi R^3}{\pi R^2} = \frac{2}{3}R \qquad (7)$$

which shows that the average yarding distance is 2/3 times the external distance. A similar analysis will show that the factor is the same for a setting in the shape of a circular sector.

PERCENT ERROR

The bias introduced by using a factor of 0.707 instead of the correct factor of 2/3 is plus 6 percent. Under most engineering disciplines, a bias of this magnitude would be intolerable, but in view of the other quantities which go into a logging cost analysis, it is probable that a 6-percent error in the average yarding distance factor will have little effect on the overall accuracy of logging cost estimates. However, it is recommended that the correct factor of 2/3 (0.667) be used in the future.

PNW-25 June 1965

VARIATION IN VEGETATION FOLLOWING SLASH FIRES

NEAR OAKRIDGE, OREGON

By

Harold K. Steen

   The following photographic sequences illustrate how vegetation differed following slash fires on two logged areas 9 miles apart. As part of a regional study to determine effects of slash burning,[1] two pairs of plots were established on the Willamette National Forest near Oakridge, Oreg. Both areas were clearcut in 1949, and the slash was burned in October of the same year. One plot of each pair was burned along with the rest of the logging unit; the unburned plot in each pair was adjacent to the burned plot and provided a control for comparison of fire effects. The two pairs of plots shown here were selected from 13 in the Oakridge vicinity because of the obvious differences in plant cover. These differences are typical of the Oakridge vicinity.

---

   [1] Morris, William G. Influence of slash burning on regeneration, other plant cover, and fire hazard in the Douglas-fir region (a progress report). U.S. Forest Serv. Pac. NW. Forest & Range Expt. Sta. Res. Paper 29, 49 pp., illus. 1958.

UNBURNED   PAIR A   BURNED

FIGURE 1.-These photographs were taken in midsummer 1950, or during the first growing season
following burning. Unburned plots have a little trailing blackberry, starflower, Pacific rhododendron,
and vine maple. Two percent of burned A and 23 percent of burned B had a hard burn (organic
material destroyed and some soil coloration). One of these hard-burned spots may be seen in the
lower right of burned A (arrow). Vine maple may be seen in the foreground of unburned B; in the
background is a burned portion of the logging unit.

UNBURNED   PAIR B   BURNED

UNBURNED   PAIR A   BURNED

FIGURE 2.--Two growing seasons since the slash fire, there are some differences both between and among pairs. Unburned A has changed little in 1 year and burned A has some groundsel, trailing blackberry, and Cascades mahonia (locally called Oregon grape). On unburned B, groundsel, trailing blackberry, and vine maple are readily visible, on burned B, groundsel forms a dense cover as contrasted to a light cover on A.

UNBURNED   PAIR B   BURNED

UNBURNED   PAIR A   BURNED

FIGURE 3.--In the fourth growing season, vine maple and willowweed (locally called fireweed) are seen on unburned A, and groundsel replaced by willowweed, trailing blackberry, and modest whipplea on burned A. Douglas-fir seedlings are just visible (arrows) on both the burned and unburned plots. Vine maple and willowweed are dominant on unburned B. On burned B, ceanothus (probably both varnishleaf and snowbrush), blueberry elder, peavine, willowweed, and groundsel have replaced the heavy cover of groundsel found 2 years previously.

UNBURNED   PAIR B   BURNED

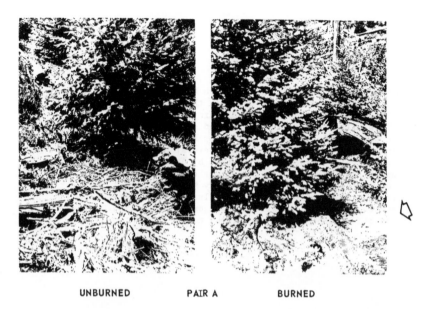

UNBURNED   PAIR A   BURNED

FIGURE 4.--By the 13th growing season, the Douglas-fir seedlings, which were barely visible in figure 3, are now of sapling size. Ninety-two-percent stocking by natural conifers occurs on unburned A (determined by 4-milacre subplot examinations) and 100-percent on burned A. Cascades mahonia and vine maple on unburned A and western bracken and modest whipplea on burned A may be seen in the photographs. The hard-burned spot is still evident in the lower right of burned A (arrow), showing that severe burns may have long-term effects. Pair B is brushy with vine maple covering the unburned plot and ceanothus the burned plot. There are about one-third as many conifer seedlings on unburned B as on unburned A, and two-thirds as many seedlings on burned B as on burned A.

UNBURNED   PAIR B   BURNED

SUMMARY

Typical variation in vegetation following slash burning is shown by comparison of paired photographs of two areas in the same locality. Except for vine maple on pair B, both pairs of burned and unburned plots were apparently similar initially. The second growing season after burning, groundsel formed a much heavier cover on burned B than on burned A. During the fourth growing season, several herbaceous species grew on burned A while burned B was invaded by brush. Thirteen years after the slash fire, the two pairs showed marked differences; conifers were well established on pair A while heavy brush covered pair B. These variations in vegetation following slash fires illustrate the predicament faced by the forest-land manager when deciding whether or not to use slash burning as a management tool.

GLOSSARY OF COMMON AND SCIENTIFIC NAMES

Blueberry elder	*Sambucus glauca*
Cascades mahonia	*Mahonia nervosa*
Douglas-fir	*Pseudotsuga menziesii*
Fireweed	*Epilobium angustifolium*
Groundsel	*Senecio* spp.
Modest whipplea	*Whipplea modesta*
Pacific rhododendron	*Rhododendron macrophyllum*
Peavine	*Lathyrus* spp.
Snowbrush ceanothus	*Ceanothus velutinus*
Trailing blackberry	*Rubus macropetalus*
Varnishleaf ceanothus	*Ceanothus velutinus* var. *laevigatus*
Vine maple	*Acer circinatum*
Western bracken	*Pteridium aquilinum* var. *pubescens*
Western starflower	*Trientalis europaea* var. *latifolia*
Willowweed	*Epilobium* spp.

FOREST AND RANGE EXPERIMENT STATION · U.S.DEPARTMENT OF AGRICULTURE · PORTLAND, OREGON

PNW-26   July 1965

WILDERNESS LAND ALLOCATION IN A MULTIPLE USE FOREST

MANAGEMENT FRAMEWORK IN THE PACIFIC NORTHWEST

by

Jay M. Hughes

INTRODUCTION

Since the early 1920's, public forest-land managers in the United States (particularly, those responsible for the administration of the National Forests) have been wrestling with a difficult problem of land use decision making. This problem is contained in the question: Why and how should particular tracts of land be allocated to a special kind of recreation use category called "wilderness"? Even though no "formula" has yet been found to answer this question, many allocation decisions have been made, resulting in a "wilderness system"[1] on the National Forests of the United States of over 14.5 million acres. A little more than 14 percent of this acreage is on the National Forests of Oregon and Washington.

Many of these decisions have aroused nationwide controversies. More such decisions are yet to be made. Even if there were no more decisions of this kind to make, a close examination of the question yields results useful to public forest-land managers who must choose among competing

---

[1] Includes wilderness areas, as defined by the 1964 Wilderness Act (78 Stat. 890; P.L. 88-577), and primitive areas.

uses for particular tracts of public land. Such decisions are becoming
more frequent and more difficult. This report highlights a recent
study[2] of this land allocation problem.

STUDY FRAMEWORK AND OBJECTIVES

Although this study examined and classified all the various historical concepts of wilderness, it was concerned mainly with "institutionalized wilderness," which was defined as an area having:

1. Been designated as wilderness with the purpose of maintaining
   its wildernesslike character;
2. A definite _name_ which associates it in the minds of administra-
   tors and others with a definite location;
3. Definite _boundaries_, usually known on the ground by local resi-
   dents and visitors and capable of being identified on a map;
4. Some direct or indirect _legal authority_ for designation and
   enforcement of management provisions;
5. A definite _plan_ or philosophy for its management.

The method used for this study involved three general stages:
(1) an examination of wilderness and land use ideologies and concepts,
with the objective of organizing viewpoints and identifying kinds of
criteria and how they were used; (2) a detailed examination and
appraisal of selected Forest Service wilderness classification cases
in the Pacific Northwest Region to see how past decisions had been
made and what the bases for decision were; and (3) particular consideration of economics analysis as a tool for measuring relevant facts and
making choices among alternative land uses.

SOME RESULTS

American wilderness and its literature make up a colorful "safari
land" for those who wish to hunt their quarry with the special weapons
of a wide range of disciplines. Psychiatrists explore the therapeutic
values to users; political scientists search for the strategies of
opponents in particular conflicts; sociologists test behavioral models
of man on the wilderness user; ecologists use the wilderness as a norm
for observing biological succession; economists measure the economic
impact of wilderness classification; philosophers muse upon the value
of wilderness solitude; etc.

---

[2] Hughes, Jay M. Wilderness land allocation in a multiple use
forest management framework in the Pacific Northwest. 1964. (Unpublished Ph. D. thesis on file Mich. State Univ., East Lansing.
597 pp., illus.)

An exhaustive examination of American wilderness literature identified 15 recurring issues and themes, which underscore the interdisciplinary nature of the general subject. These were classified and briefly characterized as follows:

1. Anthropocentricity--a concept stressing the man-centeredness of wilderness.
2. Public access to decision making--raising the questions of how and where the "public" may participate in the decision-making processes of a bureaucracy.
3. Minority rights--a justification for wilderness in view of the relative few who use wilderness.
4. Vicarious use--also a justification for wilderness since many who don't use wilderness like to know it exists.
5. The negligibility argument--a line of reasoning which contrasts economic with noneconomic values and contends economic values are negligible.
6. Intrarecreation conflict--different categories of recreationists come into conflict in particular places, and this creates a major problem to be solved.
7. Protection by legislation--reflecting concern for maximum assurance of permanence.
8. Multiple use or single use--which is wilderness?
9. Freedom of choice--wilderness widens the range of recreation experience possibilities.
10. Conservation ethics--a kind of moralistic attitude based upon the idea that wilderness is valuable to man and will become more precious.
11. Sanctuary, sanity, and health--stresses the therapeutic values of the wilderness experience.
12. Science and the control-plot idea--wilderness is seen as a standard of reference for biological change in nonwilderness environments.
13. Local and national interests--which should predominate when these conflict?
14. Wilderness use capacity--the big unknown.
15. Size, location, and configuration of area--variables which influence the productivity of wilderness satisfaction.

Examination of past classification cases, as well as the literature, reveals the need to clarify the choices that are to be made and to make explicit the contributing factors to the decisions. The true nature of the choice is that decisions are made between land use alternatives, using economic and noneconomic values together, rather than between dollar and nondollar value alternatives. Under the logic of choice of economics, we would choose that alternative which maximizes the economic where noneconomic values are equal or that which maximizes the noneconomic where economic values are equal. However, these rules of choice are inadequate where a choice must be made between land use alternatives when neither economic nor noneconomic consequences are equal.

Economics analysis does not provide the complete basis for choice. However, a number of economics methodologies are very useful, maybe indispensable, in this decision-making problem. Several recreation valuation methods were critiqued. They may be classified as follows:

1. Location or spatial differentiation analysis.
2. Precedential valuation--relative valuation based on precedent.
3. Market value of recreation.
4. User expenditures.
5. Cost of development and operation.
6. National income and product accounting.
7. Economic base study approach.

The valuation of recreation is but one part of decision making. A framework is needed in which to use all the economic and noneconomic values.

Four economics choice mechanisms were thus examined for their relevance to the wilderness land allocation decision. These are called:

1. Benefit-cost analysis.
2. Budgeting.
3. Least-opportunity-cost ranking.
4. Joint production analysis.

It was concluded that all of these methodologies encouraged more explicit economic consequences of wilderness allocation. The historical record of wilderness discussions and decisions revealed that methodologies such as the national income, economic base, and budgeting techniques seemed to be favored. However, the overall study conclusion was that all methods proved deficient in terms of providing a theoretically complete valuation of the alternatives, wilderness versus non-wilderness.

Finally, some of the economic consequences of allocating land to institutionalized wilderness status in the Pacific Northwest were estimated. For example, a principal land use alternative to wilderness in the Pacific Northwest is timber production. Using a value-added approach, to obtain an ultimate market "impact" measure of using present timbered wilderness areas for timber production or wilderness recreation, gave a ratio of over 17:1 in favor of timber production. However, this is not interpreted to mean that there has been a misallocation of resources, but simply that society has been willing to pay this "price" to have the wilderness thus far established.

SPACING AND UNDERSTORY VEGETATION AFFECT GROWTH

OF PONDEROSA PINE SAPLINGS

by

James W. Barrett

What is the best spacing of ponderosa pine *(Pinus ponderosa)*[1] for maximum production of usable wood? How does understory vegetation influence tree growth at different spacings? These questions are the subject of a spacing study installed in suppressed ponderosa pine saplings on the Pringle Falls Experimental Forest in central Oregon.

Principal objectives of the study are to determine (1) time required for trees at various densities to occupy a given amount of growing space and (2) size of trees produced at the end of this period. Even though the study has not yet fulfilled these objectives, early results merit the attention of ponderosa pine forest managers.

This research note presents a 4-year record of diameter and height increment of residual saplings following overstory removal and thinning.

EXPERIMENTAL AREA

The study is at an elevation of about 4,400 feet on an east-facing slope. Precipitation averages 24 inches per year. Most rainfall occurs in late fall, winter, and spring. Summers are dry. Soil is a Regosol

---

[1] Authorities for common and scientific names in this publication are: for trees, "Check List of Trees of the United States (Including Alaska)," by Elbert L. Little, Jr.; for shrubs, "Standardized Plant Names," by Harlan P. Kelsey and William A. Dayton.

developed in dacite pumice originating from the eruption of Mount Mazama (Crater Lake). The soil, averaging 33 inches in depth, is underlain by a sandy loam paleosol developed in volcanic ash containing cinders and basalt fragments.

The unthinned timber stand was typical old-growth ponderosa pine, with a dense 40- to 70-year-old understory of about 7,000 saplings per acre. Heights of overstory trees indicated that site quality throughout the study area uniformly averaged site IV.[2] Understory vegetation was mostly antelope bitterbrush *(Purshia tridentata)*, snowbrush ceanothus *(Ceanothus velutinus)*, and pine manzanita *(Arctostaphylos parryana* var. *pinetorum)*, although sedges, grasses, and other herbs were present.

STUDY ESTABLISHMENT AND DESIGN

Thirty 1/5-acre rectangular plots with at least 1,000 well-distributed saplings per acre were established (fig. 1). Overstory was carefully harvested, and plots were thinned to randomly assigned densities of 1,000, 500, 250, 125, and 62 trees per acre.[3] Each

Figure 1.--Typical ponderos stand before harvest of overstory and applicat spacing treatments to the suppressed sapling unde

[2] Meyer, Walter H. Yield of even-aged stands of ponderosa pine. U.S. Dept. Agr. Tech. Bul. 630, 60 pp., illus. 1938.

[3] Barrett, James W. Intensive control in logging ponderosa pine. Iowa State Jour. Sci. 34: 603-608, illus. 1960.

spacing treatment was replicated six times. Average diameters and heights of residual trees for the various stand densities in 1959 were as follows:

	Diameter (Inches)	Height (Feet)
Trees per acre:		
1,000	1.9	11.6
500	1.7	12.2
250	2.0	10.9
125	2.3	13.2
62	2.2	11.7

No reserve trees were over 3.1 inches d.b.h.

Understory vegetation was removed from three plots of each spacing treatment, and these plots were kept as free as possible of subsequently developing vegetation. Understory vegetation left on the remaining plots of each spacing treatment was measured as percent cover by line point sampling using 100 points per plot.[4]

Logging of overstory and thinning of saplings started in the fall of 1957 and was completed in the fall of 1958 (fig. 2). All thinning slash was removed from the study plots and burned.

Figure 2.--Sapling stand directly after thinning to 1,000 trees per acre. Thinning slash has been removed and understory vegetation left.

[4] Heady, Harold F., Gibbens, Robert P., and Powell, Robert W. A comparison of the charting, line intercept, and line point methods of sampling shrub types of vegetation. Jour. Range Mangt. 12: 180-188, illus. 1959.

The first diameter and height measurement of all residual saplings was in the fall of 1959 and the second (four growing seasons later) in the fall of 1963.

Diameters at breast height were measured with steel tape to the nearest 0.1 inch. Heights were measured with a sectioned aluminum pole to the nearest 0.1 foot.

RESULTS

Sapling response to spacing treatments was shown quantitatively by height and diameter measurements and morphologically by crown vigor. After release, saplings produced long, large needles resulting in a distinct improvement in crown vigor, most apparent at the lower densities (fig. 3). Some individual saplings, thinned to a wide spacing and having better than average crowns before release, showed remarkable response in diameter growth after thinning (fig. 4).

Figure 3.--Trees at a density of 62 per acre show vigorous crown development 4 years after treatment. Compare tree vigor with that of trees in figure 2.

Figure 4.--Section from a 4-inch ponderosa pine sapling, released from competition about 6 years, shows the capacity of a suppressed tree to respond to release.

Diameter Increment

Stand density had a highly significant effect on diameter increment (fig. 5). Where understory vegetation (brush and herbs) was left undisturbed, trees grew at the rate of 3.0 inches d.b.h. per decade where 62 trees per acre were left. Where 1,000 trees per acre remained with understory vegetation, diameter increment was only 1.5 inches per decade.

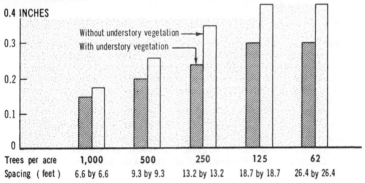

Figure 5.-- Average annual diameter increment of ponderosa pine saplings following thinning.

The effect of competition was also evident within the range of spacing treatments. For example, trees at a density of 250 per acre made significantly less diameter growth than those at 125 per acre and were, therefore, showing the effects of competition after only a few years. Saplings growing at densities of 125 per acre and less were probably not in competition with each other during the 4-year measurement period.

The removal of understory vegetation significantly increased diameter increment throughout the range of tree spacings. In addition, there was a highly significant trend for understory vegetation to have a more pronounced effect on diameter increment at the wider spacings.

Average percent cover of understory vegetation also increased with wider tree spacing. Although this trend was nonsignificant (5-percent level), it suggested that when tree spacing is increased to stimulate diameter growth, development of understory vegetation may also be stimulated. Where undisturbed, understory vegetation cover increased from 29 percent in 1959 to 38 percent in 1963. Vegetation was about three-fourths brush and one-fourth grasses and other herbs.

A further analysis of diameter increment was made, considering only the 62 largest (in 1959) equally distributed trees per acre from each of the stand density treatments. These 62 largest trees per acre will probably constitute a major portion of the stems that will make up the final harvest. They showed a highly significant increase in diameter increment with decreasing stand densities. Therefore, growth of even the largest trees--those usually occupying the most favorable position in the stand--was not independent of tree spacing.

Height Increment

Height growth was also significantly (1-percent level) affected by stand density. Height increment increased with wider spacing (fig. 6). Average growth of saplings ranged from a low of 0.20 foot per year where 1,000 trees per acre were left to a high of 0.5 foot where 62 trees remained. Some vigorous, full-crowned trees grew 0.9 foot per year at the widest spacing.

An analysis of height increment of the largest trees in each density, similar to the analysis of diameter increment of the largest trees reported above, showed that height increment of the largest trees also increased significantly (5-percent level) with decreased stand density.

Understory vegetation had a highly significant effect on height growth. On plots where understory vegetation was removed, height increment was increased by about one-third at densities of 500, 250, 125, and 62 trees per acre.

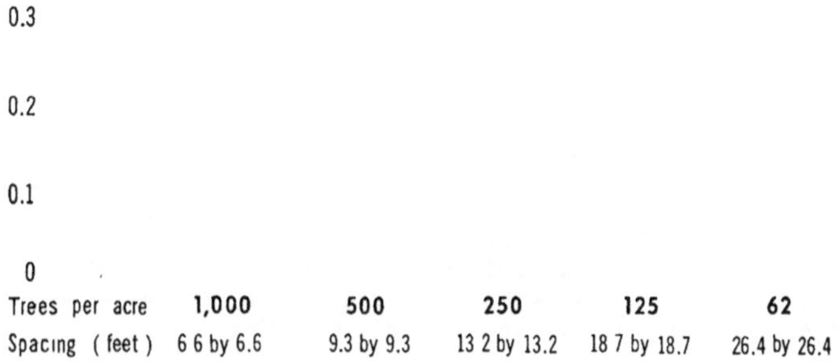

0.3

0.2

0.1

0

| Trees per acre | 1,000 | 500 | 250 | 125 | 62 |
| Spacing (feet) | 6 6 by 6.6 | 9.3 by 9.3 | 13 2 by 13.2 | 18 7 by 18.7 | 26.4 by 26.4 |

Figure 6. -- Average annual height increment of ponderosa pine saplings following thinning.

Mortality

No tree mortality occurred in this study. Extensive precautions were taken to protect the stand from damage by porcupines and snowbend, the two greatest threats to maintaining the designated tree densities. Mortality will probably occur in the future as tree crowns expand and lower crown class trees succumb to competition. Continued observation of these plots will disclose the effect of spacing on mortality.

CONCLUSIONS AND DISCUSSION

Tree spacing and presence of understory vegetation are major factors influencing diameter and height growth of suppressed ponderosa pine saplings after overstory harvest. Although this conclusion is based on only a 4-year measurement period following thinning treatment, data appear reliable enough to make short-term growth predictions. Subsequent observations will improve accuracy of such predictions for application to the sizable acreage of similar stands. Repetition of study techniques used here will probably be necessary to determine applicable growth predictions for other sites and soil types.

Continued observation of this study will provide a wide range of information. For example, we will obtain a better understanding of the effects of spacing on tree form, limb size, and branching habits, including death and natural pruning of lower limbs. Of perhaps equal importance will be the determination of optimum tree densities for production of not only wood but also vegetation, useful as forage for livestock and wildlife and for soil building.

Data presented here are useful for confirming or modifying existing management guidelines within limits. Eventually, the broad range of spacings included in this study will provide yield information for a wide variety of economic demands for wood.

U. S. FOREST SERVICE

Pacific North West Research Note

FOREST AND RANGE EXPERIMENT STATION · U.S. DEPARTMENT OF AGRICULTURE · PORTLAND, ORE

PNW-28   August 1965

FORCES IN BALLOON LOGGING

by

Charles N. Mann

This note is furnished to provide a better understanding of the mechanics of yarding with a balloon. The sources of the individual forces involved are discussed, and a possible combination of these forces to produce lift and movement of the log is illustrated. Figure 1 shows a typical configuration for balloon logging.

BALLOON-INDUCED FORCES

The following balloon forces combine vectorially to produce a tension in the tether line:

1. Net static lift force (F_s): Vertical force due to buoyancy of gas less weight of bag and rigging.

2. Inertia force (F_i): Force produced by accelerating the balloon. Mathematically, this is

$$F_i = m\ a$$

where: m = mass of gas

+ mass of balloon

+ mass of air accelerated with the balloon

a = balloon acceleration

The mass of air accelerated with the balloon is determined by using inertia coefficients which depend on the shape of the balloon. The airmass is obtained by multiplying the mass of air displaced by the inertia coefficient. The inertia coefficients are determined along the principal axes of a body. For accelerations in other directions, the acceleration is first resolved into components along the principal axes, then the force components are calculated in the principal directions, and finally, the force is obtained by vector addition. To determine this force, the magnitude and direction of the balloon acceleration must be known as well as the balloon inertia coefficients and the angle between the balloon axis and the acceleration vector.

3. Aerodynamic lift force (F_1): A force component perpendicular to the direction of air motion past the balloon which is produced by the air motion. Mathematically, this component is

$$F_1 = C_L\ \frac{\rho}{2}\ v^2\ V_H^{2/3}$$

where: C_L is the lift coefficient and varies with the angle of attack and the balloon configuration
ρ is the mass density of air
v is the air velocity relative to the balloon
V_H is the balloon volume

4. Aerodynamic drag force (F_d): A force component in the direction of air motion past the balloon which is produced by the air motion. Mathematically, this component is

$$F_d = C_D \frac{\rho}{2} v^2 \, V_H^{2/3}$$

where: C_D is the drag coefficient and also varies with the angle of attack and balloon configuration

The relative air velocity in the lift and drag force equations above is the vector sum of the ambient wind and motion of the balloon relative to the ground. The direction of this relative velocity is not necessarily horizontal. These forces can be determined if the magnitude and direction of the relative air velocity, the balloon attitude relative to the velocity, and the coefficients for the balloon attitude are known.

All of these forces can combine to produce an upward force as in the example illustrated in figure 2.

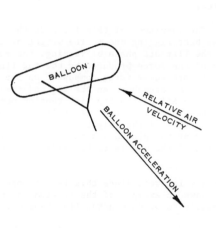

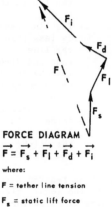

FORCE DIAGRAM
$$\vec{F} = \vec{F_s} + \vec{F_l} + \vec{F_d} + \vec{F_i}$$

where:

F = tether line tension

F_s = static lift force

F_l = aerodynamic lift force

F_d = aerodynamic drag force

F_i = inertia force

Figure 2.--Example of vector addition of balloon forces.

FORCES AT BUTT RIGGING

The butt rigging is the junction point of the balloon tether line, the main line, the haulback line, and the tag line to which the logs are attached. The source of the tether line tension is fully described in the discussion above. At the butt rigging, this tension is reduced from that at the balloon due to the weight of the tether line. A description of the forces in the remaining lines while yarding the logs into the landing is given below:

1. Main line tension: This force is produced by the yarder through the main line drum and by the weight of the cable. The force at the butt rigging may be less than at the yarder due to: (1) friction if the line contacts the ground, (2) friction in the blocks, (3) inertia of the line during periods of acceleration, and (4) difference in elevation between yarder and butt rigging.

2. Haulback line tension: The force in this line is due to (1) friction between the line and the ground; (2) friction in the blocks; (3) haulback drum induced forces caused by friction, braking, or interlocking with the main drum; and (4) the weight of the cable. The cable weight will alter the tension at the butt rigging by the product of the unit cable weight and the difference in elevation between the butt rigging and the yarder. During periods of acceleration, inertia of the haulback line will cause an additional tension in this line.

3. Tag line tension: The magnitude of this force at the log is less than at the butt rigging due to the weight of the tag line. During the lift-off phase of yarding, the magnitude and direction of the force produced by the tag line must be sufficient to produce a force component on the log to overcome the friction force between the log and the ground. For log acceleration, the tag line tension must also overcome the inertia of the log. After lift-off, the force in this line must equal the weight of the log if the log is to remain free of the ground and must exceed half the weight of the log if the log is to be yarded with one end off the ground.

Tag line tension is of primary interest since this is the force that lifts the logs. Figure 3 shows an example of the tension in the other three lines adding vectorially to produce a tag line tension.

This general force description does not consider phenomena which will cause transient variations in the forces such as oscillation of the balloon-log system or sudden impact of the log with a ground obstruction.

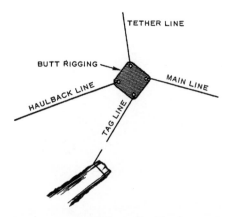

TETHER LINE

BUTT RIGGING

HAULBACK LINE

MAIN LINE

TAG LINE

Figure 3.--Example of vector addition of line tensions.

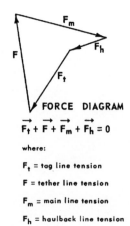

F_m

F_h

F

F_t

FORCE DIAGRAM

$$\vec{F_t} + \vec{F} + \vec{F_m} + \vec{F_h} = 0$$

where:

F_t = tag line tension

F = tether line tension

F_m = main line tension

F_h = haulback line tension

August 1965

CHRISTMAS STORM DAMAGE ON THE H. J. ANDREWS

EXPERIMENTAL FOREST

by

R. L. Fredriksen

The storm preceding Christmas, 1964, brought flood damage of major proportions to watersheds in the Douglas-fir zone of western Oregon. The H. J. Andrews Experimental Forest (Berntsen and Rothacher, 1959), located in the upper McKenzie River drainage about 50 miles east of Eugene, Oreg., is typical of upstream areas damaged by the storm. Twelve years of precipitation and runoff records at this site enable us to evaluate this storm. In this case history, we have attempted to show, at least in part, why this storm caused such extensive damage.

THE STORM

The meteorological explanation of the weather conditions causing this flood was summarized in the Portland Oregonian in the Sunday edition of January 2, 1965. This storm was preceded by a period of below-freezing temperatures. A warm front from the Pacific Ocean, overriding an artic airmass, brought the snowline down to near sea level. Snowfall changed to continuous rain, beginning about midnight Sunday, December 20, as air temperature began a rising trend. The result was an extreme example of a rain-on-snow storm in which melt water from a moderate snowpack was added to rainfall runoff when the air temperature warmed from freezing to the mid-50's F. Streamflow resulting from this storm exceeded measured maximum peaks for 50 years' standing and set new records at a number of locations throughout Oregon. This rampaging flood surge caused widespread erosion in stream channels and destroyed roads, bridges, and personal property valued in the millions of dollars.

This storm was one of the most severe of six that have occurred in the Willamette Valley in the last 104 years. It is not known how severe erosion and sedimentation was during earlier flood-producing storms because logging in watersheds of headwater streams had not yet begun and access was only by trail.

On the experimental forest, fresh snow began falling on a moderate snowpack on December 18 as temperatures gradually warmed to near melting (fig. 1). By the morning of December 20, after 1.3 inches of water had fallen as snow, temperatures continued to rise, and snow changed to mixed rain and snow. Streams began to rise on Monday morning, December 21, as rainfall intensity increased. An abrupt temperature rise at noon the same day (fig. 1), followed by maximum rainfall intensities near midnight, brought streams to the highest flow measured in 12 years of record.

This peak flow was the result of 8.25 inches of rain in more than 2 days plus an undetermined amount of snowmelt water. Of 1.5 feet of snow at 1,500-foot elevation on the morning of December 21, only scattered patches remained on the morning of December 22. Unfortunately, we have no measure of water content of this snow but estimate that it contained an equivalent of 3 or 4 inches of water. Rain plus snowmelt water, totaling more than a foot, was released on the land surface while streams in the three experimental watersheds reached peak flows.

THE EXPERIMENTAL WATERSHEDS

The watersheds in the H. J. Andrews Experimental Forest are typical examples of headwater areas sustaining extensive damage during the storm. They have deep soils, developed from tuffs and breccias, which contain a high percentage of silt and clay. Overland flow has not been observed on these watersheds even at the time of peak flows. This is probably the result of extremely porous soils together with moderate precipitation intensities characteristic of this climate. Mean annual temperature is about 48° F. at 1,600 feet. At this elevation there is seldom a continuous winter snowpack. Annual rainfall averages 92 inches, but 95 percent of this water falls during the cool season from September to May.

Although the watersheds vary in size from 149 to 250 acres, they are similar topographically. They face to the northwest (fig. 2). Maximum side slopes on each range from 85 to 105 percent and the average gradient of the stream channels from 28 to 35 percent.

For 7 years after watershed studies began, the old-growth Douglas-fir canopy in the experimental watersheds remained unbroken. During 1959, 1.6 miles of roads were completed in watershed 3 (Berntsen and Rothacher, 1959), and a fourth of the area was logged and burned in 1962. About 75 percent of the timber in watershed 1 has been harvested by skyline crane since logging began in 1961. Watershed 2 remains in a natural condition as the control watershed.

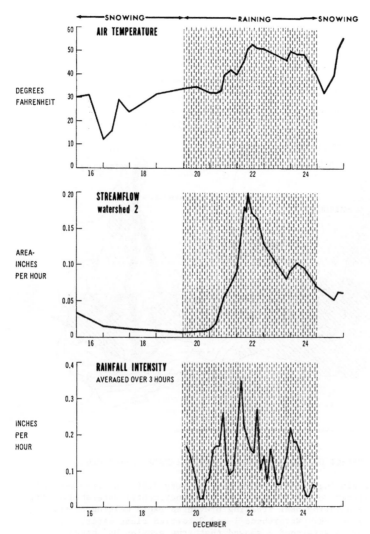

Figure 1.--Weather conditions during the 1964 Christmas storm and streamflow from watershed 2.

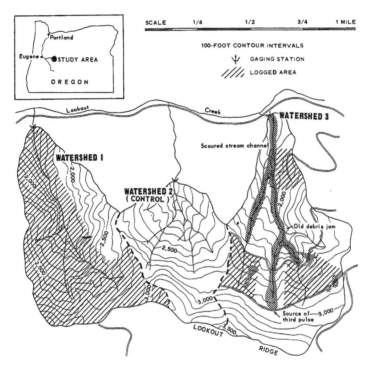

Figure 2.--Experimental watersheds, H.J. Andrews Experimental Forest.

EFFECT OF THE STORM ON THE EXPERIMENTAL WATERSHEDS

The beginning of this storm was not very different from many of the past storms we have recorded on the experimental watersheds. Air temperature hovering near freezing prevented rapid melting of the heavy wet snowpack. Watersheds 1 and 2 carried clear water, but a muddy stream in watershed 3 showed that some erosion had begun.

We were impressed by the severity of the situation about midnight of December 21 when rainfall intensities reached 0.47 inch per hour and air temperatures had warmed 10° to 12° (fig. 1). The streamflow hydrograph at watershed 2 began to rise very rapidly in response to the rain and melting snow. Streamflow in watersheds 1 and 2 reached a peak of 0.26 and 0.20 area-inch per hour by midmorning of December 22. Rainfall, which averaged 0.28 inch per hour for the 6-hour period previous to the storm peak, was only slightly greater than the rate of outflow from watershed 1.

When we inspected the gaging stations at 2 a.m. on December 22, the watershed 3 gaging station had been destroyed by a large debris slide. There were three distinct slide pulses from this watershed. The first, already mentioned, contained mainly rotten logs. The second, a larger pulse of logs and trees, struck the existing debris jam about 8 a.m., December 22. According to eyewitnesses, who narrowly escaped this pulse, about half the debris lodged behind the road fill while the other half was carried over the top of the fill and into the main stream below. Figure 3 shows the debris jam as it then appeared. The largest quantity of debris—mainly gravel and boulders—lodged behind the debris jam during the night of December 22-23 from the third pulse, which filled in the stream channel behind the road fill with about 27,500 yards of this material.

Figure 3.--Debris from watershed 3 as it appeared on December 22, 1964.

Erosion source areas in watershed 3 are indicated on figure 2. Stream channels through which the slide pulses moved were probably the main source of wood debris. Although part of the main channel had been scoured[1] by a previous slide in 1961 (Fredriksen 1963), one large debris jam remained from this slide. The first two slide pulses

---

[1] Since slides generally scour stream channels to bedrock, this phenomenon is frequently referred to as channel scour.

carried material from this debris jam plus debris accumulated in the channels. The third pulse originated from a timbered area which was recognized as an unstable area in the summer of 1964. Numerous other small failures were noted (fig. 2), but their contribution to the total load of eroded material moved by the storm was small.

Watershed 1 and 2 streams, by contrast, carried little sediment. Though the total storm sediment load coming from watershed 2 (control) was small by comparison with events in watershed 3, the total load was larger than has been measured during the past 8 years. Several yards of gravel passed through the flume near the storm peak--probably from streambank cutting--but no evidence of mass soil movement was noted during several inspection trips. No evidence of accelerated erosion was noted in watershed 1. Although peak runoff was only slightly less than the rate of applied rainfall, the water would have met drinking water standards except for very short periods during the storm.

Behavior of the experimental watersheds during the storm was fairly typical of other watersheds in the vicinity. A hasty check of headwater stream channels showed that 10 out of 20 were severely scoured by debris movement in the channel, similar to that observed in watershed 3.

WHAT MADE THIS STORM DIFFERENT?

The 1964 Christmas storm was one of the most destructive witnessed in 100 years of recorded history in western Oregon. It would be of interest to compare this storm with other storms which have occurred during past years. We will compare peak streamflows and precipitation amounts causing the peak. This is a technique frequently used to compare storms. Also we will discuss the erosion potential of frozen soil since forest soils along the Cascade front were subjected to subfreezing temperatures for several days before the storm.

Precipitation vs. Runoff

Peak streamflows in watershed 2 are compared with the maximum 6-hour precipitation falling before the peak (fig. 4). This watershed was selected for the comparison because vegetation cover has remained undisturbed during the past 12 years. Lines are drawn at 100, 80, and 60 percent of the rate of applied rainfall so that storms of different size can be compared. The 1964 Christmas storm reached flow rates greater than have been measured before but at smaller 6-hour amounts than have been measured during previous storms. Apparently snowmelt water made up the difference. The storm of December 19, 1961, was the only other storm which caused runoff rates greater than 60 percent of potential runoff. This event, also a rainfall-snowmelt storm, caused many examples of channel scour and mass movements in the vicinity and scoured the channel in watershed 3 (Fredriksen 1963).

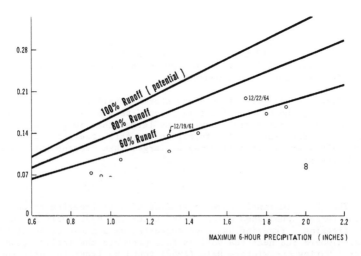

Figure 4.--Peak flows compared with maximum 6-hour rainfall, watershed 2.

Storm Size

Because rainfall from the Christmas storm lasted about 4 days, other 4-day storms measured in the experimental forest were grouped into size classes (fig. 5). Of 44 storms measured during 12 years,

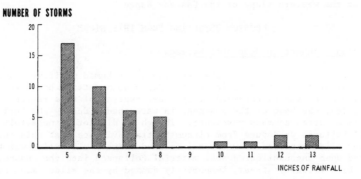

Figure 5.--Frequency of 4-day storms by size class, 1952.64.

6 delivered more than 10 inches; 2, including the Christmas storm, measured more than 13 inches. Considering the short span of records at the experimental forest, we believe 4-day storms which deliver 13 inches are probably not unusual.

Miller (1964) classifies 4-day storms totaling between 10 and 12.5 inches, along the Cascade front in Oregon, as events with a 100-year return period. Since six 4-day storms larger than 10 inches have been measured in the experimental forest in 12 years, the size of storms with a 100-year return period may be larger than present information would suggest.

Frozen Soil

Though we currently have no studies of soil freezing at the experimental forest, published evidence indicates the hydrologic potential of soil freezing. Freezing has been suggested as a cause of accelerated erosion where ice near the soil surface prevents the infiltration of water. During one winter, Hale (1950) found no frost in soils supporting Douglas-fir stands along the Cascade front even when the protective influence of vegetation cover had been removed by logging. Striffler (1959) in the central United States also found little or no concrete frost, which restricts the internal drainage of soils, in highly aggregated forest soils similar to soils under Douglas-fir stands. However, frozen soil has been observed at the H. J. Andrews Experimental Forest during snow-free winter periods of sustained below-freezing temperature. Though the soil is frozen, spaces between the soil granules remain free of ice and the soil retains the ability to conduct water. So frozen soil probably did not prevent passage of water into the soil mantle along the western slope of the Cascade Range.

EROSION RESULTING FROM THIS STORM

Erosion Sequence on Headwater Streams

Thornbury (1954) describes erosion under humid maritime climate typical of the north Pacific coast. Rapid down-cutting by streams and valley extension by headward erosion are typical of this region. Erosion from the head of the drainage in watershed 3 during the Christmas storm occurred as mass movements. Though we did not witness this head-wall failure, we deduce from circumstantial evidence that this channel scour slide resulted from several related events. The slide was triggered when unconsolidated soil material collapsed into the channel. The high-velocity stream, temporarily dammed by the slide, soon saturated the already wet slide material, and the entire mass moved down the channel taking with it all debris in its path.

Wood debris in these drainages, such as fallen trees and logging debris, adds bulk to the moving mass--thereby scouring a larger area of these deeply incised channels. Tree-length logs snatched from creek

-8-

banks carry more soil material into the drainage and disturb more area along the stream margins. Road fills and bridges, where roads cross the stream, can seldom withstand the impact of the moving debris. Consequently, the mass of these structures is frequently added to the bulk of material moving down the drainage. Rothacher (1959) has aptly discussed the debris problem in small drainages.

We witnessed the end of a slide which occurred in another watershed in a nearby logging unit. Upon hearing low rumbling sounds and earth tremors, we rushed to the scene only in time to witness the last one-third of the slide travel. The slide moved very rapidly and as a single mass through nearly one-quarter mile of channel in less than a minute.

Erosion Sequence in Lower Gradient Streams

Mud and debris flows in headwater streams contribute to erosion in lower gradient channels. Floating wood debris from source watersheds, together with old debris already in the channel, move downstream until an obstruction is encountered. Debris jams, which form behind these obstructions, are collecting points for streambed gravels and boulders. As the stream channel is plugged, the water level behind the debris jam rises and eventually finds a new channel. Rock and soil material, removed when the new channel is cut, adds to the streambed material already in motion down the stream. Channel cutting undermines the roots of trees adjacent to the channel. Trees falling across the channel serve as natural barriers for the formation of new debris jams. So, in addition to the force of water moving down the channel, debris greatly accelerates the rate of channel erosion. Damage or total destruction of roads and bridges adjacent to or crossing these low-gradient channels was the result of channel cutting, sometimes by water alone but more frequently by debris together with the flood run-off. As use of forest land in mountainous terrain becomes more intensive, damage to forest improvements from these widely spaced storms can be expected to become more severe.

MAGNITUDE OF EROSION DURING THIS STORM

In Experimental Watersheds

The magnitude of erosion and resulting sedimentation during the Christmas storm can be evaluated by comparison with 9 years of sedimentation records from the three experimental watersheds. Suspended sediment carried annually from these watersheds with winter storms has ranged from 0.006 to 0.120 ton per acre and the heavier streambed material from 0.3 to 2.4 cubic feet per acre. The annual sediment load is related to the number and size of storms occurring during a winter. When snowmelt water is added to rainfall during these long-duration storms, erosion is greatly increased by mass movements. One slide in December 1961 carried 10 cubic feet per acre of streambed gravels and 1.1 tons per acre of suspended sediment through the watershed 3 channel. Erosion in watershed 3 during the Christmas storm deposited about 3,000 cubic feet per acre of gravel, rock, and logs in the stream channel--300 times the amount measured during the 1961 slide. Minor importance of sedimentation in the other two watersheds shows that erosion rate is extremely variable, even in adjacent watersheds which are topographically very similar. Though there were no slides in watershed 1 during the Christmas storm, late in January 1965 another storm, nearly as large, caused a slide which deposited several tons of material in the stream channel. As was pointed out previously, the number of channel scour events in other headwater streams in the experimental forest were about in the same proportion to these observed on the experimental watersheds.

In Lower Gradient Channels

Lower gradient channels carried very large quantities of solid material during the storm. Though we lack quantitative data, from evidence of channel erosion along the main channel and sediment contributed from mass movements in headwater streams, we conclude that the total sediment load was many times the load observed during past storms. The deafening sound of boulders grinding together as they moved down the streambed was evidence of the magnitude of erosion taking place.

SUMMARY

Erosion during the 1964 Christmas storm was the result of a combination of climatic circumstances which has occurred in the past and undoubtedly will occur again. Six major flood-producing storms have occurred in the Willamette Valley since 1861--an average of one every 17 years. Of these, the Christmas storm was probably one of the largest.

Sedimentation in significant quantities along the west slope of the Cascade Range occurs as a result of runoff from prolonged low-intensity rain together with snowmelt water. The Christmas storm was of this type. Sedimentation began in high-gradient headwater streams. Large quantities of soil, rock, and wood debris moved into lower gradient channels collecting runoff from headwater streams. Moving debris in lower gradient channels was responsible for accelerated channel erosion and damage or destruction of forest roads and bridges.

Rainfall amounts reaching 12 to 13 inches in 4 days cause moderate local erosion and sedimentation, but when snowmelt water is added to this overabundant rainfall, damage is severe. Frequency of 4-day rainfall amounts this large is greater than regional rainfall records would indicate.

We can expect that erosion and sedimentation will be more severe in future years as the density of forest transportation structures is increased to provide access to timber stands not yet under sustained yield management.

LITERATURE CITED

Berntsen, Carl M., and Rothacher, Jack.
    1959. A guide to the H. J. Andrews Experimental Forest. U.S.
        Forest Serv. Pac. NW. Forest & Range Expt. Sta., 21 pp.,
        illus.

Fredriksen, R. L.
    1963. A case history of a mud and rock slide on an experimental
        watershed. U.S. Forest Serv. Res. Note PNW-1, 4 pp., illus.

Hale, Charles E.
    1950. Some observations on soil freezing in forest and range
        lands of the Pacific Northwest. U.S. Forest Serv. Pac. NW.
        Forest & Range Expt. Sta. Res. Note 66, 17 pp., illus.

Miller, John F.
    1964. Two to 10-day precipitation for return periods of 2 to 100
        years in the contiguous United States. U.S. Weather Bureau
        Tech. Paper 49, 29 pp., illus.

Rothacher, Jack.
    1959. How much debris down the drainage? The Timberman 60(6):
        75-76, illus.

Striffler, W. D.
    1959. Effects of forest cover on soil freezing in northern lower
        Michigan. Lake States Forest Expt. Sta., Sta. Paper 76,
        16 pp., illus.

Thornbury, William D.
    1954. Principles of geomorphology. 618 pp. New York: Wiley &
        Sons.

U. S. FOREST SERVICE

Pacific **N**orth **W**est — Research Note

FOREST AND RANGE EXPERIMENT STATION · U.S. DEPARTMENT OF AGRICULTURE · PORTLAND, OREGON

PNW-30   October 1965

SAMPLE SIZES FOR TIMBER CRUISES

by

Floyd A. Johnson

Point sampling is now being used for about half of all timber cruises on National Forests in Oregon and Washington. The usual point sampling procedure is to establish a systematic grid of points over the entire timber sale area, to count trees at all points, and to measure all trees at some fraction of all points.

In preparing for a cruise of this kind, decisions must be made on how many points to take for the large sample of "count" points and for the smaller subsample of "measurement" points. These decisions are important, because money and manpower will be wasted if too many points are taken or if the ratio of large-to-small sample sizes is not optimum. In other words, overcruising will produce an estimate of total sale volume which is more precise than it really need be, and disproportionate cruising will produce an estimate of total sale volume which is not as precise as it could be for a given cruising cost. If the samples contain too few points, the estimate of total sale volume will be too unreliable for the uses to which it will be put. This report may help the cruiser select proper sample sizes.

Total sale volume was chosen as the critical estimate for determining proper sample sizes, even though total sale volume is not the most important estimate obtained from these timber cruises. The total volume actually sold is normally established by scaling all logs from a sale area after they are cut, and the main purpose of the cruise is to estimate dollar value per unit of volume. However, a sample large enough to produce an acceptable estimate of dollar value per unit of volume will probably not be large enough for an acceptable estimate of total sale volume, and it is for this reason that the estimate of total sale volume becomes critical.

Tables 1 through 4 show the number of measurement points (k) to include in the sample when the amount of sampling error (E) has been specified and when an appropriate index (C_a) to the variation of point volumes around average point volume has been selected.

Table 1.--Number of measurement points (k), by index of variation (C_a) and sampling error (E), when a measurement point costs three times more than a count-only point (r = 3.00)

Index of variation	Sampling error (standard error of estimated total sale volume expressed as a proportion of estimated total sale volume)							
	0.01	0.02	0.03	0.04	0.05	0.06	0.08	0.10
	- - - - - - - - Number of measurement points - - - - - - - -							
0.20	200	50	22	12	8	6	-	-
.25	312	78	35	20	12	9	5	-
.30	450	112	50	28	18	12	7	-
.35	612	153	68	38	24	17	10	6
.40	800	200	89	50	32	22	12	8
.45	1,012	253	112	63	40	28	16	10
.50	1,250	312	139	78	50	35	20	12
.55	1,512	378	168	95	60	42	24	15
.60	1,800	450	200	112	72	50	28	18
.65	2,112	528	235	132	84	59	33	21
.70	2,450	612	272	153	98	68	38	24
.75	2,812	703	312	176	112	78	44	28
.80	3,200	800	356	200	128	89	50	32
.85	3,612	903	401	226	144	100	56	36
.90	4,050	1,012	450	253	162	112	63	40
.95	4,512	1,128	501	282	180	125	71	45
1.00	5,000	1,250	556	312	200	139	78	50

NOTE: Multiply the indicated number of measurement points by 3 to find the total number of points.

Table 2.--Number of measurement points (k), by index of variation (C_a)

and sampling error (E), when a measurement point costs 5.33

times more than a count-only point (r = 5.33)

Index of variation	Sampling error (standard error of estimated total sale volume expressed as a proportion of estimated total sale volume)							
	0.01	0.02	0.03	0.04	0.05	0.06	0.08	0.10

- - - - - - - - Number of measurement points - - - - - - - - -

Index of variation	0.01	0.02	0.03	0.04	0.05	0.06	0.08	0.10
0.20	175	44	19	11	7	5	-	-
.25	273	68	30	17	11	8	-	-
.30	394	98	44	25	16	11	6	-
.35	536	134	60	34	21	15	8	5
.40	700	175	78	44	28	19	11	7
.45	886	222	98	55	35	25	14	9
.50	1,094	273	122	68	44	30	17	11
.55	1,324	331	147	83	53	37	21	13
.60	1,575	394	175	98	63	44	25	16
.65	1,849	462	205	116	74	51	29	18
.70	2,144	536	238	134	86	60	34	21
.75	2,461	615	273	154	98	68	38	25
.80	2,800	700	311	175	112	78	44	28
.85	3,161	790	351	198	126	88	49	32
.90	3,544	886	394	222	142	98	55	35
.95	3,949	987	439	247	158	110	62	39
1.00	4,376	1,094	486	273	175	122	68	44

NOTE: Multiply the indicated number of measurement points by 4 to find
       the total number of points.

Table 3.--Number of measurement points (k), by index of variation (C_a)

and sampling error (E), when a measurement point costs 8.33

times more than a count-only point (r = 8.33)

Index of variation	Sampling error (standard error of estimated total sale volume expressed as a proportion of estimated total sale volume)							
	0.01	0.02	0.03	0.04	0.05	0.06	0.08	0.10

- - - - - - - - Number of measurement points - - - - - - - - -

Index of variation	0.01	0.02	0.03	0.04	0.05	0.06	0.08	0.10
0.20	160	40	18	10	6	-	-	-
.25	250	63	28	16	10	7	-	-
.30	360	90	40	23	14	10	6	-
.35	490	123	54	31	20	14	8	5
.40	640	160	71	40	26	18	10	6
.45	810	203	90	51	32	23	13	8
.50	1,000	250	111	63	40	28	16	10
.55	1,210	303	134	76	48	34	19	12
.60	1,440	360	160	90	58	40	23	14
.65	1,690	423	188	106	68	47	26	17
.70	1,960	490	218	123	78	54	31	20
.75	2,250	563	250	141	90	63	35	23
.80	2,560	640	284	160	102	71	40	26
.85	2,890	723	321	181	116	80	45	29
.90	3,240	810	360	203	130	90	51	32
.95	3,610	903	401	226	144	100	56	36
1.00	4,000	1,000	444	250	160	111	63	40

NOTE: Multiply the indicated number of measurement points by 5 to find the total number of points.

Table 4.--Number of measurement points (k), by index of variation (C_a) and sampling error (E), when a measurement point costs 12.00 times more than a count-only point (r = 12.00)

Index of variation	Sampling error (standard error of estimated total sale volume expressed as a proportion of estimated total sale volume)							
	0.01	0.02	0.03	0.04	0.05	0.06	0.08	0.10
	- - - - - - - - Number of measurement points - - - - - - - - -							
0.20	150	37	17	9	6	-	-	-
.25	234	59	26	15	9	7	-	-
.30	337	84	38	21	14	9	5	-
.35	459	115	51	29	18	13	7	5
.40	600	150	67	37	24	17	9	6
.45	759	190	84	47	30	21	12	8
.50	937	234	104	59	38	26	15	9
.55	1,134	284	126	71	45	32	18	11
.60	1,350	337	150	84	54	37	21	14
.65	1,584	396	176	99	63	44	25	16
.70	1,837	459	204	115	74	51	29	18
.75	2,109	527	234	132	84	59	33	21
.80	2,400	600	267	150	96	67	37	24
.85	2,709	677	301	169	108	75	42	27
.90	3,037	759	338	190	122	84	47	30
.95	3,384	846	376	212	135	94	53	34
1.00	3,750	937	417	234	150	104	59	37

NOTE: Multiply the indicated number of measurement points by 6 to find the total number of points.

The total number of points can be found from the relationship between total points and measured points given at the bottom of each table. Thus, from table 1 the number of measured points, k, is 78 when E is 0.04 and when C_a is 0.50. Total number of points (n) is then 3k, or 234.

Each of the four tables is for a particular situation with regard to the relative cost of taking a measured point versus taking a count-only point. If the ratio of point costs is 3.00, table 1 should be used. Tables 2, 3, and 4 are for point cost ratios of 5.33, 8.33, and 12.00, respectively. This range of cost ratios should cover the true cost ratio, whatever it is. These particular cost ratios were selected because they correspond to the integer n/k ratios 3, 4, 5, and 6.

Thus, a cruiser has only to select from these four cost ratios the one he feels is most appropriate. This will automatically establish the ratio of total points to measurement points, and it will also identify the particular table he should use for determining the number of measured points. If none of the four cost ratios is appropriate, new tables can be prepared from equations given in the final section of this report.

Sampling error, or E, in these tables is the standard error of estimated total volume for the entire sale expressed as a proportion of estimated total sale volume. The index of variation, C_a, is the familiar coefficient of variation for point volumes.

In this case,

$$ C_a = \frac{F}{\bar{u}_d} \sqrt{\frac{\sum_{}^{k}(x_i - \bar{x})^2}{(k-1)}} \quad - - - - - - - - - - - - \quad (1) $$

where C_a = coefficient of variation as calculated from a set of sample data

F = basal area factor

x_i = sum of the volume/basal area ratios over all trees at a particular point

$\bar{x}$ = average of the x_i's as calculated from all points in the sample

$\bar{u}_d$ = estimated average volume per acre

k = number of points at which trees were measured for volume.

-6-

The accumulated experience from past cruises can be used to help select an appropriate coefficient of variation (C_a) for entering tables 1 through 4. Some information of this kind has been assembled in table 5, but each cruiser will likely have values for C_a which are even more appropriate.

There are actually two coefficients of variation involved in the problem under consideration here. As stated above, one of these is C_a, the index to the variation of point volumes around average point volume. The other is an index to the variation of point volumes around a ratio line of relationship between point volume and point count. It has been given the symbol C_b.

Ideally, advance estimates of C_b should be used along with C_a and E to predict sample sizes. However, all that is presently known about C_b has already been shown in table 5, and this does not offer much encouragement for predicting C_b separately. About all that can be done until more information on C_b becomes available is to assume some fixed relationship between C_a and C_b.

Eighteen of the 23 C_a/C_b ratios in table 5 are clustered closely around 2.0, and the remaining five are considerably higher. Perhaps this justifies the assumption that C_a is normally twice C_b. In any event, tables 1 through 4 were based on this assumption. Later, when more information of the type shown in table 5 is available, it may be possible to identify, in advance, situations which will lead to C_a/C_b ratios other than 2.0. Tables 1 through 4 will not give proper sample sizes for these situations, and new solutions will be required. These new solutions can be developed from the statistical argument presented in the next section of this report.

Table 5.--Planning factors from completed timber cruises for predicting sample sizes in future timber cruises

Cruise No.	National Forest	Timber type [1]	Average net volume per acre	Basal area factor	Average number trees per point	c_a [2]	c_b [3]	c_a/c_b
			M bd. ft.					
1	Gifford Pinchot	DF	46	40.0	5.6	0.64	0.28	2.3
2	Willamette	DF-WH	74	50.0	6.0	.41	.13	3.2
3	Gifford Pinchot	WH-DF	54	38.5	7.8	.38	.08	4.8
4	Siuslaw	DF	53	40.0	4.3	.52	.11	4.7
5	Wenatchee	PSF-DF-WH	52	40.0	6.1	.48	.24	2.0
6	Willamette	DF	72	50.0	6.0	.41	.19	2.2
7	Umpqua	DF	44	40.0	4.2	.64	.33	1.9
8	Wenatchee	PSF	62	40.0	6.0	.44	.22	2.0
9	Rogue River	DF	28	20.0	5.8	.45	.27	1.7
10	Willamette	DF	91	60.0	6.8	.47	.21	2.2
11	Winema	DF-WF	11	20.0	2.3	.97	.28	3.5
12	Wenatchee	PSF-WH	51	40.0	5.6	.55	.22	2.5
13	Willamette	DF-WH	77	60.0	6.3	.41	.20	2.0
14	Winema	PP	6	10.0	3.1	.68	.21	3.2
15	Siuslaw	DF-WH	70	40.0	4.9	.62	.35	1.8
16	Mount Hood	DF	36	40.0	4.9	.60	.28	2.1
17	Mount Baker	WH	50	35.0	6.8	.36	.21	1.7
18	Mount Hood	DF	71	40.0	7.5	.49	.21	2.3
19	Winema	WF	12	20.0	2.9	.68	.33	2.1
20	Siskiyou	DF	42	36.5	5.0	.43	.22	2.0
21	Mount Hood	WF-DF	68	50.0	5.8	.43	.25	1.7
22	Umpqua	DF	31	20.0	6.8	.64	.35	1.8
23	Gifford Pinchot	DF	66	40.0	7.4	.42	.25	1.7

[1] DF = Douglas-fir, WH = western hemlock, WF = white fir, PP = ponderosa pine, PSF = Pacific silver fir (species are shown in the timber type designation only if they represent 30 percent or more of the total sale volume. Species are listed in order of greatest volume).

[2] Coefficient of variation for point volumes on measurement points.

[3] Index to the variation of point volumes around a ratio line of relationship between point volume and point count.

Statistical Argument

Standard error of estimated average volume per acre for the sampling problem under consideration here was shown in a previous publication[1] to be

$$S_{\bar{u}_d} = F \sqrt{\frac{\sum\limits_{}^{k}(x_i-\bar{x})^2}{n(k-1)} + \frac{\sum\limits_{}^{k}(x_i-Rw_i)^2}{k(k-1)}} \quad \left[\frac{n-k}{n}\right] \quad - - - - - - - - \quad (2)$$

$$\text{where } R = \frac{\sum\limits_{}^{k}x_i}{\sum\limits_{}^{k}w_i}$$

w_i = tree count at any point.

(other symbols were defined earlier in this report)

If equation 2 is divided by estimated average volume per acre and squared, the following result is obtained:

$$E^2 = \frac{(C_a^2-C_b^2)}{n} + \frac{C_b^2}{k} \quad - - - - - - - - - - - - - - - - - - \quad (3)$$

where E = standard error of estimated average volume taken as a proportion of average volume (this, of course, is the same as standard error of estimated total sale volume taken as a proportion of total sale volume).

C_a = See equation 1

$$C_b = \frac{F}{\bar{u}_d} \sqrt{\frac{\sum\limits_{}^{k}(x_i-Rw_i)^2}{(k-1)}} \quad - - - - - - - - - - \quad (4)$$

---

[1] Johnson, F. A. Standard error of estimated average timber volume per acre under point sampling when trees are measured for volume on a subsample of all points. U.S. Forest Serv., Pac. NW. Forest & Range Expt. Sta. Res. Note 201, 6 pp. 1961.

Cochran[2] has shown that E will be a minimum when

$$n = k \; \frac{\sqrt{(C_a^2 - C_b^2)r}}{C_b} \; - - - - - - - - - - - - - - - - - (5)$$

where r = average cost of measuring all trees at a point
divided by average cost of merely counting trees
at a point.

On substituting equation 5 in equation 3,

$$k = \frac{1}{E^2} \left[\frac{(C_a^2 - C_b^2)C_b}{\sqrt{(C_a^2 - C_b^2)r}} + C_b^2 \right] \; - - - - - - - - - - - - -(6)$$

If this value for k is then used in equation 5 to find n, the sampling effort will be properly apportioned between count points and measured points.

If a fixed C_a/C_b ratio of 2 is assumed, equation 5 reduces to

$$n = k(1.732) \sqrt{r} \; -(7)$$

and equation 6 reduces to

$$k = \frac{C_a^2}{E^2} \left[\frac{0.433}{\sqrt{r}} + 0.25 \right] \; - - - - - - - - - - - - - - - - -(8)$$

---

[2] Cochran, W. G. Sampling techniques. 413 pp., illus. New York: John Wiley & Sons, Inc. 1963.

Cochran covers this point in his chapter 12 on double sampling. Note that Cochran's Vn is the equivalent of

$$\bar{u}_d^2 C_b^2$$

and that his Vn' is the equivalent of

$$\bar{u}_d^2 (C_a^2 - C_b^2).$$

乡 /

FOREST AND RANGE EXPERIMENT STATION · U.S.DEPARTMENT OF AGRICULTURE · PORTLAND, OREGON

PNW-31   December 1965

THE EFFECT OF LOGGING AND SLASH BURNING ON UNDERSTORY VEGETATION
IN THE H. J. ANDREWS EXPERIMENTAL FOREST

by

C. T. Dyrness

Plant succession on clearcut areas is presently under study on two experimental watersheds in the H. J. Andrews Experimental Forest. One watershed (No. 1, 237 acres) is currently being completely logged. On the second (No. 3, 250 acres), timber was harvested from three clearcuts, 13, 20, and 28 acres in size, in the winter of 1962-63 following the conventional staggered-setting system. This paper reports on early trends in vegetation development after logging of these three clearcut units. A future paper will deal in more detail with the results of the study, exploring such questions as whether or not successional patterns vary with understory plant community present before logging.

The study area is typical of the Western Cascades geologic province. The area is topographically mature with extremely steep slopes and sharp ridges. Soils in the clearcut units are largely derived from breccias and tuffs with varying amounts of influence from basalt and andesite. The soils are of medium texture, extremely porous, and are generally at least moderately deep.

The timber stand before logging was dominantly Douglas-fir[1] mixed with varying amounts of western hemlock. Douglas-fir ages at harvest ranged from 100 to 500 years, with the older age classes being most common. Hemlock in the stand was generally younger. Other coniferous species present included western redcedar, Pacific yew, and sugar pine. Hardwoods were of scattered occurrence and included bigleaf maple, Pacific dogwood, golden chinkapin, and red alder.

---

[1] Scientific names for all species mentioned are shown in table 1.

STUDY METHODS

Sixty-three permanent milacre plots were located in the three cutting units during the summer of 1962 prior to disturbance. These plots
were located at 100-foot intervals along randomly placed transects
which traversed the cutting units from one boundary to another.

Plot arrangement followed a modified nested quadrat design. The
large plot was 1 milacre in size (6.6 feet square). Crown cover of all
shrubs and trees up to 20 feet in height occurring within this plot was
estimated and recorded by species. One-quarter of the milacre plot was
subdivided into nine subplots, each 1.1 feet square. Percent cover of
herbs and grasses occurring on each subplot was also estimated and recorded by species. The cover is crown cover; i.e., an estimate of the
percentage of the total plot area covered by the foliage of a given
species.

Understory vegetation was inventoried during the summers of 1962
(undisturbed vegetation before logging), 1963 (after logging but before
slash burning), and 1964 (after slash burning).

PRELOGGING VEGETATION

Vegetation sampling before logging disclosed the presence of five
distinct understory communities in the three cutting units. A brief
summary of some of the more outstanding characteristics of these communities follows:

   1. Rhododendron-salal. This community is characterized by an
      extremely dense shrub cover dominated by rhododendron and salal.
      Other shrub and understory tree species generally present in-
      clude vine maple, hemlock, and chinkapin. The herbaceous layer
      is generally not well developed and plants are scattered. The
      two most common species are American twin-flower and western
      gold-thread. This community is generally indicative of dry
      growing conditions.

   2. Vine maple-salal. The most outstanding characteristic of this
      community is the dense cover of vine maple and salal. Other
      woody species having some importance are long-leaved Oregon
      grape and Pacific yew. Herbaceous species are of limited oc-
      currence, probably due to the very dense shrub cover. Only
      three species occurred in 10 percent or more of the observation
      plots: twin-flower, evergreen violet, and rattlesnake plantain.
      This community occurs on sites with medium effective moisture
      and fertility levels.

   3. Vine maple-Oregon grape. This community is characterized by
      a moderately dense shrub and small tree cover over very scat-
      tered herbaceous plants. The most important tall woody species

-2-

are vine maple, hemlock, and Pacific yew. Oregon grape is the only common low shrub. Herbaceous cover averages only 3.5 percent, with twin-flower and gold-thread being the most abundant species. Sites occupied by the vine maple-Oregon grape community are moderately moist.

4. Gold-thread. This community has both a sparse shrub layer and a sparse herb layer. Very often the forest floor appears virtually bare except for scattered stems of young hemlock and Oregon grape. Closer inspection generally reveals a small amount of gold-thread and twin-flower. Other plants occur only sporadically. This plant grouping occupies the same type of sites as the vine maple-Oregon grape community, but is situated under a denser tree canopy.

5. Sword-fern. This community is the only one of the five which has a well-developed herbaceous layer. Western sword-fern is by far the most abundant plant. Other species present in significant amounts are twin-flower, gold-thread, evergreen violet, inside-out flower, cleavers,[2] and Oregon oxalis. Characteristics of the shrub layer vary, probably largely due to differences in the density of the tree canopy. For example, vine maple averaged 26 percent cover but it occurred on only half of the plots. Sword-fern is the climax understory community on moist habitats, and it is generally situated along drainage channels and on north-facing slopes.

VEGETATION AFTER LOGGING AND SLASH BURNING

Crown cover, by species, is summarized for the three units before logging (1962), after logging (1963), and after slash burning (1964) in table 1. Results of the first postlogging sampling (1963) show that very few invading plants were present and, consequently, almost all vegetation encountered was a remnant from the preexisting stand. The cover of all species was greatly decreased by logging. However, low shrubs apparently withstood logging more successfully than taller shrubs such as vine maple and rhododendron. Cover values for salal, Oregon grape, and western dewberry decreased the least. It is interesting to note that in unit L222 the "before logging" and the "after logging" cover values for salal were identical.

A marked recovery in the coverage of low shrubs and herbs began during the first growing season after slash burning (1964) (table 1).

---

[2] Locally known as bedstraw.

Table 1.--Understory plant cover on three cutting units before logging, after logging, and after slash burning[1]

(In percent)

Vegetation	Unit L141			Unit L221			Unit L222		
	1962 Before logging	1963 After logging	1964 After burning	1962 Before logging	1963 After logging	1964 After burning	1962 Before logging	1963 After logging	1964 After burning
TREE SPECIES									
Western hemlock									
Tsuga heterophylla (Raf.) Sarg.	12.6	0.2	0.5	3.3	0.2	0.5	17.8	4.2	1.2
Western redcedar									
Thuja plicata Donn	.2	0	0	3.7	0	0	5.8	0	0
Pacific yew									
Taxus brevifolia Nutt.	.9	.2	.05	4.6	.05	0	.4	0	0
Douglas-fir									
Pseudotsuga menziesii (Mirb.) Franco	.2	.05	.4	.05	.2	.3	0	.1	.2
Bigleaf maple									
Acer macrophyllum Pursh	0	0	1.9	.4	.05	.05	0	0	1.9
Golden chinkapin									
Castanopsis chrysophylla (Dougl.) A. DC.	.8	0	0	.6	.1	0	0	0	0
Pacific dogwood									
Cornus nuttallii Audubon	7.0	.05	0	0	0	0	0	0	0
Total, tree species	21.7	.5	2.8	12.6	.6	.8	24.0	4.3	3.3
SHRUB SPECIES									
Vine maple									
Acer circinatum Pursh	11.1	.3	.3	18.6	1.4	.4	12.3	.4	1.2
Long-leaved Oregon grape									
Berberis nervosa Pursh	3.0	1.3	.5	6.3	1.2	.6	8.2	1.8	.7
Salal									
Gaultheria shallon Pursh	12.6	3.1	1.2	3.4	1.1	.8	.3	.3	.1
Western rhododendron									
Rhododendron macrophyllum G. Don	10.3	1.5	.3	10.2	1.0	.2	.6	.3	0
Red huckleberry									
Vaccinium parvifolium Smith	5.3	.4	.2	1.3	.8	.2	.9	.1	.1
Western dewberry									
Rubus ursinus Cham. & Schlecht.	.9	.5	3.2	.4	.4	.9	.4	.1	.4
Snow bramble									
Rubus nivalis Dougl.	.1	0	.5	1.1	.2	.4	.3	0	0
Western blackcap									
Rubus leucodermis Dougl.	0	0	0	.5	.05	.2	0	0	.1
Thimble berry									
Rubus parviflorus Nutt.	0	0	0	0	0	.05	.4	0	.2
Snowbrush									
Ceanothus velutinus var. *laevigatus* (Hook.) Torr. & Gray	0	0	.3	0	0	.3	0	0	0
California hazel									
Corylus cornuta var. *californica* (A. DC.) Sharp	.2	0	0	0	0	0	0	0	0
Little wild rose									
Rosa gymnocarpa Nutt. in T. & G.	.2	0	0	0	0	0	0	0	0
Serviceberry									
Amelanchier alnifolia Nutt.	0	0	0	.1	0	0	0	0	0
Snowberry									
Symphoricarpos albus (L.) Blake	0	0	.05	0	0	0	0	0	0
Total, shrub species	43.7	7.1	6.6	41.9	6.2	4.0	23.4	3.0	2.8
HERBACEOUS SPECIES									
Western sword-fern									
Polystichum munitum (Kaulf.) Presl.	7.2	.2	.7	6.8	1.5	1.0	5.2	1.7	(2/)
Western gold-thread									
Coptis laciniata Gray.	1.1	.2	.1	1.4	.7	.6	1.2	.4	.3
American twin-flower									
Linnaea borealis var. *longiflora* (Torr.) Hulten	3.0	.05	1.3	1.1	.2	1.0	.2	0	0
Evergreen violet									
Viola sempervirens Greene.	.1	0	(2/)	.05	.05	.05	.05	0	(2/)
Western prince's pine									
Chimaphila umbellata var. *occidentalis* (Rydb.) Blake	.4	.05	0	.2	.05	(2/)	(2/)	0	0
Broad-leaved star-flower									
Trientalis latifolia Hook.	.2	.5	.7	.3	.2	1.0	0	(2/)	.1
Western coolwort									
Tiarella unifoliata Hook.	(2/)	0	.6	.1	(2/)	.05	.1	0	(2/)
Cleavers[2]									
Galium aparine L.	.05	.05	1.2	.5	.05	.1	.6	0	.6
Inside-out flower									
Vancouveria hexandra (Hook.) Morr. & Dec.	1.1	.05	0	.2	.05	.6	.05	0	0
Whipple-vine									
Whipplea modesta Torr.	.6	.2	(2/)	.6	0	(2/)	(2/)	0	.1

Note: See footnotes at end of table.

(In percent)

Vegetation	Unit L141			Unit L221			Unit L222		
	1962 Before logging	1963 After logging	1964 After burning	1962 Before logging	1963 After logging	1964 After burning	1962 Before logging	1963 After logging	1964 After burning
HERBACEOUS SPECIES (Cont)									
Grasses	.6	.05	.2	1.1	.7	.4	(2/)	0	0
Oregon oxalis *Oxalis oregana* Nutt ex T & G	1.8	.7	2.3	0	0	0	0	0	0
Wood groundsel *Senecio sylvaticus* L.	(2/)	0	.8	0	.05	1.6	0	0	3.1
Fire-weed *Epilobium angustifolium* L	.3	0	.9	0	0	2.1	0	0	.1
Tall annual willow-herb *Epilobium paniculatum* Nutt. ex T & G	0	0	.8	0	(2/)	.5	0	0	1.4
Willow-herb *Epilobium watsonii* Barbey in Brew & Wats	0	0	.9	0	0	1.1	0	0	.3
Western bleeding-heart *Dicentra formosa* (Andr.) Walpers	0	0	.1	0	0	.1	0	0	.1
Pearly everlasting *Anaphalis margaritacea* (L.) B & H.	0	0	0	0	0	.05	0	0	0
Harebell *Campanula* sp. [Tourn.] L.	0	0	(2/)	0	0	(2/)	0	0	.3
Vanilla-leaf *Achlys triphylla* (Smith) DC.	.1	(2/)	(2/)	(2/)	0	(2/)	0	0	0
Bear-grass *Xerophyllum tenax* (Pursh) Nutt.	.9	0	0	0	0	0	0	0	0
Little prince's pine *Chimaphila menziesii* (R. Br.) Spreng	.1	0	0	.05	0	0	0	0	0
Rattlesnake plantain *Goodyera oblongifolia* Raf	05	(2/)	0	.3	0	0	0	0	0
Western trillium *Trillium ovatum* Pursh	.5	(2/)	(2/)	(2/)	0	0	.2	.1	(2/)
Round-leaved synthyris *Synthyris reniformis* (Dougl) Benth	.2	(2/)	(2/)	(2/)	0	0	0	0	0
Larger twisted-stalk *Streptopus amplexifolius* (L.) DC.	0	0	0	(2/)	(2/)	0	0	0	0
Large pyrola *Pyrola asarifolia* Michx.	(2/)	(2/)	(2/)	.2	(2/)	(2/)	0	0	(2/)
Western white anemone *Anemone deltoidea* Hook.	(2/)	0	0	0	(2/)	0	.05	(2/)	(2/)
White-flowered hawkweed *Hieracium albiflorum* Hook.	0	0	.05	(2/)	(2/)	(2/)	0	0	(2/)
Miner's lettuce *Montia perfoliata* (Donn) How.	0	0	0	0	(2/)	0	0	0	.7
Varied-leaved collomia *Collomia heterophylla* Hook	0	0	0	0	.1	0	0	0	.7
Lady-fern *Athyrium filix-femina* (L.) Roth.	(2/)	0	0	.9	0	0	0	0	0
Western wild ginger *Asarum caudatum* Lindl.	0	0	0	(2/)	0	0	(2/)	0	0
One-flowered clintonia *Clintonia uniflora* (Schult.) Kunth.	(2/)	0	0	0	0	0	0	0	0
Three-leaved coolwort *Tiarella trifoliata* L.	0	0	0	0	(2/)	0	0	0	0
Total, herbaceous species	18.3	2.0	10.0	13.8	3 6	10.2	7.6	2.2	7.1
Total understory cover	83.7	9 6	19.4	68 3	10 4	15.0	55 0	9.5	13.2

[1] Nomenclature follows the most recent taxonomic manuals available, as follows· herbs and most shrubs from Pterdiophyta through Monocotyledonae, "A Manual of the Higher Plants of Oregon," by Morton E. Peck, Ed. 2, 936 pp., illus , 1961, herbs and shrubs from Salicaceae through Compositae, "Vascular Plants of the Pacific Northwest," by C. Leo Hitchcock, Arthur Cronquist, Marion Ownbey, and J. W Thompson, 4 v , illus., 1955-1964, trees and a few of the shrubs, "Check List of Native and Naturalized Trees of the United States (Including Alaska)," by Elbert L. Little, Jr., U S. Dept Agr. Handb. 41, 472 pp., 1953

[2] Trace

[3] Locally known as bedstraw.

Some species, present in the undisturbed stand in small amounts, had substantially increased their coverage. Species with more cover after slash burning than they had in the undisturbed stand include western dewberry, star-flower, bedstraw, and Oregon oxalis. Herbaceous cover was also increased by a number of invading species, including wood groundsel, fire-weed, willow-herb, tall annual willow-herb, western bleeding-heart, and pearly everlasting. Snowbrush was the only shrub invader found consistently on the plots.

Cover trends for selected species in unit L141 are shown in figure 1. The adverse effect of logging and burning on shrubs such as Oregon grape and salal is clearly shown. However, tree canopy removal had the opposite effect on western dewberry. This species had more than three times as much cover after slash burning as it had in the undisturbed stand. Sword-fern showed some recovery in coverage following burning; however, it is doubtful whether this trend will be maintained in the future. This same pattern was observed in the case of twin-flower. Interestingly, star-flower has shown a slight increase in cover for each year following logging.

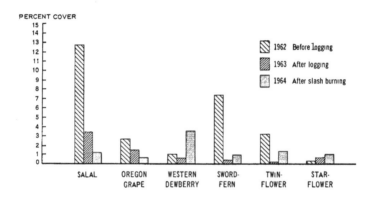

Figure 1.--*Cover of selected species occurring on unit L141 before logging (1962), after logging (1963), and after slash burning (1964).*

Figure 2 illustrates the 3-year trends for understory tree cover, shrub cover, and herb cover. For shrub and tree species, the general pattern was a marked decrease in cover the first year after logging, followed by generally small decreases after slash burning. Herbaceous cover also decreased appreciably the first year after logging. However, after slash burning, there was a marked increase in herbaceous cover in all three units. In units L221 and L222, herb cover values for 1964 approached predisturbance levels.

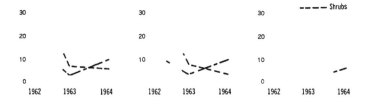

*Figure 2.--Total tree cover (less than 20 feet high),
shrub cover, and herbaceous cover on three cutting
units before logging (1962), after logging (1963),
and after slash burning (1964).*

SPECIFIC DISTURBANCE EFFECTS

Following logging or burning in a clearcut area, degree of disturbance ranges from none to severe. Each milacre sampling plot was
classified on the basis of type and amount of disturbance in an effort
to correlate logging and slash burning disturbance with characteristics
of the vegetation. Soil surface disturbance and slash burning classes,
developed for other studies, were used. Logging disturbance classes
are undisturbed, slightly disturbed, deeply disturbed, and compacted.[3]
Slash burning classes are undisturbed, disturbed-unburned, lightly
burned, and severely burned.[4]

Degree of disturbance exerts a major influence on the amount of
vegetation present during the first 2 years following logging (table 2).
After logging, plant cover on largely undisturbed plots was more than
three times as great (28.4 percent) as coverage on slightly disturbed
plots (9 percent). On deeply disturbed or compacted plots, plant cover

[3] Defined in: Dyrness, C. T. Soil surface condition following
tractor and high-lead logging in the Oregon Cascades. Jour. Forestry
63: 272-275, illus. 1965.

[4] Defined in: Dyrness, C. T., and Youngberg, C. T. The effect
of logging and slash-burning on soil structure. Soil Sci. Soc. Amer.
Proc. 21: 444-447, illus. 1957.

totaled only 1.6 percent. Differences are even more striking after slash burning. Whereas total plant cover averaged 41.7 percent on undisturbed plots, total coverage averaged only 6.8 percent on lightly burned plots. Severely burned plots had an average of only 1.1 percent cover, indicating almost no recovery the first season following this severe disturbance.

Table 2.--<u>Plant cover following logging and slash burning on plots</u>

<u>within four disturbance classes</u>

(In percent)

Disturbance class	All tree species	All shrub species	All herbaceous species	Total
After logging (1963):				
Undisturbed	5.3	19.1	4.0	28.4
Heavy slash and logs	2.8	2.7	.1	5.6
Slightly disturbed	1.0	4.2	3.8	9.0
Deeply disturbed or compacted	.4	1.1	.1	1.6
After slash burning (1964):				
Undisturbed	7.7	14.6	19.4	41.7
Disturbed-unburned	.8	3.0	15.4	19.2
Lightly burned	1.4	2.5	2.9	6.8
Severely burned	.1	.6	.4	1.1

A consideration of the influence of disturbance on the distribution of individual species reveals some interesting differences (fig. 3). Some species, such as vine maple, show a very low tolerance to disturbance and are confined almost exclusively to undisturbed sites. Others, western dewberry and sword-fern, for example, occur to a limited extent in disturbed areas, but are virtually excluded from burned-over locations. Invading herbaceous species, such as wood groundsel and fire-weed, are apparently not uniform in their site requirements, if we can tell from these early results (fig. 3). It is interesting to note, however, that only a limited amount of these plants occurred on lightly or severely burned plots. This may be partially due to destruction of seed present on the plots prior to burning. On the basis of the results of other studies, we can predict that these species will expand rapidly into burned areas during the next 2 to 3 years.

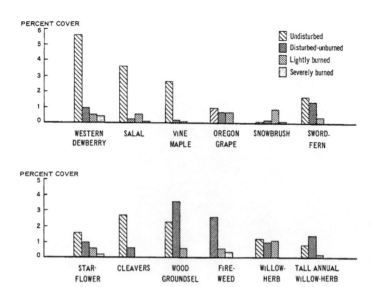

Figure 3.--The effect of disturbance on mean cover values for 12 plant species (values are averages for all three cutting units).

Average values for entire cutting units do not provide a complete picture of vegetation changes because of the variety of existing conditions. One way to gain a better understanding of plant dynamics is to study changes in species composition and plant cover from year to year on individual plots. Individual plot trends can easily be followed on the permanently located milacre plots used in this study. The records indicate that, although certain broad trends are fairly uniform, each plot exhibits a large degree of uniqueness related to disturbance history, site characteristics, prelogging vegetation, and just plain chance.

Vegetational changes on three typical plots are shown in figures 4 through 12. Plot 1-1 on unit L141 (figs. 4 and 5) originally supported vegetation classified as the vine maple-salal understory community. Even though the ground surface after logging was 100 percent undisturbed, all species excepting long-leaved Oregon grape decreased appreciably in cover (fig. 6). The year after slash burning, western dewberry increased in cover, and invading wood groundsel covered about one-tenth of the plot area.

*Figure 4.--The vine maple-salal
understory community. This
community was originally
present on plot 1-1, unit
L141.*

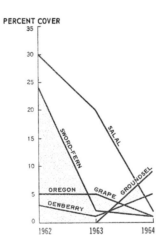

*Figure 6.--Vegetation present on
(before logging), 1963 (after
slash burning).*

Prelogging vegetation on plot 1-1 in unit L221 (figs. 7 and 8) was originally classified in the gold-thread community; shrubs occurred in only very small amounts and the dominant species was twin-flower. The entire plot was disturbed to some extent by logging and, as a result, plant cover was reduced to a low level during the summer of 1963 (fig. 9). Because almost the entire plot escaped the slash fire and the exposed mineral soil offered a favorable seedbed, six new species invaded the plot during the summer of 1964. Wood groundsel was by far the most common. In addition, certain species originally present resumed vigorous growth. Twin-flower made the most spectacular recovery, increasing its coverage over 10 times between the 1963 and 1964 measurements.

re 7.--The gold-thread understory ommunity. This community was origi- lly present on plot 1-1, unit L221.

Figure 8.--Plot 1-1, unit L221, August 1964 (first year after slash burning).

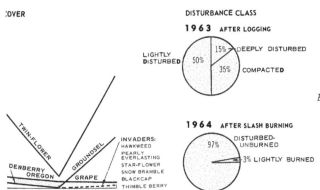

Figure 9.--Vegetation present on plot 1-1, unit L221 in 1962 (before logging), 1963 (after logging), and 1964 (after slash burning).

A vigorous understory, typical of the rhododendron-salal community, occupied plot 4-4 in unit L221 (figs. 10 and 11) prior to logging. As on the first plot discussed, plant cover greatly decreased, even though logging resulted in no appreciable soil disturbance (fig. 12). Sixty percent of the plot surface was burned over by the slash fire, and the other 40 percent remained undisturbed. The failure of residual species to increase their cover during the 1964 growing season and the presence of only one invading species, western dewberry, is noteworthy. This may be due largely to the fact that very little mineral soil was exposed on this plot. However, additional invading species such as wood ground-sel may be expected, at least in the burned portion, during the second season following burning.

CONCLUSIONS

It is apparent from the data presented that disturbance history is at least as important as species composition of the undisturbed stand in determining plant distribution on these clearcut units. As plant succession advances, the influence of logging and slash burning disturbance will decrease and other site factors, such as soil charac-teristics and aspect, will become increasingly important in controlling plant cover and composition.

igure 10.--The rhododendron-salal
    understory community. This com-
    munity was originally present on
    plot 4-4, unit L221.

Figure 11.--Plot 4-4, unit L221
    in August 1964 (first year
    after slash burning).

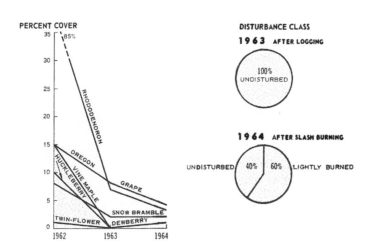

FOREST AND RANGE EXPERIMENT STATION · U.S. DEPARTMENT OF AGRICULTURE · PORTLAND, OREGON

PNW-32   January 1966

SPOTLIGHTING DEER:

Potentials for management in western Oregon[1]

by J. Edward Dealy

INTRODUCTION

Spotlighting of Columbian black-tailed deer (*Odocoileus hemionus columbianus*) has been tested as a sampling technique in the H. J. Andrews Experimental Forest on the west slope of the Oregon Cascades.[2] Research was conducted from May through October for 2 consecutive years.

The method, which requires a spotlight at night, is particularly suitable for openings in dense timber stands, such as on the west slope of the Cascade Range in relatively young logged units (3 to 5 years old). These openings, flush with shrubby and herbaceous food and cover, concentrate deer in small areas, providing excellent opportunity for observation. The particular herd studied inhabited a summer range above the line of heavy winter snows and therefore exhibited definite fall and spring migrations.

---

[1] Primary research was conducted under the auspices of the Oregon Cooperative Wildlife Research Unit, Oregon State University, Corvallis, Oreg.

[2] Dealy, J. Edward. The influence of logging practices on Columbian black-tailed deer (*Odocoileus hemionus columbianus* Richardson) in the Blue River area of Oregon. 1959. (Unpublished master's thesis on file at Oreg. State Univ., Corvallis.)

REVIEW OF LITERATURE

Few studies have been conducted on spotlighting deer as a sampling technique. Anderson,[3] studying Columbian black-tailed deer under different environmental conditions than those reported in this paper, determined that the deer were influenced significantly in their standing and bedding habits by moonlight, temperature, and humidity changes. The latter two were particularly important during the day previous to sampling. He found differences of 36 percent in standing-to-bedded ratios from the first to the fifth hours of darkness. The extreme changes occurred during the spring to early summer period. He found changes of less than 20 percent during the summer to early fall period.

Progulske and Duerre[4] studied spotlighting of white-tailed and mule deer in South Dakota meadows. They found that moonlight, temperature, cloud cover, precipitation, dew, and relative humidity were important factors, and that temperature exerted the strongest influence on deer behavior.

EQUIPMENT AND PROCEDURES

A vehicle, 7 X 50 binoculars, and a spotlight were used. A pickup with adequate safety bracing in the bed was preferred because the technician could stand up and better spot deer. The spotlight consisted of a sealed-beam unit with a bakelite pistol grip and a 20-foot cord reaching to the vehicle's cigarette lighter or battery terminals.

The sampling encompassed 27 logged units. These units included four habitats separated according to vegetative cover, slope aspect, and topographic characteristics. All had season-long water available. Habitats are described as follows:

I. North slope, low elevation; characterized by dense seasonal cover and slopes averaging 30 percent.

II. North slope, high elevation; characterized by sparse seasonal cover and slopes averaging 57 percent.

---

[3] Anderson, Carl F. Nocturnal activities of the Columbian black-tailed deer, *Odocoileus hemionus columbianus* Richardson, affecting spotlight census results in the Oregon Coast range. 1959. (Unpublished master's thesis on file at Oreg. State Univ., Corvallis.)

[4] Progulske, Donald R., and Duerre, Donald C. Factors influencing spotlighting counts of deer. J. Wildlife Manage. 28: 27-34. 1964.

III. South slope, low elevation; characterized by moderate seasonal cover and slopes averaging 42 percent.

IV. South slope, high elevation; characterized by sparse seasonal cover and slopes averaging 25 percent.

A 30-mile route was mapped through the 27 units. Observation points were carefully located in each logged unit to give technicians a complete area coverage. The number and location of points varied between units and habitats according to topography and road location. Sampling was begun at approximately 9 p.m. each observation night and terminated at various times, depending on the number of deer seen and the time spent observing each individual. The minimum time spent was 2 hours when no deer were seen, and the maximum was 5-1/2 hours when 60 were counted. At each observation point, the vehicle was stopped and the accessible area searched thoroughly. The technician used the light to pick up eye reflection. He swept the visible area with the light, using short, fast, horizontal, flipping motions and gradually working up and down the slopes from the roadside to the edge of the logged unit or the effective limit of light, approximately one-quarter mile. With the deer facing the observer, eye reflection was easily seen, even with the light moving extremely fast. All detected eye reflections were counted. Those deer close enough to permit observations of physical details were classified as to sex, age, condition, and whether or not they were standing or bedded.

FACTORS AFFECTING COUNTS

Individual error.--Three individuals were selected to test operator error for this spotlight sampling method. Two were adults, and one was a 14-year-old boy; none had experience in this type of work. Each was given approximately 30 minutes of instruction covering techniques of searching for deer and the method of handling the spotlight. Also, each individual received approximately 15 minutes of practical experience in the field.

Instruction was conducted on simulated deer eyes. One-inch squares of white reflecting tape, the type used for vehicle safety, were used to simulate deer eyes. Two squares were glued 5 inches apart (center to center) on the crossbar of each of 55 "T" stakes. The stakes were placed in the field in 10 separate sample groups, each group with 4 to 8 pairs of "eyes" to eliminate the possibility of operators anticipating total numbers per sample.

The three technicians were taken as a group to each of the 10 sampling points. All of them sampled at each point before moving to the next. While the first technician was searching for simulated eyes, the other two kept their eyes covered. Out of a total of 55 pairs of "eyes" sampled by each of three persons, only 1 pair was

missed by one individual. That pair was hidden behind dense shrub-
bery, and only one "eye" was visible.

It was evident that if personnel are given thorough, yet not
necessarily extensive, procedural training and practical experience,
they can produce comparable data with respect to total number of eye
reflections.

Deer standing vs. lying down.--One factor that is sure to affect
spotlight deer counts, especially in heavy cover, is the proportion
of total deer that are standing rather than lying down. It took an
average of approximately 4 hours to cover the sampling route. To
determine whether or not the deer showed any particular pattern with
respect to standing or lying down, a given area was sampled for the
first 4 hours of uniform darkness during the July-October period.
The results are shown in figure 1.

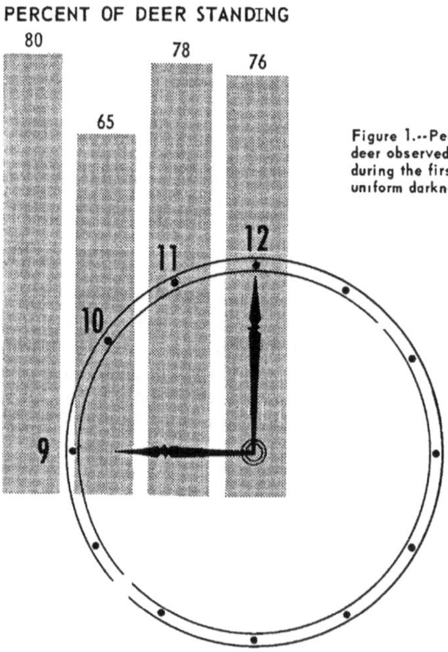

PERCENT OF DEER STANDING

Figure 1.--Percent of total
deer observed standing
during the first 4 hours of
uniform darkness, July-October.

The maximum difference, in percent of standing deer, between any two 1-hour units was 15 percent. Anderson (see footnote 3) found a similar difference during the July-October period and a much greater difference during the spring. Progulske and Duerre (see footnote 4) concluded that spotlighting should be restricted to a 4-hour period beginning 1 hour after sunset, because nearly 79 percent of all deer they counted were observed during this period. Numbers seen dropped off rapidly the fifth hour.

MANAGEMENT APPLICATIONS

Habitat preference.--The following data on habitat preference of Columbian black-tailed deer illustrate the type of information that can be obtained with spotlighting. These data were gathered with the expenditure of only 10 man-days each by two persons.

Total numbers of deer seen in habitats I through IV during the summer-fall season were 230, 64, 168, and 61, respectively. Number was highest in the north-slope, low-elevation habitat. The high-elevation habitats were least preferred and by about equal numbers of deer.

Habitat preferences by months during the total observation period are shown in figure 2. The low elevations were preferred over the

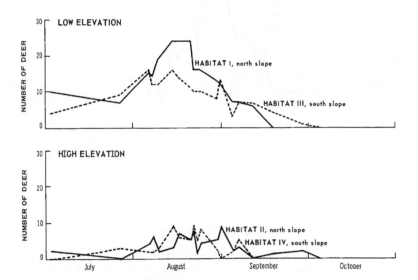

Figure 2.-Two pairs of habitats showing seasonal preference of deer and differences in use intensity.

high; and the north slope was preferred over the south during early and midsummer, probably due to more lush and palatable forage, moderate temperatures, and more cover for protection. However, during early September, north and south slopes appeared to be about equally used. Preference shown for the south slope during late September and early October is questionable since sample numbers were very low. The sample numbers from high-elevation, north- and south-slope units were small and erratic. Data from samples which have low numbers and are erratic seem to have limited value other than to indicate small populations.

Seasonal population trends.--The season-long patterns of deer use in all habitats were combined to illustrate the spotlight method for following seasonal population trends in the experimental forest (fig. 3). Observed animal numbers for both years increased gradually to midsummer and then dropped sharply through late August and September to October when samples showed no deer. Animal track observations confirmed the same seasonal fluctuation. Generally, most intense use occurred from July through mid-September.

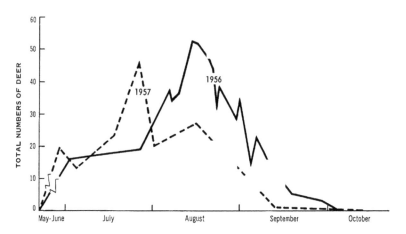

Figure 3.--Season-long deer use patterns for the H. J Andrews Experimental Forest

SAMPLING INTENSITY

A sample as defined here includes all observations of deer for one night. Sampling intensity will ordinarily be influenced by a number of factors, including the time and financing available for

-6-

the job, study area size, accuracy desired, sample route length necessary to cover the area of interest, and type of information sought. Only the latter will be treated here. The other factors vary with, and must be tailored for, each separate set of study conditions.

For following seasonal use preferences among habitats, numerous samples seem desirable; in this study, semiweekly sampling was considered acceptable.

For studying population trends over the entire season, fewer samples are probably adequate. Data shown in figure 3, from samples taken on an average of less than once a week for 2 years, produced useful information on general trends; however, sampling once weekly seems more desirable for a minimum.

If it is desirable to study the effect on deer activity of natural phenomena, such as a predicted severe temperature drop, a full moon, a storm, or other disturbance, then samples should probably be taken every night during the critical period because these phenomena occur rapidly and over a short period.

It should be pointed out here that reliability of the method will be increased both with more frequent samples than the minimums recommended and through carefully minimizing as many variables as possible.

METHOD LIMITATIONS

1. Observations from areas of low population density seem to be very erratic. Spotlighting will probably not yield reliable data in this situation other than to indicate a small population.

2. Value of comparing habitats of markedly different cover characteristics is obviously limited because, if populations are equal, the habitat with the best hiding cover would show fewer deer.

3. Changes in many environmental factors that influence spotlight counts of deer are not readily apparent at the time of observation. For this reason, data derived from spotlight counts must be recognized as indicative of very general trends rather than precise estimates.

ADVANTAGES

1. The technique of spotlighting deer is easily learned and easily applied.

2. Many observations can be taken within a comparatively uniform period with respect to deer activity (first 4 hours of uniform darkness) because deer are most active at night and are least disturbed then by vehicular activity.

3. Night-light sampling provides a maximum area coverage in a minimum time period.

4. A wide variety of information can be obtained with this technique, probably as wide or wider a variety than any single method now in use for studying deer population dynamics on natural ranges. Use intensity, movements, population trends, nocturnal activity, preferences, and seasonal relationships can be studied.

5. Very few deer were disturbed in the study area by a spotlight, even at quite close range. There was adequate time to observe many animals for sex and age grouping, which indicates that this method has possibilities for herd composition and productivity studies.

RECOMMENDATIONS

1. To minimize variability, which is difficult to measure, population samples should be taken on nights with similar weather and light conditions and when there has been no marked change in temperature and humidity during the day immediately previous to the sample.

2. With due regard for the limitations inherent in it, spotlighting can provide very useful information concerning population trends, habitat preference, and other facets of deer management such as herd composition.

3. As a management tool, spotlighting falls in the category of track counts, daylight trend counts, aerial counts, and pellet counts, all of which are currently in use with varying degrees of confidence.

FOREST AND RANGE EXPERIMENT STATION • U.S. DEPARTMENT OF AGRICULTURE • PORTLAND, OREGON

PNW-33   January 1966

BITTERBRUSH NUTRITION LEVELS UNDER NATURAL AND THINNED PONDEROSA PINE

By J. Edward Dealy

INTRODUCTION

Game and land managers have long wondered why deer generally prefer food in openings or along edges instead of under a heavy timber over-story. Is their preference due to a single overriding factor or a com-bination of factors?

This study was conducted in mid-September, 1963, to determine nutri-tional differences in antelope bitterbrush *(Purshia tridentata)*[1] as influenced by different ponderosa pine *(Pinus ponderosa)* stocking levels.

We felt this information, in turn, might give us a lead to further research which would help solve the riddle of deer feeding habits. Since 1960, approximately 130,000 acres of National Forest ponderosa pine stands have been thinned in the Northwest. An understanding of the effect of thinning on forage nutrition may aid in the proper manipulation of deer habitat.

---

[1] Authorities for common and scientific names are:

Shrubs, forbs, and grasslike plants--Kelsey, Harlan P., and Dayton, William A. Standardized plant names. 675 pp. New York: J. Horace McFarland Co. 1942.

Trees--Little, Elbert L., Jr. Checklist of native and naturalized trees of the United States (including Alaska). U.S. Dep. Agr. Handb. 41, 472 pp. 1953.

Grasses--Hitchcock, A. S. Manual of the grasses of the United States. U.S. Dep. Agr. Misc. Pub. 200 (rev.), 1051 pp., illus. 1951.

The work was done in central Oregon on the Pringle Falls Experimental Forest at an elevation of 4,400 feet. Precipitation averages 24 inches annually, much of it occurring as rain. The average annual winter snowpack is approximately 24 inches deep.

The area, with old-growth ponderosa pine, averaged a site IV[2] and had reproduction of 1- to 5-inch d.b.h. as dense as 20,000 stems per acre. The shrub, grass, and forb understory crown cover averages 83, 1, and 16 percent, respectively. Primary understory species are listed as follows:

Shrubs

Antelope bitterbrush *(Purshia tridentata)*
Snowbrush ceanothus *(Ceanothus velutinus)*
Pine manzanita *(Arctostaphylos parryana* var. *pinetorum)*

Grasses and Grasslike Plants

Western needlegrass *(Stipa occidentalis)*
Ross sedge *(Carex rossi)*
Squirreltail *(Sitanion hystrix)*

Forbs

Virginia strawberry *(Fragaria virginiana)*
Spreading dogbane *(Apocynum androsaemifolium)*
Common yarrow *(Achillea millefolium)*
Penstemon *(Penstemon* spp.*)*

The study site is in the upper edge of the ponderosa pine /antelope bitterbrush/western needlegrass plant association where it grades into ponderosa pine/snowbrush ceanothus/western needlegrass.

The soil, a Regosol developed from dacite pumice, is classified as the Lapine series. This pumice was deposited approximately 7,300 years ago during an eruption of Mount Mazama. Depth averages 33 inches. The pumice soil is underlain by a sandy loam Paleosol developed in older volcanic ash. The Lapine series typically has a thin litter layer; a 2-inch-thick A_1 horizon of dark grayish-brown loamy coarse

[2] Meyer, Walter H. Yield of even-aged stands of ponderosa pine. U.S. Dep. Agr. Tech. Bull. 630, 60 pp., illus. 1938.

sand; an AC horizon, 8 to 14 inches thick, containing some coarse
pumice fragments; a C_1 horizon, 4 to 8 inches thick, of fine and medium
pumice gravel; and a light-grey C_2 horizon, 6 to 10 inches thick, of
fine pumice gravel.[3]

PROCEDURES

Plots used in this study make up a small portion of a study in
tree spacing which was designed and installed for timber management
research.[4]

The mature overstory was completely removed from a portion of the
pine stand in order to apply thinning treatments to the reproduction.
Spacings used in this study were 13.2 feet and 26.4 feet and had been
in place four growing seasons prior to sample collection.

Twenty-seven bitterbrush samples were collected for analysis;
three in each of three plots under natural pine stands and 13.2- and
26.4-foot spacing treatments. Each sample included only current-year
leader material from at least five different plants. An analysis,
using procedures outlined by the Association of Official Agricultural
Chemists,[5] was made on samples, revealing data on percent crude fiber,
ash (primarily mineral salts), crude fat, crude protein, and N.F.E.
(nitrogen free extract). All analyses were made on ovendry material.

Effects of tree thinning on each of five nutrient groups, in terms
of nutrient percentages, were compared in an F test of significance at
the 0.05 level of probability (table 1).

Estimates of basal area of the pine were used for comparing
treatments.

RESULTS

Results of the chemical analyses are shown in table 1. Analysis
of bitterbrush revealed a significantly higher percent ash and N.F.E.

---

[3] Barrett, James W., and Youngberg, C. T. Effect of tree spacing and understory vegetation on water use in a pumice soil. Soil Sci.
Soc. Amer. Proc. 29: 472-475, illus. 1965.

[4] Barrett, James W. Spacing and understory vegetation affect
growth of ponderosa pine saplings. Pacific Northwest Forest & Range
Exp. Sta., U.S. Forest Serv. Res. Note PNW-27, 6 pp., illus. 1965.

[5] Association of Official Agricultural Chemists. Official
methods of analysis. Ed. 9, edited by W. Horwitz. 832 pp. Washington,
D.C. 1960.

Table 1.--<u>Average percentage of five nutrient groups in bitterbrush</u>

<u>under two thinning levels of ponderosa pine saplings and a</u>

<u>natural mature stand with thick sapling reproduction</u>

Nutrient groups	Natural stands	Thinned saplings	
		13.2-foot spacings	26.4-foot spacings
N. F. E.[1]	50.31*	47.69	46.98
Crude protein	9.76	9.40	9.40
Crude fat	5.80	4.90	4.96
Crude fiber	21.64*	27.21	26.90
Ash	4.20*	3.05	3.11

* Significant at 0.05 level of probability.

[1] Nitrogen free extract.

and lower percent crude fiber content under the natural stand of pine than under the thinned stands. There appeared to be a consistently higher level of crude fat under the natural stand as compared with the thinned stands, although the differences were not significant. There were no significant differences in nutrient groups between thinning treatments.

Tree basal area values for the natural stand and 13.2- and 26.4-foot spacings were 127.5, 12.5, and 3.8 square feet, respectively.

In order to show relationships more clearly, data for tree basal area, crude fiber, ash, and N.F.E. are compared graphically in figure 1. Crude fiber increased and ash and N.F.E. content decreased with a decrease in tree basal area.

DISCUSSION

Bitterbrush samples were taken for analysis in mid-September as the plants approached their fall-winter dormancy. Sampling at this stage minimized any differences in nutrient content between sites

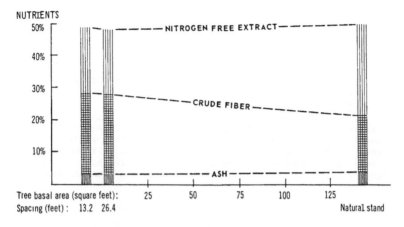

NUTRIENTS

Tree basal area (square feet):   25   50   75   100   125

Spacing (feet):   13.2   26.4   Natural stand

Figure 1.--Changes in crude fiber, N.F.E. (nitrogen free extract),
and ash content of bitterbrush in relation to changes in ponderosa
pine basal area.

resulting from different seasonal growth stages. Soil moisture
analysis[6] showed all available moisture was used by mid-September
in the natural stand of pine and 80 percent used in the thinned stands.

In general, plants grown in the shade are more succulent and thus
would be expected to have less fiber than those grown in the sun. Because of their succulence, it would seem reasonable to assume they
might be preferred by deer over their more fibrous neighbors, although
observations of deer feeding habits do not support this assumption.

Crude protein content of bitterbrush did not vary significantly
in this study between the shady, natural pine stand and the more sunny,
thinned stands. However, at least two observers, Dealy[7] and Einarsen,[8]

[6] See footnote 3.

[7] Dealy, J. Edward. The influence of logging practices on
Columbian black-tailed deer (*Odocoileus hemionus columbianus* Richardson) in the Blue River area of Oregon. 1959. (Unpublished master's
thesis on file at Oreg. State Univ., Corvallis.)

[8] Einarsen, Arthur S. Crude protein determination of deer food
as an applied management technique. N.Amer. Wildlife Conf. Trans.
1946: 309-312.

have reported higher protein in shrubby material from open areas, and there has been some speculation that deer can detect and actually seek those plants with a higher food value.

Perhaps the ash, which is significantly higher in material from the natural stand, contains some mineral component that is distasteful to a deer. There are many unanswered questions that will best be resolved only by fundamental studies that delve into the basis for food selection by ruminants. Such studies are now in the planning stage.

| **FOREST AND RANGE EXPERIMENT STATION** · U.S. DEPARTMENT OF AGRICULTURE · PORTLAND, OREGON

PNW-34   January 1966

BARK FACTORS FOR DOUGLAS-FIR

by

Floyd A. Johnson

Recent emphasis on the measurement of upper stem tree diameters with optical dendrometers[1] has directed attention to procedures for converting these outside-bark diameters to inside-bark diameters.

One procedure that has been used requires an assumption that the ratio of diameter inside bark to diameter outside bark (henceforth called bark factor) remains the same up the stem. If this is true, bark factor measured at some reachable point on the lower stem (e.g., 4.5 feet) could be applied to diameter outside bark at any point on the upper stem to estimate diameter inside bark at that point. Thus

$$d_i = d_o B_{LS} \quad - \quad (1)$$

where d_i = diameter inside bark at any point on the upper stem

d_o = diameter outside bark at the upper stem point

B_{LS} = lower stem bark factor

Equation 1 may be satisfactory for some tree species, but a regression analysis has indicated that upper stem and lower stem bark factors are not the same on young-growth Douglas-fir trees.

---

[1] Grosenbaugh, L. R. Some suggestions for better sample tree measurement. Soc. Amer. Foresters Proc. 1963: 36-42.

Data from 540 trees were used in this analysis. Six basic
independent variables were recorded for each tree along with a single
upper stem bark factor (i.e., the dependent variable) which was taken
at varying distances up the stem. The six basic independent variables
were:

L = distance up the stem from ground

A = tree age

D = diameter at breast height outside bark

H = total tree height from ground to tip

d_o = diameter outside bark at a point on the upper stem
where the upper stem bark factor was taken

B_{LS} = bark factor at stump

The 540 trees used in this study ranged from 13 to 143 years in
age and from 2 to 40 inches in outside-bark diameter at breast height.
They are believed to be reasonably representative of the young-growth
timber type in western Oregon and western Washington.

Stump bark factor was used as an independent variable in the
analysis merely because bark factor at 4.5 feet was not available.
Perhaps it can be assumed that bark factor at 4.5 feet and bark factor
at stump would have been approximately the same.

The regression analysis led to the following equation:

$$B_{US} = \left[6931 - 2.5A + 10.6D - 311(L/H)^2 + 1343(L/H)(d_o/D) + 2326B_{LS}\right]10^{-4} -$$

where B_{US} = upper stem bark factor

Better estimates of upper stem, inside-bark diameters should
result if B_{US} is used to replace B_{LS} in equation 1. This would be
facilitated by an electronic computer because equation 2 is rather
unwieldy.

If total height (H) is not available as a predictor variable,
either because it is too difficult to measure or for some other reason,
equation 2 cannot be used, and equation 3 will then be appropriate:

$$B_{US} = \left[6194 - 2.6A + 3.2L + 2378(d_o/D) - 1545(d_o/D)^2 + 2533B_{LS}\right]10^{-4} - - -$$

Equation 4 can be used if both tree age and total height are unavailable:

$$B_{US} = \left[5590 + 0.6L + 2030(d_o/D) - 1542(d_o/D)^2 + 3413B_{LS}\right]10^{-4} - - - - -(4)$$

Percentages of the total bark factor variation accounted for were 40 by equation 2, 37 by equation 3, and 27 by equation 4.

When equations 2, 3, and 4 were applied to an 80-year-old Douglas-fir tree which had a breast-high bark factor of 0.90, a breast-high diameter outside bark of 20.9 inches, a total height of 131 feet, and a series of measurements, L and d_o, up the stem, the following results were obtained:

L	d_o	Bark factor			Diameter inside bark (inches)			
		Equation 2	Equation 3	Equation 4	Equation 2	Equation 3	Equation 4	Equation 1
18.3	17.6	0.9198	0.9231	0.9289	16.2	16.2	16.3	15.8
30.5	16.7	.9279	.9277	.9318	15.5	15.5	15.6	15.0
46.1	15.0	.9347	.9324	.9352	14.0	14.0	14.0	13.5
60.7	13.7	.9388	.9356	.9367	12.9	12.8	12.8	12.3
82.5	11.3	.9381	.9364	.9358	10.6	10.6	10.6	10.2
94.5	9.3	.9315	.9321	.9317	8.7	8.7	8.7	8.4
104.7	7.3	.9222	.9242	.9245	6.7	6.7	6.7	6.6

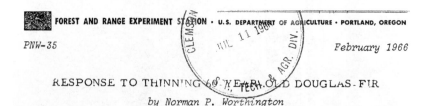

FOREST AND RANGE EXPERIMENT STATION · U.S. DEPARTMENT OF AGRICULTURE · PORTLAND, OREGON

PNW-35   February 1966

RESPONSE TO THINNING 60-YEAR-OLD DOUGLAS-FIR

by *Norman P. Worthington*

Thirty years of growth after the first thinning in a 60-year-old
Douglas-fir stand on site IV show that heavy thinning substantially
depressed gross increment in ensuing years. However, a moderate thinning reduced gross increment only slightly. Growth was well above
normal on both moderately thinned and unthinned stands, but was a
little less than normal on heavily thinned areas. Pecords single out
the increased increment obtainable on actual stands as compared with
normal yield table estimates. Main advantages in the thinnings were:
(1) salvage of mortality; (2) reallocation of stand growth potential
to fewer, larger, and higher quality trees; and (3) realization of
earlier returns through thinning. Presumably, the stand was too old
for heavy thinning to speed up residual tree growth sufficiently to
compensate for loss of increment on trees cut.

Four of six areas, located at the base of Mount Walker, Olympic
National Forest, near Quilcene, Wash., were thinned in 1934 and 1937.[1]
Basal areas removed were 31 and 37 percent on moderately thinned plots
9 and 10; 44 and 50 percent on heavily thinned plots 6 and 7 (figs. 1
and 2). Thinning, chiefly from below, removed mostly suppressed and
intermediate trees, but also included some dominants and codominants
to eliminate "wolf" trees and improve spacing. Plots 5 and 8 were
left untouched as checks. A second light thinning in 1949 and a
third in 1958, on three plots, improved spacing, removed poorer grade
trees of lower crown class, and salvaged dead or dying trees. The
original stand on plot 7 was 20 percent less in basal area and cubic
volume than an average for the five other plots.

---

[1] Worthington, Norman P., and Isaac, Leo A. Experimental thinnings in young Douglas-fir. Northwest Sci. 26: 1-9, illus. 1952.

Figure 1.-Mount Walker plot 10, first thinned moderately (31 percent basal area) in 1937. Photo was taken in 1949, during a second thinning. Gross cubic volume increment after 30 years was 91 percent of that in an unthinned area visible in right background.

Figure 2.-- Mount Walker plot 7 as it appeared after heavy thinning (50 percent basal area) in 1934; shows open condition of residual stand. Gross 30-year increment in cubic volume was 75 percent of that in unthinned stand, with greatest growth loss occurring during first 5 years after thinning.

Gross increment on both moderately thinned stands was within 9 percent of the unthinned stands in terms of cubic volume and practically identical in terms of Scribner board feet. The heavily thinned plots fell 25 percent below in cubic volume growth, or 20 percent in Scribner scale (table 1). Net increment was generally highest on moderately thinned plots, lower on unthinned plots, and lowest on heavily thinned plots.

Mortality was plainly lower on all thinned areas, averaging less than one-half that on unthinned plots. Further, roughly one-half of all mortality on thinned stands was, or could be, salvaged. Unsalvaged losses averaged 8 cubic feet, or 19 board feet Scribner, per acre per year for all thinned areas. Irrevocably lost were 38 cubic feet, or 47 board feet, on unthinned areas. Still, losses cannot be considered serious in either case.

Growth percent rates show greater efficiency of growing stock among all thinned stands. Average annual gross rates were 2.2 percent for cubic volume, or 3.2 percent for board feet, after thinning, but only 1.8 and 3.1 percent, respectively, in unthinned stands. The better rates for the thinned stands are, of course, directly related to reduced tree numbers.

Average stand diameter growth was 23 percent greater on thinned areas (3.48 inches versus 2.65 inches). There was an actual increase in growth, although part of the difference is the effect of eliminating most suppressed trees in initial thinning.

Restricting plot computations to only the 100 largest trees per acre confirms the greater efficiency of both volume and gross increment on thinned as opposed to unthinned stands:

	Percent of stand represented by the 100 largest trees		
	Unthinned plots 5 and 8	Lightly thinned plots 9 and 10	Heavily thinned plots 6 and 7
1964 stand:			
Basal area	59	75	97
Cubic volume	63	78	98
Board-foot volume (International)	68	81	99
Board-foot volume (Scribner)	83	89	100
Gross increment (1934–64):			
Basal area	58	61	83
Cubic volume	59	68	85
Board-foot volume (International)	64	72	84
Board-foot volume (Scribner)	69	71	88

Table 1.—Thirty-year increment and mortality record, Mount Walker thinning plots (1934-64)[1]

Plot number	Item	Site index, 1964 (Feet)	Basal area cut (Percent)	Stems (Number)	Basal area (Sq. ft.)	Volume[2]		
						Cubic (Cu. ft.)	International (Bd. ft.)	Scribner (Bd. ft.)
5 (unthinned)	Beginning stand	111	0	365	205.3	6,903	38,690	16,668
	Gross increment	--	--	--	102.6	4,595	33,379	24,760
	Mortality	--	--	105	29.8	883	4,136	1,348
	Net increment	--	--	--	72.8	3,712	29,243	23,412
6 (heavily thinned)	Stand after first thinning	114	44	144	116.9	4,337	27,184	13,321
	Gross increment	--	--	--	81.2	3,425	26,646	19,499
	Mortality	--	--	29	17.8	652	6,780	1,942
	Net increment	--	--	--	63.4	2,773	19,866	17,557
	Thinnings, 1949 and 1958	--	--	21	20.3	801	5,111	2,934
	Salvaged mortality[3]	--	--	3	5.3	210	1,402	951
7 (heavily thinned)	Stand after first thinning	113	50	126	86.4	3,025	18,190	9,632
	Gross increment	--	--	--	78.6	3,416	24,092	17,552
	Mortality	--	--	14	4.3	143	760	400
	Net increment	--	--	--	74.3	3,273	23,332	17,152
8 (unthinned)	Beginning stand	103	0	678	216.3	6,615	32,463	10,773
	Gross increment	--	--	--	103.6	4,548	30,480	21,388
	Mortality	--	--	332	52.0	1,420	4,680	1,471
	Net increment	--	--	--	51.6	3,128	25,800	19,917
9 (moderately thinned)	Stand after first thinning	101	37	312	114.6	4,608	24,650	7,581
	Gross increment	--	--	--	102.9	4,164	29,491	22,490
	Mortality	--	--	38	18.5	636	3,763	2,298
	Net increment	--	--	--	84.4	3,528	25,728	20,192
	Thinnings, 1949 and 1958	--	--	58	28.7	968	5,354	934
	Salvaged mortality	--	--	2	1.8	71	459	286
	Salvable mortality, 1964[4]	--	--	6	9.1	352	2,342	1,568
10 (moderately thinned)	Stand after thinning	111	31	217	157.8	5,764	35,343	17,295
	Gross increment	--	--	--	99.5	4,202	29,105	23,515
	Mortality	--	--	14	11.4	400	2,491	1,517
	Net increment	--	--	--	88.1	3,802	26,614	21,998
	Thinnings, 1949 and 1958	--	--	47	27.9	979	5,056	1,435
	Salvable mortality, 1964	--	--	3	7.2	278	1,900	1,315

1/ Plots 9 and 10, thinned in 1937, are adjusted to a 30-year basis.
2/ Cubic volume is for entire stem, International rule for trees 6.6 inches d.b.h. and larger to a 5-inch top, and Scribner rule for trees 11.6 inches d.b.h. and larger to an 8-inch top.
3/ Salvaged mortality is included in both "mortality" and "thinnings."
4/ Dead trees included in "mortality" which would have been salvaged had another thinning been made.

With wider spacing, the increases in d.b.h. increment most strik-
ingly illustrate the effects of thinning (fig. 3). A significant rise
is evident, beginning with a very close similarity in rates for both unthinned plots, to the greatest increase for plot 7, which was thinned to
the fewest trees and smallest average diameter. No significance should
be attached to the differences in slope of individual plot lines, except
possibly for plot 9 where most of the 100 largest trees were concentrated
toward the small end of the diameter range.

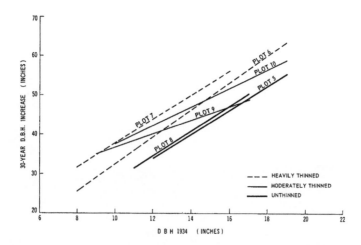

Figure 3.-- D. b. h. increase, 100 largest trees. Mount Walker thinning plots, 1934-64.

It can be reasonably inferred that the moderate thinnings on plots
9 and 10 were better suited to the low-site condition than were the
heavier cuttings on plots 6 and 7. Moderate thinnings also compared
much more favorably with unthinned stands in gross yield. Gross cubic-
foot increment after moderate thinning, though only 82 percent of the
unthinned standard during the first 15 years, was 103 percent in the
last 15 years, whereas increment after heavy thinning improved from 66
percent to within 82 percent during the latter period. Such recovery
reaffirms the tardy response elsewhere noted among older, young-growth
stands.[2]

[2] Worthington, Norman P., and Staebler, George R. Commercial
thinning of Douglas-fir in the Pacific Northwest. U.S. Dep. Agr. Tech.
Bull. 1230, 124 pp., illus. 1961. (See pp. 25-26.)

FOREST AND RANGE EXPERIMENT STATION · U.S. DEPARTMENT OF AGRICULTURE · PORTLAND, OREGON

PNW-36   *February 1966*

THINNING RESPONSE IN 110-YEAR-OLD DOUGLAS-FIR

by Richard L. Williamson

A study was established in 1952 near Boundary Creek in the Panther Creek area on the Wind River Experimental Forest near Carson, Wash. Site index averages 140, and aspect is westerly at elevations around 2,000 to 2,400 feet. Two minor drainages traverse the study area from east to west, creating various northwesterly and southwesterly aspects. The almost pure Douglas-fir stand was fairly well stocked before thinning, averaging 86 percent of normal basal area, although individual plot percentages ranged from 62 to 100.

This paper concerns only one objective of the study--to determine how much stands could be reduced in basal area without impairing increment.

The first report[1] on this study, based on data up to and including 1958, described a lack of response to thinning and recommended only anticipation of mortality when partial cutting in stands of this age is planned. More recent measurements, however, imply somewhat greater response, though the recommendation may remain the same.

Nine contiguous rectangular treatment areas of at least 7.7 acres each were established in a 3 by 3 pattern (fig. 1). A 1-by 10-chain plot (1 acre) was located on the long axis of each treatment area, providing at least a 3-chain buffer strip on both sides of every plot and a small, but varying, buffer at the ends.

---

[1] Yerkes, Vern P. Growth after thinning in 110-year-old Douglas-fir. U.S. Forest Serv. Pacific Northwest Forest & Range Exp. Sta. Res. Note 189, 3 pp., illus. 1960.

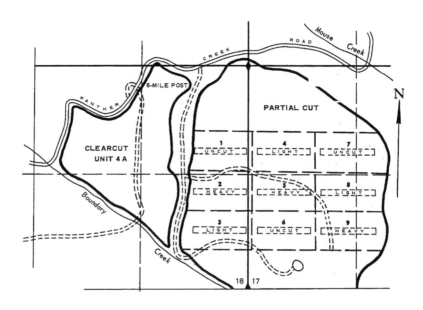

Figure 1.--*Boundary Creek thinning, Wind River Experimental Forest.*

Each north-south tier of three plots was treated as a block, with the three treatments randomized within each to create a randomized block design.

Heavy thinning reduced three plots to 55 percent of normal basal area; light thinning reduced three other plots to 74 percent of normal; and the three remaining plots served as checks.

Plot establishment was followed immediately by thinning in the fall of 1952. Insect-killed trees were salvaged in 1953 from most of the plots, including the check plots.

Plot remeasurements were made in 1955, 1958, and 1963. Only diameters at breast height and mortality were recorded until 1963, when tree heights were also measured.

Table 1 shows the considerable variation between plots prior to treatment. Cubic-foot volume per acre before cutting ranged from 8,500 to 14,400, averaging 11,500. Scribner volume per acre ranged from 43,600 to 77,400 board feet, averaging 58,300. In addition, two stands had much lower site indices than the other stands.

All plots are near, or have passed, the culmination of net mean annual increment in both cubic-foot and Scribner volumes (table 2). In addition, no plot is growing at a gross rate faster than 1.35 percent of the 1952 residual cubic-foot volume, with the average growth rate being 1.04 percent. Therefore, any thinning effects here would be of interest primarily to agencies whose circumstances preclude harvest of stands in this age class for another 20 years or more, principally because of even-flow sustained-yield objectives.

Also, all measures of gross annual increment over the entire 11-year period have been less on the thinned plots than on the unthinned (table 2). Gross periodic annual cubic-foot growth has been 119, 98, and 79 cubic feet, respectively, for the unthinned, lightly thinned, and heavily thinned plots.

The data tabulated below show that average gross periodic annual increment on the thinned plots increased during the latest of the shorter periods, and increment on the unthinned plots steadily decreased.

Period	Unthinned	Lightly thinned	Heavily thinned
	---------- (Cubic feet) ----------		
1952-55	155	104	88
1956-58	110	77	73
1959-63	104	108	76

Table 1.--Stand statistics for Boundary Creek thinning treatments at age 110 and 121 years

(acre basis)

Plot numbers by treatment and date	Site index	Total stand				Volume[1]	
		Trees	Basal area	Average d.b.h.	Average height	Cubic	Scribner
	Feet	Number	Sq.ft.	Inches	Feet	Cu.ft.	Bd.ft.
CHECK AREA							
Plot 1:							
Before cut, 1952		115	304	22.0	146	14,424	77,450
After cut, July 1952		105	285	22.3	146	13,547	72,923
After 11 years, Aug. 1963	152	103	313	23.6	150	14,829	81,339
Plot 6:							
Before cut, 1952		147	257	17.9	134	11,855	59,310
After cut, 1952		140	239	17.7	133	10,984	57,304
After 11 years, Aug. 1963	145	131	260	19.1	138	12,148	61,952
Plot 7:							
Before cut, 1952		78	180	20.5	142	8,530	44,879
After cut, Aug. 1952		75	174	20.6	142	8,260	43,530
After 11 years, Aug. 1963	143	70	185	22.0	145	8,830	47,649
Average:							
Before cut, 1952		113	247	20.0	141	11,603	60,547
After cut, 1952		106	233	20.1	140	10,930	57,030
After 11 years, 1963	147	101	253	21.4	144	11,936	63,647
LIGHT THINNING							
Plot 3:							
Before cut, 1952		124	293	20.8	142	13,692	72,879
After cut, 1952		85	222	21.9	145	10,400	56,160
After 11 years, Aug. 1963	150	82	241	23.2	149	11,353	62,181
Plot 4:							
Before cut, 1952		106	260	21.2	143	12,384	66,168
After cut, 1952		82	215	21.9	145	10,266	55,295
After 11 years, Aug. 1963	151	77	241	23.9	150	11,501	63,466
Plot 8:							
Before cut, 1952		165	291	18.0	134	13,309	65,921
After cut, 1952		121	227	18.5	136	10,453	52,443
After 11 years, Aug. 1963	134	114	236	19.7	139	11,010	55,998
Average:							
Before cut, 1952		132	281	19.8	140	13,128	68,323
After cut, 1952		96	221	20.5	142	10,373	54,633
After 11 years, 1963	145	91	241	22.0	146	11,288	60,548
HEAVY THINNING							
Plot 2:							
Before cut, 1952		183	224	15.0	123	9,658	43,646
After cut, 1952		100	144	16.3	128	6,374	29,832
After 11 years, Aug. 1963	121	98	161	17.3	132	7,249	34,798
Plot 5:							
Before cut, 1952		131	211	17.2	131	9,604	47,261
After cut, 1952		84	163	18.8	137	7,549	38,039
After 11 years, Aug. 1963	143	82	179	20.0	140	8,398	43,289
Plot 9:							
Before cut, 1952		207	240	14.6	122	10,337	47,587
After cut, 1952		124	155	15.1	124	6,759	31,350
After 11 years, Aug. 1963	114	113	161	16.1	128	7,136	33,989
Average:							
Before cut, 1952		174	225	15.4	125	9,866	46,165
After cut, 1952		103	154	16.6	130	6,894	33,074
After 11 years, 1963	126	98	167	17.7	133	7,594	37,359

[1] Cubic Volume is entire stem Volume of trees 1.5 inches d.b.h. and larger; Scribner Volume is for trees 9.6 inches d.b.h. and larger to an 8-inch top.

-4-

Table 2.—Increment and mortality by treatment and subplot, Boundary Creek thinning, 1952-63

(acre basis)

Treatment and plot number	Net periodic annual growth			Periodic annual mortality			Gross periodic annual growth			Net mean annual increment[1]		
	Basal area	Volume		Basal area	Volume		Basal area	Volume		Basal area	Volume	
		Cubic	Scribner		Cubic	Scribner		Cubic	Scribner		Cubic	Scribner
	Sq.ft.	Cu.ft.	Bd.ft.	Sq.ft.	Cu.ft.	Bd.ft.	Sq.ft.	Cu.ft.	Bd.ft.	Sq.ft.	Cu.ft.	Bd.ft.
Check area:												
1	2.5	116	765	0.2	7	30	2.7	123	795	2.74	130	710
6	1.9	106	665	.6	27	117	2.5	133	782	2.30	108	551
7	1.0	52	374	1.1	50	263	2.1	102	637	1.58	75	405
Average	1.8	91	601	.6	28	137	2.4	119	738	2.20	104	555
Light thinning:												
3	1.7	87	547	.2	5	17	1.9	92	564	2.57	121	652
4	2.4	112	743	.3	9	31	2.7	121	774	2.36	112	614
8	1.4	51	323	.7	32	161	2.1	83	484	2.48	115	.574
Average	1.8	83	538	.4	15	70	2.2	98	608	2.47	116	613
Heavy thinning:												
2	1.5	80	451	.1	1	0	1.6	81	451	1.99	87	402
5	1.4	77	477	.1	4	10	1.5	81	487	1.87	86	434
9	.5	34	240	.9	40	163	1.4	74	403	2.03	88	415
Average	1.1	64	389	.4	15	58	1.5	79	447	1.96	87	417

[1] In 1963 at age 121 years.

This relationship applies to all three unthinned plots and to five of the six thinned plots. One heavily thinned plot declined in growth during the latest period, though to a lesser extent than the unthinned plots. Also, there is no statistically significant difference in gross increment for the latest period between the unthinned and the lightly thinned plots. Current annual growth rates for both are about 106 cubic feet and 650 board feet, Scribner rule. Contributing, no doubt, to a drop in increment for all plots during the period 1956-58 was a decrease in precipitation of 50 percent from normal during the growing season for 2 of the 3 years. There is nothing to suggest that these stands were affected by the drastic freeze of 1955.

Because the heavily thinned plots averaged considerably lower in site index than the other plots, it seems unrealistic to compare their gross increment during the latest, or any, period with that of the un- thinned plots, as was done with the lightly thinned plots. For this reason, a comparison was made with increment indicated by normal gross yield tables.[2] Average periodic annual gross increment for the latest period is 85, 86, and 81 percent of normal for the unthinned, lightly thinned, and heavily thinned plots, respectively. This suggests that if all plots were of comparable site index, there would be no signifi- cant differences in gross cubic-foot volume increment for the latest period. This seems noteworthy for stands of this age after a 32-per- cent cut in basal area to only 52 percent of normal basal area. It is unfortunate there is no record of growth prior to treatment.

Thinning response is also indicated by increment cores from 10 dominant and codominant trees chosen in 1964 from the thinned areas. Radial growth since thinning averaged 137 percent of the growth for an equal period before thinning. This does not represent an average re- sponse because these trees were chosen on the basis of above-average release.

Mortality on the unthinned plots (310 cubic feet) has been nearly twice that of the thinned plots (165 cubic feet) for the 11-year period, but very little has been due to suppression, an indication of light stocking. Bark beetles, *Poria weirii* root rot, scattered windthrow, and blister rust of occasional white pine have accounted for most of the mortality.

After 6 years, growth on the lightly thinned (21 percent by basal area) plots caught up with growth on the unthinned plots (tabulation, p. 3). Because this growth is concentrated on fewer trees, value

---

[2] Staebler, George R. Gross yield and mortality tables for fully stocked stands of Douglas-fir. U.S. Forest Serv. Pacific North- west Forest and Range Exp. Sta. Res. Paper 14, 20 pp., illus. 1955.

increment, presumably, will be a little higher on the thinned than on the unthinned plots. The situation is less clear with the heavily thinned plots. This study is not capable of pinpointing where permanent growth would be impaired by thinning in stands this old.

The facts reported here, although inconclusive, may help landowners decide whether they should try only to anticipate mortality with intermediate cuttings in this age class or whether they should try to increase early monetary returns through reduction of growing stock without impairing growth of the residual stand.

shame

 **FOREST AND RANGE EXPERIMENT STATION** · U.S. DEPARTMENT OF AGRICULTURE · PORTLAND, OREGON

PNW-37

S.I., TECH. & AGR. DIV.

April 1966

A COMPARISON OF SITE CURVES FOR DOUGLAS-FIR

by

Robert O. Curtis, Associate Mensurationist

INTRODUCTION

The use of the height-age relationship for determination of site quality has long been generally accepted for Douglas-fir in the Pacific Northwest. It provides the basis of site classification in yield studies and in management planning.

There are numerous published height-age curves for the species, both in North America and in Europe (see, for example, the listing given by Smith et al. 1960).[1] These exhibit a diversity of shapes, presumably reflecting both differences in method of preparation and in the site and stand conditions from which the original data were taken.

The site index curves in general use in the Pacific Northwest are those given by McArdle et al. (1961). These are proportional curves, originally prepared in the 1920's from single determinations of average height and age for a sample of natural stands thought to represent comparable average site quality over the range of ages.

Curves prepared by these methods are subject to two main types of possible errors:

1. The shape of the average curve used as the basis of the system may be incorrect; this can result from unequal representation of sites in the different age classes in the sample.

---

[1] Names and dates in parentheses refer to Literature Cited, p.7.

2. The common assumption that height-over-age curves are proportional for all sites may be incorrect; polymorphic (nonpropor-
   tional) curves may be more suitable.

The shape of existing site curves may best be judged by comparison
with height growth data obtained from remeasurements of permanent plots,
or by comparison with height curves obtained from stem analyses. A
number of such comparisons, though of limited scope, have been or can
readily be made:

1. The University of British Columbia has done a considerable
   amount of stem analysis work at Haney, British Columbia. Results and comparisons with existing curves have been reported
   by Heger,2/ Smith (1962), and Smith and Walters (1964).

2. The British Columbia Forest Service (1953, pp. 41-42) has published an average height curve based upon records from remeasured
   permanent plots.

3. Warrack (1959) has prepared an average height curve based on
   stem analyses made at Cowichan Lake, Vancouver Island, British
   Columbia.

4. Spurr (1952) prepared "natural" height-age curves for Douglas-
   fir, based on the data available at that time from remeasured
   permanent plots of the Pacific Northwest Forest and Range
   Experiment Station in Washington and Oregon. Most of these
   data were from stands over 45 years of age.

All the above curves exhibit a generally similar pattern of divergence from the standard curves (McArdle et al. 1961); lower heights at
the younger ages suggest that the latter may underestimate site quality
of young stands. Polymorphic curves based on floristic site types,
prepared by Spilsbury and Smith (1947) and by Eis (1962), also appear
to indicate the same general pattern.

It is interesting to note that Spurr's curves are very similar in
shape to the average height-age curve of Munger (1911), possibly the
first such curve ever published for Douglas-fir in the Pacific Northwest (fig. 1), and to Hanzlik's 1914 curves.

_____

2/ Heger, L. A comparison of conventional and natural height-age
curves for Douglas-fir. 71 pp. 1959. (Unpublished master's thesis
on file at Univ. Brit. Columbia, Vancouver.)

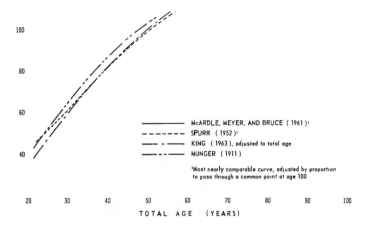

100

80

60

—————— McARDLE, MEYER, AND BRUCE (1961)'
— — — — — SPURR (1952)'
— · — · — KING (1963), adjusted to total age
40 ——— ·· ——— MUNGER (1911)

'Most nearly comparable curve, adjusted by proportion
to pass through a common point at age 100

20   30   40   50   60   70   80   90   100
TOTAL AGE   (YEARS)

*Figure 1.--Comparison of shapes of some Douglas-fir
height-age curves for Washington and Oregon.*

Recently, James King of Weyerhaeuser Co. has prepared a new set of
site curves[3] for second-growth Douglas-fir, based on measurements of
internode length and age at breast height of the largest 20 percent (by
diameter) of trees from 50-tree samples. When compared with McArdle's
curves (after adjustment to a comparable age basis), these exhibit a

---

[3] King, J. E. Preliminary site index tables for Douglas-fir.
20 pp. 1963. (Unpublished report on file at Weyerhaeuser Co., Forestry
Research Center, Centralia, Wash.)
King, J. E. Site index curves for Douglas-fir in the Pacific
Northwest. (In preparation for publication, Weyerhaeuser Co., Forestry
Research Center, Centralia, Wash.)

pattern of divergence similar to the other curves cited, even more pronounced in very young stands.

McArdle[4] has recorded the procedure used in constructing his site curves. Of the original data, a portion was discarded in order to get what he considered comparable average site quality in the different age classes. Of the data used in preparing the final curves, relatively little was from stands under 40 years of age. Hence, the hypothesis that the shape of the published curves may not be correct for young stands appears plausible.

THE COMPARISON

In connection with a study of gross yield of Douglas-fir,[5] a comparison was made of the standard curves with King's preliminary curves, using data available from remeasured permanent plots in stands under rotation age.

Where estimates of site index have been made at successive remeasurements of the same plot, one would expect--if the site curves used correctly represent the average curve of height growth--that estimated site index would be unrelated to age. From figure 1, it is apparent that, if the King curves are correct, successive estimates of site index made on the same plot with the standard curves would tend to rise with increasing age. Conversely, if the older curves are correct, estimates based on the King curves would tend to decrease as age increased. Since differences between curves are most pronounced in the younger ages, the relationship of site index to age might be expected to approximate linearity when logarithm of age is taken as the independent variable.

Data used in the comparison consisted of successive measurements of permanent plots located in well-stocked, unmanaged Douglas-fir stands for which there were available four or more successive estimates of site index at intervals of 5 years or more. These plots consisted of the 31 listed by Williamson (1963), together with 6 control plots from thinning studies. Height and site index values were taken from applicable Forest Service progress reports.

----

[4] McArdle, R. E. Site index curves by anamorphosis. (Memorandum dated Feb. 26, 1926, on file at the Pacific Northwest Forest and Range Exp. Sta., Portland, Oreg.)
[5] Curtis, Robert O. A study of gross yield in Douglas-fir. 152 pp. 1965. (Unpublished Ph.D. thesis on file at Univ. Wash., Seattle.)

Values used for SI_{50} (site index estimated by King's curves) were obtained by applying the King curves to the mean height of dominants and codominants given in the progress reports. In these well-stocked stands, the 20 percent of all stems with largest diameter usually consisted of dominants and larger codominants. Hence, use of mean height of dominants and codominants results in a slight but consistent underestimate of site index as defined by King. Since interest was in relative change rather than absolute value, this bias was not considered serious for purposes of the desired comparison.

A consistent relationship of successive estimates of site index on the same plot to stand age (or its logarithm) would indicate that the site curves used do not correctly represent the course of height growth. In other words, the site curves should be considered unsatisfactory if the value of b is significantly different from zero in the equation:

$$Y_{ij} = u + P_i + bX_{ij} + e_{ij}$$

where Y_{ij} is estimated site index of plot i at measurement j; u is mean site index for all plots and ages; P_i is deviation of mean site index of plot i from the overall mean u; X_{ij} is logarithm of age of plot i at measurement j; e is an independent normal random variable.

The hypothesis that the average value of b for these 37 plots is zero was tested by covariance analysis for two sets of values:

1. Values of SI_{100} (site index by McArdle's curves) and logarithms of corresponding ages.

2. Values of SI_{50} and logarithms of corresponding ages.

Results obtained were:

1. For McArdle's curves (SI_{100})

   F = 78.5 with degrees of freedom 1, 201

where $F_{.01} = 6.76$

2. For the King curves (SI_{50})

   F = 3.46 with degrees of freedom 1, 201

where $F_{.05} = 3.89$

Thus, estimates of site index obtained by use of McArdle's curves were found to be significantly related to logarithm of age, whereas those obtained with King's curves were not.

For each individual plot, regressions of SI_{100} and SI_{50} on logarithm of age were calculated. For SI_{100}, 16 of the 37 regressions had slopes significantly different from zero, with 13 positive and 3 negative. For SI_{50}, 14 had slopes significantly different from zero, with 7 positive and 7 negative.

DISCUSSION AND CONCLUSIONS

For these 37 plots, the King curves represent the observed pattern of height growth better than do the standard curves. However, it is clear that the height-age curve for an individual plot may differ considerably from either the King or standard curves.

The comparison covers a rather restricted range of ages, with relatively little data from stands less than 45 years old. The age range 20 to 50 years, in turn, is that in which King's curves diverge most radically from McArdle's. Consequently, the analysis does not necessarily demonstrate that the King curves are superior. It does show that--within the age range of the majority of these plots-- average observed height growth diverges from McArdle's curves in a manner consistent with both King's curves and the other curves discussed earlier.[6] If, as this suggests, the divergence extends down into younger ages, then it follows that the standard curves overestimate height growth and underestimate site index of younger stands. The resulting errors in estimation of site index could be greater than for the older stands used in this comparison.

From figure 1, it is evident that possible differences in curve shape above about 50 years of age are much less important; even if real, they are not likely to introduce large errors in site classification.

If the standard curves do consistently underestimate site index of young stands, then it also follows that the curves of normal basal area and normal yield (McArdle et al. 1961)--being based on classification by these site curves--contain corresponding distortions in the same age range. Since the age range 20 to 50 years is also the period of most rapid cubic-volume increment, estimates of cumulative gross yield could also be seriously affected.

---

[6] The data used in this analysis included much of that used by Spurr (1952), plus additional data accumulated since. Hence, the result obtained is not independent of Spurr's work.

With the increasing importance of young Douglas-fir stands and
growing interest in their management and yields, further comparisons
of the standard and alternative site curves appear desirable. Emphasis
should be on stands under 50 years of age. Meanwhile, King's new curves
appear promising as a prospective replacement for the older curves.

LITERATURE CITED

British Columbia Forest Service.
    1953. Report of the Forest Service, year ended December 31st,
        1952. 171 pp., illus.

Eis, Slavoj.
    1962. Statistical analysis of several methods for estimation of
        forest habitats and tree growth near Vancouver, B.C.
        Univ. Brit. Columbia, Fac. Forest., Forest. Bull. 4,
        76 pp., illus.

Hanslick [Hanzlik], E. J.
    1914. A study of the growth and yield of Douglas fir on various
        soil qualities in western Washington and Oregon.
        [A review.] Forest. Quart. 12: 440-451.

McArdle, Richard E., Meyer, Walter H., and Bruce, Donald.
    1961. The yield of Douglas-fir in the Pacific Northwest. U.S.
        Dep. Agr. Tech. Bull. 201 (rev.), 74 pp., illus.

Munger, Thornton T.
    1911. The growth and management of Douglas fir in the Pacific
        Northwest. U.S. Dep. Agr. Forest Serv. Circ. 175,
        27 pp., illus.

Smith, J. Harry G.
    1962. Preparation of a method for predicting stand development
        from stem analysis. Univ. Brit. Columbia, Fac. Forest.,
        13 pp.

_____ and Walters, John.
    1964. A technique for predicting growth of Douglas fir, western
        hemlock, and western red cedar near Haney, B.C. by use
        of stem analysis. Univ. Brit. Columbia, Fac. Forest.
        Res. Pap. 67, 31 pp., illus.

_____ Ker, J. W., and Heger, L.
    1960. Natural and conventional height-age curves for Douglas-fir
        and some limits to their refinement. Fifth World
        Forest. Congr. Proc. (Seattle.) 1: 546-551.

Spilsbury, R. H., and Smith, D. S.
     1947. Forest site types of the Pacific Northwest. Brit. Columbia
          Forest Serv. Tech. Pub. T30, 46 pp., illus.

Spurr, Stephen H.
     1952. Forest inventory. 476 pp., illus. New York: Ronald Press
          Co.

Warrack, G. C.
     1959. Forecast of yield in relation to thinning regimes in
          Douglas fir. Brit. Columbia Forest Serv. Tech. Pub.
          T51, 56 pp.

Williamson, R. L.
     1963. Growth and yield records from well-stocked stands of
          Douglas-fir. Pacific Northwest Forest & Range Exp.
          Sta. U.S. Forest Serv. Res. Pap. PNW-4, 24 pp., illus.

| FOREST AND RANGE EXPERIMENT STATION U.S. DEPARTMENT OF AGRICULTURE · PORTLAND, OREGON

PNW-38   *April 1966*

A RECORD OF PONDEROSA PINE SEED FLIGHT

by

James W. Barrett, Associate Silviculturist

When natural seedfall is needed to restock denuded forest areas, effective seeding distance becomes very important.

This note reports on 1958 dissemination of ponderosa pine seed into a 65-acre tract, bare of overstory, in central Oregon.

PAST WORK

Published information on ponderosa pine seed dispersal into large openings is scarce because most managed stands have been selectively cut and distant seed flight was of minor concern. Earlier workers *(1, 7, 3)* agree that most seed falls within 2 chains[1] of its source. However, theoretical calculations of ponderosa pine seed flight, based on Siggins' *(6)* work, indicate that seed from a 100-foot tree could, with a 20-mile-an-hour wind, be disseminated up to a distance of about 9 chains. Fowells and Schubert *(3)* point out that theoretical flight distances do not account for factors such as wind gusts, updrafts, and air turbulence. Working in California, these investigators estimated that little seed is dispersed more than about 4.5 chains. Isaac *(5)*, studying the dissemination of winged ponderosa

---

[1] The "chain" used as a unit of measure in the text is 66 feet long and composed of 100 subdivisions or links 7.92 inches long. The study was established using a 2-chain surveyors' tape supplemented by correction graduations for use in slope chaining with the topographic Abney level.

pine seed from a pilot balloon at an elevation of 150 feet in a 3.5-mile-an-hour wind, found the greatest concentration of seed at a distance of 4.5 chains from the point of release. At 7.6 chains, 12.5 percent of the seed was recovered. No seed was found at 9.1 chains.

Workers (7, p. 7) in Idaho found that 82 percent of ponderosa pine seed falling within 7.6 chains of the timber edge was confined to an area only 1.5 chains from the source. Curtis and Foiles (1), also in Idaho, studied dissemination of ponderosa pine seed into scarified 0.25- to 3-acre clearcuttings. Two or more overstory trees were left on the margin of the area to provide seed and shade for the seedlings. They concluded that "...most of the seed from a tree falls within a chain of it...."

EXPERIMENTAL AREA

The 1958 central Oregon study was made on the Pringle Falls Experimental Forest within a 65-acre oval-shaped tract where the overstory trees had been completely removed. This cutting area provided a good opportunity to study natural seed flight over greater distances than previously reported. The area is on a gentle east-facing slope at an elevation of about 4,400 feet and 600 feet below the summit of Pringle Butte. Prevailing winds, in autumn, at time of greatest seedfall, are from the southwest.

The timber stand surrounding the study area averaged 20,000 board feet per acre and consisted of overmature and mature ponderosa pine trees averaging 110 feet high.

STUDY METHODS

Seed dispersal was sampled on both eastern and western edges of the 65-acre study area. Two parallel seedtrap lines, 2 chains apart, extended 8 chains from the eastern timbered edge toward the middle of the cleared area (fig. 1). Two additional trap lines extended completely across a narrower portion of the cleared area. In both cases, seedtraps were placed at the timbered edge and at 2-chain intervals out into the cleared area.

Twenty-six traps of two sizes were used. Eight traps had horizontal surface dimensions of 4 feet by 4 feet and were placed at locations 6 and 8 chains from timbered edge. The other 18 traps were smaller, 2 feet by 3 feet, and were located at distances less than 6 chains from the timbered edge. Seedtraps were in place by June 1, 1958, and were inspected for seed on October 10 and November 6, 1958, and again on May 11, 1959.

A few cones occurred on the ponderosa pine saplings within the cleared area. These cones were removed prior to seedfall to avoid confounding seed catches from the mature trees at the timbered edge.

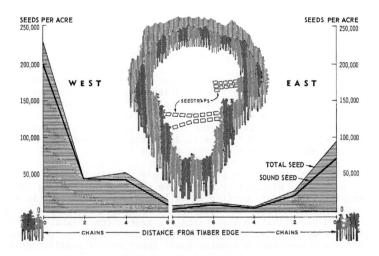

Figure 1.--Dissemination of ponderosa pine seed into area from east and west edges during 1958.

RESULTS

A good crop of ponderosa pine seed was produced in 1958 on the experimental forest. Prevailing westerly winds accounted for heaviest seedfall on the west edge of the cleared area where seed catches averaged almost 200,000 seeds per acre (fig. 1).[2] Quantity of seed dropped sharply with distance from source--43,500 seed per acre at 2 chains, and 15,000 at 6 chains. Seed catch at the eastern edge averaged 71,000 seeds per acre, diminished to 23,000 at 2 chains and only 5,400 at .8 chains from the edge.[3]

A cutting test revealed that 86 percent of the total seed collected at 2 chains from the timber edge was sound. Seed soundness at 8 chains decreased to 67 percent.

---

[2] All seedfall statistics in text are sound seed only.

[3] Average of four trap lines originating on the eastern edge.

CONCLUSIONS AND DISCUSSION

The most apparent conclusion is that ponderosa pine seed does not disseminate naturally over extensive distances. For conditions in the vicinity of the study area, it seems logical that clearcuts should be small patches or narrow strips less than 5 chains wide at right angles to the prevailing winds if abundant natural regeneration is desired. Elsewhere, size of clearcut may vary depending on amount of summer rain, slope, and other environmental factors (8).

On the other hand, site preparation may greatly increase effective seed disseminating distance by increasing the seed-to-seedling ratio. For example, Hallin (4), working in California, observed a ratio of seed (130,000) to 4-year-old seedlings of 100 to 1, where rodents were poisoned and scarification kept competing vegetation "light." These practices resulted in an adequately stocked stand. However, attempts to duplicate these results several years later with a seedfall of about 45,000 seed per acre were only "moderately successful."

Exceptionally good seed-to-seedling ratios in group clearcuttings in central Idaho were attributed by Foiles and Curtis (2) to a comparatively cool, moist summer. However, they state, "...it would have been impossible to anticipate the combination of events that culminated in the unusually abundant seedling establishment...." Thus, there is an element of luck associated with good seed-to-seedling ratios in having sites prepared when seed production and environmental factors are ideal.

The seed flight information resulting from the Pringle Falls study is directly applicable to ponderosa pine in central Oregon. This knowledge may also be helpful elsewhere in determining how natural seedfall can be used in combination with other cultural measures to obtain prompt restocking of ponderosa pine.

LITERATURE CITED

(1) Curtis, James D., and Foiles, Marvin W.
        1961. Ponderosa pine seed dissemination into group clear-
            cuttings. J. Forest. 59: 766-767.

(2) Foiles, Marvin W., and Curtis, James D.
        1965. Natural establishment of ponderosa pine in central
            Idaho. Intermountain Forest and Range Exp. Sta.
            U.S. Forest Serv. Res. Note INT-35, 4 pp., illus.

(3) Fowells, H. A., and Schubert, G. H.
        1956. Seed crops of forest trees in the pine region of Cali-
            fornia. U.S. Dep. Agr. Tech. Bull. 1150, 48 pp.,
            illus.

(4) Hallin, William E.
      1959. The application of unit area control in the management
            of ponderosa-Jeffrey pine at Blacks Mountain Experi-
            mental Forest. U.S. Dep. Agr. Tech. Bull. 1191,
            96 pp., illus.

(5) Isaac, Leo A.
      1930. Seed flight in the Douglas fir region. J. Forest. 28:
            492-499, illus.

(6) Siggins, Howard W.
      1933. Distribution and rate of fall of conifer seeds. J. Agr.
            Res. 47: 119-128, illus.

(7) U.S. Forest Service.
      1940. Annual report. Intermountain Forest and Range Exp. Sta.

(8) Wagg, J. W. Bruce, and Hermann, Richard K.
      1962. Artificial seeding of pine in central Oregon. Oreg.
            State Univ. Forest. Res. Lab. Res. Note 47, 47 pp.,
            illus.

324

■ **FOREST AND RANGE EXPERIMENT STATION** · U. S. DEPARTMENT OF AGRICULTURE · PORTLAND, OREGON

PNW-39

April 1966

POSSIBLE GROUSE DAMAGE ON TRUE FIRS

by Carroll B. Williams, Jr.

INTRODUCTION

Wildlife damage to coniferous seedlings and saplings frequently interferes with regeneration of forests in the Pacific Northwest. Radwan (1963)[1] reviewed the literature and summarized research on wild mammal damage to forest trees, but there has been little documentation of grouse damage or control. This paper documents the author's observations of debudded true firs and associated species near Mount Hood, Oregon, during the spring of 1964. There is strong circumstantial evidence that the damage was caused by grouse.

Grouse normally inhabit forest lands, and population increases on recently logged and burned areas have been recorded (Hatter 1955). Grouse eat buds and needles of seedlings thus impeding height growth of the injured trees (Lawrence et al. 1961). Douglas-fir (*Pseudotsuga menziesii* (Mirb.) Franco) is a preferred food of grouse throughout the year in the Pacific Northwest (Martin et al. 1951). Plantations of Douglas-fir seedlings on Vancouver Island have been subject to heavy and repeated damage by sooty blue grouse (*Dendragapus obscurus fuliginosus* Ridgeway), particularly in the spring (Fowle 1960). However, damage to saplings and larger trees has, so far, not been reported to be important.

Grouse damage to true firs and associated upper-slope species in the Pacific Northwest has not been previously reported, although at least two studies of feeding habits mention a preference for true fir needles.

---

[1] Names and dates in parentheses refer to Literature Cited, p. 6.

Beer (1943) reported that at high elevations in Washington and northern Idaho grouse preferred true fir, although many Douglas-fir were present. Stomach analyses of sooty blue grouse from areas containing true firs also have shown that the birds feed largely on true fir needles, although Douglas-fir needles are consumed in appreciable quantities, too (Beer 1943; Stewart 1944).

STUDY AREA

An old burn, situated 2 miles west of Government Camp, Oregon, and 4 to 5 miles southwest of Mount Hood, is the site of a seasonal height-growth study of coniferous saplings. It is surrounded by a mature forest of Douglas-fir, western hemlock (*Tsuga heterophylla* (Raf.) Sarg.), and western redcedar (*Thuja plicata* Donn). The area experiences much cold air drainage down the snow-covered slopes of Mount Hood, and frost occurs at any time of the year. The wide assortment of tree species growing on the old burn suggests that it may be a tension zone between the Douglas-fir forest below and the upper-slope or subalpine forests above. Natural regeneration of Douglas-fir, western hemlock, mountain hemlock (*T. mertensiana* (Bong.) Carr.), western redcedar, noble fir (*Abies procera* Rehd.), Pacific silver fir (*Abies amabilis* (Dougl.) Forbes), subalpine fir (*Abies lasiocarpa* (Hook.) Nutt.), western white pine (*Pinus monticola* Dougl.), Engelmann spruce (*Picea engelmannii* Parry), ponderosa pine (*Pinus ponderosa* Laws.), and lodgepole pine (*Pinus contorta* Dougl.) occurs mixed in seedling to pole sizes. Sooty blue grouse were often heard and occasionally seen during the summers of 1963 and 1964.

OBSERVATIONS

In the spring of 1964, the author visited the area to begin a second season's leader-growth measurement on coniferous saplings. The terminal and, often, many lateral buds were missing on numerous study trees as well as those in the surrounding stand (fig. 1). Injured trees ranged from approximately 5 feet to over 30 feet in height. Damage was particularly noticeable on trees in a powerline right-of-way that bisected the southern third of the area.

Comparison of the leader measurement with that of the preceding year showed that only the buds were cleanly nipped off. Comparison of the injuries with damage descriptions in a key to wildlife injuries to seedlings and saplings (Lawrence et al. 1961) points clearly to grouse as the damaging agent. The type of damage, its occurrence on trees up to 30 feet tall, and its concentration in seedling stands within a right-of-way are signs of grouse presence. The location of the study area coupled with these grouse signs indicates a grouse

wintering area. Samples of the injury were examined by mammalogists[2]
at Oregon State University and tentatively identified as grouse damage.

A 12- to 15-foot accumulation of snow was reported on the area
during the winter and spring of 1963-64.[3] Apparently, the high snow

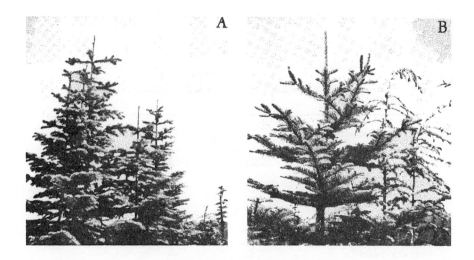

*Figure 1.--A clump of Pacific silver fir saplings (A) and a noble fir
sapling (B) exhibiting animal damage--removal of terminal buds.
Both photos were taken July 19, 1964. By this time, several of
the top lateral branches on the noble fir were beginning to turn
upward. No lateral branches of any Pacific silver fir did so
during the 1964 growing season.*

[2] Edward Hooven and Hugh Black, forest wildlife ecologists,
Oregon Forest Research Laboratory, examined the damage specimens
collected by the author.

[3] Personal communication with Raymond Steiger, Assistant Ranger,
Zigzag District, Mount Hood National Forest, June 4, 1964.

accumulations forced the grouse to feed on the terminal and top lateral buds of the taller trees that were not covered. As the snow melted, grouse were able to feed on progressively smaller trees.

Some tree species showed a greater incidence of damage than others. The true firs and pines, which have fairly large terminal buds, received the most damage. Apparently, grouse concentrated on trees with large attractive buds. In order to check this seeming preference for true firs and pines, a 100-percent survey for incidence of grouse damage was made on all trees growing within a half chain of the powerline for a distance of approximately 720 feet (table 1).

Table 1.--Incidence of possible grouse damage to coniferous saplings near Government Camp, Oreg., 1964 [1]

Tree species	Total trees	Damaged trees	
	Number	Number	Percent
Pacific silver fir	91	48	52.7
Subalpine fir	7	4	57.1
Noble fir	7	4	57.1
Douglas-fir	230	27	11.7
Lodgepole pine	26	6	23.1
Western white pine	9	--	--
Western redcedar	85	--	--
Western hemlock	148	--	--
Mountain hemlock	36	--	--

[1] Observed during a survey of all trees growing within a half chain each side of a 720-foot section of a powerline bisecting the study area.

The tally clearly showed that grouse preferred buds of true firs to those of other species, including Douglas-fir. Whether this preference was based on the attractiveness of true fir buds, their nutritive value, or availability was not ascertained. However, in California, Hoffmann (1961) found that in wintering areas Sierra blue grouse *(Dendragapus obscurus sierrae)* cropped white fir *(Abies concolor)* needles and buds only in the upper part of the trees. He analyzed white fir needle samples, collected from different heights and exposures, and found that needles from higher branches contained a significantly higher crude protein content. Hoffmann reasoned that grouse may

-4-

select them for that reason, although other considerations such as greater insolation and warmth may have played a part.

Apparently, Pacific silver fir does not recover as rapidly from this type of injury as other species (figs. 1 and 2). Top lateral

Figure 2.--A subalpine fir and lodge-
pole pine with debudded terminal
shoots. The subalpine fir (right)
was one of the few true fir trees
in the study area that showed apical
elongation by a top lateral bud by
the end of the growing season. In
contrast, the damaged lodgepole pine
(below, left), within several weeks
(closeup below, right), showed rapid
progress of lateral in assuming domi-
nance over damaged terminal. Adven-
titious buds and subsequently new
needles developed on the lodgepole
pine damaged terminal towards the
end of the growing season. None
developed on any of the true firs.

buds or branches began growing upward (apically) on all the injured Douglas-firs and lodgepole pines at the beginning of the 1964 growing season. Generally, the new terminal buds grew close enough to the wound of the old ones so little stem deformity and height growth loss should occur on these trees. This observation is supported by a recent assessment of deer damage on five Douglas-fir plantations on Vancouver Island. Animal feeding did not seriously affect the survival or height growth of young Douglas-firs (Mitchell 1964). Apical growth by top lateral buds or branches occurred only sporadically among the true firs. None was seen on Pacific silver firs.

These observations suggest that debudding is at least a localized problem in upper-slope forests, that damage to true fir is greater than to pine and Douglas-fir, and that hemlock and western redcedar may be left undamaged.

LITERATURE CITED

Beer, James.
    1943. Food habits of the blue grouse. J. Wildlife Manage. 7: 32-44, illus.

Fowle, C. David.
    1960. A study of the blue grouse (*Dendragapus obscurus* (Say)) on Vancouver Island, British Columbia. Can. J. Zool. 38: 701-713, illus.

Hatter, J.
    1955. Problems in the management of sooty grouse in British Columbia. Annu. Conf. West. Ass. State Game & Fish Comm. Proc. 35: 262-265.

Hoffmann, Robert S.
    1961. The quality of the winter food of blue grouse. J. Wildlife Manage. 25: 209-210, illus.

Lawrence, William H., Kverno, Nelson B., and Hartwell, Harry D.
    1961. Guide to wildlife feeding injuries on conifers in the Pacific Northwest. West. Forest. & Conserv. Ass., Wash. Forest Protect. Ass., Ind. Forest. Ass., Univ. Wash. Coll. Forest., .44 pp., illus.

Martin, Alexander C., Zim, Herbert S., and Nelson, Arnold L.
    1951. American wildlife and plants. 500 pp., illus. New York, Toronto [etc.]: McGraw-Hill Book Co., Inc.

Mitchell, K. J.
  1964. Height growth losses due to animal feeding in Douglas fir
         plantations, Vancouver Island, B.C. Forest. Chron. 40:
         298-307, illus.

Radwan, M. A.
  1963. Protecting forest trees and their seed from wild mammals.
         (A review of the literature) Pacific Northwest Forest &
         Range Exp. Sta. U.S. Forest Serv. Res. Pap. PNW-6, 28 pp.

Stewart, Robert E.
  1944. Food habits of blue grouse. Condor 46: 112-120, illus.

PNW-40   *June 1966*

SNOW DAMAGE TO CONIFEROUS SEEDLINGS AND SAPLINGS

by *Carroll B. Williams, Jr.*

Heavy snow fell on upper slopes of the Cascade Range during late winter and early spring of 1964, and lower than normal spring temperatures retarded snowmelt (U.S. Weather Bureau 1964). Summer temperatures also were low, and areas normally free of snow by July retained snow until mid-August or even through the entire summer. As a result, trees bore large accumulations of snow for longer than average periods of time. Many of them were injured.

OBSERVATIONS

During the 1964 growing season, general observations were made of snow damage to and recovery of young conifers growing on several old cutovers in upper-slope forests. All cutovers contained young, open, mixed stands of conifers, generally Pacific silver fir *(Abies amabilis)*, Douglas-fir *(Pseudotsuga menziesii)*, noble fir *(Abies procera)*, western hemlock *(Tsuga heterophylla)*, and western white pine *(Pinus monticola)*. Douglas-fir, Pacific silver fir, and western hemlock were usually most abundant. Species composition on the cutover areas generally mirrored that of the surrounding mature stands.

More detailed observations were made of free-growing seedlings on one cutover--Lava Lakes unit 9 near the Santiam-Clear Lake highway junction in the central Oregon Cascades. Seedling damage was rated as follows:

None . . . . . . No visible injury
Very light . . . Stem slightly bent or one to several lateral
                 branches stripped from stem
Light . . . . . Stem bent severely; one to several lateral
                 branches may be stripped from stem
Moderate . . . . Stem fractured; one to several lateral branches
                 may be stripped from stem
Severe . . . . . Stem broken off

Ratings were made before 1964 height growth began, except for western white pine whose growth elongation started a week or two before snowmelt permitted access to the area. The same seedlings were measured for height growth during the 1963 and 1964 seasons for another study. This permitted relating snow damage to height growth. However, lack of trees in some ratings and failure of some terminal buds to elongate in 1964 prevented tests of statistical significance.

SNOW DAMAGE

Leaning, bent, and fractured stems and broken branches were common on many trees after snowmelt. Some tree species and tree sizes suffered more damage than others. Few trees below 4 feet were damaged by snow. Damage was most severe on trees from 4 to 20 feet in height. Occasionally, pole-size trees sustained a broken top or were stripped of a few branches. Trees of sawtimber size were uninjured except for a few broken branches.

In upper-slope forests, Douglas-fir seedlings and saplings were injured most severely. At Lava Lakes, Douglas-fir was the only species in the severe damage class--25 percent of the trees studied (table 1). Many Douglas-firs had fractured or broken stems, with fractures often occurring at several places along the stem. Some stems were broken off. Recovery of fractured or bent stems was noticeable approximately 1 week after bud bursting, and in 3 to 4 weeks stems were nearly straight (fig. 1). Apparently some of the food reserves accumulated during the previous fall and winter were translocated to the bent areas of the stem and helped to straighten the stem rather than to increase height growth. This was indicated by the average reduction in height growth of Douglas-firs in 1964 being inversely proportional to damage intensity (table 1).

In general, noble fir saplings suffered fewer snow injuries than did Douglas-fir, but more than western hemlock, western white pine, and Pacific silver fir in many upper-slope areas. Some noble fir poles had broken tops, but they were infrequent. On Lava Lakes unit 9, most noble fir injuries consisted of bent leaders or stems (fig. 2); no stem fractures were seen. Failure of terminal buds to elongate on several study trees in 1964 obscured any relationship between damage intensity and reduced height growth.

Few western hemlocks were seriously damaged by snow. However, one at Lava Lakes suffered moderate injuries consisting of fractures at several places along the stem. It recovered by the end of the growing season (fig. 3). It was common for pressure of snow to cause hemlocks to lean, but the trees recovered completely by the second to third week of the growing season. It appears that the supple stems of this species tolerate heavy snow without breaking. Height growth of hemlock apparently was not affected as much as associated tree species by snow damage. Actually, the 1964 rate of height growth of many hemlocks increased over that of 1963 (table 1).

-2-

Table 1.--<u>Average 1963 and 1964 height growth for trees rated according</u>

<u>to degree of snow damage observed at the Lava Lakes plot</u>

Tree species	Snow damage ratings, spring, 1964	Trees studied	Mean height growth		
			1963	1964	$\frac{1964}{1963}$x100
		Percent	----- Cm ----		
Western white pine	None	18.2	30.8	38.8	126.0
	Very light	54.5	43.7	37.9	86.7
	Light	18.2	44.4	37.1	83.6
	Moderate	9.1	58.4	30.5	52.2
	Severe	--	--	--	--
Western hemlock	None	33.3	14.0	29.1	207.8
	Very light	33.3	30.5	24.9	81.6
	Light	25.0	16.0	29.1	181.9
	Moderate	8.4	62.6	14.0	22.4
	Severe	--	--	--	--
Pacific silver fir	None	--	--	--	--
	Very light	57.1	35.2	23.9	67.7
	Light	35.7	33.7	22.1	65.6
	Moderate	7.2	28.0	17.0	60.7
	Severe	--	--	--	--
Douglas-fir	None	--	--	--	--
	Very light	8.3	28.5	31.4	110.2
	Light	41.7	28.6	22.5	78.6
	Moderate	25.0	35.5	16.1	45.3
	Severe	25.0	38.5	4.3	11.1
Noble fir	None	--	--	--	--
	Very light	45.5	39.	17.	43.7
	Light	54.5	43.8	26.0	59.6
	Moderate	--	--	--	--
	Severe	--	--	--	--

A

B

Figure 1.--Recovery of a Douglas-fir sapling fractured in two places: A, Appearance on July 4, 1964, before bud flushing; B, approximately 2 weeks later, 1 week after bud flushing; C, recovered tree on September 12, 1964, 2 weeks after height growth had ceased. This moderately damaged tree grew 41.0 centimeters in height during 1963, only 14.2 centimeters in 1964.

C

Figure 2.--A lightly damaged noble fir and its subsequent recovery and height growth compared with that of an adjacent very lightly damaged western white pine: _A_, The two trees late in 1963; _B_, appearance on July 4, 1964, 1 week after bud break on the noble fir--the 1963 noble fir leader was severely bent by snow, the pine's leader was only slightly bent; _C_, recovery after several weeks (July 18, 1964); and _D_, by the end of the 1964 growing season.

Figure 3.--_A_, Undamaged western hemlock sapling in late 1963; _B_, the
same tree on July 18, 1964, 4 weeks after bud break--stem was
fractured in three places; _C_, same sapling at the end of the
1964 growing season. The tree grew 62.6 centimeters in 1963
and only 14.0 centimeters during 1964.

Western white pine was not heavily damaged by the snow. Common injuries seen at Lava Lakes were bent stems on some trees (fig. 4A) and stripped lateral branches on others. All Pacific silver firs at Lava Lakes suffered some damage, but injuries were mainly bent stems that recovered by the end of the growing season (fig. 4B). The 1964 height growths of damaged trees of these two species were generally less than in 1963 (table 1).

Figure 4.--_A_, Very light snow damage on a western white pine. The injuries were mainly bent stems. _B_, Tree on right shows the common type of injury on Pacific silver fir.

DISCUSSION

A high percentage of seedlings growing in several high-elevation areas in the Cascade Range were injured by large snow accumulations during the winter of 1964. Approximately 90 percent of those observed and measured on Lava Lakes unit 9 suffered various intensities of damage. Tabulation of the 1963 and 1964 height data of damage-rated trees indicated differences between tree species in the amount of damage suffered. This was shown by the percentage of study trees of a particular species in each rating and by reductions in the 1964 height growth compared with the 1963 growth of the injured trees. Reductions in height growth were generally commensurate with damage intensity.

Watt (1951) compared the 1948-49 winter damage with western white pine, western hemlock, grand fir (Abies grandis), and other species including Douglas-fir growing in association on plot 14, Deception Creek Experimental Forest, Idaho. He observed that all species were about equally damaged. However, Douglas-fir observed in this study in the Cascade Range suffered more snow damage than any of its associated species.

Planting true firs, pure or in mixture with Douglas-fir, is recommended in the Douglas-fir region of the Pacific Northwest at elevations where noble fir or Pacific silver fir naturally occur mixed with the Douglas-fir (Douglas-fir Second-Growth Management Committee 1947). These true firs are considered more resistant than Douglas-fir to snowbreak and winter injury. Observations reported here support this recommendation.

Western hemlock suffered the least snow damage of any species at Lava Lakes. Few bent or fractured trees of this species were seen. Also, although there was considerable variation, the 1964 height growth increased on two-thirds of the measured hemlocks, whereas, it was generally reduced on associated species. Since an acceleration in height growth is expected from seedlings and saplings growing in the uncrowded conditions of the cutovers, an actual reduction is especially important. Height growth of all measured "undamaged" trees was not reduced in 1964.

Perhaps the most surprising development observed was the rapid recovery made by the damaged trees. In most cases, severely bent trees and those with fractured stems had straightened by the third week of bud elongation. Lateral branches on trees whose main stems were broken had turned upward and were competing for tree dominance by the end of the growing season. Presumably, only the trees which suffered broken stems would have any lasting deformity.

Similar observations on tree recovery were reported by Fenton (1959). He observed that most 3- to 6-year-old Virginia pine (Pinus virginiana) seedlings, severely bent by heavy snows the previous winter, returned to a near-normal position during the first 2 months of the growing season. Although snow injury was minor to seedlings, saplings were severely damaged. Fenton believes that basal sweep, a defect common to larger Virginia pine, may be due to snow damage early in the life of the tree. Basal sweep is often seen on seedlings and saplings in the upper-slope forests of Washington and Oregon.

Since none of the study trees were cut, formation of reaction wood induced by heavy snow load was not observed. Young upper-slope conifers are often subject to heavy snow loads and consequent bending. Compression wood forms on the underside of bent trees and helps straighten the stem (Brown et al. 1949). Trees which are unable to straighten themselves form this wood indefinitely (Paul 1959). Since most trees observed in this study recovered quickly, compression wood formation will not be a major defect unless damage occurs repeatedly.

Snow damage may become more of a problem in upper-slope forests as management of these forests is intensified. Douglas-fir, a species observed here to be more susceptible to snow damage than its associates, is currently used to regenerate most upper-slope cutovers. Literature on snow damage shows that degree and timing of thinning can influence amount of damage. Generally, newly thinned--particularly, heavily thinned--sapling stands are especially vulnerable. Trees become more resistant to snow damage as their root systems expand and stems become stouter. Frequent, light thinnings, beginning at an early age, will help make stands more resistant to snow breakage and windfall (Rosenfeld 1944; Zeidler 1944; Roe and Stoeckeler 1950).

LITERATURE CITED

Brown, H. P., Panshin, A. J., and Forsaith, C. C.
    1949. Textbook of wood technology. Vol. 1, 652 pp., illus.
           New York, Toronto [etc.]: McGraw-Hill Book Co., Inc.

Douglas-fir Second-Growth Management Committee.
    1947. Management of second-growth forests in the Douglas-fir
           region. U.S. Forest Serv. Pacific Northwest Forest &
           Range Exp. Sta., 151 pp., illus.

Fenton, Richard H.
    1959. Heavy snowfalls damage Virginia pine. U.S. Forest Serv.
           Northeast. Forest Exp. Sta. Sta. Pap. 127, 7 pp., illus.

Paul, Benson H.
    1959. The effect of environmental factors on wood quality. U.S.
           Forest Serv. Forest Prod. Lab. Rep. 2170, 48 pp.

Roe, Eugene I., and Stoeckeler, Joseph H.
    1950. Thinning over-dense jack pine seedling stands in the Lake
           States. J. Forest. 48: 861-865, illus.

Rosenfeld, W.
    1944. Erforschung der Bruchkatastrophen in den Ostschlesischen
           Beskiden in der Zeit von 1875-1942. Forstwiss. Centralbl.
           u. Thorandter Forstl. Jahrb. 1944(1): 1-31, illus.
           [English abstract in Biol. Abstr. 19: 19914. 1945.]

U.S. Weather Bureau.
    1964. Climatological data, Oregon. Vol. 7, Nos. 2-7.

Watt, Richard F.
    1951. Snow damage in a pole stand of western white pine. U.S.
           Forest Serv. Norch. Rocky Mountain Forest & Range Exp. Sta.
           Res. Note 92, 4 pp.

Zeidler, G.
    1944. Die Fichtenwirtschaft in Südwestfalen. Gedanken zu den
           Katastrophen der letzten Jahre. Forstarchiv 20(1/2): 15-29,
           illus. [English abstract in Biol. Abstr. 19: 14383. 1945.]

A FORMULA FOR THE DOUGLAS-FIR TOTAL CUBIC-FOOT VOLUME TABLE FROM BULLETIN 201

by

Robert O. Curtis, Mensurationist

The total cubic-foot volume table given by McArdle et al.[1] has been in common use in the Douglas-fir region for many years. In recent years, use of tables and interpolation has increasingly been supplanted by automatic data processing. For such use, volume equations are far more convenient than are tables.

Because of a need for a volume equation equivalent to the table previously used, an equation has been derived representing table 12 of Bulletin 201. Since this table was prepared by graphical methods, it cannot be exactly reproduced by a mathematical equation. However, the equation given below does closely approximate the values of the original table and is suitable for use with electronic computers.

The equation is:

$$\log V = -\,2.10299 + 3.94426(\log D) + 0.16352\left(\frac{H}{100}\right)$$

$$-\,0.80523(\log D)^2 - 0.04705\left(\frac{100}{H}\right) - 0.10849(\log D)\left(\frac{100}{H}\right)$$

$$+\,0.27677\left(\frac{1}{\log D}\right) + 0.02815\left(\frac{H}{100}\right)^2 + 0.00140\left(\frac{D}{10}\right)^2\left(\frac{H}{100}\right)$$

---

[1] McArdle, Richard E., Meyer, Walter H., and Bruce, Donald. The yield of Douglas fir in the Pacific Northwest. U.S. Dep. Agr. Tech. Bull. 201 (rev.), 74 pp. 1961.

where:

V is total cubic-foot volume, including stump and tip.

D is diameter at breast height in inches.

H is total height in feet.

Common logarithms (base 10) are used.

The equation was checked by calculating differences between predicted volumes and the values given in the table; it agrees closely over the range of diameters and heights within the heavy line in the original table. A partial tabulation of these percentage differences is given in table 1.

Volumes calculated by this equation for individual trees 3 inches to 30 inches d.b.h. are listed in table 2 by 1/10-inch intervals of diameter and by 10-foot intervals of height. Since the relationship of volume to height is not strongly curvilinear, straight-line interpolation within 10-foot intervals of height will not introduce appreciable errors.

Table 1.--Partial tabulation of differences between volumes given by equation and by original table, expressed as percent of original table value

D.b.h. (inches)	Total height in feet										
	20	40	60	80	100	120	140	160	180	200	220
	-------------------------------- Percent ---------------------------------										
4	-7.3	-0.4	-10.0	--	--	--	--	--	--	--	--
6	--	1.8	-1.0	--	--	--	--	--	--	--	--
8	--	3.2	3.7	-2.9	--	--	--	--	--	--	--
10	--	--	2.4	.3	1.8	0.4	--	--	--	--	--
12	--	--	1.6	1.0	2.1	.4	--	--	--	--	--
16	--	--	--	-1.8	-1.2	.4	-0.2	0.6	--	--	--
20	--	--	--	--	-2.3	.2	-.4	-.1	0.5	--	--
24	--	--	--	--	--	0	.9	.2	.4	1.2	--
28	--	--	--	--	--	-.1	1.4	-.2	-3.0	-.1	--
32	--	--	--	--	--	--	1.1	-.3	-1.4	-.5	0.3
36	--	--	--	--	--	--	--	-.1	-.5	-.6	-.4
40	--	--	--	--	--	--	--	1.3	.2	-.7	-.9
44	--	--	--	--	--	--	--	2.1	1.0	-.8	--
48	--	--	--	--	--	--	--	--	--	-.4	--
52	--	--	--	--	--	--	--	--	--	-.1	--

TABLE 2. SOLUTIONS OF THE VOLUME EQUATION. TOTAL CUBIC FEET, INCLUDING STUMP AND TIP

DBH (inches)	TOTAL HEIGHT IN FEET																			
	20	30	40	50	60	70	80	90	100	110	120	130	140	150	160	170	180	190	200	210
2.6	0.43	0.64																		
2.7	.45	.67																		
2.8	.47	.71																		
2.9	.50	.75																		
3.0	.52	.79																		
3.1	.54	.83																		
3.2	.57	.88																		
3.3	.60	.93																		
3.4	.63	.98																		
3.5	.66	1.03																		
3.6	.69	1.08	1.38	1.64	1.86															
3.7	.72	1.13	1.46	1.72	1.96															
3.8	.75	1.19	1.53	1.82	2.07															
3.9	.78	1.25	1.61	1.91	2.18															
4.0	.82	1.31	1.69	2.01	2.29															
4.1	.85	1.37	1.78	2.11	2.41															
4.2	.89	1.43	1.86	2.22	2.53															
4.3	.92	1.50	1.95	2.33	2.66															
4.4	.96	1.56	2.04	2.44	2.79															
4.5	1.00	1.63	2.13	2.55	2.92															
4.6	1.03	1.70	2.23	2.67	3.06	3.42														
4.7	1.07	1.77	2.32	2.79	3.20	3.57														
4.8	1.11	1.84	2.42	2.91	3.34	3.73														
4.9	1.15	1.91	2.52	3.03	3.48	3.90														
5.0	1.19	1.99	2.63	3.16	3.63	4.07														
5.1	1.23	2.06	2.73	3.29	3.78	4.24														
5.2	1.27	2.14	2.84	3.42	3.94	4.42														
5.3	1.32	2.22	2.95	3.56	4.10	4.60														
5.4	1.36	2.30	3.06	3.70	4.26	4.78														
5.5	1.40	2.38	3.17	3.84	4.42	4.97														
5.6		2.46	3.29	3.98	4.59	5.16														
5.7		2.55	3.40	4.12	4.76	5.35														
5.8		2.63	3.52	4.27	4.94	5.55														
5.9		2.72	3.64	4.42	5.11	5.75														
6.0		2.80	3.77	4.58	5.29	5.96														
6.1		2.89	3.89	4.73	5.48	6.17														
6.2		2.98	4.02	4.89	5.66	6.38														
6.3		3.07	4.14	5.05	5.85	6.59														
6.4		3.16	4.27	5.21	6.04	6.81														
6.5		3.26	4.40	5.37	6.24	7.03														
6.6		3.35	4.54	5.54	6.43	7.26	8.05	8.83												
6.7		3.44	4.67	5.71	6.63	7.49	8.30	9.11												
6.8		3.54	4.81	5.88	6.83	7.72	8.56	9.40												
6.9		3.64	4.94	6.05	7.04	7.95	8.83	9.69												
7.0		3.73	5.08	6.23	7.25	8.19	9.09	9.98												
7.1		3.83	5.22	6.41	7.46	8.43	9.36	10.28												
7.2		3.93	5.36	6.59	7.67	8.67	9.64	10.58												
7.3		4.03	5.51	6.77	7.88	8.92	9.91	10.89												
7.4		4.13	5.65	6.95	8.10	9.17	10.19	11.20												
7.5		4.23	5.80	7.14	8.32	9.42	10.48	11.51												

TABLE 2. SOLUTIONS OF THE VOLUME EQUATION. TOTAL CUBIC FEET, INCLUDING STUMP AND TIP--Continued

DBH (inches)	TOTAL HEIGHT IN FEET																			
	20	30	40	50	60	70	80	90	100	110	120	130	140	150	160	170	180	190	200	210
7.6			5.95	7.32	8.55	9.68	10.76	11.83												
7.7			6.10	7.51	8.77	9.94	11.05	12.15												
7.8			6.23	7.70	9.00	10.20	11.34	12.47												
7.9			6.40	7.90	9.23	10.46	11.64	12.80												
8.0			6.55	8.09	9.46	10.73	11.94	13.13												
8.1			6.71	8.29	9.69	11.00	12.24	13.47												
8.2			6.86	8.49	9.93	11.27	12.55	13.81												
8.3			7.02	8.69	10.17	11.54	12.86	14.15												
8.4			7.18	8.89	10.41	11.82	13.17	14.50												
8.5			7.34	9.09	10.65	12.10	13.49	14.85												
8.6			7.50	9.30	10.90	12.38	13.80	15.20	16.60	18.03										
8.7			7.66	9.50	11.15	12.67	14.12	15.56	16.99	18.46										
8.8			7.83	9.71	11.40	12.96	14.45	15.92	17.39	18.89										
8.9			7.99	9.92	11.65	13.25	14.78	16.28	17.79	19.33										
9.0			8.16	10.13	11.90	13.54	15.11	16.65	18.19	19.77										
9.1			8.32	10.35	12.16	13.83	15.44	17.01	18.60	20.21										
9.2			8.49	10.56	12.41	14.13	15.77	17.39	19.01	20.66										
9.3			8.66	10.78	12.67	14.43	16.11	17.76	19.42	21.11										
9.4			8.83	11.00	12.94	14.73	16.45	18.14	19.84	21.56										
9.5			9.00	11.22	13.20	15.04	16.79	18.52	20.26	22.02										
9.6			9.17	11.44	13.46	15.34	17.14	18.91	20.68	22.48	24.35									
9.7			9.35	11.66	13.73	15.65	17.49	19.29	21.11	22.95	24.86									
9.8			9.52	11.89	14.00	15.96	17.84	19.69	21.54	23.42	25.37									
9.9			9.70	12.11	14.27	16.27	18.19	20.08	21.97	23.89	25.88									
10.0			9.87	12.34	14.54	16.59	18.35	20.47	22.40	24.37	26.40									
10.1			10.0	12.6	14.8	16.9	18.9	20.9	22.8	24.9	26.9									
10.2			10.2	12.8	15.1	17.2	19.3	21.3	23.3	25.3	27.5									
10.3			10.4	13.0	15.4	17.5	19.6	21.7	23.7	25.8	28.0									
10.4			10.6	13.3	15.7	17.9	20.0	22.1	24.2	26.3	28.5									
10.5			10.8	13.5	15.9	18.2	20.4	22.5	24.6	26.8	29.1									
10.6			10.9	13.7	16.2	18.5	20.7	22.9	25.1	27.3	29.6									
10.7			11.1	14.0	16.5	18.9	21.1	23.3	25.5	27.8	30.1									
10.8			11.3	14.2	16.8	19.2	21.5	23.7	26.0	28.3	30.7									
10.9			11.5	14.4	17.1	19.5	21.9	24.2	26.5	28.8	31.2									
11.0			11.7	14.7	17.4	19.9	22.2	24.6	26.9	29.3	31.8									
11.1			11.9	14.9	17.7	20.2	22.6	25.0	27.4	29.8	32.4									
11.2			12.2	15.2	17.9	20.5	23.0	25.4	27.9	30.4	32.9									
11.3			12.2	15.4	18.2	20.9	23.4	25.9	28.4	30.9	33.5									
11.4			12.4	15.6	18.5	21.2	23.8	26.3	28.8	31.4	34.1									
11.5			12.6	15.9	18.8	21.6	24.2	26.7	29.3	31.9	34.6									
11.6				16.1	19.1	21.9	24.6	27.2	29.8	32.5	35.2	38.1								
11.7				16.4	19.4	22.3	25.0	27.6	30.3	33.0	35.8	38.7								
11.8				16.6	19.7	22.6	25.4	28.1	30.8	33.5	36.4	39.3								
11.9				16.9	20.0	23.0	25.8	28.5	31.3	34.1	37.0	40.0								
12.0				17.1	20.3	23.3	26.2	29.0	31.8	34.6	37.6	40.6								
12.1				17.4	20.6	23.7	26.6	29.4	32.3	35.2	38.1	41.3								
12.2				17.6	20.9	24.0	27.0	29.9	32.7	35.7	38.7	41.9								
12.3				17.9	21.2	24.4	27.4	30.3	33.2	36.2	39.3	42.6								
12.4				18.1	21.6	24.7	27.8	30.8	33.8	36.8	39.9	43.2								
12.5				18.4	21.9	25.1	28.2	31.2	34.3	37.4	40.5	43.9								

TABLE 2. SOLUTIONS OF THE VOLUME EQUATION. TOTAL CUBIC FEET, INCLUDING STUMP AND TIP--Continued

DBH (inches)	20	30	40	50	60	70	80	90	100	110	120	130	140	150	160	170	180	190	200	210
12.6				18.7	22.2	25.5	28.6	31.7	34.8	37.9	41.2	44.5	48.1	51.8						
12.7				18.9	22.5	26.0	29.0	32.1	35.3	38.5	41.8	45.2	48.8	52.6						
12.8				19.2	22.8	26.2	29.4	32.6	35.8	39.0	42.4	45.9	49.5	53.4						
12.9				19.4	23.1	26.5	29.8	33.1	36.3	39.6	43.0	46.5	50.3	54.2						
13.0				19.7	23.4	26.9	30.3	33.5	36.8	40.2	43.6	47.2	51.0	55.0						
13.1				19.9	23.7	27.3	30.7	34.0	37.3	40.7	44.2	47.9	51.7	55.8						
13.2				20.2	24.1	27.7	31.1	34.5	37.9	41.3	44.9	48.6	52.5	56.6						
13.3				20.5	24.4	28.0	31.5	35.0	38.4	41.9	45.5	49.2	53.2	57.4						
13.4				20.7	24.7	28.4	31.9	35.4	38.9	42.5	46.1	49.9	53.9	58.2						
13.5				21.0	25.0	28.8	32.4	35.9	39.4	43.0	46.8	50.6	54.7	59.0						
13.6					25.3	29.2	32.8	36.4	40.0	43.6	47.4	51.3	55.4	59.8						
13.7					25.7	29.5	33.2	36.9	40.5	44.2	48.0	52.0	56.2	60.6						
13.8					26.0	29.9	33.7	37.3	41.0	44.8	48.7	52.7	56.9	61.4						
13.9					26.3	30.3	34.1	37.8	41.6	45.4	49.3	53.4	57.7	62.2						
14.0					26.6	30.7	34.5	38.3	42.1	46.0	50.0	54.1	58.5	63.1						
14.1					27.0	31.1	35.0	38.8	42.6	46.6	50.6	54.8	59.2	63.9						
14.2					27.3	31.4	35.4	39.3	43.2	47.2	51.3	55.5	60.0	64.7						
14.3					27.6	31.8	35.8	39.8	43.7	47.8	51.9	56.2	60.8	65.6						
14.4					28.0	32.1	36.3	40.3	44.3	48.4	52.6	56.9	61.5	66.4						
14.5					28.3	32.6	36.7	40.8	44.8	49.0	53.2	57.7	62.3	67.2						
14.6					28.6	32.9	37.2	41.3	45.4	49.6	53.9	58.4	63.1	68.1						
14.7					29.0	33.4	37.6	41.8	45.9	50.2	54.5	59.1	63.9	68.9						
14.8					29.3	33.8	38.0	42.3	46.5	50.8	55.2	59.8	64.7	69.8						
14.9					29.6	34.1	38.5	42.8	47.0	51.4	55.9	60.5	65.5	70.6						
15.0					30.0	34.5	38.9	43.3	47.6	52.0	56.5	61.3	66.2	71.5						
15.1					30.3	34.9	39.4	43.8	48.2	52.6	57.2	62.0	67.0	72.4						
15.2					30.6	35.3	39.8	44.3	48.7	53.2	57.9	62.7	67.8	73.2						
15.3					31.0	35.7	40.3	44.8	49.3	53.8	58.6	63.5	68.6	74.1						
15.4					31.3	36.1	40.7	45.3	49.8	54.5	59.2	64.2	69.4	74.9						
15.5					31.6	36.5	41.2	45.8	50.4	55.1	59.9	64.9	70.2	75.8						
15.6					32.0	36.9	41.7	46.3	51.0	55.7	60.6	65.7	71.0	76.7	82.7					
15.7					32.3	37.3	42.1	46.8	51.5	56.3	61.3	66.4	71.8	77.6	83.7					
15.8					32.7	37.7	42.6	47.3	52.1	57.0	62.0	67.2	72.7	78.4	84.6					
15.9					33.0	38.1	43.0	47.8	52.7	57.6	62.7	67.9	73.5	79.3	85.6					
16.0					33.3	38.5	43.5	48.4	53.2	58.2	63.3	68.7	74.3	80.2	86.5					
16.1					33.7	38.9	43.9	48.9	53.8	58.9	64.0	69.4	75.1	81.1	87.5					
16.2					34.0	39.3	44.4	49.4	54.4	59.5	64.7	70.2	75.9	82.0	88.4					
16.3					34.4	39.7	44.9	49.9	55.0	60.1	65.4	70.9	76.7	82.9	89.4					
16.4					34.7	40.1	45.3	50.4	55.6	60.8	66.1	71.7	77.6	83.8	90.4					
16.5					35.1	40.5	45.8	51.0	56.1	61.4	66.8	72.5	78.4	84.7	91.3					
16.6						40.9	46.3	51.5	56.7	62.0	67.5	73.2	79.2	85.6	92.3					
16.7						41.4	46.7	52.0	57.3	62.7	68.2	74.0	80.1	86.5	93.3					
16.8						41.8	47.2	52.5	57.9	63.3	68.9	74.8	80.9	87.4	94.3					
16.9						42.2	47.7	53.1	58.5	64.0	69.6	75.5	81.7	88.3	95.3					
17.0						42.6	48.1	53.6	59.0	64.6	70.3	76.3	82.6	89.2	96.2					
17.1						43.0	48.6	54.1	59.6	65.3	71.0	77.1	83.4	90.1	97.2					
17.2						43.4	49.0	54.6	60.2	65.9	71.8	77.9	84.3	91.0	98.2					
17.3						43.8	49.5	55.2	60.8	66.6	72.5	78.6	85.1	91.9	99.2					
17.4						44.2	50.0	55.7	61.4	67.2	73.2	79.4	85.9	92.9	100.2					
17.5						44.6	50.5	56.2	62.0	67.9	73.9	80.2	86.8	93.8	101.2					

DBH (inches)	20	30	40	50	60	70	80	90	100	110	120	130	140	150	160	170	180	190	200	210
											TOTAL HEIGHT IN FEET									
17.6						45.1	51.0	56.8	62.6	68.5	74.6	81.0	87.6	94.7	102.2					
17.7						45.5	51.4	57.3	63.2	69.2	75.3	81.8	88.5	95.6	103.2					
17.8						45.9	51.9	57.8	63.8	69.8	76.1	82.5	89.4	96.6	104.2					
17.9						46.3	52.4	58.4	64.4	70.5	76.8	83.3	90.2	97.5	105.2					
18.0						46.7	52.9	58.9	65.0	71.1	77.5	84.1	91.1	98.4	106.2					
18.1						47.1	53.4	59.5	65.6	71.8	78.2	84.9	91.9	99.4	107.2					
18.2						47.6	53.8	60.0	66.2	72.5	79.0	85.7	92.8	100.3	108.3					
18.3						48.0	54.3	60.5	66.8	73.1	79.7	86.5	93.7	101.2	109.3					
18.4						48.4	54.8	61.1	67.4	73.8	80.4	87.3	94.5	102.2	110.3					
18.5						48.8	55.3	61.6	68.0	74.5	81.1	88.1	95.4	103.1	111.3					
18.6						49.2	55.8	62.2	68.6	75.1	81.9	88.9	96.3	104.1	112.3	121.2	130.7	140.9		
18.7						49.7	56.2	62.7	69.2	75.8	82.6	89.7	97.1	105.0	113.4	122.3	131.9	142.2		
18.8						50.1	56.7	63.3	69.8	76.5	83.3	90.5	98.0	105.9	114.4	123.4	133.1	143.5		
18.9						50.5	57.2	63.8	70.4	77.1	84.1	91.3	98.9	106.9	115.4	124.5	134.3	144.8		
19.0						50.9	57.7	64.4	71.0	77.8	84.8	92.1	99.8	107.8	116.4	125.6	135.5	146.1		
19.1						51.3	58.2	64.9	71.6	78.5	85.6	92.9	100.6	108.8	117.5	126.8	136.7	147.4		
19.2						51.8	58.7	65.4	72.2	79.2	86.3	93.7	101.5	109.8	118.5	127.9	137.9	148.7		
19.3						52.2	59.2	66.0	72.9	79.8	87.0	94.5	102.4	110.7	119.6	129.0	139.1	150.0		
19.4						52.6	59.6	66.5	73.5	80.5	87.8	95.3	103.3	111.7	120.6	130.1	140.3	151.3		
19.5						53.0	60.1	67.1	74.1	81.2	88.5	96.2	104.2	112.6	121.6	131.3	141.6	152.7		
19.6								67.6	74.7	81.9	89.3	97.0	105.0	113.6	122.7	132.4	142.8	154.0		
19.7								68.2	75.3	82.6	90.0	97.8	105.9	114.6	123.7	133.5	144.0	155.3		
19.8								68.8	75.9	83.2	90.8	98.6	106.8	115.5	124.8	134.7	145.2	156.6		
19.9								69.3	76.5	83.9	91.5	99.4	107.7	116.5	125.8	135.8	146.5	158.0		
20.0								69.9	77.2	84.6	92.3	100.2	108.6	117.5	126.9	136.9	147.7	159.3		
20.1								70.4	77.8	85.3	93.0	101.1	109.5	118.4	127.9	138.1	148.9	160.6		
20.2								71.0	78.4	86.0	93.8	101.9	110.4	119.4	129.0	139.2	150.2	162.0		
20.3								71.5	79.0	86.6	94.5	102.7	111.3	120.4	130.0	140.4	151.4	163.3		
20.4								72.1	79.6	87.3	95.3	103.5	112.2	121.4	131.1	141.5	152.7	164.7		
20.5								72.6	80.3	88.0	96.0	104.3	113.1	122.3	132.2	142.7	153.9	166.0		
20.6								73.2	80.9	88.7	96.8	105.2	114.0	123.3	133.2	143.8	155.2	167.4		
20.7								73.8	81.5	89.4	97.5	106.0	114.9	124.3	134.3	145.0	156.4	168.7		
20.8								74.3	82.1	90.1	98.3	106.8	115.8	125.3	135.4	146.1	157.7	170.1		
20.9								74.9	82.8	90.8	99.1	107.7	116.7	126.3	136.4	147.3	158.9	171.4		
21.0								75.4	83.4	91.5	99.8	108.5	117.6	127.2	137.5	148.4	160.2	172.8		
21.1								76.0	84.0	92.2	100.6	109.3	118.5	128.2	138.6	149.6	161.4	174.2		
21.2								76.6	84.6	92.9	101.3	110.2	119.4	129.2	139.6	150.8	162.7	175.5		
21.3								77.1	85.3	93.6	102.1	111.0	120.3	130.2	140.7	151.9	163.9	176.9		
21.4								77.7	85.9	94.2	102.9	111.8	121.2	131.2	141.8	153.1	165.2	178.3		
21.5								78.3	86.5	94.9	103.6	112.7	122.2	132.2	142.9	154.3	166.5	179.6		
21.6									87.2	95.6	104.4	113.5	123.1	133.2	143.9	155.4	167.7	181.0		
21.7									87.8	96.3	105.2	114.3	124.0	134.2	145.0	156.6	169.0	182.4		
21.8									88.4	97.0	105.9	115.2	124.9	135.2	146.1	157.8	170.3	183.8		
21.9									89.0	97.7	106.7	116.0	125.8	136.2	147.2	158.9	171.6	185.1		
22.0									89.7	98.4	107.5	116.9	126.7	137.2	148.3	160.1	172.8	186.5		
22.1									90.3	99.1	108.2	117.7	127.7	138.2	149.4	161.3	174.1	187.9		
22.2									90.9	99.8	109.0	118.5	128.6	139.2	150.4	162.5	175.4	189.3		
22.3									91.6	100.5	109.8	119.4	129.5	140.2	151.5	163.7	176.7	190.7		
22.4									92.2	101.2	110.5	120.2	130.4	141.2	152.6	164.8	178.0	192.1		
22.5									92.9	101.9	111.3	121.1	131.3	142.2	153.7	166.0	179.2	193.5		

TABLE 2. SOLUTIONS OF THE VOLUME EQUATION. TOTAL CUBIC FEET, INCLUDING STUMP AND TIP--Continued

DBH (inches)	20	30	40	50	60	70	80	90	100	110	120	130	140	150	160	170	180	190	200	210
								TOTAL HEIGHT IN FEET												
22.6									93.5	102.6	112.1	121.9	132.3	143.2	154.8	167.2	180.5	194.8	210.3	227.0
22.7									94.1	103.4	112.9	122.8	133.2	144.2	155.9	168.4	181.8	196.2	211.8	228.7
22.8									94.8	104.1	113.6	123.6	134.1	145.2	157.0	169.6	183.1	197.6	213.3	230.3
22.9									95.4	104.8	114.4	124.5	135.0	146.2	158.1	170.8	184.4	199.0	214.8	231.9
23.0									96.0	105.5	115.2	125.3	136.0	147.2	159.2	172.0	185.7	200.4	216.4	233.6
23.1									96.7	106.2	116.0	126.2	136.9	148.2	160.3	173.2	187.0	201.8	217.9	235.2
23.2									97.3	106.9	116.8	127.0	137.8	149.3	161.4	174.4	188.3	203.3	219.4	236.9
23.3									97.9	107.6	117.5	127.9	138.8	150.3	162.5	175.6	189.6	204.7	220.9	238.5
23.4									98.6	108.3	118.3	128.7	139.7	151.3	163.6	176.8	190.9	206.1	222.5	240.2
23.5									99.2	109.0	119.1	129.6	140.6	152.3	164.7	178.0	192.2	207.5	224.0	241.9
23.6									99.9	109.7	119.9	130.5	141.6	153.3	165.8	179.2	193.5	208.9	225.5	243.5
23.7									100.5	110.4	120.7	131.3	142.5	154.3	166.9	180.4	194.8	210.3	227.1	245.2
23.8									101.2	111.1	121.4	132.2	143.4	155.4	168.0	181.6	196.1	211.7	228.6	246.8
23.9									101.8	111.9	122.2	133.0	144.4	156.4	169.1	182.8	197.4	213.1	230.1	248.5
24.0									102.4	112.6	123.0	133.9	145.3	157.4	170.3	184.0	198.7	214.6	231.7	250.2
24.1									103.1	113.3	123.8	134.8	146.3	158.4	171.4	185.2	200.0	216.0	233.2	251.9
24.2									103.7	114.0	124.6	135.6	147.2	159.5	172.5	186.4	201.3	217.4	234.8	253.5
24.3									104.4	114.7	125.4	136.5	148.1	160.3	173.6	187.6	202.7	218.8	236.3	255.2
24.4									105.0	115.4	126.2	137.3	149.1	161.5	174.7	188.8	204.0	220.3	237.9	256.9
24.5									105.7	116.1	126.9	138.2	150.0	162.5	175.8	190.0	205.3	221.7	239.4	258.6
24.6									106.3	116.8	127.7	139.1	151.0	163.6	177.0	191.3	206.6	223.1	241.0	260.2
24.7									106.9	117.6	128.5	139.9	151.9	164.6	178.1	192.5	207.9	224.6	242.5	261.9
24.8									107.6	118.3	129.3	140.8	152.9	165.6	179.2	193.7	209.2	226.0	244.1	263.6
24.9									108.2	119.0	130.1	141.7	153.8	166.7	180.3	194.9	210.6	227.4	245.6	265.3
25.0									108.9	119.7	130.9	142.5	154.8	167.7	181.4	196.1	211.9	228.9	247.2	267.0
25.1									109.5	120.4	131.7	143.4	155.7	168.7	182.6	197.4	213.2	230.3	248.7	268.7
25.2									110.2	121.1	132.5	144.3	156.6	169.8	183.7	198.6	214.5	231.7	250.3	270.4
25.3									110.8	121.9	133.3	145.1	157.6	170.8	184.8	199.8	215.9	233.2	251.9	272.1
25.4									111.5	122.6	134.0	146.0	158.5	171.8	185.9	201.0	217.2	234.6	253.4	273.8
25.5									112.1	123.3	134.8	146.9	159.5	172.9	187.1	202.2	218.5	236.1	255.0	275.5
25.6									112.8	124.0	135.6	147.7	160.4	173.9	188.2	203.5	219.9	237.5	256.6	277.2
25.7									113.4	124.7	136.4	148.6	161.4	174.9	189.3	204.7	221.2	239.0	258.1	278.9
25.8									114.1	125.5	137.2	149.5	162.4	176.0	190.5	205.9	222.5	240.4	259.7	280.6
25.9									114.7	126.2	138.0	150.4	163.3	177.0	191.6	207.2	223.9	241.9	261.3	282.3
26.0									115.3	126.9	138.8	151.2	164.3	178.1	192.7	208.4	225.2	243.3	262.9	284.0
26.1									116.0	127.6	139.6	152.1	165.2	179.1	193.9	209.6	226.6	244.8	264.4	285.7
26.2									116.6	128.3	140.4	153.0	166.2	180.1	195.0	210.9	227.9	246.2	266.0	287.4
26.3									117.3	129.1	141.2	153.8	167.1	181.2	196.1	212.1	229.2	247.7	267.6	289.2
26.4									117.9	129.8	142.0	154.7	168.1	182.2	197.3	213.3	230.6	249.1	269.2	290.9
26.5									118.6	130.5	142.8	155.6	169.0	183.3	198.4	214.6	231.9	250.6	270.4	292.6
26.6									119.2	131.2	143.6	156.5	170.0	184.3	199.5	215.8	233.3	252.1	272.4	294.3
26.7									119.9	132.0	144.5	157.3	171.0	185.4	200.7	217.1	234.6	253.5	273.9	296.0
26.8									120.5	132.7	145.2	158.2	171.9	186.4	201.8	218.3	236.0	255.0	275.5	297.8
26.9									121.2	133.4	146.0	159.1	172.9	187.5	202.9	219.5	237.3	256.5	277.1	299.5
27.0									121.8	134.1	146.8	160.0	173.8	188.5	204.1	220.8	238.7	258.1	278.7	301.2
27.1									122.5	134.8	147.6	160.9	174.8	189.6	205.2	222.0	240.0	259.4	280.3	303.0
27.2									123.2	135.6	148.4	161.7	175.8	190.6	206.4	223.3	241.4	260.9	281.9	304.7
27.3									123.8	136.3	149.2	162.6	176.7	191.7	207.5	224.5	242.7	262.3	283.5	306.4
27.4									124.5	137.0	150.0	163.5	177.7	192.7	208.7	225.8	244.1	263.8	285.1	308.2
27.5									125.1	137.7	150.8	164.4	178.7	193.8	209.8	227.0	245.4	265.3	286.7	309.9

TABLE 2. SOLUTIONS OF THE VOLUME EQUATION, TOTAL CUBIC FEET, INCLUDING STUMP AND TIP--Continued

DBH (inches)	TOTAL HEIGHT IN FEET																				
	20	30	40	50	60	70	80	90	100	110	120	130	140	150	160	170	180	190	200	210
27.6										138.5	151.6	165.3	179.6	194.8	211.0	228.3	246.8	266.8	289.3	311.6
27.7										139.2	152.4	166.1	180.6	195.9	212.1	229.5	248.1	268.2	289.9	313.4
27.8										139.9	153.2	167.0	181.5	196.9	213.3	230.8	249.5	269.7	291.5	315.1
27.9										140.6	154.0	167.9	182.5	198.0	214.4	232.0	250.9	271.2	293.1	316.9
28.0										141.4	154.8	168.8	183.5	199.0	215.6	233.3	252.2	272.7	294.7	318.6
28.1										142.1	155.6	169.7	184.4	200.1	216.7	234.5	253.6	274.1	296.3	320.4
28.2										142.8	156.4	170.5	185.4	201.1	217.9	235.8	255.0	275.6	298.0	322.1
28.3										143.6	157.2	171.4	186.4	202.2	219.0	237.0	256.3	277.1	299.6	323.9
28.4										144.3	158.0	172.3	187.3	203.3	220.2	238.3	257.7	278.6	301.2	325.6
28.5										145.0	158.8	173.2	188.3	204.3	221.3	239.5	259.1	280.1	302.8	327.4
28.6										145.7	159.6	174.1	189.3	205.4	222.5	240.8	260.4	281.6	304.4	329.1
28.7										146.5	160.4	175.0	190.3	206.4	223.6	242.0	261.8	283.1	306.0	330.9
28.8										147.2	161.2	175.8	191.2	207.5	224.8	243.3	263.2	284.6	307.6	332.7
28.9										147.9	162.0	176.7	192.2	208.6	226.0	244.6	264.5	286.0	309.3	334.4
29.0										148.6	162.8	177.6	193.2	209.6	227.1	245.8	265.9	287.5	310.9	336.2
29.1										149.4	163.6	178.5	194.1	210.7	228.3	247.1	267.3	289.0	312.5	337.9
29.2										150.1	164.4	179.4	195.1	211.7	229.4	248.3	268.7	290.5	314.1	339.7
29.3										150.8	165.3	180.3	196.1	212.8	230.6	249.6	270.0	292.0	315.8	341.5
29.4										151.6	166.1	181.2	197.1	213.9	231.8	250.9	271.4	293.5	317.4	343.3
29.5										152.3	166.9	182.1	198.0	214.9	232.9	252.1	272.8	295.0	319.0	345.0
29.6										153.0	167.7	182.9	199.0	216.0	234.1	253.4	274.2	296.5	320.7	346.8
29.7										153.7	168.5	183.8	200.0	217.1	235.2	254.7	275.5	298.0	322.3	348.6
29.8										154.5	169.3	184.7	200.9	218.1	236.4	255.9	276.9	299.5	323.9	350.3
29.9										155.2	170.1	185.6	201.9	219.2	237.6	257.2	278.3	301.0	325.6	352.1
30.0										155.9	170.9	186.5	202.9	220.3	238.7	258.5	279.7	302.5	327.2	353.9
30.1										156.7	171.7	187.4	203.9	221.3	239.9	259.7	281.1	304.0	328.8	355.7
30.2										157.4	172.5	188.3	204.9	222.4	241.1	261.0	282.4	305.5	330.5	357.5
30.3										158.1	173.3	189.2	205.8	223.5	242.2	262.3	283.8	307.0	332.1	359.3
30.4										158.9	174.1	190.1	206.8	224.5	243.4	263.6	285.2	308.5	333.7	361.0
30.5										159.6	174.9	190.9	207.8	225.6	244.6	264.8	286.6	310.1	335.4	362.8

FOREST AND RANGE EXPERIMENT STATION · U.S. DEPARTMENT OF AGRICULTURE · PORTLAND, OREGON

PNW-42   *September 1966*

COMPATIBILITY OF BALLOON FABRICS WITH AMMONIA

by

Hilton H. Lysons,
Principal Industrial Engineer

Our recent logging test of a single-hull balloon[1] identified
a major problem in connection with the high cost of inflation gas.
Helium, the currently preferred gas, is not only inherently costly
to produce, it is also expensive to transport and store in high-
pressure containers.

Previous efforts to reduce the cost of balloon inflation through
the use of hydrogen met with little acceptance due to its explosive
properties under a wide range of air mixtures. Other efforts to
reduce cost by using ammonia were limited to expendable balloons
where good fabric life and high static lift were relatively unimportant.

Previous research[2] has determined that a balloon's static lift
is only one of several forces available that may be combined to lift
and move the logs. Therefore, even though ammonia provides slightly
less than half the gross static lift of helium, it merits careful
consideration for a possible application in balloon logging.

---

[1] Lysons, Hilton H., Binkley, Virgil W., and Mann, Charles N.
Logging test of a single-hull balloon. U.S. Forest Serv. Res. Pap.
PNW-30, 20 pp., illus. 1966.

[2] Mann, Charles N. Forces in balloon logging. U.S. Forest
Serv. Res. Note PNW-28, 5 pp., illus. 1965.

A brief review of the properties of ammonia[3] showed that, although it can be made to explode when mixed with air, there is little likelihood of this occurring out-of-doors due to its very narrow explosive mixture range. Ammonia also presents certain toxic hazards, but its widespread use indicates that it can be safely handled by established procedures.

The two major advantages of ammonia for balloon inflation are:

1. It is very inexpensive when compared with helium.

2. It is readily transported in liquid form from widely available sources (1 ton of anhydrous ammonia produces 45,000 cubic feet of gas).[4]

Two important unknowns exist in connection with using ammonia in logging balloons:

1. Will it provide an adequate amount of static lift in a suitable logging balloon configuration?

2. Will it be compatible with present or future balloon fabrics?

Since the first question cannot be answered without specifying the balloon's fabric and weight, the second question was investigated. By Contract No. 19-50, the Pacific Northwest Forest and Range Experiment Station requested the GCA Viron Division, GCA Corporation, in Minneapolis, Minn., to determine the compatibility of representative balloon fabrics with ammonia.

This test, conducted under the direction of James A. Menke, project manager, GCA Viron Division, was completed in February 1966. The final report[5] is on file at this Station and is available to interested logging balloon designers and users.

The following information has been extracted from GCA Viron's final report to cover the most pertinent results.

3/ Manufacturers Chemists' Association, Inc. Properties and essential information for safe handling and use of anhydrous ammonia. Chemical Safety Data Sheet SD-8, 16 pp., illus. 1952.

4/ Compressed Gas Association, Inc. Anhydrous ammonia. Pamphlet G-2, 33 pp., illus. 1956.

5/ Menke, James A., and Ruffenbach, Gene. Compatibility of balloo fabrics with ammonia. Prepared by GCA Viron Division, GCA Corp., for Pacific Northwest Forest and Range Exp. Sta., Forest Serv., U.S. Dep. Agr., Portland, Oreg., 19 pp., illus. 1966.

I. OBJECTIVE

The objective of this program was to determine the compatibility
of representative balloon materials with ammonia. Use of ammonia as
a balloon inflatant is attractive because of its low cost, availability,
and compressiblity. Anhydrous ammonia and ammonia in combination with
water will react with many organic functional groups. As such, most
organic polymers will degrade on exposure to ammonia. Selected fabrics
were exposed to anhydrous ammonia (NH_3) and ammonium hydroxide (NH_4OH)
at a temperature of 125° F. for 8 weeks. Physical properties of the
fabrics were determined before, during, and after exposure.

II. TEST EQUIPMENT

A. Environmental chambers

Five transparent inflatable chambers were used to contain the
sample materials. Samples were hung from the top or submerged in
trays of water on the bottom of the chambers. Inflatable rather
than rigid containers were used to visually indicate ammonia leak-
age or absorption in water and thereby facilitate maintenance of
a high ammonia concentration. Each chamber had an inflation tube
extending outside the oven for refilling. Figure 1 shows the
environmental test setup.

B. Oven

The five containers were placed in a large oven and held at
125° F. Because ammonia is explosive (at a concentration of 16
to 25 percent with air), the electric heat source was placed
outside the oven and an open forced-air system was used. The
temperature of the oven was controlled by a thermostat. The
temperature was also monitored by a Brown Recorder to check
temperature range and stability.

C. Material testing equipment

1. A floor model TTC Instron was used to measure tensile
    strength (accuracy, 1 percent of full scale).

2. A Cambridge fabric permeameter was used to measure
    helium permeability (accuracy, 3 percent of full scale).

3. A Mettler Analytic Balance was used to measure change
    in weight (accuracy, $\pm$ 0.001 g.).

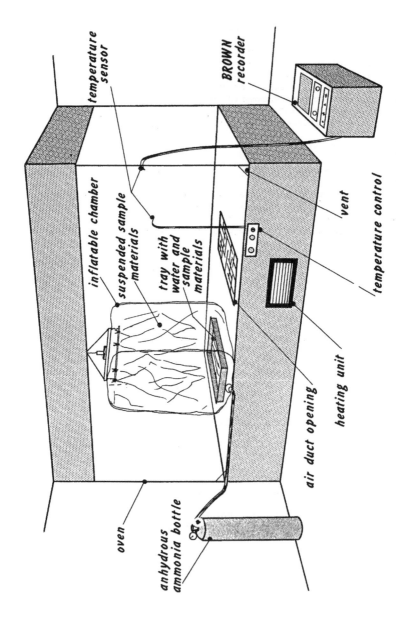

Figure 1.--Setup for testing compatibility of balloon fabrics with ammonia.

III. SELECTED MATERIALS AND ADHESIVES

Eleven representative balloon materials and three seam adhesives were tested. A description of these materials is in tables 1 and 2.

Table 1.--Selected materials

Material identi- fication number	Base fabric	Base fabric weight per square yard	Coating, side 1	Coating, side 2	Material weight per square yard
		Ounces			Ounces
1	Nylon	3.8	Urethane	Urethane	6.5
3	Nylon	5.1	Neoprene	Urethane	15.2
4	Nylon	5.1	Urethane	Uncoated	10.5
5	Nylon	5.1	Hypalon	Hypalon	19.5
6	Nylon	4.3	Urethane	Urethane	7.4
7	Nylon	3.85	Uncoated	Uncoated	3.85
8	Dacron	4.25	Uncoated	Uncoated	4.25
11	Nylon	6.4	Vinyl	Vinyl	21.0
12	Dacron	8.0	Hypalon	Hypalon	24.0
14	Glass cloth	3.1	Uncoated	Uncoated	3.1
18	Nylon	5.1	Neoprene	Neoprene	16.0

Table 2.--Selected seam adhesives

Material number	Adhesive
1, 4	Bostik 7074A and B
3	Caram 244
5, 11, 12	Fairprene 5149

Adhesives were selected for test on the basis of past experience and reliability. The seams were made by the cleaning, sanding, and coating methods described in the adhesive manufacturer's recommended procedure.

IV. TEST PROCEDURE

A. Material properties tests

The physical property tests to determine deterioration were conducted in accordance with the following test standards:

		CCC-T-191 b [1]	ASTM method [2]
1.	Strength and elongation, breaking of woven cloth; cut strip method	5102.1	
2.	Tear strength of cloth, tongue method	5134.1	
3.	Helium permeability of rubber-coated fabrics	--	D815-47
4.	Peel or stripping strength of adhesives	--	D903-49
5.	Adhesion of lapped seam	5102	
6.	Weight of cloth; small specimen method	5041	

[1] This is a Federal specification.

[2] American Society for Testing Materials.

The above tests were conducted on the fabrics both before and after the 8-week period. Tests 1, 3, and 5 were also run at 2-week intervals. Tests 2, 4, and 6 were run at the beginning of the test period and after 8 weeks' exposure.

B. Environment tests

Sample materials were placed in five sealed containers. Half the samples in each container were suspended from the top (NH_3 gas) with the remaining samples submerged in the water (NH_4OH). The water absorbed a large amount of NH_3; thus, the bags were refilled with ammonia until the water was saturated. The solubility of NH_3 in water is approximately 760 to 1 by volume. Each chamber had a temperature of 125° F. with a relative humidity of 100 percent (due to the tray of water). At 2-week intervals, samples of each material were removed from the container and the container resealed.

-6-

V. TEST RESULTS

A complete tabulation of test results is available, on request, to interested readers wishing additional information on any of the following materials:

Material No. 1

Tests were discontinued after 4 weeks because the urethane coating failed in both the NH_3 and NH_4OH environment. The urethane became brittle and cracked. It also powdered and began to fall off as shown by the weight loss. The Bostik 7074A and B adhesive became powdery almost instantly.

Material No. 3

The neoprene side survived but the urethane side was destroyed. The urethane side was brittle and cracked when folded. The deterioration affected only the urethane and not the neoprene or nylon. The Caram 244 adhesive was applied to the neoprene side only. Failure of the seams in the ammonium hydroxide was an adhesive failure. The Caram 244 became powdery after 8 weeks' immersion in NH_4OH.

Material No. 4

Tests were discontinued because the urethane coating failed. It became brittle and cracked. The Bostik 7074A and B seams separated during the first 2 weeks. The nylon was not affected.

Material No. 5

Tests were discontinued due to the failure of the hypalon coating. The white hypalon turned brown. This material absorbed a very large amount of water. The hypalon became very soft and it peeled off the nylon easily..The Fairprene 5149 adhesive turned brown in NH_3 but retained fairly significant strength. In NH_4OH the Fairprene 5149 became powdery.

Material No. 6

Tests were discontinued because the urethane coating failed. The coating began to fall off (in a powder form) during the first 2 weeks. This was shown by the weight loss.

Material No. 7

No deterioration was seen on the nylon fabric. It did become slightly stiffer after the test. (This stiffness could have been due to the presence of dissolved residues of the other samples in the NH_4OH.)

Material No. 8

The dacron was removed from test because it turned from white to brown and disintegrated.

Material No. 11

The yellow vinyl coating turned white. The vinyl became sticky to the touch and the permeability (leak rate) increased greatly. The point of seam failure could not be determined because the vinyl coating separated from the fabric and the adhesive.

Material No. 12

The fabric swelled during the first 2 weeks and then disintegrated. The hypalon turned brown and the seams had very little strength. Apparently, the seams failed because the hypalon became slimy. The Fairprene 5149 appeared to retain significant strength.

Material No. 14

The glass cloth did not show any visual deterioration, but it was much stiffer. The stiffness was probably due to the dissolved residues of other samples in the NH_4OH.

Material No. 18

The neoprene-nylon-neoprene did not show any deterioration due to the ammonia environment.

VI.   CONCLUSIONS AND RECOMMENDATIONS

The only fabric which showed favorable life test characteristics was nylon. The only coating which withstood NH_3 and NH_4OH environments was neoprene. Neoprene owes its special stability to the fact that each chlorine atom is linked to a double bonded carbon. (A halogen atom directly attached to an ethylenic carbon atom displays definitely diminished reactivity.)

In the NH_3 - 100-percent relative humidity water environment, both neoprene adhesives (Caram 244 and Fairprene 5149) showed a significant retention of strength. In ammonium hydroxide, both showed significant deterioration after 8 weeks' immersion. The ammonium hydroxide represents a severe environment in that it contains free hydroxide ions which react with many organic functional groups.

The chemical composition of the Caram 244 and Fairprene 5149 is proprietary by their manufacturers. It is thought that neoprene rubber is their major component.

This preliminary effort indicates that future use of NH₃ as an inflatant is reasonable. The neoprene-coated nylon fabric showed no deterioration in either NH₃ gas or NH₄OH after 8 weeks. Future work is indicated in two areas:

1. Neoprene is not considered to have good weathering character-istics. Composites of neoprene-nylon fabric-weatherable coating should be evaluated with the neoprene side exposed to the NH₃ environment.

2. An extensive evaluation of neoprene-base and other rubber-base adhesives should be pursued. Methods of crosslinking these rubber-base adhesives would be desirable from the stand-point of minimizing NH₃ attack and minimizing creep in the seams.

FOREST AND RANGE EXPERIMENT STATION · U.S. DEPARTMENT OF AGRICULTURE · PORTLAND, OREGON

PNW-43   *September 1966*

LABOR REQUIREMENTS IN THINNING DOUGLAS-FIR
AND WESTERN HEMLOCK ON TWO EXPERIMENTAL FORESTS
IN WESTERN WASHINGTON   *by Norman P. Worthington*

INTRODUCTION

Throughout the Douglas-fir subregion of western Oregon and western Washington, commercial thinnings of young-growth stands of Douglas-fir and western hemlock are increasing. Both research findings and operating experience have demonstrated increased stand productivity and profit from the thinnings.

The Pacific Northwest Forest and Range Experiment Station has been engaged in research over the past 20 years to discover some of the silvicultural and economic factors which would influence thinning practice. We have accumulated a series of time and production records from several studies of thinning methods.

NATURE OF STUDIES

This paper analyzes and discusses data obtained during thinning of young Douglas-fir and western hemlock in central western Washington using three skidding methods. Information is presented on how total labor requirements are affected by (1) volume thinned per acre and (2) average d.b.h. of trees cut.

During the period 1951 through 1965, records were obtained from seven different operators in 25 thinning operations.[1] Eleven of

---

[1] Size of Douglas-fir areas ranged from 31 to 44 acres and hemlock stands from 11 to 25 acres.

these were in 45- to 75-year-old site II Douglas-fir, with small quantities of cedar and western hemlock and up to 20 percent of alder, on the McCleary Experimental Forest near McCleary, Wash.[2/] Stand volumes were 5,000 to 8,000 cubic feet per acre in trees averaging 20 inches d.b.h. The remaining 14 thinning operations were in pure 50- to 60-year-old site II western hemlock on the Hemlock Experimental Forest near Hoquiam, Wash.,[3/] with stand volumes of 7,500 to 10,000 cubic feet per acre in trees averaging 18 inches d.b.h.

DESCRIPTION OF THINNING METHODS

The most obvious difference in the methods was in the skidding operation. Skidding was either by horse, crawler tractor, or a four-wheel rubber-tired tractor known as a Tree Farmer. Other operations were similar.

Trees were marked prior to cutting, and thinning was completed primarily during June through October of each year. Crews varied from one to five men, but generally were three: a tree feller, a horse skinner or tractor operator and loader, and a truck driver. Truck roads were already constructed before thinning began, at the rate of 1 mile for each 135 acres, and roadbuilding by contractors was not required.

Contractors were local loggers experienced in thinning or partial cutting. Generally they purchased the stumpage, based on individual tree marking tallies. Logs and pulpwood were disposed in the best market available to them. However, in about 20 percent of the cases, the thinnings were by a contract piece rate, with delivery to a market specified by the timber owner. All thinnings at McCleary were made into saw or veneer logs, whereas at Hemlock, 80 percent went into pulpwood. Trees were usually cut by powersaws into 12- to 20-foot lengths but occasionally 8-foot or 32-foot lengths. Loading generally was by a forklift hydraulic loader but occasionally with a portable swing boom or self-loading truck. Hauling was by 2-1/2-ton truck alone, or truck with either semi- or full trailer. In all instances, the operations were similar to those currently in use in the area, except that there was a tendency to use light equipment and small crews. The only unusual feature was the use of horses for skidding in some operations (fig. 1).

[2/] Maintained by the U.S. Forest Service in cooperation with the Simpson Timber Co.

[3/] Maintained by the U.S. Forest Service in cooperation with the St. Regis Paper Co.

Figure 1.--The only unusual feature was the use of horses for skidding on some operations.

Description of the thinning jobs (table 1) reveals considerable variation. Aside from the involvement of seven different contractors over the 15-year period, there were important differences in crew size and management skill. Also, there were differences in skidding methods and machinery, as well as in trucking distance and types of hauling equipment. These many differences may increase the value of the study, since any valid inferences are thus more generally applicable.

RECORDS

Daily time records were secured from each contractor, not only for the overall operation, but for the various functions of felling and bucking, skidding, loading, hauling, and miscellaneous. The breakdown of full daily time on the job included rest time, travel time, and all delays. At the end of each job, time for each operation was compared with cubic-foot volume[4] produced.

---

[4] At McCleary, where output was measured in board feet, conversion to cubic feet was based upon average log diameter produced. Board-foot/cubic-foot ratios averaged 5.6 and ranged from 5.4 to 5.8.

Table 1.--<u>Time and related data for thinning studies, McCleary and Hemlock Experimental Forests</u>

Year	Experimental Forest	Average d.b.h. of thinning	Average skidding distance	Total thinnings	Trucking distance one way	Total man-hours involved	Average time					
							Felling and bucking	Skidding	Loading	Hauling	Miscellaneous	Total
		Inches	Feet	Cu. ft.	Miles		Man-hours per 100 cu. ft.					
HORSE SKIDDING OPERATION												
958	Hemlock	9.0	175	12,231	70	684	1.27	1.71	0.96	1.35	0.30	5.59
958	Hemlock	9.0	200	19,536	40	1,158	.80	2.56	.96	1.19	.41	5.92
958	Hemlock	9.3	175	12,276	15	581	.96	2.08	.53	.70	.45	4.72
960	Hemlock	10.3	225	3,956	15	219	.78	3.06	.53	.81	.35	5.53
956	Hemlock	11.0	280	20,859	15	949	1.11	1.61	.82	.60	.41	4.55
957	Hemlock	11.5	300	21,490	15	951	1.05	1.78	.70	.70	.20	4.43
960	Hemlock	11.9	300	22,671	15	898	.72	1.66	.52	.79	.27	3.96
959	Hemlock	12.3	280	13,890	20	506	.77	1.14	.58	.79	.36	3.64
CRAWLER TRACTOR SKIDDING OPERATION												
1960	McCleary	14.1	300	23,244	17	874	.78	1.29	.64	.79	.26	3.76
1955	McCleary	14.3	300	20,439	5	669	.89	1.20	.41	.44	.33	3.27
1957	McCleary	14.3	500	23,539	5	776	.98	.94	.55	.51	.32	3.30
1959	McCleary	14.3	200	22,182	17	812	.73	1.25	.62	.79	.27	3.66
1962	Hemlock	15.4	280	14,298	15	412	.55	1.00	.43	.59	.31	2.88
1951	McCleary	15.6	460	39,107	5	1,375	.87	1.28	.53	.33	.51	3.52
1954	McCleary	15.7	200	21,091	5	738	.95	.88	.68	.50	.49	3.50
1953	McCleary	16.6	300	34,285	5	996	.67	.96	.35	.47	.46	2.91
TREE FARMER (4-WHEEL TRACTOR) SKIDDING OPERATION												
1964	Hemlock	11.1	200	15,932	95	521	.72	1.21	.47	.71	.16	3.27
1964	Hemlock	12.8	175	17,448	95	499	.64	.75	.50	.79	.18	2.86
1963	Hemlock	13.1	300	19,306	15	770	1.05	1.29	.67	.68	.28	3.97
1965	Hemlock	14.6	280	13,351	100	354	.49	.48	.48	1.00	.20	2.65
1964	McCleary	15.1	410	24,943	22	633	.64	1.03	.17	.49	.21	2.54
1965	Hemlock	15.1	300	26,785	100	721	.35	.46	.57	1.10	.21	2.69
1965	McCleary	15.1	400	28,955	22	679	.54	.99	.16	.46	.21	2.26
1962	McCleary	16.5	500	27,838	17	589	.47	.79	.17	.44	.25	2.12
1963	McCleary	17.4	375	40,672	22	936	.56	.92	.15	.52	.15	2.30

RESULTS AND DISCUSSION

Total time[5]/ per unit of volume and amount cut per acre were not significantly correlated at either location (fig. 2).

The plotted data at both locations clearly indicate lower man-hour requirements for Tree Farmer skidding over that for crawler tractors or horse skidding.

In a recent comparable study in western Washington,[6]/ it was also observed that amount cut per acre had little effect on man-hour requirements. This seems consistent with the flexibility of thinning methods which are characterized by small crews, light and inexpensive equipment, and high mobility.

This ease and speed of movement reduces time involved in traveling from tree to tree and in collecting an efficient turn for skidding to the landing. Also, improvements in loading procedure, permitting quick and efficient movements along roads, negate necessity for large-volume road decks as in the past.

Range of observed data for both locations restricts inferences to operations removing approximately 5 to 16 cords per acre which, under current commercial thinning practices, encompass very light to moderately heavy removal. By grouping the 25 projects by skidding method (table 1), a significant statistical relationship between average d.b.h. removed and labor requirements for horse skidding (1-percent level) and for Tree Farmer (5-percent level) was revealed. Crawler tractor showed no significance, perhaps due to limited range of data (fig. 3). As could be expected, man-hours decreased as d.b.h. increased. Slope of the regression lines is quite similar for Tree Farmer and crawler tractor skidding and much steeper for horse skidding, perhaps because of smaller and less efficient diameters in this latter method.

As an example of actual man-hours involved in thinning, a 12-inch-d.b.h. tree average required 3.30 man-hours per 100 cubic feet for the Tree Farmer method, and horse skidding required 4.01 man-hours or 21 percent more. Since the crawler tractor method was not involved in diameters below 14 inches, no direct comparison is possible with horse skidding. However, at this 14-inch diameter, it required 3.56 man-hours, or 20 percent more, than did the Tree Farmer method at the same size.

---

[5]/ Total time included all functions of the thinning operation from felling to delivery to the processing mill.

[6]/ Worthington, Norman P. Cost of thinning 50-year-old Douglas-fir for pulpwood at Voight Creek Experimental Forest. Pacific Northwest Forest & Range Exp. Sta. Res. Note 215, 4 pp. 1961.

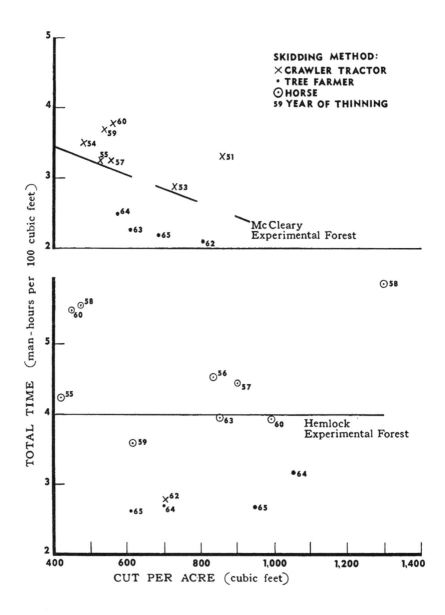

Figure 2.--Relation of total time per 100 cubic feet to cut per acre.

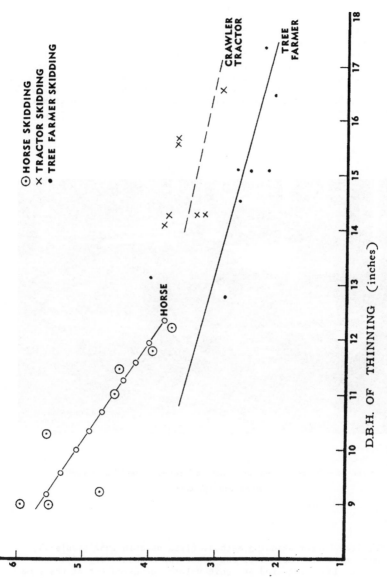

⊙ **HORSE SKIDDING**
✕ **TRACTOR SKIDDING**
• **TREE FARMER SKIDDING**

CRAWLER TRACTOR

TREE FARMER

HORSE

D.B.H. OF THINNING (inches)

Figure 3.--Relation of total time per 100 cubic feet to d.b.h. of thinning.

Labor requirements per diameter class (fig. 3) indicate the superiority of the Tree Farmer in labor efficiency over use of horses or crawler tractors. The difference in labor requirements between horses and tractors appears to be slight, but a good comparison is not possible due to lack of overlap on common tree diameters handled. Low efficiency for crawler tractors in this particular case may be because of larger, less efficient crews, ill suited to small timber and light cuts (fig. 4). The higher labor ratio for horse skidding was often partially offset by the low overhead, smaller crews, and greater adaptability to thinning by the horse-using operators.

Figure 4.--The crawler tractor is not well suited to thinning in small timber and light cuts.

The Tree Farmer skidding method, first used in 1962 (table 1), represents an improvement over the other two methods (fig. 5). Not only is less labor required per unit volume harvested but at the same time it allows a greater efficient-skidding radius, thus reducing amount of roadbuilding required. This method, or a similar one, may be expected to predominate in the thinning field, at least in the immediate future.

Figure 5.--The Tree Farmer represents an improved method of skidding, requiring less labor and allowing a greater efficient-skidding radius.

Diameters used in the above analyses are averages for each thinning method and are valid only for diameter ranges as shown in figure 3. All thinning projects reported were repeats, except for the 1951 and 1953 sales at McCleary and the 1957 sale at Hemlock. Thus, skidroads, landings, and any benefits from greater felling efficiency inherent in a previously thinned stand were available for all jobs except the three cited examples.

Apparently, labor requirements for Tree Farmer thinning are fairly close to those of harvest of typical old-growth timber (table 2).

-9-

Table 2.--<u>Logging output per man-hour in extraction of typical</u>

<u>old-growth timber and young-growth thinnings in</u>

<u>Oregon and Washington</u>

Job function	Old growth[1]		Young growth[2] (Tree Farmer method)
	West side	East side	
	Board feet, Scribner Rule		
Falling, bucking, yarding, and loading	483	586	403
Hauling	1,342	1,095	956
All job functions	224	277	259

[1] Adapted from table 5 of: Smith, Richard C., and Gedney, Donald R. Manpower use in the wood-products industries of Oregon and Washington 1950-1963. Pacific Northwest Forest & Range Exp. Sta. U.S. Forest Serv. Res. Paper PNW-28, 48 pp., illus. 1965.

[2] Seventeen-inch-d.b.h. average tree.

This comparison is not precise since average old-growth tree diameters are larger for east- and west-side[7] examples as compared with thinning diameters. Undoubtedly, thinning operations may be in some cases as efficient as mature timber harvest despite smaller tree diameter because of no road allowance in the thinning case as opposed to sizable allowances in mature timber harvest. Furthermore, smaller crews, almost universal use of contract system, and less general overhead expense inherent in thinning make possible substantial reduction in overall labor requirements. The readily accessible areas of young timber, which are substantial, thus may be thinned at a labor cost somewhat comparable to that for harvesting more remote mature timber.

[7] East and west of the Cascade Range in Oregon and Washington.

The relative importance of individual job functions clearly shows skidding (31-39 percent) and felling and bucking (21-24 percent) as the major users of manpower in thinning operations (table 3). Hauling, loading, and miscellaneous follow in that order. The high figure of 24 percent for hauling under the Tree Farmer method is due to exceptionally long hauls experienced on these jobs.

Table 3.--Percent of total time for various job functions in

thinning by three skidding methods[1]

Job function	Horse	Crawler tractor	Tree Farmer
	------------------ Percent ----------------		
Felling and bucking	21	24	23
Skidding	39	34	31
Loading	14	16	16
Hauling	16	18	24
Miscellaneous	10	8	6
Total	100	100	100

[1] Twelve- and 14-inch-d.b.h. average tree for horse and Tree Farmer methods and crawler tractor method, respectively.

MEANING AND APPLICATION OF RESULTS

1. Since labor requirements are but little influenced by cut per acre, this item does not require major consideration in laying out a thinning operation, at least within the range of volumes studied--400 to 1,300 cubic feet per acre or, roughly, 2,250 to 7,250 board feet. Ability to make light cuttings could conceivably reduce the interval between thinnings.

2. Labor requirement in thinning decreases with increase in average d.b.h. of tree taken. Hence, a thinning which yields a larger tree will make more efficient use of labor than a smaller tree thinning. Findings of this study may be a useful guide in marking of trees, timing of thinning, and choice of thinning method. As an example, in an early thinning when

-11-

diameters are close to a marginal economic size, it may be feasible to thin from above, using a crown or selection thinning, rather than from below, thus starting the thinning regime earlier.

3. There is a slight trend toward increased labor efficiency in extraction over the period (1951-64) for the entire job. Most improvement has been in the felling and bucking and loading operations.

4. More studies are needed in manpower requirements for thinning young Douglas-fir and western hemlock. Studies which relate these factors to individual tree diameter would be of greater value than comparisons with average diameters of entire stand thinning as presented here. Until such findings are available, however, rough approximations as presented should prove useful. It is impossible to intelligently thin or partially cut without some guides on how size of cut trees may influence labor requirements. Many a thinning operation will fail without serious consideration of this simple relationship.

* * *

FOREST AND RANGE EXPERIMENT STATION · U.S. DEPARTMENT OF AGRICULTURE · PORTLAND, OREGON

PNW-44   November 1966

A COMPUTER PROGRAM

FOR CALCULATING ALLOWABLE CUT

USING THE AREA-VOLUME CHECK METHOD

by Daniel E. Chappelle, Economist

In connection with a study of timber management planning on Pacific Northwest National Forests, a computer program has been written which calculates allowable cut by the area-volume check method, assuming volume regulation. This scheduling method is rather extensively used by public and private owners in the region to calculate allowable cut, especially for old-growth Douglas-fir forests in transition to young-growth forests.

DESCRIPTION OF THE METHOD

The area-volume check method of calculating allowable cut consists of the following steps:[1]

1. Derive a first approximation of allowable annual cut, or trial cut. There are several ways to do this--the most common for old-growth Douglas-fir forests involves Hanzlik's formula.[2] Another way would be to use the annual cut for the previous year. In fact, an intelligent estimate may be adequate for this purpose.

2. Arrange data for the forest stands in order of cutting priority. In the Pacific Northwest, this has generally meant arranging stand data by decreasing age. In this manner, the oldest stands are scheduled to be cut first. Data include the total area and percentage of area which is thinnable by age class, rotation age, regeneration period, and factors which influence yields.

---

[1] Western Forestry & Conservation Association. Reports of the West Coast Forestry Procedures Committee on various recommended forest practices and techniques. Rep. V. Determination of allowable cut for forests in the Douglas fir region, pp. 16-38. 1950.

[2] Davis, Kenneth P. American forest management. 482 pp., illus. New York, Toronto [etc.]: McGraw-Hill Book Co., Inc. 1954.

3. Calculate the time required to cut each age class, using the first approximation of annual allowable cut. Knowing time required to cut each age class, and present average age of stands, calculate the average age of the stands when cut.

4. Calculate yield of stand when cut. Yield equations that are generally used specify "age when cut" as an independent variable.

5. Once all age classes are run through the above process, check to see if the cumulated years to cut the forest are equal to the rotation length or conversion period desired. Also, check the area cut per year for reasonableness.

6. If criteria regarding volume and area cut are not met, then change the trial cut in a systematic way and rerun the analysis. Continue this process until the desired conditions are met.

DESCRIPTION OF THE *ARVOL* COMPUTER PROGRAM

ARVOL is a computer program for calculating allowable cut by the area-volume check method. The program is coded in *FORTRAN IV* for an IBM 7040 installation.

The program characteristics are:

1. A maximum of 40 age classes can be analyzed in this program. These age classes apply to the beginning of the rotation being analyzed. Any increment between age classes may be used, and the increment need not be constant between age classes.

2. Up to eight age classes predicted to have zero net growth (i.e., mortality equal to gross growth) are acceptable.

3. Two different equations may be used to calculate yields of stands under extensive management.

4. Either a separate yield equation for intensively managed stands may be entered, or a normal yield equation may be entered.

5. Both thinned and unthinned stands may be included in any one analysis.

6. A range of alternative rotation ages or conversion periods may be evaluated. A table is produced for each rotation alternative desired.

7. Regeneration period is entered as an input, and hence may be varied as desired by the user.

-2-

8. Precision of the final allowable cut may be set as desired by the user.

9. Problems may be stacked; i.e., a number of analyses may be completed in one computer run.

10. Minimum cutting age may be specified by the user.

11. Negative age classes may be assigned in those cases where a period longer than the assumed regeneration period is likely to occur.

ARVOL inputs:

1. Number of problems to be run.
2. Trial allowable cut.
3. Regeneration period.
4. Forward and backward increments to adjust allowable cut.
5. Age class identifiers which key to the yield equations.
6. An identifier which specifies which yield equations are to be used for intensively managed stands.
7. Beginning and ending rotation ages and intervening increment.
8. Minimum cutting age.
9. Area distribution by age class.
10. Percentage of area intensively managed by age class.
11. Yields of stands assumed to have zero net growth over the rotation or conversion period.
12. Coefficients of two empirical yield equations.
13. Coefficients of yield equation for intensively managed stands, or normal yield equation coefficients.

ARVOL outputs:

1. Area distribution by beginning age class.
2. Yield per acre when cut by beginning age class.
3. Total yield when cut by beginning age class.
4. Years required to cut the total yield by beginning age class.
5. Cumulated years required to cut the total yield by beginning age class.
6. Area to cut annually by beginning age class.
7. Average age when cut by beginning age class.
8. Total area.
9. Total volume.
10. Final allowable cut.
11. Rotation age.
12. Average area to cut each year over the conversion period.
13. Average yield per acre.
14. Average yield per acre per year.

OPERATION OF THE *ARVOL* COMPUTER PROGRAM

The *ARVOL* program provides for printing only the final allowable cut and related data. The number of trial cuts required to arrive at the final cut is a function of two items: (1) accuracy of the starting approximation of allowable cut, which is a required input to the program, and (2) the level of precision desired by the user. The program begins at the level of cut set by the user as a first approximation and converges to final allowable cut by the forward and backward increments. If the first approximation is too low, the convergence will proceed forward, by the forward increment, until final cut is encountered or exceeded. If final cut is encountered, the final cut and associated outputs are printed, and the next rotation length or problem is considered. If the final cut is exceeded, the program proceeds to the final cut by the backward increment.

In view of the program behavior, as outlined above, it is easily seen that the precision desired in the allowable cut figure may be controlled by the levels of forward and backward increments set by the user.

The time requirements for a problem of any given size cannot be estimated with any certainty because speed of solution is dependent on the first approximation of allowable cut and the level of precision set by the user. Typical operating times are as follows:

Number of age classes	Intensive management	Number of rotation lengths	Execution time (minutes)[1]
25	Yes	23	4.73
24	No	23	.72
26	Yes	13	3.95

[1] Does not include compilation time.

AVAILABILITY OF *ARVOL*

Requests for the source program listing, *FORTRAN IV* source deck, and user's manual may be addressed to the Director, Pacific Northwest Forest and Range Experiment Station, U.S. Forest Service, P.O. Box 3141, Portland, Oregon 97208.

FOREST AND RANGE EXPERIMENT STATION · U.S. DEPARTMENT OF AGRICULTURE · PORTLAND, OREGON

PNW-45   *December 1966*

A SIMPLE, PROGRESSIVE,

TREE IMPROVEMENT PROGRAM FOR DOUGLAS-FIR

by Roy R. Silen
Principal Plant Geneticist

Present Douglas-fir tree improvement programs appeal primarily to the very large forest ownerships. There is need for a simple, low-cost program which appeals to medium and smaller forest-land owners if tree improvement is to become generally practiced in the Northwest. There is need also for a ready alternative to programs based upon clonal Douglas-fir seed orchards because technical problems, though probably solvable, are becoming serious. This paper proposes and describes such a program in which substantial improvement in steady increments appears assured from known performance patterns of tree families in the half-century-old Douglas-fir heredity study.[1]

---

[1] Munger, Thornton T., and Morris, William G. Growth of Douglas fir trees of known seed source. U.S. Dep. Agr. Tech. Bull. 537, 40 pp., illus. 1936.

Silen, Roy R. Regeneration aspects of the 50-year-old Douglas-fir heredity study. In Western Reforestation. West. Forest. & Conserv. Ass. Reforest. Coordinating Com. Proc. 1964: 35-39. 1965.

Silen, Roy R. A 50-year racial study of Douglas-fir in western Oregon and Washington. (Abstr.) West. Forest Genetics Ass. Proc. 1965: 6-7. 1966.

U.S. Forest Service. The 1912 Douglas-fir heredity study. In Annual Report 1963, the Fifty and Fiftieth Year(s). Pacific Northwest Forest & Range Exp. Sta., pp. 4-7, illus. 1964.

It departs from previous programs in that it (1) provides immediate and ample supplies of seed from cone-producing trees along roadsides rather than from seed orchards, (2) emphasizes testing of parent trees by the hundreds through performance of their offspring instead of stressing rigorous initial selection, (3) leaves decisions on details of parent tree selection to foresters of future generations, and (4) leads directly and logically into a long-term breeding program covering many tree generations.

THE PROGRAM IN BRIEF

The program can be briefly described as follows. Enough cone-producing trees would be chosen along the road system of a forest ownership to provide adequate seed supplies for all planting needs of a sustained yield program. This group of trees will henceforward be referred to as the seed source group. At the same time, a group-- two or three times larger and referred to henceforward as the reserve tree group--would also be chosen for the program. The degree of selection could range from random to rigorous, as decided by the landowner. Some improvement would be expected in the initial seed collections if we assume some positive correlation between selected parent and their offspring.

The basis for steady and progressive improvement of the seed source group of parents over the years would be a test of every parent in both groups by performance of their wind-pollinated offspring in several test sites on the forest ownership. Each evaluation of this progeny test, possibly at 5-year intervals, would provide opportunities to eliminate poor parents in the seed source group and to substitute better parents from the reserve tree group. All parents would be carefully preserved. Genetic improvement becomes progressively more assured from the earliest to the final evaluation of the progeny test, although half a century or more may elapse before the final results of growth and survival are available.

As test results accumulate, numerous opportunities are provided to phase into sound breeding programs, based on tested parents or families, or into various seed orchard programs. Steps in the program are outlined in more detail on pages 12 and 13.

RESEARCH BACKGROUND

Many of the details of this proposed program are based on unpublished results from the Douglas-fir heredity study. Some of the most important findings from this study are:

1. Some parents in every race tested could have provided appreciable genetic gains, even though their progeny have only one known parent. Within a race, best families from wind-pollinated parents outproduce poorest families in timber volume per acre at 50 years by

ratios of 2:1 and sometimes over 3:1. Even from randomly selected parents within a race, the one best parent in four would have provided more than 10 percent increased volume over the average of unselected parents. However, the data provide no satisfactory substitute for a long-term progeny test to determine which parents actually produce best families for a particular site. Hence, the study provides a major simplification--a sound tree improvement program can be based upon seed collections from progeny-tested mature parent trees located in the forest.

2. Progeny tests employing wind-pollinated seed are practical. Although tests using controlled-pollinated seed would provide more information for the plant breeder, a test using wind-pollinated seed will separate poor and good parents. Using wind-pollinated seed for a progeny test facilitates testing hundreds of parents of the same crop year with minimum of time, initial effort, expense, and highly trained personnel.

3. A long progeny test is required because early results are often reversed in later years. Survival differences, although generally unimportant for the first quarter century, account for more and more differences as stands approach the half century mark. At the family level, inherent survival differences already account for one-quarter or more of the volume-per-acre differences. At the racial level, the local races now are surviving best. Thus, the study furnishes evidence that improvement should be based upon a long-term test of parents well distributed among the local race to assure that they are well adapted to the site.

4. There is no assurance that a family that displays a clear superiority on one site will do well on another. A small percentage of families are above average on several sites, but the great majority that do well on one site are average or poor on others. The only way to determine such behavior is to test families on several sites.

ASSUMPTIONS

The proposed tree improvement program is based also upon these assumptions:

1. That the most important consideration at the start of a breeding program is to screen a large number of parent trees by progeny test. This provides a large genetic base as a major safeguard against production of a poorly adapted or otherwise undesirable strain from subsequent selections and reselections after investing years of effort.

2. That substantial improvement of any race is possible with wind-pollinated seed provided the best quarter of the parents are used as ascertained by long-term progeny test.

3. That a progeny test must, as a minimum, evaluate survival differences, at least up to age 30 and perhaps to age 60.

4. That a seed source unit, within which movement of planting stock should be limited, should have generally the same local climate and probably normally correspond to some management unit of about 75,000 to 150,000 acres. The data for this assumption is fragmentary for Douglas-fir. The effect on program cost per pound of seed from using larger or smaller areas is very large.

5. That 75 to 100 parent trees of climbable size in the seed source group will furnish enough seed for the sustained yield planting program on a seed source unit.

6. That 300 trees, well dispersed over the seed source unit, constitute a large enough genetic base for a long-term breeding program. This number still limits first-generation selection of parents at end of the test to the best 25 percent of the 300 parents in order to have a genetic base of at least 75 parent trees.

7. That, in choosing parents for the seed source group, trees will not be selected very rigorously from the population because of their roadside location and cone-bearing requirements. Detailed discussion of pros and cons of this assumption are given later.

8. That any practical program must provide seed in ample quantities within as few years as possible. Economic analysis has shown all tree improvement programs where ample seed supplies are long delayed to be costly and often uneconomical.

9. That there is a positive parent-progeny correlation which will result in some improvement in the progeny of the seed source group of trees even if the parental selection is not very rigorous. No data as to the strength of this correlation is yet available for traits in mature trees.

10. That a practical progeny test involving 300 parents can be made under conditions found in the region. Difficulties in finding homogeneous test sites in the rugged terrain of the Douglas-fir region and expense of installing such a test on heterogeneous sites may make this assumption one deserving much analysis. However, this problem is one which will eventually face any selection or breeding program.

DETAILS OF THE PROGRAM

Based upon the above background and research, the following steps are the minimum required to implement the program: (1) selection of seed source and reserve groups of trees, (2) repeated collection of seed from the seed source group, (3) establishment of a progeny test, (4) periodic evaluation of the progeny test with reselection of the seed source group, (5) initiation of a program for long-term breeding. Alternative steps are also discussed.

Selection

The selection of about 300 parent trees divided between a seed source group (75 to 100) and a reserve group (200 to 225) would be made among easily climbed trees 30 to 60 years old, well distributed along forest roads, each capable of bearing a bushel or more of cones. There is no reason why a high intensity of selection could not be used if conditions permit. However, the population of trees that meet these requirements is usually restricted on most Northwest forest units. Selection beyond the best 1 in 20 would probably not usually be practical for the combination of traits ordinarily included in selection programs when this large a number of parent trees is desired. The practicing forester should be aware that arguments do exist for low intensity of selection just as they do for high selection intensity in an initial program. Otherwise, he may place more weight on the disadvantages of low selection intensity than present knowledge would justify. The next three paragraphs, therefore, discuss some of the arguments for a low selection intensity.

Simply from the standpoint of costs and returns, there is no data at present upon which to base the decision of whether a dollar spent in more intensive selection is better than the same dollar spent in progeny testing a greater number of trees selected less rigorously. Present figures on heritability of traits and the expertise with which foresters can assess the environmental component expressed for a trait in a single tree raise many questions about the effectiveness of any level of present-day selection. Intensive selection procedures require concentrating at the outset on a very few traits, a somewhat dangerous limitation in view of changes in market demands even in the last decade. The preference of some families for a single site, as displayed in the 50-year-old study, raises additional problems.

The only kind of selection in Douglas-fir on which there is long-term data is random selection. In the Douglas-fir heredity study the items for which selection was made (age, stand condition, or soil type) amounted to no conscious selection for growth, form, or survival. With volume differences at age 50 of 2:1 or larger between families within every race, there seems little question that adequate gains could be expected even from random selection to justify the proposed program.

Without corresponding data on the outcome of intensive selection, increasing departure from random selection introduces an additional risk. The 50-year-old study shows that (1) adapted races and families survive best, (2) ability to survive becomes increasingly important in influencing volume differences after 30 years, and (3) unexpected extremes of climate, which occur at infrequent intervals, are very important in this survival. Exact traits that permit one genotype to survive and another to perish over a rotation in the wild may be rather difficult to ascertain at present stage of knowledge. A sobering thought is that natural selection is generally against almost every trait that deviates far from the average, including unusual growth. The low selection intensity built into the plan would appear to be a safeguard against including an overly high proportion of any trait that deviates far from the average.

With these uncertainties and risks, a rather low selection intensity for the 300 trees is certainly acceptable, if not prudent. However, foresters would not be human if they did not wish to exercise their skill and experience in initially selecting good phenotypes for inclusion in the program. Hence, inclusion of as intensively selected a seed source group of trees as roadside selection will permit is probably inevitable. The advisability of including a randomly selected group of trees among the reserve parent group is discussed under alternative steps.

Seed Collection

Initially, wind-pollinated seed would be collected from all 300 trees in the small amount adequate for the progeny test. Such collection would best be made during a good crop year to maximize cross-pollination and minimize possible bias toward inherently prolific cone producers. One of the advantages of using wind-pollinated seed is that collections from all the parents can be made in a single crop year.

From the 75 to 100 trees of the seed source group, all the cones would be collected any year they produce appreciable seed to provide the supply of seed for the planting program. Higher seed costs than commercial collection should be expected because commercial seed collections are usually confined to heavily bearing trees with large cones to reduce costs. The seed source group of trees would have greater variation in range of cone size and crop, and smaller cone lots would be handled. However, costs would be no higher than normal for any collection from specified trees.

Whether enough seed can be obtained from 75 to 100 roadside trees is a debatable assumption. An estimate of seed yields in British

-6-

Columbia[2/] indicates that rather large trees might be required--
perhaps 20- to 30-inch diameters--for even the 25 to 50 pounds of seed
needed yearly. This amount of seed is based upon needs of a 100,000-acre
forest, assuming a planting program of 1,250 acres a year and an 80-year
rotation. There are several alternatives if seed quantities prove
insufficient. The total number of parent trees can be increased, or
cones can be collected from more than the 75 to 100 trees of the
seed source group. It is fairly certain that if provided ample growing space for several decades, 75 original parent trees of the seed
source group, representing a 1:4 selection among the 300 trees, would
develop enough crown to produce seed in required quantities. As
another alternative, an auxiliary group of selected, but untested,
trees could be used while the seed source group of trees gained
crown size.

Progeny Testing

The proposed program emphasizes the progeny test rather than
intensive initial selection.

Any design of test might be employed that adequately ranks
parent trees in terms of progeny performance on the forest ownership.

Because the testing phase is the most important cost of the
proposed program, as well as the major informational requirement, the
reader needs some idea of what minimal effort may be involved in a
progeny test. Hence, a few remarks are ventured concerning problems,
size, and evaluation.

The Douglas-fir region has some complications associated with
progeny testing that are common to rugged topography and high rainfall
forests. It is difficult to find uniform testing areas of 10 acres
and larger in most of the forested areas of this region. Intensive
cultivation or scarification of the plots, though desirable, is often
impossible because of stumps and the heavy accumulation of slash.
Problems with drought and animal damage to seedlings are often severe.
Initial growth of Douglas-fir seedlings is slow, and brush invasion
sometimes becomes a serious problem providing highly variable
competition to various parts of the plot. Any progeny test design
must cope with these complications.

A standard progeny test for the wind-pollinated seed needs to
be designed; possibly, by some genetics group like the Western Forest
Genetics Association. It should provide a sensitive test for families

---

2/ Kozak, A., Sziklai, O., Griffith, B. G., and Smith, J. H. G.
Variation in cone and seed yield from young, open-grown Douglas firs on
the U.B.C. Res. Forest. Univ. Brit. Columbia Fac. Forest. Res. Paper 57,
8 pp. 1963.

that perform well at several sites and a less sensitive test for families
that perform outstandingly at a single site. Preference in early
selection would probably be toward families that perform well on a
variety of sites. The 50-year-old-study results suggest that, as a
bare minimum, a test could be based upon as few as 40 seedlings per
parent if survival is excellent, or about 12,000 trees at each site,
possibly planted with complete randomization. At least three sites
would be needed to sample the seed source unit. A test with 36,000
tagged seedlings would entail a workload comparable to that of the
Douglas-fir heredity study, which is not excessive for a small
company. A more sensitive, larger test would be justified if suitable outplanting sites are available.

Periodic Evaluation

Gradually, as confidence is gained in progeny test results, choice
of parents for the seed source group will change from phenotypic to
genotypic selection. An evaluation of the progeny test is contemplated
at 2 years in the nursery, to remove parents with low germination or
weak seedlings from the seed source group. At 5 years in the field,
a further evaluation of the progeny will probably reveal a small percentage of very outstanding or weak families on which to base further
replacement of parents in this group. The first major reliance upon
the progeny test would come with the 10-year examination, when reasonable seedling-to-mature tree correlations appear obtainable. Subsequent examinations at 5-year intervals, up to the half century mark,
can be expected to substantially improve the genotypic selection. The
first generation goal is a completely tested group of parents from
which the landowner can select any combination of traits displayed in
the best families.

Future Breeding

At least for the first 20 years, the main seed supply would
come from parent trees. Eventually, seed from seed orchards and
breeding programs would replace this supply. Hand-pollinated-progeny
tests could be started early in the program to explore specific
combining ability of some parental combinations, pinpoint gene-
environment interactions, and to interpret wind-pollination results.
When outstanding families are identified, future breeding programs
could be planned to achieve specific objectives such as early volume
production, desirable form, or custom-grown wood. Whether best gains
would come from parental combinations or from crosses of best individuals of the offspring is a question that can be decided only by the
outcome of such tests. The plan itself permits complete flexibility
since all parent trees are preserved.

Alternative Steps

Alternative pathways are available from initial selection onward.
For example, there are good reasons to consider inclusion of a portion

of parents selected at random. As a group, their progeny furnish a yardstick for comparing all future progress in breeding. For example, the genetic gain would be computed at each evaluation of the progeny test. Inclusion of a substantial portion of randomly selected parents, for example 100 trees, assures inclusion of the complete gene pool of a race at the beginning of the program. This is a safeguard against unknowingly limiting genetic variability and is a hedge against future technological changes which may demand tree traits now in little demand. Because a fair proportion of excellent families did show up in the random selection used in the 50-year-old study, the inclusion of a randomly selected group of parents involves little risk and would provide a sporting challenge to the forester's selection system. Are his selections better or worse than random selection?

The development of a seedling or clonal seed orchard is an alternative that presents itself early in the progeny test. One of the plots on good topography could be successively thinned of poorest performing families starting soon after the first decade. Once the best parents are identified, a grafted seed orchard could be established if larger supplies of seed are needed.

Another alternative is open to a landowner who might wish to incorporate existing grafted seed orchards into this type of tree improvement program. Selections already made for the seed orchard form a nucleus of parents that could be included as part of the 300 trees to be tested. Conversely, number of clones in some orchards might be increased by adding the best phenotypes from the reserve group of trees when losses in the orchard are replaced. Seed collected from the orchard might be preferred early in the program to seed collected from parent trees along the road system. Including seed orchard trees in the progeny test would be complicated by the need to hand-pollinate the orchard clones with a pollen mix comparable with wind-pollinated seed in the parent locality. Since many seed orchards now have too few clones for a long-range breeding program, some elements of this plan may provide a way to make the necessary transition to a more adequate breeding program.

DISCUSSION

The main theme of the proposal is an attempt to simplify procedures and reduce risks through using seed from wind-pollinated parent trees already producing cones in abundance. Fifty-year results of the Douglas-fir heredity study indicate a clear, safe pathway to virtually certain substantial improvement. We would be remiss if the information were not synthesized into a proposal for those desiring a simple, low-cost, low-risk program that fits Northwest conditions. We would also be remiss if we left the impression that other plans involving cross-pollination between highly selected parents may not turn out to be superior in the long run. This is quite possible. As a rule, such programs do involve greater investments of effort and facilities, and rely more heavily on genetic theory. The simple program outlined here extends the range of programs available, with the hope that the low-investment, low-risk features will broaden the tree improvement efforts in Douglas-fir to the smaller ownerships or to applicable portions of larger ownerships. Furthermore, the program can easily be split up so that several landowners in the same area can each choose and test a portion of the 300 trees in a cooperative effort.

The fact that it has also some important side benefits makes for easy acceptance of such disadvantages as wind pollination from forest trees and low selection intensities. The proposal is highly flexible. At the outset, selection intensity can be varied to fit local desires. Progeny testing can be done to any intensity and by any well-conceived plan. More sophisticated breeding can begin on the trees at any time.

What might easily be overlooked is the flexibility of the end product. If families differ appreciably in such traits as growth, survival, taper, and straightness, future stands can be tailor made through choosing a mixture of parents for seed source. For example, a parent tree whose family survives poorly or grows slowly may be added to the seed mix to accomplish the same purpose as a precommercial thinning. Families that produce Christmas tree types might be added for an early cash crop. Families that produce high proportions of trees suited for poles and pilings may be included, as well as those that produce maximum volume at end of rotation. Thus, the forester can produce many different products on the same acre instead of a single product as is the usual goal of tree breeding. He can choose and collect seed from all these types displayed in the progeny as long as all the parent trees are carefully preserved. All these decisions are made by the forester of the future based upon the markets of the future rather than now.

The proposal has a great many built-in safeguards against change, overcommitment, or failure. If all types of parents are tested and preserved, the heavy responsibility in other plans attendant with initial selection of which traits and which trees to include in the program is avoided. Early mistakes are of a transient importance since correct selections can be substituted later on the basis of progeny test results. Low selection intensity hedges against the possibility that intensive selection is associated with parents at such extreme positions in the population array that their types are naturally selected against. Testing of large numbers of trees safeguards against ending with too small a genetic base. Growth in crown size of parent trees hedges against the loss of trees through selection and accident so that seed for the planting program will continue to be produced in ample quantities. Having the entire program within the confines of the forest ownership, rather than geared to a complex, widely based cooperative program, guards against the impermanence of human organizations. The increasing certainty of identifying the truly superior parents for both growth and long-term survival, regardless of whether the right assumptions were made initially, is a hedge against the worst possibility of all--failure.

Accounting aspects also should not be overlooked. Parent trees and progeny test located on the seed source unit become a salable asset, increasing the land value each passing year far out of proportion to the parent tree values alone. What increased value, for example, would be attached to a 100,000-acre forest ownership today if a certain group of parent trees growing there were demonstrated as capable of enhancing future production of that piece of land by 10 percent? Increased land value would begin to develop almost at the outset of the program.

As a final comment, genetic improvement of most crop plants has required the testing of thousands of parents for their genetic traits. At present, only a few hundred parent trees are being tested in the Douglas-fir region in seed orchard or experimental programs. The future competitive position of the region will be enhanced when several thousand parent trees, distributed over a wide range of sites, are being tested. This goal is not likely to be attained until a highly profitable incentive is provided to the forest-land owner. It is hoped that the features of this proposal can provide a financial incentive to test large numbers of parent trees.

SUMMARY

The proposal for a simple, progressive, tree improvement program for a forest unit of 75,000 to 150,000 acres starts with selection of 300 trees along roads of a forest ownership and collection of seed needed for future planting from the best 75 to 100 of these trees. Initial improvement would be based upon phenotypic selection and assumed parent-progeny correlation. A progeny test of all 300 trees would provide information for progressive and certain improvement at 5-year intervals in choosing the genetically superior parents. All 300 selected trees would be saved for perhaps half a century so that any combination of tested parents could be used to produce whatever combination of products is desired in the stand. The proposal is an outgrowth of the findings of a 50-year study of Douglas-fir families of known parentage. Thus, estimates of gain and problems of implementation are, to a large extent, known.

OUTLINE OF PROPOSED PROGRESSIVE TREE IMPROVEMENT
PROGRAM FOR A SEED SOURCE UNIT

Year	Activity	Options
1st	Choose 300 cone-producing parents at roadsides (75 to 100 in seed source group plus 200 to 225 in reserve group). Provide for permanent marking and excellent protection of all 300 trees.	Selection can range from random to high intensity. A randomly selected group of about 100 trees may form part of reserve group.
1st	Collect seed for progeny test from all 300 trees.	
1st	Collect and bulk all seed produced from seed source group. (Plan for subsequent collection every fair or good crop thereafter).	If seed requirements not met, use alternatives suggested in text.
2d	Sow bulked seed in nursery for planting program.	
2d	Sow 300 seed lots in nursery for progeny test.	Establish special nursery progeny test, carried to 3-0 or beyond for first evaluation of parents as possible alternative to 5-year examination of field test.
4th	Outplant seedlings from seed source trees as required for sustained yield program.	
4th	Measure progeny-test seedlings. Consider for elimination from seed source group parents showing very low seed yield, or whose progeny show poor germination or very poor growth.	Mild selection based on family performance may replace some phenological selected parents.
4-5th	Outplant progeny test using some standard design.	Further selection on basis of 3-0 nursery progeny test.
7th	5-year measurement of progeny-test seedlings. Replace 10 to 20 percent of poorest parents from seed source group with better parents of reserve group.	Use any desired combinati of phenotypic or progeny-test selection.

-12-

Year	Activity	Options
12th	10-year field measurement. Base primary selection of seed source group on progeny test.	Begin breeding program between best parents or families.
17th	15-year field measurement.	Begin seedling seed orchard by thinning out poorest families on one plot.
22d	20-year field measurement. Go entirely to selection based on progeny test.	
27th-52d	Replace parent trees of seed source group as changes occur in progeny test.	Continue breeding program.

FOREST AND RANGE EXPERIMENT STATION · U.S. DEPARTMENT OF AGRICULTURE · PORTLAND, OREGON

PNW-46

January 1967

TRANSLOCATION OF DYE IN GRAND AND SUBALPINE FIRS
INFESTED BY THE BALSAM WOOLLY APHID
by
Russel G. Mitchell, Entomologist

ABSTRACT

Tree-killing populations of balsam woolly aphid on the stems of grand and subalpine firs cause traumatic xylem tissue resembling compression wood. Anatomical characteristics of this wood suggest that damage from 3 to 4 years of infestation might inhibit sap flow and thus significantly reduce tree vigor. To test whether water conduction is affected by aphid attack, 20 infested and 20 noninfested grand and subalpine firs were injected with acid fuchin dye and the path of the dye traced throughout the stems.

Dye patterns confirmed that stem-infesting populations of the balsam woolly aphid materially affect water-conducting tissue. Among the characteristics of the dye columns were:

1. Infested trees absorbed about half as much dye as noninfested trees.
2. Dye columns did not ascend as high in infested trees as in noninfested trees.
3. Fewer rings conducted dye in infested trees than noninfested trees, about 50 percent fewer in some parts of the stem.
4. Aphid-affected xylem either blocked the dye columns completely or forced the column into a narrow band of springwood.
5. The helical pattern of ascent that is so uniform in normal trees was rather erratic in aphid-infested trees.

Because more rings actively conduct water at the bottom of the tree than higher in the stem, a given amount of aphid infestation at the bottom would be less damaging than the same population above. This may explain why grand fir is more tolerant to aphid attack than subalpine fir. Infestations on the former usually start near the bottom; those on the latter are usually high on the stem.

INTRODUCTION

Anatomy of the xylem in grand fir (*Abies grandis* (Dougl.) Lindl.)
and subalpine fir (*A. lasiocarpa* (Hook.) Nutt.) is greatly affected by
stem-infesting populations of the balsam woolly aphid (*Adelges piceae*
(Ratzeburg)) (Doerksen and Mitchell 1965). Particularly evident is
the effect on water-conducting tracheids. Tracheid length may be short-
ened 40 percent and, because of greatly thickened cell walls, lumen
space is reduced some 65 percent. In cross section, tracheids are
characteristically round in shape, as if differentiation occurred under
pressure. These and other features, such as increased volume of ray
tissue (2.4 times greater) and proliferation of traumatic resin canals,
both of which preempt space. ordinarily occupied by tracheids, suggest
the likelihood of constriction in the water column of infested trees.
If true, such constriction would become increasingly significant with
each year of infestation. Observed symptoms in infested trees, such
as drooping leaders (Mitchell 1966), positive sap pressures in midsummer
(when pressure is normally negative), and water-soaked appearance of
heartwood in grand fir, further suggest changes in the normal water-
conduction pattern.

This paper describes an investigation made in 1963 to trace water-
conduction patterns by injecting dye into the main stem of 10 infested
and 10 noninfested grand and subalpine firs. It is similar to an investigation by Balch (1952) on aphid-infested balsam fir. Primary objective of the study was to achieve a better understanding of the normal
water-conducting patterns of these species and to gain some idea how
these patterns are affected by balsam woolly aphid infestations. It
was also hoped the investigation would reveal the significance of certain
symptoms of vigor decline in aphid-infested true firs and thereby define
a point of departure for specific physiological studies.

METHODS AND PROCEDURES

Following procedures described by Vité (1959), 10 subalpine firs
and 10 grand firs (5 infested and 5 noninfested of each species) were
injected with a 1-percent solution of acid fuchsin stain.[1] The grand
firs varied from 20 to 45 years in age and were growing in a farm
woodlot near Monroe, Oregon. The subalpine firs were 30 to 60 years

---

[1] In an earlier test, a fluorescent material in water (Calcofluor)
was also tried. This material worked as well or better than dye, but
owing to difficulties in detection under the field conditions, its use
was discontinued.

old, growing adjacent to a mountain meadow in the upper Santiam drainage, Oregon. Most trees were growing in the open and had full crowns. All infested trees had been infested long enough to show visible symptoms of crown decline. Height growth was sharply reduced, new growth on secondary and many primary branches was halted, needle density was reduced, and there was a distinct chlorotic color in the most severely damaged trees. Descriptions of the trees are presented in table 1.

Table 1.—Description trees tested for movement of injected dye

Species	Tree No.	Age	D.b.h.	Height	Crown length	Crown position[1]	Competition	Condition
		Years	Inches	Feet	Feet			
GRAND FIR, NONINFESTED:	1	32	11.7	64	64	CD	Slight from one side	Full vigor
	2	35	9.0	66	64	CD	Close on one side	Full vigor
	3	28	10.4	57	57	CD	Close from three sides	Full vigor
	4	28	9.4	66	66	CD	Close from two sides	Full vigor
	5	24	7.2	54	54	CD	Moderate from two sides	Full vigor
GRAND FIR, INFESTED:	1	36	13.4	[2]/53	47	CD	Slight from one side	Seriously to moderately weakened by 7 years of stem attack
	[3]/2							
	3	29	12.0	[2]/50	50	CD	Close on two sides	Moderately weakened by 7 years of stem attack
	4	27	8.4	50	45	Int.	Close all sides	Slightly to moderately weakened by 6 years of stem attack
	5	45	7.5	50	30	CD	Close from three sides	Moderately to severely weakened by 5 years of stem attack
SUBALPINE FIR, NONINFESTED:	1	53	10.4	63	60	CD	Open grown	Full vigor
	2	45	7.4	42	42	CD	Open grown	Full vigor
	3	34	6.5	33	33	CD	Open grown	Full vigor
	4	50	10.5	57	50	CD	Close from two sides	Full vigor
	5	60	6.8	57	38	Int.	Close from all sides	Full vigor
SUBALPINE FIR, INFESTED:	1	45	13.5	53	53	CD	Open grown	Moderately weakened by 5 years of stem infestation
	2	44	9.0	35	35	CD	Open grown	Moderately weakened by 5 years of stem infestation
	3	47	8.4	39	39	Int.	Moderate from two sides	Moderately to seriously weakened by 5 years of stem infestation
	[4]/4							
	5	52	7.0	44	34	Int.	Close from all sides	Moderately weakened by 5 years of stem infestation

[1]/ Key. CD = codominant; Int = intermediate.
[2]/ Top broken out.
[3]/ Not evaluated; sap pressure could not be overcome.
[4]/ Not evaluated; tree too distressed to carry dye.

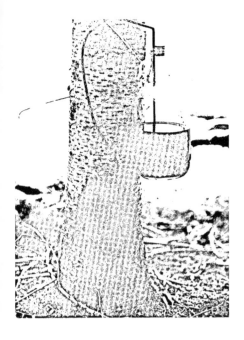

Dye was injected into the trees through a hole made with an increment borer. The hole was about 1 foot above ground level and extended to the pith, thus permitting every growth ring an opportunity to carry the dye. A 1/4-inch plastic tube carried the dye to the injection hole from an elevated 1-gallon reservoir (fig. 1).

Figure 1.--Apparatus for injecting dye into study trees.

Subalpine fir was injected August 1 and grand fir August 14, 1963. About 2 weeks after injection, trees were felled and cross-section disks cut from the main stems at 3-foot intervals, starting 1 foot above the injection hole. Each disk was numbered and the position directly above the injection site was marked with a nail as the zero axis. Data were recorded for: (1) Height of disk in tree, (2) age of disk, (3) number of years that portion of the stem had been infested by the balsam woolly aphid (i.e., number of rings having traumatic, reaction wood,[2] (4) number of rings carrying dye, and (5) degree of spiral in the water-conducting column, starting with the outermost ring and measuring every other ring thereafter (i.e., measuring spiral in rings formed in 1963, 1961, 1959, etc.). For determining spiral, it was considered that a line drawn from the pith to the nail was 0°; a complete revolution, 360°.

---

[2] Traumatic wood, called rotholz in the literature, is produced in the area where the aphids have settled. The affected rings are generally quite wide and composed of an abnormally dense, reddish wood.

GENERAL CHARACTERISTICS OF DYE MOVEMENT

Noninfested trees generally absorbed about twice as much dye as the infested trees. Total uptake in noninfested trees during the 2-week test period was one-half to three-fourths gallon per tree for subalpine fir and 1 to 1-1/2 gallons for grand fir. Dye was taken up faster in noninfested trees than in infested trees, as evidenced by the rate reservoirs emptied.

Dye was carried close to the top (to the 2- and 3-year-old whorls) in all noninfested trees but was never observed in terminal growth. In infested trees, the dye seldom reached beyond the 6- to 10-year-old whorls, often stopping 10 to 15 feet below the tree top.

Near the injection point on infested trees, the dye frequently spread out over a wide area of the inner rings, as if under pressure. This was especially apparent with subalpine fir (fig. 2B). With grand fir, it was sometimes difficult to get dye into the tree due to sap pressure pushing it back into the reservoir. Observations on one infested tree were never completed because of this problem.

"Rotholz," the aphid-induced traumatic wood, noticeably interfered with dye conduction. The dye column in a rotholz ring, if not stopped completely, was usually confined to the narrow band of springwood. Also, the dye column usually spread along the rings in unusually wide arcs (figs. 2B and 3B). Sometimes the column became separated into two or three small adjacent columns. Dye seemed to be conducted more easily through rotholz areas in the lower bole than rotholz areas in the upper bole.

One infested subalpine fir which appeared alive, though seriously weakened, was, in fact, dead. When this tree was injected, the outer, 1-year-old ring carried the dye up the stem about 3 feet; the 2-year-old ring, about 2 feet; and the older rings, about 1 foot.

With noninfested trees, whenever the dye column contacted a limb, dye was carried into the outermost needles of the limb. Dye was rarely found in the needles of infested trees. Dye was not detected in the phloem or cortical tissues of either infested or noninfested trees.

NUMBER OF RINGS CARRYING DYE

Noninfested Trees

Only sapwood rings actively carried dye. Vertical movement in heartwood rings was no more than 1 or 2 inches. There was minor transportation of dye through the pith and the checks around the pith in the injection area, but the distance seldom exceeded 12 inches.

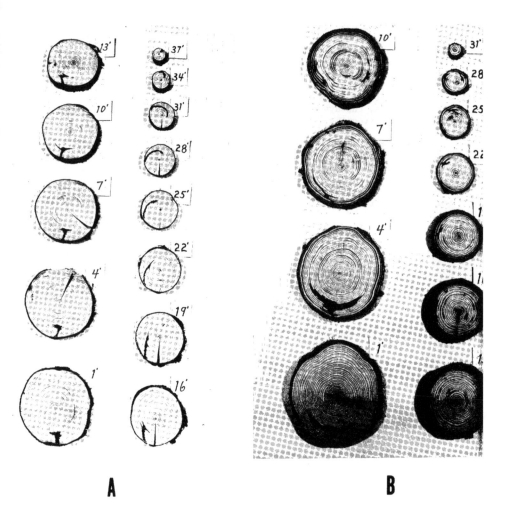

Figure 2.--*A*, Dye pattern in normal subalpine fir (tree No. 2).
B, Dye pattern in aphid-affected subalpine fir (tree No. 2).
Dark wood in outer rings (4 to 22 feet) reflects stem in-
festations.

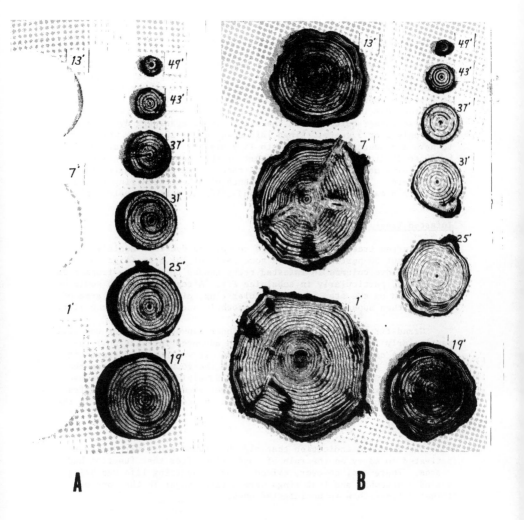

Figure 3.--*A*, Dye pattern in normal grand fir (tree No. 2). *B*, Dye pattern in aphid-affected grand fir (tree No. 1). Dark, irregular outer rings (rotholz) reflect the presence of aphids.

More rings were active in dye transport at the bottom than higher in the trees (figs. 4 and 5), but the percentage of rings involved in conduction increased with height, except at the very top of the trees. The number of years a particular annual ring was capable of conduction became fewer as it appeared higher in the tree and nearer the pith. It appeared that the ring next to the pith was active for only 1 year-- i.e., the year it was formed. Rings laid down 3 to 4 years from the pith also rather quickly lost their ability to transport dye, often after only 2 or 3 years. Rings laid down in the 20th year were found to have a conducting life of 10 to 15 years; i.e., until there would be 30 to 35 growth rings in that part of the stem. Occasionally, rings ceased being active at one level and then became active again at a higher level. But there was no instance of a heartwood ring in the injection area becoming active in conduction at a higher point on the stem.

Infested Trees

Infested trees had fewer rings conducting dye than noninfested trees, about 50 percent fewer in some parts of the stem (figs. 4 and 5). Also, dye columns in infested trees tended to be quite fragmented vertically, particularly in subalpine fir. A conduction path would be established up the stem in a particular ring, disappear in an area of rotholz, then appear again above the rotholz section in the same ring.

Grand fir tended to use the old, inner sapwood rings for conduction, particularly in the upper stem where (in advanced infestations) the outer rings contained traumatic tissue.[3] It was not characteristic of grand fir to reestablish conduction in the younger rings once the dye column had passed the rotholz zone. Subalpine fir tended to use the outer rings in both the upper and lower stem. In advanced infestations, the outer rings generally showed the rotholz condition in the lower regions of the stem, where it was most easily penetrated or circumvented.[4]

There was no indication that old, heartwood rings were being reactivated to carry on the role of conduction after that function had ceased. There was, however, evidence that conducting life was being extended somewhat and that rings were active longer in the tops of infested trees than in noninfested ones.

---

[3] As a general rule, grand fir infestations start low on a tree and move upwards with time, whereas infestations on subalpine fir start high and move downwards.

[4] Refer to footnote 3.

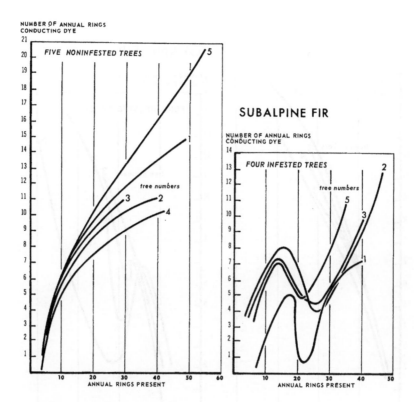

Figure 4.--*Number of annual rings actively conducting dye in normal and aphid-infested subalpine firs as related to the number of annual rings present.*

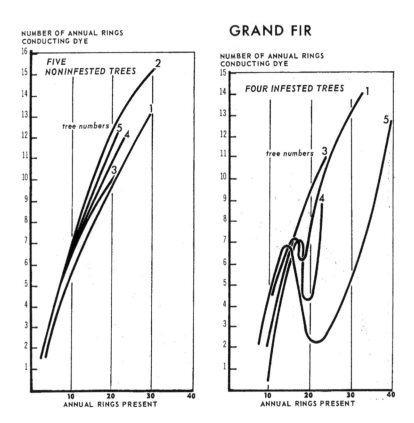

GRAND FIR

Figure 5.--*Number of annual rings conducting dye in normal and aphid-infested grand firs as related to the number of annual rings present.*

-10-

Generally, both grand and subalpine fir, infested and noninfested, carried dye up the stem in a helical pattern, turning clockwise (figs. 2 and 3 and 6 through 10). The closer the rings were to the pith, the sharper the angle of dye ascent. Accordingly, ascent in rings high in the tree was sharper than in lower rings.

The helical characteristic of the ascent was most pronounced in trees with full crowns. In closely grown trees, where the crown was 50 percent or less of the total tree height, the dye column tended to go straight up the unfoliated stem and start turning in the crown region. In one instance, the dye column even turned counterclockwise before it got to the crown: figure 6 illustrates the spiral in a 55-year-old subalpine fir that was 40 feet tall with a 20-foot crown. The spiral in the youngest ring (1963) was counterclockwise for a full 360° and continued to within 7 feet of the tree top before it began turning clockwise.

The erratic spirals in the rotholz regions showed that balsam woolly aphid infestations altered the normal conduction patterns to some degree (figs. 8 and 10), although rings formed early in the infestation or prior to attack had normal patterns.

NORMAL SUBALPINE FIR NONINFESTED

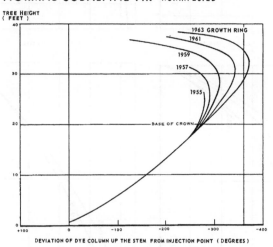

Figure 6.--*Spiral ascent of tracheidal conduits in the main stem of a normal subalpine fir growing in a closed stand near Mount Hood in Oregon. Tree was injected before the main experiment as a test of techniques.*

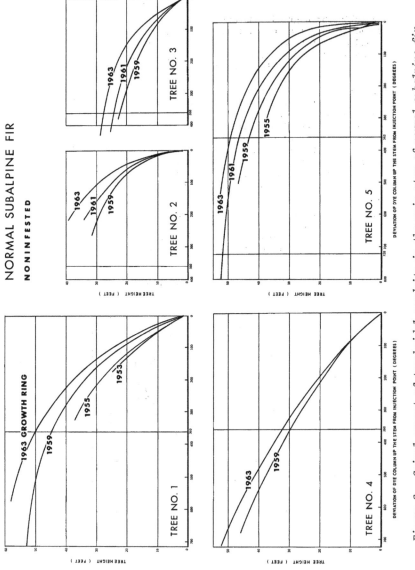

Figure 7.—Spiral ascent of tracheidal conduits in the main stem of normal subalpine fir.

SUBALPINE FIR
INFESTED BY BALSAM WOOLLY APHID

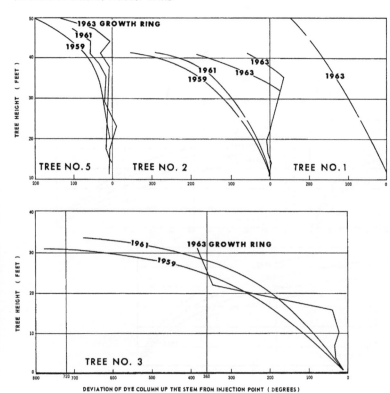

Figure 8.--*Spiral ascent of tracheidal conduits in the main stem of aphid-infested subalpine fir.*

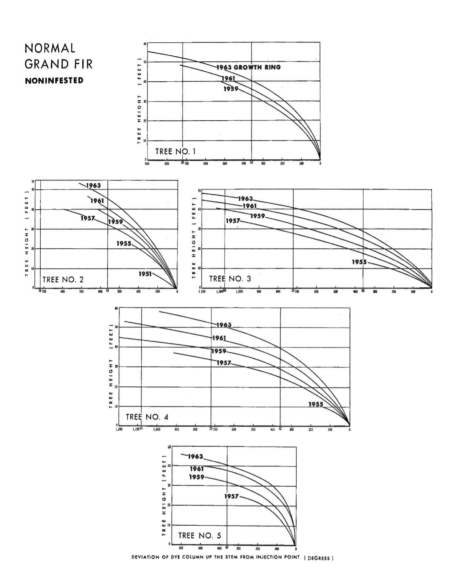

Figure 9.--*Spiral ascent of tracheidal conduits in the main stem of normal grand fir.*

-14-

GRAND FIR
INFESTED WITH BALSAM WOOLLY APHID

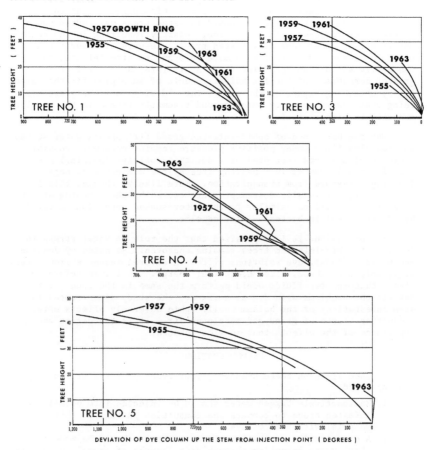

Figure 10.--Spiral ascent of tracheidal conduits in the main
stem of aphid-infested grand fir.

DISCUSSION AND CONCLUSIONS

The dye patterns in noninfested trees agreed rather well with findings of Vité and Rudinsky (1959), but in infested trees the patterns were different. Balsam woolly aphid infestations materially disrupt a tree's water-conducting tissue. This suggests that the changed anatomy in the xylem of aphid-infested trees may indeed cause severe water stresses within the tree, possibly resulting in the characteristic droop of tops of infested trees. Results also suggest a possible reason why grand fir is more tolerant to stem infestations of the woolly aphid than subalpine fir: Aphid infestations affect a greater percentage of the tracheidal conduit of subalpine fir than grand fir by attacking higher on the stem. The old rings obviously are not being reactivated to carry water around traumatic tissue in the regular conduits in either species.

Why the heartwood of aphid-infested grand fir appears water soaked and contains fluid under positive pressure remains unknown. Possibly there is always some root pressure, but this positive (pushing) pressure is usually masked in a healthy tree by the dominance of negative (pulling) pressure from transpiration. More likely, though, this is an expression of localized stem pressure caused by the wounding effect of aphid infestations--similar to the water-soaked condition reported by Carter (1945) in bacteria-infected elms.

In conclusion, it is emphasized that the role of water stress in decline of aphid-infested trees remains unproven. As noted by Johnson and Rediske (1964), dye solutions differ in several respects from water, e.g., molecular shape, size, electrical charge. It is, therefore, unlikely that the two fluids would perform the same in the tree. But despite the problems with dye as a tracer, the study demonstrated that stem infestations of the balsam woolly aphid adversely affects water-conducting tissue of grand and subalpine fir. It is the degree and importance of the effects that remains unknown.

RECOMMENDATIONS

To shed light on these unknowns, four types of tests or studies are suggested:

1. Radioactively tagged water should be injected into normal and infested trees to compare the conduction pattern of this material with that of dye.
2. A quantitative evaluation of water stress should be made in which water is pulled through unit lengths of normal and aphid-affected sapwood with a suction pump.
3. Investigation should be made of water stress in the crowns of the same trees used for pump tests. The techniques described by Scholander et al. (1965) seem appropriate.
4. Experimentation is needed to determine water-conduction patterns in suppressed trees and trees growing on poor sites.

It is becoming apparent that such trees can survive heavy
infestations longer than trees on good sites or trees in
dominant and codominant crown classes.

LITERATURE CITED

Balch, R. E.
    1952. Studies of the balsam woolly aphid, *Adelges piceae* (Ratz.)
           and its effects on balsam fir, *Abies balsamea* (L.) Mill.
           Can. Dep. Agr. Pub. 867, 76 pp.

Carter, J. C.
    1945. Wetwood of elms. Ill. Natur. Hist. Surv. 23: 401-448.

Doerksen, Allan H., and Mitchell, Russel G.
    1965. Effects of the balsam woolly aphid upon wood anatomy of
           some western true firs. Forest Sci. 11: 181-188, illus.

Johnson, Norman E., and Rediske, J. H.
    1964. Tests of systemic insecticides for the control of the
           Douglas-fir cone midge, *Contarinia oregonensis* Foote.
           Weyerhaeuser Co. Res. Note 56, 13 pp., illus.

Mitchell, Russel G.
    1966. Infestation characteristics of the balsam woolly aphid in
           the Pacific Northwest. Pacific Northwest Forest & Range
           Exp. Sta. U.S. Forest Serv. Res. Pap. PNW-35, 18 pp.,
           illus.

Scholander, P. F., Hammel, H. T., Bradstreet, Edda D., and Hemmingsen, E.A.
    1965. Sap pressure in vascular plants. Science 148: 339-345.

Vité, J. P.
    1959. Observations on the movement of injected dyes in *Pinus*
           ponderosa and *Abies concolor*. Contrib. Boyce Thompson
           Inst. 20: 7-26.

Vite, J. P., and Rudinsky, J. A.
    1959. The water-conducting systems in conifers and their impor-
           tance to the distribution of trunk injected chemicals.
           Contrib. Boyce Thompson Inst. 20: 27-38.

* * *

PNW-47   *January 1967*

LOW STAND DENSITY SPEEDS LODGEPOLE PINE TREE GROWTH

by Walter G. Dahms, Silviculturist

INTRODUCTION

To the silviculturist, judicious control of tree density throughout the life of a forest stand provides one of the primary avenues for optimizing returns from timber growing. Tree density is especially critical in the culture of lodgepole pine because stagnation from overcrowding is probably more pronounced in this species than in any other western conifer.

The first of a series of experiments, designed to provide foresters with better basic information on growth-growing stock relationships in lodgepole pine (Pinus contorta), was started in a 22-year-old stand in central Oregon in 1959. This note reports findings from the first 5-year growth period.

THE EXPERIMENT

The stand chosen for this experiment originated after a fire in 1934 on an area that can support either ponderosa or lodgepole pine. Site quality for ponderosa pine (Pinus ponderosa) is in the very high, site class IV[1]/ range. Similarly, site quality for lodgepole pine is considerably above average for central Oregon.

1/ Site quality determined with aid of site index curves contained in "Yield of Even-Aged Stands of Ponderosa Pine," by Walter H. Meyer, U.S. Dep. Agr. Tech. Bull. 630 (rev.), 59 pp., illus. 1961.

The experiment consists of ten 1/10-acre plots. Each of five level-of-growing-stock treatments was assigned to two plots at random.

Treatments were defined in terms of bole area. Bole area is the cambium area of the main stem. Lexen,[2] the originator of this density measure, explained many of its advantages as a basis for thinning control.

For the convenience of those not familiar with bole area, equivalents in terms of basal area and crown competition factor (CCF)[3] are also included in the various tables. Figure 1 further aids in visualizing the kind of treatment applied.

Figure 1.--The 4,000-square-foot bole area treatment, shown at left, resulted in an average spacing of 18.7 feet.

---

[2] Lexen, Bert. Bole area as an expression of growing stock. J. Forest. 41: 883-885. 1943.

[3] Crown competition factor, in essence, compares growing space available to a tree with the area of shadow the crown of an open-grown tree of the same breast-high diameter would cast on level ground with the sun directly overhead. Because growing space available to a single tree is not readily determinable, the comparison is made on a group basis. A CCF of 100 means tree growing space and open-grown-tree shadow area are the same. A CCF of 50 means tree growing space is twice the open-grown-tree shadow and a CCF of 200 means growing space is half the open-grown-tree shadow area. Crown competition factor is further described by Krajicek, J. E., Brinkman, K. A., and Gingrich, S. F., in "Crown competition--a measure of density." Forest Sci. 7: 35-42. 1961.

Growing-stock levels initially chosen for testing were 7,500, 12,500, 17,500, 22,500, and 27,500 square feet of bole area per acre. After examination of the first 5-year growth data, levels were dropped to 4,000, 8,000, 12,000, 16,000, and 20,000 square feet, respectively. We plan to cut back to these latter levels at the end of each 5-year period.

Pretreatment density (table 1) was not high enough to provide the higher density treatments on all plots. Accordingly, there was very little difference between the two highest growing-stock levels after the 1959 thinning (table 2). However, stand density increased substantially by 1964 and was high enough on all plots to meet the revised 1964 treatment definitions.

Table 1.--Stand statistics before thinning lodgepole pine

in central Oregon, 1959 (per-acre basis)

Growing-stock level	Plot	Number of stems	Average d.b.h.	Basal area	Bole area	CCF	Site index[1]
			Inches	Sq. ft.	Sq. ft		
1	8	1,650	3.4	101.4	20,606	187	61
(lowest)	10	1,580	3.5	102.6	20,931	184	60
	Average	1,615	3.4	102.0	20,768	185	60
2	2	1,350	3.4	87.1	18,463	157	62
	4	1,010	4.0	90.0	16,586	142	71
	Average	1,180	3.7	88.6	17,524	150	66
3	1	1,670	3.5	110.3	24,522	196	65
	6	1,550	3.4	110.2	21,255	192	65
	Average	1,610	3.4	110.2	22,888	194	65
4	3	1,940	3.2	106.8	24,447	206	65
	5	1,370	3.4	85.8	17,820	157	61
	Average	1,655	3.3	96.3	21,134	182	63
5	7	1,630	3.3	94.6	21,925	179	60
(highest)	9	2,140	2.9	96.5	22,355	204	58
	Average	1,885	3.1	95.6	22,140	192	59

[1] Site index at index age 50 years determined with the aid of height-over-age curves contained in: Dahms, Walter G. Gross and net yield tables for lodgepole pine. U.S. Forest Serv. Res. Pap. PNW-8, 14 pp., illus. 1964.

-3-

Table 2.--Stand statistics of lodgepole pine in central Oregon after

1959 thinning, before 1964 thinning, and after 1964 thinning

(per-acre basis)

Growing-stock level	Number of stems	Average spacing	Average d.b.h.	Average height	Basal area	Bole area	CFF	Volume[1]
		Feet	Inches	Feet	Sq. ft.	Sq. ft.		Cu. ft.
Immediately after 1959 thinning:								
1	405	10.4	4.2	26.0	41.7	7,330	64	537
2	610	8.4	4.4	28.2	70.0	12,454	102	979
3	925	6.9	4.0	27.2	85.3	16,538	136	1,152
4	1,345	5.7	3.4	24.6	92.4	19,305	164	1,186
5	1,705	5.1	3.0	22.8	93.6	20,248	182	1,122
Just before 1964 thinning:								
1	405	10.4	5.2	32.4	62.0	10,496	84	875
2	610	8.4	5.0	34.1	88.6	16,343	121	1,362
3	920	6.9	4.5	33.2	107.4	21,822	158	1,657
4	1,315	5.8	3.8	30.3	113.6	24,700	184	1,656
5	1,645	5.1	3.4	27.9	115.4	25,078	201	1,527
Immediately after 1964 thinning:								
1	125	18.7	6.2	34.5	26.8	4,302	33	409
2	235	13.6	5.9	38.0	45.7	7,972	58	734
3	420	10.2	5.2	36.0	64.6	12,236	88	1,023
4	675	8.0	4.5	33.5	78.8	16,100	116	1,200
5	1,060	6.4	4.0	30.4	95.0	19,970	154	1,326

[1] Volume of entire stem, inside bark.

Excess trees cut to achieve desired densities were the diseased and small individuals of poor thrift. Goal was to leave the best trees with as uniform spacing as possible.

Tree measurements taken at the beginning and ending of the growth period fall into two categories. One consists of height and diameter of all plot trees. The other includes diameter and bark thickness at intervals up the stems of five sample trees per plot. Formulas calculated from the sample trees express volume and bole area of entire stem as a function of diameter and height for each measurement date. These formulas were used to calculate plot volume and bole area.

-4-

Soil moisture was measured with a neutron probe.[4] The first measurement was made in the spring of 1961, shortly after the winter snow had melted. This reading was a good estimate of the fully charged soil's water-holding capacity. Another measurement was taken at the[5] end of the growing season just before fall rains began. A water use[5] estimate was obtained as the difference between the beginning and ending soil moisture measurements.

Differences between the spring 1961 and spring 1962 soil moisture measurements were very small. Furthermore, winter precipitation always substantially exceeded soil water-holding capacity. Therefore, the spring 1962 measurement was accepted as the initial soil water charge for succeeding years. An estimate of water use for a particular growing season was obtained as the difference between the spring 1962 measurement and a measurement at the end of the growing season in question.

RESULTS

Diameter growth was greatest in the lowest level of growing stock and least in the highest level. Principal difference was between the lowest stand density level and the other four treatments (fig. 2). This relationship was consistent and statistically significant whether diameter growth of all trees or only that of the largest diameter trees per acre (100, 200, or 300) were compared.

Height growth ranged from a low of 4.7 feet per tree on one plot to a high of 6.5 feet on another. Height growth averaged 5.8 feet over all plots. Differences between treatments were small and statistically nonsignificant. This relationship was true whether all trees or only a limited number of tallest trees were considered.

4/ Oregon State University, through Dr. C. T. Youngberg, supplied the neutron probe. Methods of soil moisture measurement closely followed those described in "Effect of Tree Spacing and Understory Vegetation on Water Use in a Pumice Soil," by James W. Barrett and C. T. Youngberg (Soil Sci. Soc. Amer. Proc. 29: 472-475, illus. 1965), except that sampling points were mechanically distributed over individual plots rather than being located at the center of a square formed by four trees.

5/ Water use here means difference between water in the soil at the end of snowmelt in the spring and end of the growing season. Direct evaporation from the soil is included. Not included were additions to soil moisture in the form of growing-season precipitation. However, very little precipitation fell during the growing season.

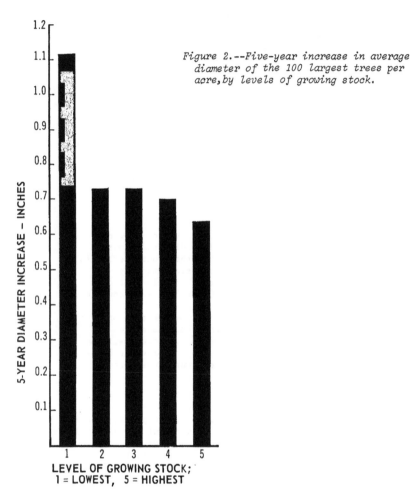

Figure 2.--*Five-year increase in average diameter of the 100 largest trees per acre, by levels of growing stock.*

Volume increment of a limited number of largest trees was substantially greater on plots with lowest levels of growing stock (fig. 3). For example, the 100 largest trees per acre on the lowest level-of-growing-stock plots added almost as much volume as the 200 largest trees at the highest density level. This tendency was statistically significant. Thus, the main goal of stand density control, transfer of volume increment from many small useless trees to a lesser number of larger, potentially higher valued trees, was accomplished.

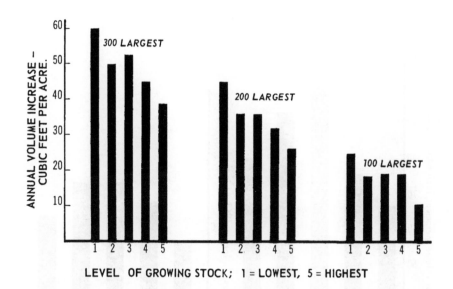

Figure 3.--*Volume increase of the 100, 200, and 300 largest (diameter) trees per acre, by growing-stock level.*

Volume increment of all trees was somewhat less on the lowest and highest levels-of-growing-stock treatments than on the intermediate ones (fig. 4). However, statistical analysis failed to show that differences were significant.

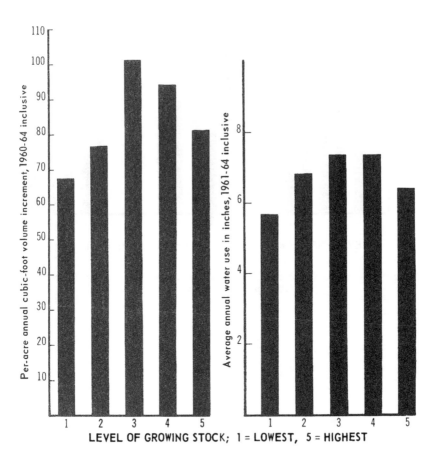

Figure 4.--*Volume increment and soil moisture use, by growing-stock level.*

Stand-density increase was very rapid (table 3). Density
increased on the lowest level-of-growing-stock treatment from 7,300
square feet of bole area per acre to 10,500 square feet in 5 years.
This was 61 percent of the difference between initial density and
beginning density of the next higher level-of-growing-stock treatment. In terms of basal area, the comparable increase amounted to
72 percent.

Table 3.--Five-year change in stand density by growing-stock

level for lodgepole pine in central Oregon (per-

acre basis)

Growing-stock level	Bole area			Basal area		
	1959	1964	Increase	1959	1964	Increase
	M square feet			Square feet		
1 (lowest)	7.3	10.5	3.2	41.7	62.0	20.3
2	12.5	16.3	3.8	70.0	88.6	18.6
3	16.5	21.8	5.3	85.3	107.4	22.1
4	19.3	24.7	5.4	92.4	113.6	21.2
5 (highest)	20.3	25.1	4.8	93.6	115.4	21.8

Records of soil moisture use, including surface evaporation,
are available for only four of the five growing seasons included in
the growth record. Nevertheless, a regression of 5-year volume
increment on 4-year water use, by plots, showed a significant
correlation (fig. 5), indicating that more soil moisture was used
where more wood was produced.

When moisture use is tabulated by individual years (table 4),
additional insight is furnished on the probable influence of stand
density on water use (and ultimately on wood production). In 1961
(second growing season after the original thinning) and again in
1965 (immediately following the second thinning), differences in
moisture use between treatments were significant. Low soil moisture
use by the low density treatment during these years was the principal
reason for differences. In the intervening years, differences in
moisture use among treatments were not statistically significant.
These trends suggest that the heaviest thinning treatment lowered
stand density enough to reduce water use for the first year or two;

however, recovery of roots and crowns was sufficiently rapid to eliminate treatment-caused differences or reduce them to nondetectable size by the third year after thinning.

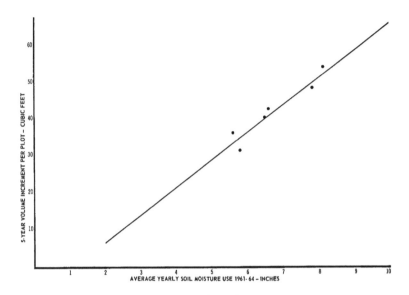

Figure 5.--Regression of volume increment on water use.

Table 4.--<u>Average moisture use by treatments and years for</u>

<u>lodgepole pine in central Oregon (inches)</u>

Treatment	1961	1962	1963	1964	1965
1 (lowest density)	5.2	6.4	4.6	6.6	3.5
2	7.2	7.4	5.6	7.0	5.4
3	7.4	8.0	6.0	7.7	6.1
4	7.4	8.2	6.0	7.6	6.0
5 (highest density)	6.3	7.5	5.0	6.9	6.2

DISCUSSION

First results from this experiment confirm that good rates
of diameter growth can be attained in young lodgepole pine if trees
have ample growing space. They also demonstrate that growth
capacity of the site is redistributed very rapidly following a broad
range of thinning intensities. Total volume of wood produced per
acre over the 5-year period was not significantly different among
growing-stock levels, although annual moisture use records suggest
a temporary reduction probably occurred in the lowest level. Moisture
records further demonstrate that volume production per unit area is
closely related to use of water during the growing season.

In terms of Oregon markets, trees in the experimental stand
are well below merchantable size. A primary management goal in
such premerchantable stands would usually be to eliminate stems that
die before they reach usable size and concentrate growth capacity on
only those stems that will contribute to intermediate or final
harvests. During this premerchantable stage of development, total
wood production per acre is of secondary importance. Initial results
indicate this goal can be achieved with very low levels of growing
stock and suggest either that initial spacings of lodgepole pine
should be very wide or that precommercial thinnings may have to be
repeated at frequent intervals.

FOREST AND RANGE EXPERIMENT STATION · U.S. DEPARTMENT OF AGRICULTURE · PORTLAND, OREGON

PNW-48   *February 1967*

AN ANALYSIS OF TWO LOGGING ROAD STANDARDS
FOR BLM'S TILLAMOOK PROJECT[1]

by
Con H. Schallau, Principal Economist

INTRODUCTION

Currently, most logging road construction on public lands in the Pacific Northwest is financed from the proceeds of timber sales. In 1965, for instance, only 9.8 percent of the National Forest and 14.0 percent of the Bureau of Land Management mileage of new road construction in Washington and Oregon were built with appropriated funds.

Generally, appropriated funds are used to finance road construction where circumstances dictate a higher standard of road than can be underwritten by a timber sale appraisal, cost allowance deduction; e.g., where multiple use traffic is heavy. But does financing roads with appropriated funds necessarily justify a higher standard of construction than that which the timber operator would build, other things being equal? A recent analysis of roading alternatives for the Tillamook Young-Growth Management Project sheds some light on this question.

---

[1] This project was established in Tillamook County, Oreg., by the U.S. Department of Interior's Bureau of Land Management (BLM) to use and test the latest technical and economic young-growth timber management concepts. The Pacific Northwest Forest and Range Experiment Station is assisting in the evaluation phases of the project.

Choice of building lower cost road would
expose three times as much timber but
result in higher maintenance costs

Funds (approximately $475,000) became available for advance
roading a portion of the Bureau of Land Management's 56,000-acre
Tillamook project area during fiscal year 1967. The area to be roaded
supports a full range of age classes. Therefore, the roads[2] would
provide access for thinning in immature stands as well as for harvest
cuts. Just how much acreage could be exposed would depend upon the
choice of road standard--the higher the standard, the higher the cost
per mile and, therefore, the fewer miles of road that could be constructed with appropriated funds. The question to resolve, therefore,
was, "Given a fixed budget, which would be the more feasible from an
economic standpoint, (1) 8 miles of high-standard 'timber access'
roads [see table 1 for a comparison of road specifications] or (2) 24
miles of 'low design-speed'[3] roads?"

Cost per mile for timber access roads was estimated to be three
times that for low design-speed roads--$59,374 vs. $19,792. Since
$475,000 spent for constructing the latter type of road would result
in exposing three times as much timberland for more intensive management (2,886 acres vs. 962 acres), the choice of road standard would
appear rather straightforward. But two additional factors affect the
decision: (1) hauling cost and (2) road maintenance.

Generally speaking, hauling costs increase as road investment
decreases. For any given timber sale tributary to the proposed road
segments, total hauling distances will range from 20 to 40 miles.
But only 1 mile of this distance, on the average, will be over the
proposed roads. For this reason, any difference in hauling costs due
to varying the investment of the 1-mile-long road segments would undoubtedly be minor. So, for the purposes of this analysis, hauling
costs were assumed to be the same for both road standards.

---

[2] The roading situation involves a group of road segments
averaging 1 mile in length. Each segment would represent the last
leg of the permanent road system required to gain access into a
given timbershed.

[3] The average designed speed for this type of road would
range from 15 to 20 miles per hour. The average speed for the timber
access roads would range from 20 to 25 miles per hour.

Table 1.--Comparison of specifications for low design-speed
and access roads[1]

Road specification	Low design-speed road	Access road
Usable width (feet)	12	12
Maximum subgrade width (feet)	16	20
Maximum radius curve (feet)	75	100
Maximum favorable grade (percent)	15	12
Average number of curves per mile	20	11
Average number of turnouts per mile	9	13
Average number of cleared acres per mile	6-1/2	10

[1] The location of the road would be the same for both road standards.

Given the same amount of use, lower standard roads can be expected to cost more to maintain than higher standard roads.[4] For the purposes of this analysis, low design-speed roads were assumed to cost $637 per mile per year to maintain. This cost was estimated by averaging fiscal years 1963 and 1964 Bureau of Public Roads maintenance charges for purchaser-built roads in the Bureau of Land Management's Salem district. Comparable data for timber access roads were not available--this type of road generally receives more use than low design-speed road--but an average annual maintenance cost of $500 per mile was believed fairly realistic.

Economic analysis uses internal
rate-of-return criterion

The economic analysis involved a comparison of costs of and returns to the two types of road systems during a 40-year investment period commencing in 1967. A planning horizon of 40 years was selected because logging technology probably will render the roads under question obsolete within this time span.

[4] Betz, Matthew J. Highway maintenance cost--a consideration for developing areas. In "Highway Research Record No. 94," p. 10. Highway Res. Board, Nat. Acad. Sci., Nat. Res. Counc. Pub. 1310. 1965.

The essential task of the economic analysis was to determine the rate (p) which equated the present value of costs to the present value of revenues for each of the roading alternatives. This was accomplished by discounting to the present all costs and returns associated with a roading investment, using various interest rates, until the difference between the present value of costs and returns was zero. The general equation for solving such a problem is

$$0 = \left[\sum_{j=1}^{t} R_j/(1+p)^n - \sum_{j=1}^{y} C_j/(1+p)^n \right]$$

where

R_j = jth revenue stemming from roading investment, dollars
C_j = jth cost associated with roading investment, dollars
n = year of transaction
p = interest rate, decimal
t = number of revenue items
y = number of cost items

Road construction and maintenance cost assumptions have already been mentioned. However, one additional variable cost item entering into the analysis was the cost of timber sale administration. Currently, the weighted average of such costs for intermediate and harvest cuts is $2.75 per thousand board feet and, for the purposes of this analysis, is assumed to remain at this level indefinitely.

Annual stumpage revenues from tributary timber sales were assumed to remain at $156,418 for the 24 miles of low design-speed roads and $52,162 for the 8 miles of timber access roads. The flow of stumpage receipts is based upon a cutting budget generated by the age-class distribution of forest types exposed by the proposed roads. The method used for determining the volume of timber harvested annually was patterned after the technique (area-volume check) used to regulate the cut from the entire 56,000-acre Tillamook project area. Per-acre yields were modified to reflect thinning operations. A constant stumpage price of $30 per thousand board feet (International 1/8-inch log rule) was used to convert timber volumes to values.

Results of analysis disclose low design-speed road more economical when limited traffic is anticipated

High-standard, timber access roads are undoubtedly more economical than the low design-speed road for situations where moderate-to-heavy traffic is anticipated. But constructing the proposed system of timber sale roads to the timber access road standard represents

overbuilding from an economical standpoint in this instance. This
statement was substantiated by the comparison of the internal rates of
return to the two road-investment alternatives. An investment in 8
miles of high-standard access roads costing $475,200 would earn ap-
proximately 9 percent, but an investment of approximately the same
magnitude--$475,000--for constructing 24 miles of low design-speed
road would earn 27 percent.

SUMMARY

This analysis demonstrates why factors other than maintenance
costs must be considered in deciding what road standard to adopt.
The lower standard, less expensive, low design-speed roads do cost
more to maintain than access roads.[5] But, in situations where
limited use is expected, the difference in annual maintenance charges
does not justify the construction of high-standard access roads. In
the case of the Tillamook project, $475,200 invested in low design-
speed roads will expose three times as much forest land for intermediate and harvest cutting as the same amount invested in access roads,
thus generating a flow of revenues which more than compensates for a
higher maintenance budget.

---

[5] A 3-percent discount rate assumed, annual road maintenance
for the low design-speed roads would have to average $3,434 per mile
before timber access roads would be more profitable.

RADIATION SAMPLING IN A MOUNTAINOUS ZONE

by

William B. Fowler, Meteorologist

1 a broad area of similar climate, it is commonly accepted
;le station measurement of incoming solar radiation can be
:ive of conditions for a reasonable distance. In other
: climatic change is rapid, extension of single station
:s over even short distances may be suspect. Within the
:ted States, rapid climatic changes are typical.

.iminary investigation
iriation and sampling
7as made during the
.963 in a watershed
: Cascade Range crest
:on State. Radiation
'ranometers) (fig. 1)
:ated (including re-
)r) to within 5 per-
:tandard Eppley pyra-
.11 sensors recorded
:rcent of each other.

:he exception of one
ition site (2,500 feet),
is were within a 5,000-
·ot range with unob-
·mispheric view. The
ition site was included
hs (figs. 2 and 3) and
  computations without
for elevational effects.

Figure 1.--*Field installation
of radiation sensor used.*

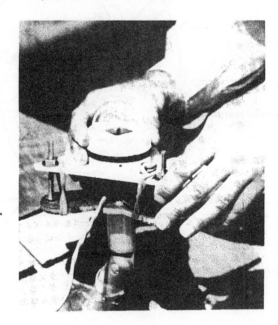

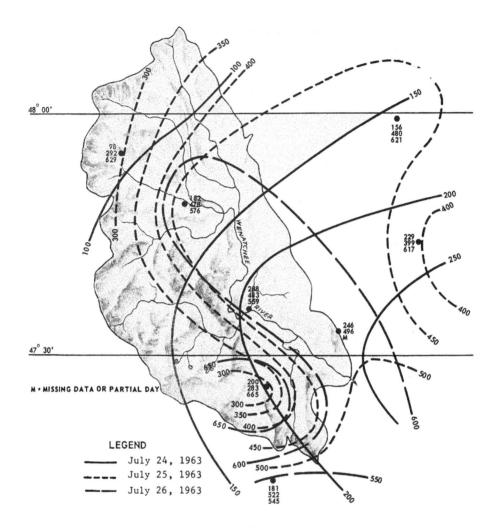

Figure 2.—*Three-day input pattern of total solar radiation ly. day*$^{-1}$ *for July 24-26, 1963.*

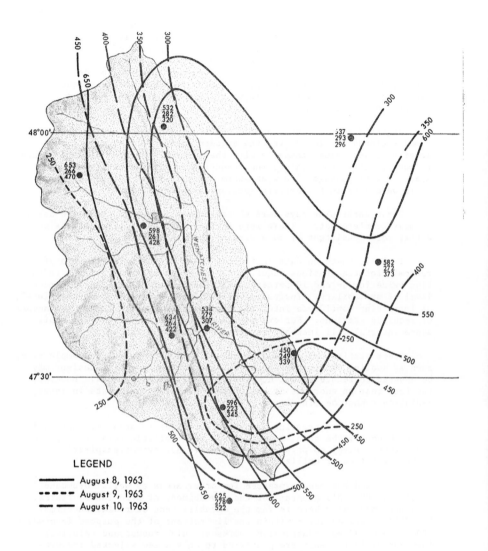

Figure 3.--*Three-day input pattern of total solar radiation ly. day*[-1] *for*
August 8-10, 1963.

The input data for two 3-day sequences (figs. 2 and 3) reflect the changing patterns of cloud development and movement within or across the watershed area. July 24 (fig. 2) represented a situation of generally low radiative input but with gradual dissipation of cloud cover with distance east from the Cascade Range crest. This is an expected and frequently occurring pattern. More marked clearing to the east was seen on July 25. On July 26 the weather system had passed through the area; all sensors showed high input values, and gradient was small over the entire watershed area.

August 8 (fig. 3) represented another commonly occurring pattern. Cumulus clouds developed over the eastern segment of the watershed lowering input values compared with the western segment. A large change to much lower overall values and reduction in gradient was shown on August 9 with passage of a weak storm. The residual effects of this storm were seen in the eastern section on August 11.

These particular days were chosen from a larger group on the basis of most complete data. There were periods when the input patterns were either more consistent or more erratic than those shown.

Table 1, based on data in figures 2 and 3, indicates numbers of randomly located stations required to determine mean daily input radiation value for 5- and 10-percent confidence intervals at the 95-percent level of probability. Increasing probability above the 95-percent level, or increasing confidence interval, increases by a large factor the number of required stations. For example, each 50-percent increase in confidence interval will increase sampling density by a factor of 4.

Other statistical procedures can be used to recalculate sample size, such as pooling within-day variance. Also, other sampling designs may be adopted to reduce actual numbers of required instruments. However, the fact that an enormous amount of natural variation exists in input radiation cannot be minimized.

The need for increasing numbers of stations in areas of rapid climatic change can be seen, especially if any realistic relationship between input energy to physical processes (i.e., evapotranspiration) is to be determined or utilized.

This need has been expressed for other areas as well. Drummond,[1] writing of UNESCO's program for the development of arid lands, states, "the main necessity here is for the establishment of radiation climatologies, representative within the limitations of the purpose in mind, from widespread observational networks at which robust and relatively inexpensive instruments are preferred to only a few selected measurement series, even if the latter are of a more precise nature."

---

[1] Drummond, A. J. Radiation and the thermal balance. Climatology: Reviews of Research, 1-20. UNESCO. 1958.

Table 1.—Number of stations for sampling radiation intensities (on the basis of figures 2 and 3) by selected 1963 dates

Date	Number of stations used	Input radiation values			Variance s^2	Number of stations required when sampling error (95-percent probability) is	
		Mean	Maximum	Minimum		10 percent of mean value	5 percent of mean value
		------- ly. day^{-1} -------					
July 24	8	185	246	98	2,846	33	133
July 25	8	429	522	292	8,863	19	77
July 26	8	599	665	559	1,638	2	7
August 8	10	578	653	450	4,061	5	19
August 9	10	264	293	223	570	3	13
August 10	10	377	522	296	6,138	17	70

FOREST AND RANGE EXPERIMENT STATION · U.S. DEPARTMENT OF AGRICULTURE · PORTLAND, OREGON

PNW-50   *March 1967*

PRIMARY MICROBIOLOGICAL SUCCESSION ON A LANDSLIDE
OF ALPINE ORIGIN AT MOUNT RAINIER

by

W. B. Bollen, *Principal Soil Microbiologist*
K. C. Lu, *Microbiologist*
J. M. Trappe, *Principal Mycologist*
R. F. Tarrant, *Principal Soil Scientist*
J. F. Franklin, *Plant Ecologist*

In December 1963, immense masses of rock and debris broke loose
from the north face of Little Tahoma Peak on the shoulder of Mount
Rainier (Crandell and Fahnestock 1965).[1] Originating from a zone
roughly 9,000 to 11,000 feet above sea level, the resulting series
of avalanches swept down Emmons Glacier to deposit an estimated 14
million cubic yards of debris over 2 square miles of the glacier and
the sparsely vegetated outwash valley below (fig. 1). Deposits reach
thicknesses of about 100 feet in the valley, whose original elevation
ranged from about 4,500 to 5,500 feet.

Figure 1.--Northeast slope of
Mount Rainier with Little
Tahoma Peak on left-center
skyline and avalanche de-
posit in valley.

[1] Names and dates in
parentheses refer to Literature Cited, p. 7.

This nearly virgin, alpine "soil," laid in a valley surrounded by montane forest, presents superb opportunity for studies of soil development, plant succession, and distribution of pesticides and other environmental pollutants, especially when coupled with concurrent observations of nearby terminal moraines left from recent recession of Emmons Glacier. To seize this opportunity in time to observe early stages of microbiological succession, we began reconnaissance soil sampling and analysis in early October 1965.[2]

The top 8 inches of deposit were sampled at three locations: (1) near the middle of the lower half of the valley deposit (fig. 2); (2) at the lower edge of the main deposit, adjacent to uncovered moraine disgorged by Emmons Glacier in 1897 (Sigafoos and Hendricks 1961); and (3) on the 1897 moraine from under a clump of Sitka alder (*Alnus sinuata* (Reg.) Rydb.) adjacent to location 2 (fig. 3). In addition, water was sampled from a turbid pond trapped in a furrow on the deposit near location 1 (fig. 2). These locations were chosen to represent new deposits and older, plant-colonized surface. The extreme heterogeneity of both avalanche and moraine precluded any attempt to sample "average" conditions.

Figure 2.--Surface of the avalanche deposit with pond trapped in furrow.

[2] We thank the staff of Mount Rainier National Park for facilities and assistance.

Figure 3.--Clump of *Alnus sinuata* on moraine adjacent to avalanche (sapling in foreground is *Pinus contorta* Dougl.).

Three collections of about 500 grams each were dug with sterile tools and combined at each location. After all stones thicker than 1 inch were discarded, each combined sample was sealed in a sterile bottle at the site. In the laboratory, 3 days later, samples were sieved with sterile precautions through a 10-mesh Tyler standard screen. Material larger than 10-mesh was dried, weighed, and discarded. After subsamples were taken for microbial analysis and determination of water content, pH, and ash, residuals were air-dried. Sample residuals from locations 1 and 3 were sieved through a series of closer meshed Tyler screens on a Porter sand shaker; fractions were weighed and then recombined (the 10-mesh residual from location 2 was insufficient for mechanical analysis). Finally, the recombined residuals and the residual from location 2 were ground to pass 100-mesh and analyzed for total carbon and nitrogen content.

Samples were dried to a constant weight at 105° C. to determine their water content. Glass-electrode determinations of pH were made with suspensions of one part soil in five parts water. Total nitrogen was determined by the Kjeldahl procedure, and total carbon by dry combustion at 950° C. For analysis of microflora, dilutions were prepared to provide 30 to 100 colonies per plate. Agar media included rose bengal and peptone-glucose-acid for molds, and sodium albuminate and trypticase soy for bacteria and *Streptomyces* (Martin 1950, Waksman and Fred 1922, Baltimore Biological Laboratory 1962).

A smaller proportion of avalanche material than moraine soil passed through the 10-mesh sieve (21 versus 63 percent), likely due to the differing origins of deposit. Though vegetation on the moraine doubtless has influenced breakdown of soil particles, studies of moraines in Alaska suggest that several more decades of plant growth must elapse before such effects become detectable (Crocker and Major 1955, Crocker and Dickson 1957, Viereck 1966).

In contrast to textural properties, chemical differences between avalanche and moraine deposits can reasonably be attributed to effects of vegetation on the moraine (table 1). Reaction of avalanche samples was near neutral, whereas the pond water had a pH of 8.2. Because the avalanche deposits are largely andesite (Crandell and Fahnestock 1965), a basic igneous rock, these relatively high pH's were expected. The moraine soil, though derived from similar rock, had a pH of 5.7. We ascribe this higher acidity largely to the deposit and decomposition of organic matter.

Table 1.--Chemical analyses of samples from deposits of Little Tahoma

avalanche and adjacent moraine in percentage ovendry weight

Sample No.	Water	pH	Ash	Total carbon	Kjeldahl nitrogen	C:N ratio
	Percent		Percent	Percent	Percent	
1	10.5	7.2	98.9	0.075	0.002	38
2	8.7	7.2	99.8	.049	.002	25
3	7.0	5.7	99.4	.263	.014	19

Total carbon was minimal in the avalanche material. Carbon content of moraine samples, though low in comparison with well-developed soils (Buckman and Brady 1960), shows the contribution of organic matter from Sitka alder and its associated mosses and lichens. A notable amount of nitrogen had accumulated in the moraine soil. Some of this may have been contributed by free-living, nitrogen-fixing micro-organisms, but most can be reasonably attributed to the alder, a nodulated, nonlegumi-nous woody plant capable of fixing atmospheric nitrogen. The concomitant lowering of the C:N ratio is particularly important for soil micro-organisms and plant succession. Sitka alder here influenced soil properties as it did on moraines in coastal Alaska (Crocker and Major 1955, Crocker and Dickson 1957) and as *Alnus rubra* did on forest soils of the Pacific Northwest (Tarrant and Miller 1963, Chen [3]).

Despite the interval of nearly 2 years between the avalanche and our sampling, the avalanche material still was at a very early stage of primary microbiological succession. Fungal populations (table 2) were analogous in both kind and number to those isolated from moraine soils in very early successional stages in coastal Alaska (Cooke and Lawrence 1959). Bacterial populations (table 3) were at levels similar to those of barren soils of the Arctic (Sushkina 1960). The profound influence of Sitka alder on microfloral populations was of a magnitude similar to that in Alaska (Cooke and Lawrence 1959).

Table 2.--Fungi isolated on dilution plates from samples of deposits of Little Tahoma avalanche and adjacent moraine in total number of colonies per ovendry gram of sample and proportion of various groups

Location No.	Medium [1]	Total colonies per gram	*Mucor* species	*Penicillium* species	*Aspergillus* species	Dematiaceae	Sterile mycelia	Other
		Number	----------------------------------- Percent -----------------------------					
1	RB	300	1		0	4	43	46
	PGA	35	u	،	10	33	24	28
2	RB	160	0	50	-	0	6	44
	PGA	80	0	81		0	19	0
3	RB	56,000	0	93		0	0	7
	PGA	36,500	0	100	0	0	0	0

[1] RB = Martin's rose bengal-streptomycin agar, pH 7.0.

PGA = peptone-glucose-acid agar, pH 4.0.

[3] Chen, Chi-Sin. Influence of interplanted and pure stands of red alder (*Alnus rubra* Bong.) on microbial and chemical characteristics of a coastal forest soil in the Douglas-fir region. 167 pp., illus. Unpublished Ph. D. thesis on file at Oreg. State Univ., Corvallis. 1965.

Table 3.—Bacteria isolated on dilution plates from samples

of deposits of Little Tahoma avalanche and adjacent

moraine in total number of colonies per ovendry

gram of sample and proportion of *Streptomyces*

Location No.	Medium[1]	Total colonies per gram	*Streptomyces* species
		Number	Percent
1	Na Alb.	76,000	10
	TSA	24,500	0
2	Na Alb.	37,500	16
	TSA	214,000	0
3	Na Alb.	3,550,000	20
	TSA	5,900,000	12

[1] Na Alb. = sodium albuminate agar, pH 7.0.

TSA = trypticase soy agar (BBL), pH 7.0.

The low population of *Penicillia* and relative abundance of Dematiaceae at location 1 were unlike those for well-developed soils. The far greater population of fungi under alder on the moraine was characteristic of forest soils, as was the high proportion of *Penicillia* (Bollen and Wright 1961). Several other genera common to forest soils were lacking, however. We detected no fungi in water from the turbid pond.

Differences in bacterial populations similarly show the striking influence of alder. *Streptomyces* were relatively poorly represented in all cases, as compared with forest and arable soils where they frequently comprise nearly half the total count (Bollen and Wright 1961, Bollen 1941). The pond water had a very high count, 192,500 bacteria/milliliter (no *Streptomyces*). This large population was likely due to the high content of inorganic suspended solids, totaling 1,440 parts per million. No coliform bacteria were detected from inoculations of pond samples into lactose broth, so use of the area by animals has evidently remained low to date.

6

By August 1966, the avalanche deposit was still unstable, with
considerable settling and slumping activity. Few vascular plants
have become established, although current-year seedlings of *Alnus
sinuata* and *Salix* spp. have taken tenuous hold in numerous locations.
The ensuing sequence of microbiological succession will undoubtedly
hinge on the same kind of soil amelioration that alder has exerted
on adjacent moraine: accumulation of nitrogen and organic matter
and lowering of the C:N ratio and pH.

LITERATURE CITED

Baltimore Biological Laboratory, Inc.
    1962. Culture media and materials and apparatus for the micro-
        biological laboratory. 244 pp. Baltimore, Md.

Bollen, W. B., and Wright, Ernest.
    1961. Microbes and nitrates in soils from virgin and young-
        growth forests. Can. J. Microbiol. 7: 785-792.

Bollen, Walter B.
    1941. Soil respiration studies on the decomposition of native
        organic matter. Iowa State Coll. J. Sci. 15: 353-374.

Buckman, Harry O., and Brady, Nyle C.
    1960. The nature and properties of soils. Ed. 6, 567 pp., illus.
        New York: The Macmillan Co.

Cooke, W. B., and Lawrence, D. B.
    1959. Soil mould fungi isolated from recently glaciated soils
        in south-eastern Alaska. J. Ecol. 47: 529-549.

Crandell, Dwight R., and Fahnestock, Robert K.
    1965. Rockfalls and avalanches from Little Tahoma Peak on Mount
        Rainier Washington. U.S. Geol. Surv. Bull. 1221-A, 30 pp.,
        illus.

Crocker, Robert L., and Dickson, B. A.
    1957. Soil development on the recessional moraines of the Herbert
        and Mendenhall Glaciers, south-eastern Alaska. J. Ecol.
        45: 169-185, illus.

——————— and Major, Jack.
    1955. Soil development in relation to vegetation and surface age
        at Glacier Bay, Alaska. J. Ecol. 43: 427-448, illus.

Martin, James P.
    1950. Use of acid, rose bengal, and streptomycin in the plate
        method for estimating soil fungi. Soil Sci. 69: 215-232,
        illus.

Sigafoos, Robert S., and Hendricks, E. L.
    1961. Botanical evidence of the modern history of Nisqually
           Glacier, Washington. U.S. Geol. Surv. Prof. Pap. 387-A:
           A1-A8, illus.

Sushkina, N. N.
    1960. Characteristics of the microflora of Arctic soils. Soviet
           Soil Sci. 1960: 392-400.

Tarrant, Robert F., and Miller, Richard E.
    1963. Accumulation of organic matter and soil nitrogen beneath
           a plantation of red alder and Douglas-fir. Soil Sci. Soc.
           Amer. Proc. 27: 231-234.

Viereck, Leslie A.
    1966. Plant succession and soil development on gravel outwash of
          the Muldrow Glacier, Alaska. Ecol. Monogr. 36: 181-199,
          illus.

Waksman, S. A., and Fred, E. B.
    1922. A tentative outline of the plate method for determining
           the number of microorganisms in the soil. Soil Sci. 14:
           27-28.

* * * * *

FOREST AND RANGE EXPERIMENT STATION · U.S. DEPARTMENT OF AGRICULTURE · PORTLAND, OREGON

PNW-51   *April 1962*

FIRE-DANGER RATING IN THE FUTURE

by

James E. Hefner
Associate Fire Systems Analyst

The forest resources of this country must be protected from
wildfire. Protection does not eliminate fire but does reduce loss
from fire. In recent years, more acres have been burned on the unprotected 3 percent of forest land than on the 97 percent under
organized fire protection. Protection from fire has saved more than
100 million acres per year. This figure is based on an average burned-
area rate of 10 percent for unprotected and 0.2 percent for protected
lands.

The fire protection job has been accomplished by public and
private expenditures of about $150 million per year. Because of
intangible values, which often exceed timber losses, the dollar savings cannot be pinpointed, but are estimated to be at least a billion
dollars per year. Obviously, fire control pays its way.

The Forest Service objective with regard to fire-danger rating
is "to provide forest officers with information on current fire danger
to guide them in making the best and most economical use of force and
facilities." The general policy is "to make maximum use of fire-danger
rating in prevention, presuppression, and suppression action." An
accurate, simple, yet complete system of fire-danger rating is needed

to help accomplish the task of fire control decision making.

Prevention, presuppression, and suppression plans are the basis for actions taken at various levels of administration during the fire season. An important part of presuppression planning by the U.S. Forest Service is the Manning and Specific Action Guide which is based on fire-danger rating. This guide specifies manpower, equipment, and action required each day depending on the level of fire danger forecast for the management unit. Both the basic protection organization and the emergency organization are considered in planning. These plans affect the actions of the fire control staff at the district, forest, and regional levels of administration.

Most fire control people are familiar with the history of fire-danger rating and are aware of recent advances made with the completion of the Spread Phase of the National System of fire-danger rating. The Spread Phase tables, providing for the computation of a Spread Index and a Buildup Index, have been adopted by most Forest Service and other Federal units and some States. Other elements of fire behavior--risk, ignition, and fire intensity--are not considered in the Spread Phase.

Where do we go from here in fire-danger rating? The National Fire-Danger Rating Project, formerly located at the Southeastern Forest Experiment Station, Asheville, N.C., has been transferred to Seattle, Wash., as a part of Pacific Northwest Forest and Range Experiment Station research. The objective of the project is to develop a fire-danger rating system adequate for application to all forest and range types in the continental United States. In doing this, the project expects to extend the efforts of those who developed the Spread Phase of the National System.

Analytical research is establishing use-related specifications for additional fire-danger rating indexes, as well as structural framework for these indexes. Research data will be drawn from appropriate fields to develop the indexes in quantitative form. It should be understood that any index, present or future, will need to be updated from time to time as new information becomes available. It should also be understood that a certain amount of study and testing will be needed to adapt any national index to local use. The testing of any new index(es) will include field trials and comparisons with historical records of weather, fire occurrence, and severity.

Fire control specialists realize that the analytical problem in danger rating is more involved than a simple component framework, involving four phases, might suggest. For example, there is some question whether risk can be separated from ignition in the early development work of the various phases of a system. Risk is defined as the number of firebrands landing on a fuel bed, and a direct method of measuring this element will ultimately be needed. The only available indicator at present, number of fire occurrences, is influenced by both risk and ignition probability. Another example of jointly determined fire-danger elements is the effect of fuel energy on rate of spread.

It is necessary to determine, by systems analysis, the indexes or integration of indexes that will be most useful to the fire control organization. An integral part of this application problem is the bridge from fire-danger indexes, based on fuel, weather, and risk conditions, to fire control planning and execution. How best to convert a physical index into on-the-ground decisions? What kind of index number system is needed by the fire dispatcher, the organization's fire chief, or the fire boss? What is the proper balance between simplicity and accuracy; between timeliness, sophistication of instrumentation, and cost? To meet objectives of cost and precision, what is the best grid of danger stations for a particular set of physical, climatic, and administrative circumstances? These and other questions are being answered by analyzing fire control as a network of decisions, with each decision requiring its own kind of fire-danger information.

This system-analysis approach is expected to lead to one or more danger-rating schemes that can be interpreted with minimum effort in terms of preparedness levels and action plans. Thus, for example, a dispatcher sending a crew on initial attack should be able, with pertinent information on fire location, size, topography, fuels, and access available to him at the moment, to convert a fire-danger-rating number into an estimate of the effort required to control the fire.

Underway at this time are two fact-finding studies to obtain information on national requirements and local variations in fire-danger rating, as a basis for future work in the project. The first study is concerned with the present status of fire-danger rating and how it is used in various parts of the country. The second study deals with how day-to-day fire control decisions are affected by fire-danger rating and what these decisions are. Future studies requiring laboratory research or collection of field data will be referred to fire research laboratories or selected cooperators.

Because this project is national in scope, cooperators will include various Federal and State fire control agencies. As in the past, similar cooperation from industry and universities is anticipated and welcomed.

* * * * *

PNW-52

April 1967

SINGLE-SPAN RUNNING SKYLINE

by

Hilton H. Lysons, *Principal Industrial Engineer*
and
Charles N. Mann, *Mechanical Engineer*

Introduction

Skylines for harvesting timber in steep terrain have proved to be effective in reducing log breakage, soil disturbance, and access road requirements. Elements of skyline logging systems vary with the needs of each operation, but generally, such systems employ a fixed or standing line for support of the load and operating lines for movement and control. This note refers to an arrangement, called a "running skyline," which does not require a standing line. A method of calculating its load-carrying capability is presented.

The Running Skyline

Two running lines, generally referred to as main and haulback, may be tensioned to support a load (fig. 1) and thereby eliminate the need for a separate standing skyline. The elimination of the standing line provides faster and easier rigging and reduces fire hazard because no operating lines run along the ground. Since the logs are supported by two lines, the lines can be smaller than a single standing line for the same job.

Equipment Considerations

Proper equipment will contribute greatly to an efficient operation. The yarder is most important in this respect due to the critical line tension requirements. An ideal yarder for this system should incorporate an efficient interlock between main and haulback drums to provide the necessary line tensions with minimum use of brakes. The yarder

Figure 1.--Running skyline system.

should also provide a means of limiting tensions to the safe working load of the lines, either by providing the operator with a tension indicator or by automatically limiting the line tension.

A variety of carriages, grapples, or butt rigging may be adapted to running skylines. As with any skyline, the weight of this suspended equipment should be kept to a minimum to permit the maximum payload.

Careful attention should be given to the design of the tailblock to insure reasonable wire rope life. Consideration should be given to use of a factor of safety higher than 3, as generally used for standing skylines, to compensate for the added bending and wear imposed on the running lines.

Capability

Much of the basic information contained in the "Skyline Tension and Deflection Handbook"[1] for standing skylines can be used to determine the payload capability of running skyline systems. A copy of this publication may be obtained from Pacific Northwest Forest and Range Experiment Station, P. O. Box 3141, Portland, Oregon 97208.

---

[1] Lysons, Hilton H., and Mann, Charles N. Skyline tension and deflection handbook. Pacific Northwest Forest & Range Exp. Sta. U.S. Forest Serv. Res. Pap. PNW-39, 41 pp., illus. 1967.

The earlier version of this handbook[2] may also be used. However, figures will have to be identified by titles only since their numbers were changed in the 1967 version.

Unlike a standing skyline, the lines of a running skyline system are not preset to provide a specific deflection or sag in the line. Instead, the deflection results from a combination of the load and the line tension. If the yarder maintains a constant tension on the lines of a loaded running skyline, the deflection at any point (the load path) will depend on the weight of load.

In the skyline handbook (footnote 1), a procedure is presented for graphically determining the allowable deflection of a standing skyline. The load path is approximated by fixing the length of the line and moving a weight along the line to check for the required clearance. Since the maximum line tension occurs when the load is at midspan, the midspan deflection is obtained for calculating the capability based on the safe working load of the line.

The situation is somewhat different for a running skyline with a constant line tension. If the same span conditions and midspan deflection for a standing and a running skyline system are assumed, a comparison of the two load paths can be made. At the midspan and the ends, the two load paths will coincide. Everywhere else, the running line load path will be somewhat above that of the standing line. Since the actual load path of a running skyline system cannot be readily determined, it is suggested that the load path of the standing skyline be substituted as a conservative approximation.

Payload capability is defined as the maximum safe vertical load on the skyline after deducting the weight of the carriage or other suspended equipment. This should not be exceeded by the total weight of the logs if carried free of the ground or an appropriate portion of the log load if one end is allowed to drag.

If the mainline passes through the carriage and down to the log, safe working load on this line must be equal to or greater than the payload capability. The payload capability of a running skyline system is determined by the location of the yarder as discussed below:

1. System with yarder at upper end.--In this case, main-line tension will be greater than haulback tension since the main line must provide the snubbing force or tangential component of the load as well as support

[2] Lysons, Hilton H., and Mann, Charles N. Skyline logging handbook on wire rope tensions and deflections. U.S. Forest Serv. Pacific Northwest Forest and Range Exp. Sta., 34 pp., illus. 1965.

part of the load normal to the skyline. The problem is approached by
finding capability based on the haulback line, then checking the main
line to see if it is adequate. Either the main line must be of a
larger size or it must be worked to a higher stress than the haulback.
Detailed steps for finding the capability of the system with the yarder
at the upper end are discussed below:

a. Make a plot of the profile following procedures for single-
span skylines given in "Skyline Tension and Deflection
Handbook." Determine allowable deflection, slope, and
horizontal span length from the plot.

b. Find payload capability based on the haulback line size,
following the detailed steps as presented in the running
skyline worksheet for yarder at upper end (fig. 2). In
calculations, obtain tension due to load for carriage not
clamped to skyline (fig. 12 or table 3 in "Skyline Tension
and Deflection Handbook").

c. Determine the tension on the main line and compare it with
the safe working load. If the main-line tension thus calculated exceeds the safe working load, any one or more of
the following steps may be taken to improve this condition:

(1) Reduce the allowable midspan deflection and recalculate the payload based on the original haulback safe
working load.[3]

(2) Select a larger sized main line to accommodate the
added tension. (Note that the main-line tension
increases with the slope when the yarder is located
at the upper end of the skyline.)

(3) Try relocating the skyline to shorten the span and
thereby reduce the tension.

(4) If the first three steps are not suitable, consideration may be given to reducing the factor of safety
and thereby increasing the working load on the main
line.

---

[3] The difference between the tension in the main line and the
haulback line is a function of the load and the slope of the span.
Since the yarder applies a constant pull on the haulback, the difference in the tensions must be reduced to reduce the main-line tension.
Use of a smaller midspan deflection reduces the payload capability
which reduces the main-line tension.

DETERMINE FROM SKYLINE PROFILE:

Allowable loaded deflection _____ percent

Horizontal span length (one station = 100 feet) _____ stations

Slope of span _____ percent

GIVEN:

Haulback line: Diameter _____ inches   Weight _____ pounds/foot

Breaking strength _____ kips (1 kip = 1,000 pounds)

Factor of safety _____   Safe working load _____ kips

Skyline carriage weight _____ kips

DETERMINE REMAINING CABLE TENSION CAPABILITY:

Safe working load (given) _____ kips

Subtract tension due to cable weight (fig. 11 or table 2):

_____ kips/sta./lb./ft. x _____ stations x _____ lbs./ft.   - _____ kips

Remaining cable tension capability _____ kips

DETERMINE GROSS LOAD CAPABILITY:

Single line gross capability

$$\frac{\text{Remaining tension capability \_\_\_\_\_ kips}}{\text{Tension/kip of load}\underline{1/} \text{ \_\_\_\_\_ kips/kip}}$$ _____ kips

Running line gross capability

Single line gross capability _____ kips x 2   _____ kips

Subtract carriage weight   - _____ kips

Payload capability _____ kips

GIVEN:

Main line: Diameter _____ inches   Weight _____ pounds/foot

Breaking strength _____ kips (1 kip = 1,000 pounds)

Factor of safety _____   Safe working load _____ kips

DETERMINE MAIN-LINE TENSION:

Tension/kip of load$\underline{2/}$ _____ x 2   _____ kips/kip

Subtract tension/kip of load$\underline{1/}$ - _____ kips/kip

Main-line tension/kip of load _____ kips/kip

Tension due to load

Main-line tension/kip of load _____ x _____ single line gross capability _____ kips

Add tension due to cable weight (fig. 11, table 2)   + _____ kips

Main-line tension $\underline{3/}$ $\underline{4/}$ _____ kips

$\underline{1/}$ Tension due to load (carriage not clamped), figure 12 or table 3.

$\underline{2/}$ Tension due to load (carriage clamped), figure 13 or table 4.

$\underline{3/}$ If main-line tension is higher than safe working load, refer to item c, page 4.

$\underline{4/}$ If main line goes through the carriage and down to the logs, refer to item d, page 6.

Figure 2.--Single-span running skyline (yarder at upper end). Note: Figure and table numbers used in this worksheet refer to those in "Skyline Tension and Deflection Handbook."

d. If the main line passes through the carriage and down to
the log load, its safe working load should be equal to or
greater than the payload capability. When employing this
type of carriage, compare the main-line tension with the
payload capability. If the main-line tension is less than
required, a reduction in the allowable loaded deflection is
indicated to reduce the payload capability and thereby reduce the required main-line tension.

2. System with yarder at lower end.--The haulback supplies the
snubbing force, in this case, and haulback tension will be greater
than main-line tension. Capability is based on the haulback-line size.
The procedure for this arrangement is given below:

a. Make a plot of the profile, following procedures for single-
span standing skylines given in the handbook. From this
plot, determine allowable deflection, slope, horizontal
span length, and vertical distance from top of skyline to
loaded carriage.

b. Find payload capability based on haulback line size, using
running skyline worksheet for yarder at lower end (fig. 3).
In calculations, obtain tension due to load for carriage
clamped to skyline (fig. 13 or table 4 in "Skyline Tension
and Deflection Handbook").

c. In this case, main-line tension is lower than haulback
tension and need not be calculated unless the main line
extends through the carriage and is used to pick up the log.
Again, with this type of carriage, main-line tension must be
equal to or greater than the payload capability. If the
main-line tension is less than required, a reduction in the
allowable loaded deflection is indicated to reduce the payload capability and thereby reduce the required main-line
tension.

The "Skyline Tension and Deflection Handbook" gives coefficients
for tension due to load under two conditions; namely, carriage clamped
to the skyline (figure 13 or table 4) and carriage not clamped to the
skyline (figure 12 or table 3). Both coefficients are used in running
skyline calculations, even though the carriage does not clamp to a
running skyline. The difference between these two coefficients is
that one considers only the load normal to the skyline (not clamped)
and the other includes the tangential or snubbing force (clamped) as
well as the load normal to the skyline. The terms "clamped" and "not
clamped," as used herein, refer only to whether the tangential load is
included with the load normal to the skyline and not to the use of any
clamping mechanism in the carriage.

DETERMINE FROM SKYLINE PROFILE:

Allowable loaded deflection   _____ percent

Horizontal span length (one station = 100 feet)   _____ stations

Slope of span   _____ percent

Vertical distance from top of skyline to midspan load point   _____ feet

GIVEN:

Haulback line: Diameter _____ inches   Weight _____ pounds/foot

                Breaking strength _____ kips (1 kip = 1,000 pounds)

                Factor of safety _____   Safe working load _____ kips

Skyline carriage weight _____ kips

DETERMINE REMAINING CABLE TENSION CAPABILITY:

Safe working load (given)   _____ kips

Subtract tension due to cable weight (fig. 11 or table 2):

     _____ kips/sta /lb./ft. x _____ stations x _____ lbs./ft.   - _____ kips

         Remaining cable tension capability   _____ kips

DETERMINE GROSS LOAD CAPABILITY:

Single line gross capability

     $\dfrac{\text{Remaining tension capability} \_\_\_\_\_ \text{ kips}}{\text{Tension/kip of load}\underline{1/} \_\_\_\_\_ \text{ kips/kip}}$ _____ kips

Running line gross capability

     Single line gross capability _____ kips x 2   _____ kips

Subtract carriage weight   - _____ kips

     Payload capability   _____ kips

         (Continue below only if main line goes through carriage
         and down to log)

GIVEN:

Main line. Diameter _____ inches   Weight _____ pounds/foot

             Breaking strength _____ kips (1 kip = 1,000 pounds)

             Factor of safety _____   Safe working load _____ kips

DETERMINE MAIN-LINE TENSION:

Tension/kip of load$\underline{2/}$ _____ x 2   _____ kips/kip

Subtract tension/kip of load$\underline{1/}$ - _____ kips/kip

     Main-line tension/kip of load   _____ kips/kip

Tension due to load

Main-line tension/kip of load _____ x _____ single line gross capability   _____ kips

Add tension due to cable weight (fig. 11 or table 2)   + _____ kips

     Subtotal   _____ kips

Subtract tension loss from upper end to carriage

Vertical distance from upper end to midspan _____ feet

     ‹ _____ lbs./ft./1,000 main-line weight   - _____ kips

     Main-line tension$\underline{3/}$ _____ kips

$\underline{1/}$ Tension due to load (carriage clamped), figure 13 or table 4.

$\underline{2/}$ Tension due to load (carriage not clamped), figure 12 or table 3.

$\underline{3/}$ If main line goes through the carriage and down to the logs, refer to item c, page 6.

Figure 3. _–Single-span running skyline worksheet (yarder at lower end). Note: Figure and table numbers used
in this worksheet refer to those in "Skyline Tension and Deflection Handbook."

FOREST AND RANGE EXPERIMENT STATION · U.S. DEPARTMENT OF AGRICULTURE · PORTLAND, OREGON

PNW-53   *May 1967*

ELEVATION EFFECTS ON RAINFALL NEAR HOLLIS, ALASKA

by

W. J. Walkotten, Forestry Research Technician[1]

and

J. H. Patric, Research Hydrologist[1]

INTRODUCTION

Most precipitation measurements in southeast Alaska are obtained near sea level. Although precipitation on this mountainous coastal region is known to increase with elevation (Federal Power Commission and U.S. Forest Service 1947), few measurements have been made on the densely forested, nearly inaccessible mountains. For a comparison of mountainside rainfall with that at sea level, measurements were made in the fall of 1965 during frequent visits to soil stability plots on a logged mountainside.

STUDY SITE

The Hollis study site (45 miles west of Ketchikan, Alaska) was clearcut in patches during 1957-60. It was on a steep (22.5°), uniform slope facing east-southeast, into the prevailing storm direction. A logging road permitted ready access over the elevational range of the study site (fig. 1). The unlogged, old-growth forest was predominately western hemlock and included Sitka spruce, Alaska-cedar, and western redcedar. The clearcut, low-brush area contained a well-stocked seedling stand of these tree species with salmonberry and huckleberry.

---

[1] Stationed at Institute of Northern Forestry, Juneau, Alaska.

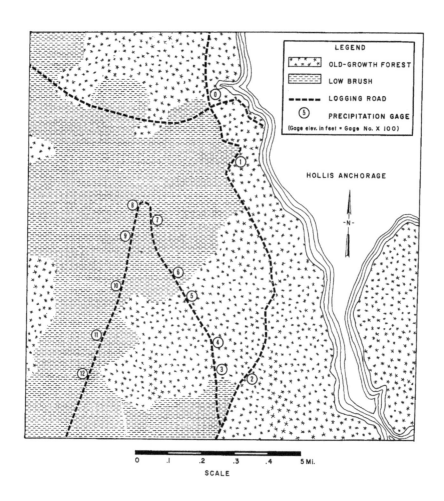

Figure 1.--*The study area. The abandoned mining town of Hollis is just below precipitation gage 1.*

METHOD

Number 10 food cans were used for rain gages, except at sea level where a standard 8-inch U.S. Weather Bureau gage was installed with a number 10 can gage nearby. This pair provided a check on the performance of the can gages. Single can gages were placed along the logging road at 100-foot-elevation intervals to 1,200-foot elevation (fig. 1). Stations 0 through 5 were in old-growth forest, 6 through 12 were in low brush. Wind was noticeably stronger at gage stations in low brush, but windspeed was not measured and gages were unshielded. Rain amounts were recorded on a per-storm basis. A storm was defined as a period of essentially continuous rain separated from other stormy periods by at least 6 hours without rain. Two storm records were discarded when snow fell at elevations above 800 feet. Standard-gage catch was measured directly in inches with a graduated stick. Can-gage catch was measured in cubic centimeters in a graduated cylinder and later converted to inches depth.

RESULTS

Records were obtained from 21 storms ranging in size from 0.04 to 2.66 inches at sea level (table 1). A total of 22.44 inches of rain was measured at sea level during the period of record. The similarity of catch between the standard gage and can gage at station 0, or at sea level, confirms Ursic and Thames' (1958) claim that number 10 cans are satisfactory for many rain-gaging purposes. Can-gage catches were grouped as shown by letter designations in table 1 to provide replicated sampling within selected elevational ranges.

Plotting gage catch by elevation intervals for various storm sizes showed considerable similarity among storms with less than 1.5 inches of rainfall and greater than 1.5 inches. For this reason, average gage catch was plotted for all storms by size classes and elevations, as shown in figure 2. Both elevation and wind influences are apparent in this figure. Gages from sea level to 500 feet were within old-growth forest, and curves for storms less than 1.5 inches and storms greater than 1.5 inches indicate gage catch increasing by 0.01 and 0.04 inch per 100 feet of elevation, respectively. Gages from 600 to 1,100 feet were exposed in low brush, but their catch nevertheless increased at the same rate as gages in old-growth forest. The offset at the old-growth forest—low brush juncture is wind effect, which uniformly reduced catch in all gages exposed in low brush but had no influence on the rate at which gage catch increased with elevation. For all storms,

Table 1.--Rainfall measurements at 100-foot-elevation intervals at Hollis, Alaska, 1965, by storm size and date

Station No.[1]	Elevation group[2]	Storms up to 1.5 inches															Storms greater than 1.5 inches					
		9/28	9/30	10/1	10/3	10/4	10/8	10/9	10/12	10/21	10/23	10/25	10/28	10/30	11/2	11/4	10/6	10/11	10/14	10/17	10/20	10/22
		Inches															Inches					
STD[3]	A	0.04	0.46	0.61	1.22	1.17	0.99	0.20	0.37	0.32	0.78	0.19	1.13	1.28	1.14	0.62	2.66	2.21	1.85	1.70	1.54	1.96
0	B	.04	.50	.61	1.24	1.16	.97	.16	.34	.31	.77	.18	1.10	1.27	1.11	.58	2.71	2.19	1.84	1.71	1.59	1.99
1	B	.07	.54	.63	1.27	1.14	.99	.18	.43	.32	.77	.19	1.11	1.25	1.17	.62	2.72	2.26	1.86	1.74	1.61	1.99
2	B	--	--	.70	1.39	1.19	1.05	.19	.38	.35	.78	.19	1.13	1.26	1.23	.65	2.72	2.30	2.02	1.73	1.63	2.07
3	C	.06	.61	.70	1.49	1.23	1.03	.20	.38	.33	.76	.18	1.12	1.24	1.22	.65	2.74	2.41	2.09	1.79	1.70	2.15
4	C	.07	.63	.68	1.48	1.29	--	.19	.39	.33	.76	.19	1.09	1.24	1.18	.66	2.72	2.41	2.08	1.77	1.66	2.16
5	C	.09	.65	.69	1.50	1.26	1.06	.20	.44	.34	.79	.20	1.12	1.25	1.21	.66	2.87	2.48	2.08	1.81	1.72	2.21
6	D	.08	.59	.66	1.37	1.10	1.05	.20	.42	--	.79	.19	1.10	1.26	1.06	.61	2.79	2.31	1.83	1.86	1.62	2.10
7	D	.07	.60	.73	1.36	1.09	1.00	.22	.36	.33	.74	.19	.98	1.22	.99	.58	2.59	2.30	1.79	1.73	1.60	2.08
8	D	.08	.60	.64	1.41	1.12	1.07	.24	.35	.34	.87	.18	1.23	1.33	1.14	.56	3.10	2.36	1.89	1.99	1.53	2.06
9	D	.09	.62	.67	1.31	.97	1.05	.26	.36	.33	.80	.18	1.08	1.30	.95	.54	2.75	2.41	1.69	1.86	1.39	1.93
10	E	.12	.70	.71	1.61	1.18	1.06	.24	.36	.35	.86	.18	1.25	1.31	1.12	.57	3.11	2.45	1.98	1.96	1.60	2.14
11	E	.12	.74	.73	1.60	1.14	1.04	.26	.33	.34	.77	.18	1.11	1.22	1.06	.60	2.89	2.54	2.01	1.77	1.64	2.18
12	E	.13	.70	.72	1.60	1.03	1.07	.26	.33	.37	.79	.18	1.11	1.26	1.04	.52	2.95	2.44	1.99	1.87	1.52	2.01

1/ Gage elevation in feet = station number x 100.

2/ Elevation group refers to mean elevation:
A = sea level
B = 100 feet
C = 400 feet
D = 750 feet
E = 1,100 feet

3/ Standard rain gage--all other stations used a No. 10 can gage.

for each inch of rain at sea level, the average rainfall increase was
0.02 inch per 100 feet of elevation. This amounted to an average increase in rainfall of 2 percent per 100-foot rise in elevation.

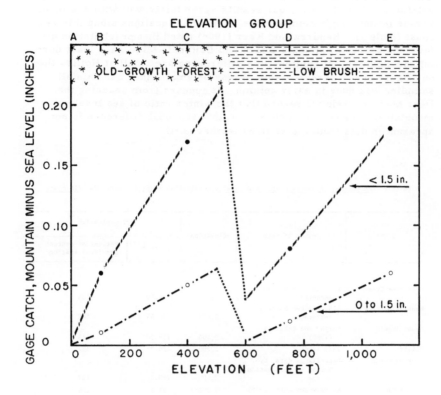

Figure 2.--*Influence of elevation and vegetation
on rain gage catch at Hollis, Alaska.*

DISCUSSION

The results indicate that sea level rainfall sampling provides only minimum estimates of mountain rainfall at Hollis. The increase of 0.02 inch of rain per 100 feet of elevation does not, however, apply to other gage locations in the Hollis vicinity. Apparently, differing land configuration causes variation among individual elevation-rainfall relations. Nevertheless, our results agree fairly well with sea level versus mountainside comparisons from other locations along this sea coast (table 2). Kendrew and Kerr (1955) noted that precipitation differences between Britannia Beach and Britannia Mine were least during the summer. If summertime differences are small at Hollis, then our figure of 117 percent (table 2) may be small since our rainfall sampling was done in early autumn. It appears from scanning the Deer Mountain rainfall record that the winter ratio of sea level—mountainside rainfall is highest, but this seasonal difference is not apparent in data from the stations farther north.

Table 2.--Comparison of mountain with sea-level precipitation along the North Pacific coast

Station	Source of data	Elevation	Precipitation	
			Inches[1]	Percent of nearest sea-level station
		Feet		
Porcupine Creek	U.S. Weather Bureau, Anchorage	1,800	39.00	184
Kensington Mine	U.S. Weather Bureau, Anchorage	2,025	74.65	146
Mount Juneau	Murphy and Schamack (1966)	3,400	128.10	313
Hollis	This study	1,200	26.35	117
Deer Mountain	Unpublished data, U.S. Bureau of Reclamation, Juneau	2,600	240.39	122
Tunnel Camp	Kendrew and Kerr (1955)	2,200	95.6	126

[1] Precipitation amounts are for various lengths of time.

Do the offsets in figure 2 actually reflect decreased gage catch caused by more wind outside the forest? Wind data are unavailable for Hollis, but we noticed that it blew most of the time and hardest outside the forest. The nearest wind recorder was on Annette Island (U.S. Weather Bureau 1965), 50 miles southeast of Hollis and across Clarence Strait. Annette data showed that sea-level wind averaged 13.4 m.p.h. from the southeast. If we assume that wind at Hollis differed little from Annette and apply Fons' (1940) results, average windspeed inside the forest would not exceed 2 m.p.h. Foster (1948, p. 46) states that at 8.94 m.p.h. wind decreases rain-gage catch by 10 percent, winds of 13.41 m.p.h. by 19 percent. Thus, the assumed windspeed increase of 11 m.p.h. outside the forest was ample to decrease rain-gage catch by approximately 10 percent as shown in figure 2.

Table 2 suggests a fairly uniform regional pattern of topographic influence on rainfall. This pattern could be more closely defined on a larger study area having large elevation spans permitting adequate statistical treatment of the data. The need for further study of the influence of elevation on precipitation is apparent when stream gages frequently measure runoff from mountains exceeding sea level rainfall (Federal Power Commission and U.S. Forest Service 1947).

LITERATURE CITED

Federal Power Commission and U.S. Forest Service.
    1947. Water powers of southeast Alaska. Fed. Power Comm.,
        Washington, D.C., 168 pp., illus.

Fons, Wallace L.
    1940. Influence of forest cover on wind velocity. J. Forest.
        38: 481-486.

Foster, Edgar E.
    1948. Rainfall and runoff. 487 pp., illus. New York: The
        Macmillan Co.

Kendrew, W. G., and Kerr, D.
    1955. The climate of British Columbia and the Yukon Territory. 222 pp., illus. Ottawa, Canada: Edmond
        Cloutier, C.M.G., O.A., D.S.P.

Murphy, Thomas D., and Schamack, Seymour.
    1966. Mountain versus sea level rainfall measurements during
        storms at Juneau, Alaska. J. Hydrol. 4: 12-20.

U.S. Weather Bureau.
    1965.   Local climatological data, Annette, Alaska. 2 pp.

Ursic, S. J., and Thames, J. L.
    1958.   An inexpensive raingage. J. Soil & Water Conserv.
        13(5): 231-232.

* * *

FOREST AND RANGE EXPERIMENT STATION · U.S. DEPARTMENT OF AGRICULTURE · PORTLAND, OREGON

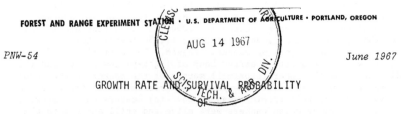

PNW-54

June 1967

GROWTH RATE AND SURVIVAL PROBABILITY

BLISTER RUST CANKERS ON SUGAR PINE BRANCHES

by
George M. Harvey, Plant Pathologist

INTRODUCTION

The potential of a white pine blister rust branch canker, caused by *Cronartium ribicola* Fischer, to reach the trunk and kill sugar pine *(Pinus lambertiana* Dougl.) saplings and poles has been conjectural. Judgment based on experience has been the only basis for such decisions in the past. Harvey and Cohen *(3)*[1] established the relationship between the extent of blister rust mycelia in sugar pine bark tissues and canker discoloration to provide guides for pruning infected branches. Since available antibiotics are not effective for eradicating the fungus in sugar pine *(2)* and pruning is not always feasible, the problem of predicting the growth rate and potential threat of a branch canker remains.

In the western white pine region of northern Idaho, quantitative information on the growth rate and survival probability of branch cankers on *Pinus monticola* Dougl. is available *(1, 4, 5)* and is used in disease and damage surveys. Similar information is needed for sugar pine to estimate the threat of branch cankers and to appraise damage.

The present study on sugar pine was made to determine: (a) the proximal[2] growth rate of cankers, and (b) the survival probability of cankers based on their distance from the trunk.

---

[1] Italic numbers in parentheses refer to Literature Cited, p. 6.

[2] "Proximal" is growth toward trunk as opposed to "distal," growth away from trunk.

METHODS

Five study groups of cankers were established in 1954 at four
different localities in southwestern Oregon. The groups included 490
naturally occurring branch cankers on 234 reproduction- or small pole-
sized sugar pines. The trees ranged from 4 to 25 feet in height (12.1
feet, average) and from 1 to 8 inches d.b.h. (2.1 inches, average).
Three of the groups were located at 2,000- to 3,000-foot elevation,
and the remaining two groups were lower (1,650 feet). Selected trees
and branch cankers were permanently tagged. The extremities of each
canker were marked with a narrow band of light-yellow paint, and the
distance from the inner (proximal) margin of the canker to the trunk
of the tree was recorded. The plots were reexamined at irregular intervals over 10 full growing seasons to: (a) measure canker growth,
and (b) determine which cankers were alive and still enroute to the
trunk or had died from suppression or other natural causes. Final
examinations were made in 1965.

RESULTS

In 1957, canker growth measurements were terminated, as many
cankers were dead or had reached the trunk. Comparison of the average
annual proximal growth of cankers on western white pine and sugar pine
was made by regression analysis (fig. 1). For both species, the average annual proximal growth of a branch canker increases with increasing
branch diameter. Buchanan's data for western white pine in northern
Idaho (1) show that the average annual proximal growth of western white
pine branch cankers is from 1.7 to 1.8 times greater than the growth
found for sugar pine cankers of the same diameter in southwestern Oregon. These differences were found to be statistically significant.

The remaining portion of the study was terminated in the spring
of 1965. By then, 82 of the original 490 cankers were on trees lost
to an earth slide, road construction, right-of-way clearing, and logging. Of the 412 remaining cankers, 146 had reached the trunk, 262
had died from natural causes, and only 4 were still alive and growing
toward the trunk (table 1).

By transforming into probits the percentage of cankers reaching
the trunk for each original canker-to-trunk-distance class, a mathematically smoothed curve was derived (fig. 2). This curve gives the
probability that a sugar pine canker a given distance from the trunk
will reach the trunk. Slipp's data from western white pine in northern Idaho (5) were adapted for treatment in the same manner so that
the two species could be directly compared (fig. 2). The two curves
were tested statistically and found to be significantly different.

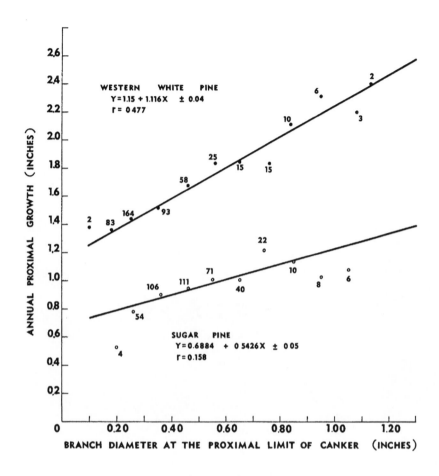

Figure 1.--Comparison of average annual proximal growth of white
pine blister rust cankers on branches of western white pine
in northern Idaho (data from Buchanan *(1)*) and on branches
of sugar pine in southwestern Oregon.

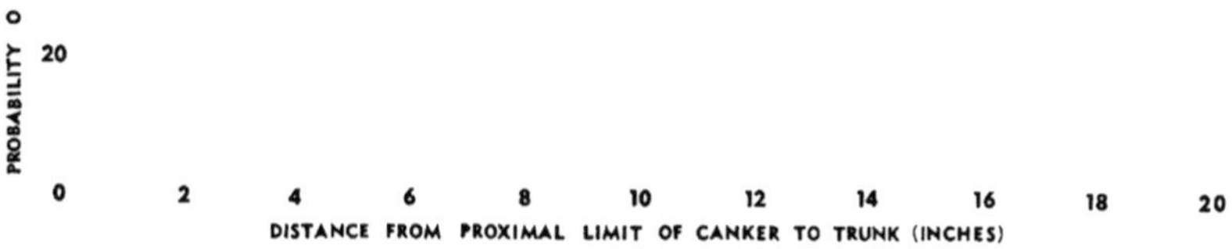

PROBABILITY O

20

0   2   4   6   8   10   12   14   16   18   20

DISTANCE FROM PROXIMAL LIMIT OF CANKER TO TRUNK (INCHES)

Figure 2.--Probability of white pine blister rust canker reaching
trunk in relation to distance from proximal limit of canker to
trunk.   Comparison of western white pine in northern Idaho
(data from Slipp (5)) and sugar pine in southwestern Oregon.

CONCLUSIONS

Blister rust branch cankers grow significantly slower on young
sugar pine in southwestern Oregon than on young western white pine in
northern Idaho. In addition, the probability that a blister rust
branch canker on sugar pine in southwestern Oregon will reach the
trunk is significantly lower than for a comparable canker on western
white pine in northern Idaho. The reasons for these differences are
not clear. Perhaps the slower canker growth rate on sugar pine may
provide a partial answer to the difference in the canker survival
probability rates--a slower growing canker has a longer period of
time in which to succumb to branch suppression or other biologic
factors.

Figures 1 and 2 provide a means for estimating the time required
for a sugar pine branch canker to reach the bole and an estimate of
the probability of this occurrence. By determining the distance from
the bole to the proximal edge of the canker, it is possible to estimate
the potential threat of an existing blister rust canker on sugar pine
in southwestern Oregon.

5

LITERATURE CITED

(1) Buchanan, T. S.
     1938. Annual growth rate of *Cronartium ribicola* cankers on
            branches of *Pinus monticola* in northern Idaho.
            Phytopathology 28: 634-641.

(2) Harvey, George M.
     1966. An evaluation of the basal stem application of Acti-dione
            and Phytoactin for control of white pine blister rust
            on sugar pine in Oregon and California. Plant Dis.
            Rep. 50: 554-556.

(3) _____ and Cohen, Leon I.
     1958. The extent of blister rust mycelia beyond bark discolora-
            tions on sugar pine. U.S. Forest Serv. Pacific North-
            west Forest & Range Exp. Sta. Res. Note 159, 4 pp.

(4) Slipp, Albert W.
     1951. Growth of cankers of white pine blister rust along
            branch leaders toward trunk in western white pine.
            Univ. Idaho Forest, Wildlife, & Range Exp. Sta. Res.
            Note 1, 3 pp.

(5) _____.
     1953. Survival probability and its application to damage
            survey in western white pine infected with blister rust.
            Univ. Idaho Forest, Wildlife, & Range Exp. Sta. Res.
            Note 7, 3 pp.

FOREST AND RANGE EXPERIMENT STATION · U.S. DEPARTMENT OF AGRICULTURE · PORTLAND, OREGON

PNW-55

AUG 14 1967

June 1967

SOIL SURFACE CONDITIONS FOLLOWING SKYLINE LOGGING

by

C. T. Dyrness, *Principal Soil Scientist*

In the Douglas-fir region of the Pacific Northwest most timber harvesting involves one of three methods: tractor, high-lead, or skyline. Tractor and high-lead methods are now used much more frequently than the skyline. Recently, however, interest in skyline logging has increased, especially in areas where the timber ready for harvest is located on steep terrain with difficult access. Because skyline yarding distances may range up to a mile, road requirements are substantially less than those for other methods. Wooldridge,[1] in comparing skyline and tractor logging near Twisp, Wash., estimated that skyline logging required only 10 percent of the road area necessary for tractor yarding.

Skyline logging has been advocated not only for its effect in decreasing soil disturbance due to road construction, but also because of its potential for minimizing soil disturbance during yarding. Typically, a skyline system involves yarding logs to a fixed overhead cable where they are raised then transported to a downhill landing Theoretically, the logs should be off the ground over most of the yarding distance; therefore, it has been assumed that skyline logging results in substantially reduced soil disturbance compared with that resulting from a conventional high-lead operation.

---

[1] Wooldridge, David D. Watershed disturbance from tractor and skyline crane logging. J. Forest. 58 369-372, illus. 1960.

THE STUDY

This paper reports on the results of a portion of a study designed to assess and compare soil disturbance caused by tractor, high-lead, and skyline logging The effects of high-lead and tractor logging on soil surface conditions have been described previously.[2] The study was conducted in the H. J. Andrews Experimental Forest, which is located on the west side of the Cascade Range, approximately 40 miles east of Eugene, Oreg.

The effects of skyline logging were studied in experimental watershed 1. This entire 237-acre watershed was clearcut between the fall of 1962 and the fall of 1966. Logs were yarded to a single landing near the mouth of the watershed by means of a 10-ton Wyssen Skyline Crane.

The timber stand was largely old-growth Douglas-fir mixed with western hemlock. Slopes in watershed 1 are steep, averaging about 63 percent There are several nearly vertical rock outcrop areas, as well as steep downward trending ridges between tributary drainages. Soils tend to be shallow and stony. The Frissell series,[3] a Regosol derived from reddish tuffs and breccias, is the most common soil in the area.

Four soil surface disturbance classes were used to determine the extent of soil disturbance after yarding:

1. Undisturbed--litter still in place and no evidence of compaction
2. Slightly disturbed--three conditions fit this class:
   a. litter removed and mineral soil exposed;
   b. mineral soil and litter intimately mixed, with about 50 percent of each; and
   c. pure mineral soil deposited on top of litter and slash.

----

[2] Dyrness, C. T. Soil surface condition following tractor and high-lead logging in the Oregon Cascades. J. Forest. 63: 272-27, illus. 1965.

[3] Provisional series, not yet correlated.

3. Deeply disturbed--surface soil removed and the subsoil exposed.
4. Compacted--obvious compaction due to passage of a log. The soil surface directly under large cull logs was assumed to be in this condition.

The percentage of the total clearcut area in each of the four disturbance classes was determined from conditions observed at 10-foot intervals along eight randomly located transects.

Slash density observations were also made within 1 square foot centered at each observation point. The four slash density classes were as follows;

1. Heavy--entire square foot covered with slash at least 1 foot deep.
2. Light--10 percent or more of the area covered with slash less than 1 foot deep.
3. Absent--total slash cover is less than 10 percent.
4. Cull log--log 12 inches or more in diameter present.

To determine the extent to which surface soil physical properties were altered by logging disturbance, 80 bulk-density samples were collected from the surface 2 inches of soil. Sampling was carried out in a representative area of Frissell soil near the mouth of the watershed. Twenty bulk-density samples were collected in 1962 before logging, and 20 samples were taken from areas representative of each of three disturbance classes after logging--undisturbed, slightly disturbed, and deeply disturbed. The compacted class was not sampled for bulk density because much of it was located directly beneath cull logs

RESULTS

Soil surface disturbance and slash density were observed at about 1,750 points in watershed 1. Values for high-lead logging in three nearby cutting units are included in the summary for comparison (table 1).

Perhaps the most surprising aspect of the soil surface disturbance data is that values for skyline and high-lead logging are, in most respects, similar Largest differences between skyline and high-lead logging are in the proportion of logged area within the deeply disturbed and compacted classes. Skyline logging resulted in some decrease in both the proportion of area classified as deeply disturbed (4.7 percent vs. 9.7 percent for high-lead) and compacted (3.4 percent vs. 9.1 percent for high-lead). Although skyline logging resulted in slightly more area within the undisturbed class as compared with high-lead logging, there was also a small increase in area within the slightly disturbed class (table 1).

Table 1.--*Percent of total cutting unit area by soil surface disturbance and slash density classes for two logging methods; H. J. Andrews Experimental Forest*

Classes	Skyline	High-lead[1]
Soil surface disturbance:		
Undisturbed	63.6	57.2
Slightly disturbed	24.4	21.5
Deeply disturbed	4.7	9.7
Compacted	3.4	9.1
Nonsoil areas[2]	3.9	2.5
Total	100.0	100.0
Slash density:		
Heavy	10.8	26.9
Light	53.8	37.7
Absent	32.2	25.9
Cull log	6.4	9.9
Total	[3]103.2	100.4

[1] Averages for three cutting units located in watershed 3 in the H. J. Andrews Experimental Forest (see text footnote 2).

[2] Stumps, rock outcrops, and streambeds.

[3] Totals more than 100 percent because "cull log" plus "heavy" or "light" slash were sometimes recorded at a single point.

4

Slash distribution figures indicate that skyline logging caused fewer accumulations of heavy slash than did high-lead (table 1). As a result, there was a corresponding increase in the proportion of the area falling within the light slash class in the skyline unit (53.8 percent vs. 37.7 percent for high-lead).

Bulk density of the surface 2 inches of soil in both the skyline and high-lead logged areas was similar for the before-logging class and for the undisturbed and slightly disturbed classes after logging (table 2). Light disturbance apparently results in very little alteration of the mineral soil, involving mainly the removal of surface litter. Deep disturbance caused an appreciable increase in bulk density for both skyline and high-lead logging methods. This greater bulk density may be attributed largely to the exposure of more dense subsoil material.

Table 2.--*Mean surface-soil bulk-density values*[1] *before and after two methods of logging; H. J. Andrews Experimental Forest*

(In grams per cubic centimeter)

Disturbance	Skyline	High-lead[2]
Before logging	0.677 ± 0.023	0.712 ± 0.016
After logging:		
Undisturbed	.730 ± .032	.753 ± .019
Slightly disturbed	.668 ± .030	.785 ± .032
Deeply disturbed	.858 ± .025	.990 ± .026

[1] Standard error of the mean.

[2] The high-lead samples were collected in an area of the McKenzie River soil (tentative series) which, like the Frissell, is derived from reddish tuffs and breccias. The Frissell and McKenzie River series have almost identical surface soil properties.

DISCUSSION

The potential for erosion following logging is largely a function of the area of exposed mineral soil. Therefore, a protective layer of slash over disturbed soil will probably prevent any substantial amount of surface erosion for at least a year or two. In this study of skyline logging, the presence or absence of slash was noted along with the degree of soil disturbance. The proportion of the logged area in which bare mineral soil was exposed was 12.1 percent of the total area of this skyline-logged unit. This value is compared with values for percent of bare mineral soil exposed, determined in another study comparing skyline and high-lead logging on the Oregon coast:[4]

	Skyline	High-lead
	(percent)	(percent)
This study	12.1	14.8
Oregon coast	6.4	15.8

In this study, about twice as much bare mineral soil was exposed by skyline logging as that determined by Ruth on the Oregon coast. The greater incidence of soil disturbance in the present study is probably due largely to the unfavorable topographic characteristics of watershed 1 for skyline logging. The canyonlike terrain and intervening ridges often made it impossible to hold the logs off the ground during the entire yarding distance, resulting in considerable soil disturbance on ridgetops directly under the skyline. The site for the coast study was much more favorable for skyline operations, having generally smooth, uniform side slopes. As a result, it was possible to keep logs free of the ground, minimizing contact between logs and soil during yarding.

Soil surface disturbance data collected for this study indicate very little difference between the skyline and high-lead logging methods. This agrees substantially with Ruth's findings on the Oregon coast. His study was replicated on four areas where half of each area was logged

---

[4] Ruth, Robert H. Silvicultural effects of skyline crane and high-lead yarding. J. Forest. 65: 251-255, illus. 1967.

by the skyline method and the other half by high-lead. At two of these sites, the skyline-logged area showed considerably less disturbance than did the high-lead. However, at the other two locations both logging methods resulted in approximately equal amounts of soil disturbance. Because of this variance, the difference between the two treatments was not statistically significant.

Soil surface conditions immediately after logging are subject to rapid change, especially if the slash is burned. The amount of bare soil exposed to the erosive action of precipitation after burning may actually be controlled more by severity of the slash burn than by the original logging disturbance. It is also important to consider the rapidity with which vegetation restores protection against erosion. Despite regeneration problems that sometimes arise, we are fortunate in western Oregon that regrowth of native vegetation in cutting units occurs rapidly. Present plans call for study of soil surface conditions following slash burning in watershed 1, as well as a yearly inventory of plant cover and species composition.

Since results of this study, along with Ruth's findings, indicate very little difference in yarding-caused disturbance when skyline logging is compared with high-lead, it may be concluded that the main advantage of the skyline method lies in the fact that it requires far less road construction than does high-lead. Binkley[5] calculated that road requirements for skyline yarding are only about one-third of those necessary for high-lead logging. This reduction is extremely important to good watershed management. Many studies have shown roads, especially those newly constructed, are often the primary source of stream sediment coming from forested uplands. For example, Fredriksen[6] reported that road construction in watershed 3 resulted in a 250-fold increase in stream sediment during the first storms after the roads were built. In addition to surface erosion

---

[5] Binkley, Virgil W. Economics and design of a radio-controlled skyline yarding system. U.S. Forest Serv. Res. Pap. PNW-25, 30 pp., illus. 1965.

[6] Fredriksen, R. L. Sedimentation after logging road construction in a small western Oregon watershed. In Proc. Fed. Inter-Agency Sedimentation Conf., 1963. U.S. Dep. Agr. Res. Serv. Misc. Pub. 970, pp. 56-59, illus. 1965.

from raw, roadside slopes, roads are also the source of many mass soil movements, some of which have far-reaching downslope effects. Therefore, any means of reducing road mileage in steep, mountainous areas of western Oregon and Washington is a goal well worth pursuing. The possibilities of skyline logging in this connection certainly deserve serious consideration.

* * * * *

FOREST AND RANGE EXPERIMENT STATION · U.S. DEPARTMENT OF AGRICULTURE · PORTLAND, OREGON

June 1967

SOIL-MOISTURE AND TEMPERATURE TRENDS

IN CUTOVER AND ADJACENT OLD-GROWTH

DOUGLAS-FIR TIMBER

by William E. Hallin, *Principal Silviculturist*

INTRODUCTION

Knowledge of soil-moisture variation and its causes is necessary for improving establishment and early growth of regeneration and for developing a better understanding of tree-site relationships in the mixed-conifer zone of southwest Oregon. In the study reported here, seasonal soil-moisture trends on a cutover were compared with those on an adjacent timbered area. Soil temperature was also measured, because the electrical resistance readings used to measure soil moisture must be corrected for temperature.

The purpose of this article is: (1) to report seasonal trends in soil moisture and temperature on a cutover and adjacent timber, (2) to show the importance of low, invading vegetation in depleting soil moisture on a cutover.

STUDY AREA

The study was conducted in the mixed-conifer zone of the South Umpqua drainage at 43°04-1/2' N. latitude and 122°42' W. longitude. Elevation is 2,800 feet. The cutover area was logged in 1957 and the slash was burned in fall of 1958. Intensity of the slash burn varied from unburned to light. Light burn is defined as a burn in which the slash is partially consumed--the litter surface is charred and there are unburned pieces below the surface.

The timber is (or was) an old-growth stand of Douglas-fir (*Pseudotsuga menziesii*), with scattered grand fir (*Abies grandis*) and incense-cedar *(Libocedrus decurrens)* trees. Sugar pine *(Pinus lambert-iana)* trees are present in the stand but not within the study boundaries. Ground cover of variable density in the uncut stand consists of salal *(Gaultheria shallon)*, Oregongrape *(Mahonia aquifolium)*, western sword-fern *(Polystichum munitum)*, and miscellaneous herbaceous plants. There are occasional fir saplings and poles and shrubs.

The vegetation on the cutover was similar in composition and density to that found on many other north-facing cutovers 2 to 5 years after the slash burn. The vegetation density on the cutover area in 1963 varied from medium to heavy. Whitebark raspberry *(Rubus leucodermis)*, deerbrush ceanothus *(Ceanothus integerrimus)*, snowbrush ceanothus *(Ceanothus velutinus)*, western swordfern, bull thistle *(Cirsium lanceolatum)*, grass species, and miscellaneous annual weeds occur as scattered individuals. Dense patches of modest whipplea *(Whipplea modesta)* and salal were present.

The soil varies from a well-drained stony loam to a stony clay at the 36-inch depth, is derived from reddish breccias, and is classified in the tentative Straight[1] series. The slope varies from approximately 30 to 60 percent. Average annual rainfall for the 3 years reported here was 40 inches at a station 4-1/2 miles south of the study area.

METHODS

Soil moisture was measured with Fiberglas electrical resistance units[2] at 6-, 18-, and 36-inch depths. Soil temperature was measured with thermistors in the resistance units.

In January 1960, 10 points 1 chain apart--5 in the timber and 5 in the cutover area--were located along a line at right angles to the cutting edge.[3] Thus, the first point in the timber and the first point in the cutover area were one-half chain from the cutting edge. Resistance units were inserted in the soil at the 6-, 18-, and 36-inch depths on the side of a hole dug with post-hole auger.

---

[1] Richlen, E. M. Soil survey report of South Umpqua area of Region 6. In-Service report, U.S. Forest Service, Region 6, Portland, Oreg. 1963.

[2] Colman, E. A., and Hendrix, T. M. The Fiberglas electrical soil-moisture instrument. Soil Sci. 67: 425-438. 1949.

[3] Records were also taken for a second line but are not reported here, as the soil for the cutover portion was a different series than for the timber.

Resistance readings were taken usually between 9 a.m. and noon, at 2- or 3-week intervals during spring and summer months of 1960, 1961, and 1963. During winter months, readings were taken at 2- to 6-week intervals, depending on accessibility of the study area. Resistance readings were corrected for temperature and converted to soil-moisture percent from the following calibration equations of soil moisture over logarithm of resistance:

Cutover:

$$6\text{-inch depth, } y = 76.48 - 12.1736x$$
$$18\text{-inch depth, } y = 64.35 - 9.9159x$$
$$36\text{-inch depth, } y = 54.83 - 7.3842x$$

Timber:

$$6\text{-inch depth, } y = 79.78 - 12.917x$$
$$18\text{-inch depth, } y = 65.65 - 9.6977x$$
$$36\text{-inch depth, } y = 58.17 - 7.1719x$$

where x equals logarithm of resistance and

y equals soil-moisture percent

Soil samples for calibration were collected during spring and summer of 1961 at each of the three depths for the 10 sampling points. Quadrant at each location for soil-moisture sample was selected randomly each time. Samples were taken at least 3 feet from the resistance unit in order not to disturb moisture relations at units. Soil moisture is expressed as the percent of ovendry weight of the soil including stones.[4]

Calibration samples consisted of average soil-moisture content for five sample points and average logarithm of resistance for the corresponding five moisture units. The five points in the cutover and the five points in the timber constituted a sample for each depth.

Results are graphically presented for soil moisture and soil temperature by plotting over time.

---

[4] Tests showed that a better estimate of soil moisture was obtained by including the stones, as the stones in this soil hold substantial amounts of moisture.

RESULTS AND DISCUSSION

Soil moisture.--Soil moisture during the growing season is of principal concern in connection with tree growth. The 1960 and 1961 seasons were typical in that there was little precipitation during the usual dry period, whereas in 1963, temperatures were below average and heavy precipitations occurred during the latter part of June.

Soil moisture declined sharply in June at the 6- and 18-inch depths (figs. 1 and 2). In 1960 and 1961, the sharp decline slowed in July and continued at a reduced rate until terminated by fall rains in late August or September. In 1963, late-June rains interrupted the normal decline in soil moisture for 6- and 18-inch depths (fig. 3). Soil moisture increased and a period of rapid decline started again in early July and ended in early September.

At the 36-inch depth, the period of rapid soil-moisture decline did not begin until early July and ended in August or September. Late-June rains in 1963 only slowed the rate of decline.

The most surprising result of this study was the similarity of the soil-moisture depletion rates and minimum soil-moisture contents for the timbered and adjoining cutover area. Bethlahmy[5] has shown that, in the year following timber harvest but before the cutover has been invaded by competing vegetation, minimum soil-moisture contents have been considerably lower on the timbered areas than on the adjoining cutover area. However, in this study, the vegetation which has invaded the cutover is shown to be as effective as the old-growth stand in depleting soil moisture at the 6- and 18-inch depths and nearly so at the 36-inch depth. Minimum soil moisture at 6 and 18 inches was the same or slightly lower on the cutover than on the timbered area. At the 36-inch depth, the minimum soil moisture was only slightly higher on the cutover area than on the timbered. In a subsequent study[6] on other cutovers, minimum levels of soil moisture were much lower on areas with vegetation than on adjoining plots from which vegetation had been removed.

During wetting periods, the soil in the timbered area usually was recharged more slowly than in the cutover area, due to precipitation interception by the trees.

---

[5] Bethlahmy, Nedavia. First year effects of timber removal on soil moisture. Int. Ass. Sci. Hydrol. Bull. 7(2): 34-38, illus. 1962.

[6] Hallin, William E. Data in preparation for publication, Pacific Northwest Forest & Range Exp. Sta., U.S. Forest Serv., Portland, Oreg.

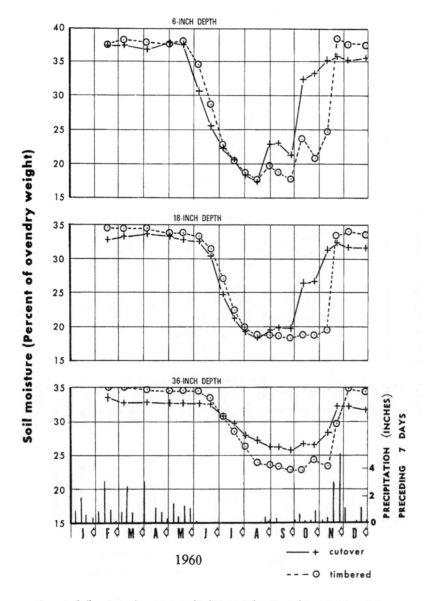

Figure 1.--Soil moisture in cutover and adjacent timber in southwest Oregon, 1960.

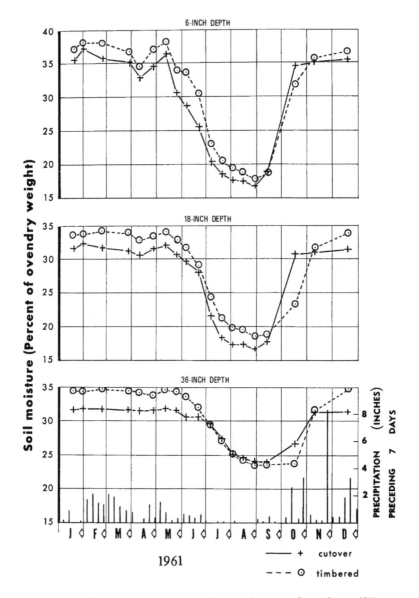

Figure 2.--Soil moisture in cutover and adjacent timber in southwest Oregon, 1961.

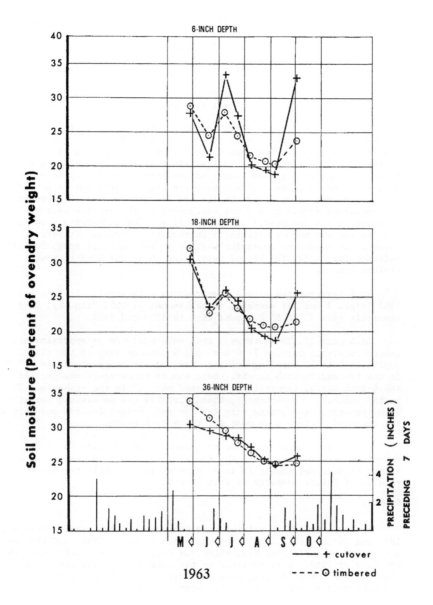

Figure 3.--Soil moisture in cutover and adjacent timber in southwest Oregon, 1963.

Results of this study confirm observational conclusions that vegetation is an important source of moisture depletion on cutover areas. In establishing regeneration, foresters must recognize the heavy drain on soil moisture caused by competing vegetation. The need for prompt establishment of regeneration after cutting before competing vegetation invades the cutover is again emphasized. Control of competing vegetation on many areas to permit establishment of regeneration or release of existing regeneration is also necessary.

Although fertilizing forest areas for increased growth is becoming an accepted practice in some areas, many foresters question its practicability in southwestern Oregon because of supposed lack of adequate soil moisture. The soil-moisture trends reported here show that, even though ultimate summer soil-moisture levels may be quite low, substantial amounts of moisture are present well into June and even to the end of June for the 18- and 36-inch depths. Consequently, soil-moisture levels during the early part of the growing season may be adequate for successful use of fertilizer for increasing growth, despite the dry summer climate in southwestern Oregon. Therefore, research is needed to determine whether or not there is adequate soil moisture for successful use of fertilizer on forest land in southwestern Oregon.

Soil temperatures.--Soil temperatures were similar in 1960 and 1961 (figs. 4 and 5); whereas, in the summer of 1963 (fig. 6), they generally were 3° to 5° F. lower than in 1960 and 1961.

On August 20, 1964, temperatures were measured at approximately 2-hour intervals between 7:30 a.m. and 5 p.m. at each of the three depths for the 10 sampling points. Maximum air temperature was 82° F. At the 18- and 36-inch depths, there was no temperature change. At the 6-inch depth, temperature increased only 1° in the timber and 2° on the cutover. Consequently, there probably was no diurnal variation from temperatures reported here for 18- and 36-inch depths, and only a few degrees' variation at most for the 6-inch depth.

Very little is known about temperature requirements for root growth of western conifers. The temperature data is presented as a record of seasonal change in soil temperature primarily for use with results of future research on root growth.

SUMMARY

Seasonal trends in moisture and temperatures are reported for 6-, 18-, and 36-inch soil depths for the years of 1960, 1961, and 1963 on a timbered and adjoining area which was cutover in 1957 and burned in the fall of 1958. Soil moisture on the cutover area was similar to that for the timbered area, thus indicating a nearly equal moisture drain by lesser vegetation on the cutover area.

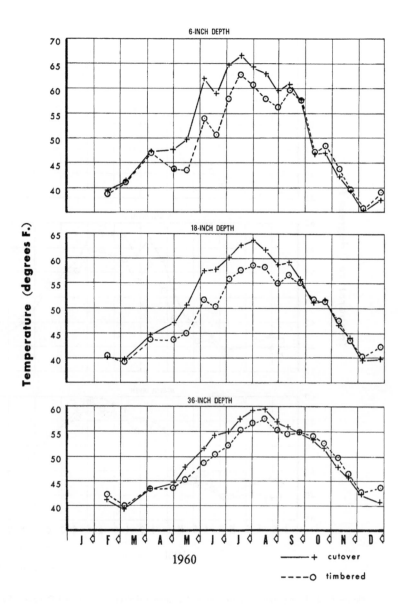

Figure 4.—Soil temperature in cutover and adjacent timber in southwest Oregon, 1960.

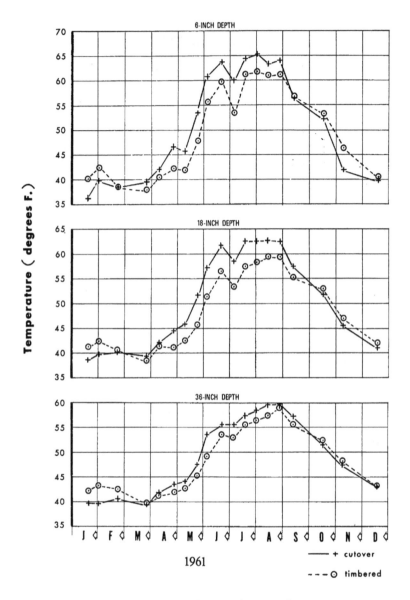

Figure 5.--Soil temperature in cutover and adjacent timber in southwest Oregon, 1961.

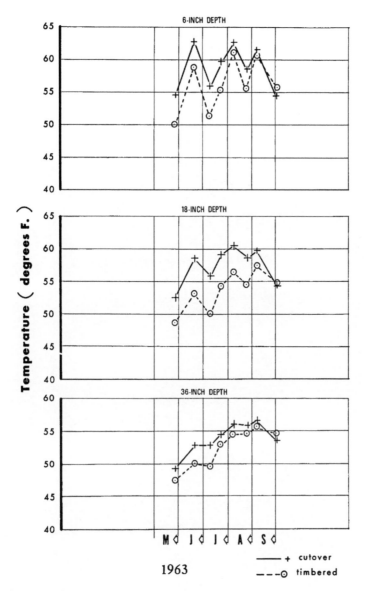

Figure 6.--Soil temperature in cutover and adjacent timber in southwest Oregon, 1963.

-11-

FOREST AND RANGE EXPERIMENT STATION · U.S. DEPARTMENT OF AGRICULTURE · PORTLAND, OREGON

PNW-57

TWO SIMPLE, TIME-SAVING TECHNIQUES
for studies of
SOIL MICRO-ORGANISMS [1]

J. L. Neal, Jr., K. C. Lu, W. B. Bollen, and J. M. Trappe

With the variety of highly sophisticated instruments now available for research, inexpensive materials are easily overlooked and are often not even reported in the literature. We have devised some simple techniques that greatly reduce the time and tedium of standard procedures in research on soil micro-organisms.

SPREADING SOIL DILUTIONS ON AGAR PLATES

After samples of soil or the rhizosphere are taken and diluted by traditional methods, aliquots of the diluted suspension can be spread over the surface of hardened agar plates for counting or isolating pure cultures of soil micro-organisms.[2] Sterile glass rods, bent at right angles into a loop with a flat side, serve well to spread the suspension evenly (fig. 1). The ease and efficiency of this operation can be markedly increased, moreover, if the agar plates are revolved on a turntable while the rod is held in a fixed position, rather than the rod itself being moved.

---

[1] Text is derived from "Two simple, time-saving techniques for studies of soil microbial populations and subsequent culture characterization" by the same authors, published in Soil Biology--Int. News Bull., Comm. III, Int. Soc. Soil Sci., No. 6, p. 38. Dec. 1966. The information is being reissued in this note so that it will be available to a wider audience and illustrations can be included.

[2] Johnson, Leander F., Curl, Elroy A., Bond, John H., and Fribourg, Henry A. Methods for studying soil microflora-plant disease relationships. 178 pp. Minneapolis: Burgess Publ. Co. 1959.

Figure 1.--Spreading an aliquot of
soil-water suspension on agar
surface with aid of glass rod
and modified spring-operated
phonograph turntable.

A variable speed phonograph has proved ideal for this purpose
(fig. 1). A circular, velvet-lined, wooden mount was fashioned with
a lip 7 mm. high to hold a standard-sized petri dish. The mount was
attached to the spindle of the phonograph turntable.

In use, an inoculated plate is placed on the turntable, the
phonograph motor switched on, and the rod held still against the agar
surface. As the petri dish revolves under the rod, the suspension is
spread evenly over the agar surface with minimal effort. When hundreds
of plates are being spread, this technique spares both time and sore
wrists! A hand-operated petri dish spinner is now commercially available.

Before use, the agar plates should be dried 8-12 hours at 37° C.
to minimize spread of motile bacteria over the agar surface after
inoculation. For best results, the liquid inoculum should be placed
near the center of the plate.

ISOLATING PURE CULTURES FROM DILUTION PLATES

Once colonies develop on the agar surface of dilution plates, further time can be saved by using pointed, white birch[3] toothpicks for obtaining pure cultures of individual organisms. The toothpicks are autoclaved in a petri dish and removed from the sterile dish with sterile tweezers as needed to probe a colony on the agar surface (fig. 2). The whole toothpick is then immersed in a tube of enriched nutrient broth, which is then stirred with a vortex mixer and incubated. After suitable incubation, aliquots are examined for purity and transferred to the rapid replicator[4] for study of the organism's physiological characteristics.

When hundreds of organisms are under simultaneous study, as is often the case in extensive research on the rhizosphere, these simple techniques and low-cost materials can yield large dividends in saved time and reduced fatigue.

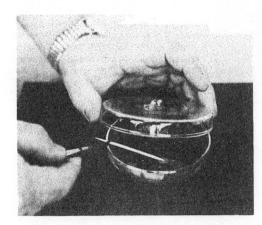

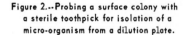
Figure 2.--Probing a surface colony with a sterile toothpick for isolation of a micro-organism from a dilution plate.

---

[3] White birch is not necessary, but woods such as cedar may be somewhat toxic to bacteria.

[4] Neal, J. L., Jr., Lu, K. C., Bollen, W. B., and Trappe, J. M. Apparatus for rapid replica plating in rhizosphere studies. Appl. Microbiol. 14: 695-696, illus. 1966.

Cle

.

AERIAL PHOTO INTERPRETATION OF UNDERSTORIES
IN TWO OREGON OAK STANDS[1]

by

H. Gyde Lund,[2] *George R. Fahnestock,*[2] *and John F. Wear*[3]

Aerial color photography has shown promise for evaluating under-story vegetation as a forest-fire fuel. Mapping understory vegetation from special aerial photography produced results reasonably similar to those obtained by an independent ground check. Differences in the methods used in the exploratory work prevented strict comparability, but agreement was close enough to suggest that further study would be fruitful. Perfection of photographic and interpretive techniques will improve ability to scout going fires and to map fuels for planning fire control systems. Information on visibility and trafficability in timber stands will be a side benefit.

In mid-July 1966, two hardwood stands in northwestern Oregon were photographed with Ektachrome Aero and Ektachrome Infrared Aero films[4]

---

[1] Sponsored by Advanced Research Projects Agency, Remote Area Conflict, ARPA Order 818. This Research Note is a condensation of the final progress report, dated December 30, 1966, on file at the Pacific Northwest Forest and Range Experiment Station, Portland, Oreg.

The authors gratefully acknowledge the aid of W. G. Morris in locating study areas and making the ground observations.

[2] Research foresters, Pacific Northwest Forest and Range Experiment Station, Portland, Oreg.

[3] Forester, Remote-Sensing Project, Pacific Southwest Forest and Range Experiment Station, Berkeley, Calif.

[4] Mention of trade names or products does not imply endorsement by the Forest Service.

at scales of 1:2,000 and 1:3,500. The photographs were taken with a Fairchild K-17 camera having a 12-inch focal length and 9- by 9-inch format. Most of the resulting photography was of excellent quality with near-maximum detail in crown shadows.

The dominant vegetation of the two stands was Oregon white oak averaging 60 feet tall, with scattered bigleaf maple, Pacific madrone, Oregon ash, and Douglas-fir. Crown closure was somewhat varied but averaged 92 percent on both areas. Understory vegetation varied rather widely in height and density. All of the woody understory was deciduous; the most important species were California hazel, Pacific serviceberry, Pacific dogwood, rose, trailing blackberry, and Pacific poisonoak. The most conspicuous herbaceous plant was western swordfern, an evergreen.

Topography consisted of dissected slopes, seldom exceeding 30 percent, between major valley bottoms and the gently rolling uplands. Total relief was about 300 feet. One area (Gray Farm) had a general southerly aspect; the other (Muddy Valley) faced east.

Gray Farm was used as a test site for selecting imagery and photo interpretation techniques to be applied on the Muddy Valley area. Photos were interpreted in the office and then taken to the field to compare with actual ground conditions. Ektachrome Aero photography at 1:3,500 was best for identifying and mapping the understory vegetation as to height and density (understory crown closure). Overstory shadows on the infrared photos were too dark to let the understory be seen adequately. Had the overstory been less dense or shorter, the infrared would have been more useful. The 1:2,000 photography had greater parallax displacement that was a hindrance to interpretation. A photo interpretation guide was developed for use with the Muddy Valley photography:

Photo characteristics	Indication
Overstory dense, uniform in spacing and color. Light-brown patches beneath canopy.	No brush beneath.
Overstory dense, uniform in spacing and color. Shadows deep; occasional green showing from ground.	Small scattered patches of brush.
Overstory with rough or feathery appearance. Shadows interrupted by various heights and shades of green to ground.	Tall and mixed brush beneath. The rougher the appearance, the taller and denser the brush.
Conglomeration of different shades of green. Heights uneven. No overstory present.	Brush of medium-to-heavy density and varied heights.

-2-

Examination of the Muddy Valley photos confirmed that Ektachrome Aero at 1:3,500 was better than the other film-scale combinations; therefore, this film and scale were used for the remainder of the study. "Pure" interpretation, i.e., without measurements, was tried first, then aerial reconnaissance in a light, fixed-wing aircraft, and finally photo interpretation with supplementary brush-height measurements.

Pure interpretation developed a technique of stereo "stare" for looking past overstory crowns and concentrating on understory characteristics. Starting at an opening and working into the stand gave better results than trying to peer down through the crowns at any one point. Caution is necessary with this method to avoid "forcing" portions of the overstory to the ground. Such forcing can give a false impression of brush where there is none or of bare ground where bare branches occur. The main disadvantage of the pure interpretation was absence of any reliable estimate of brush height.

After the initial photography, aerial reconnaissance was tried to see if the area could be mapped from a fixed-wing aircraft and to evaluate heavily shaded areas that were impossible to interpret from the photos--north-facing slopes and areas under dense maple patches. The plane, even when flying at a speed of only 60 m.p.h. and at 100 feet above the canopy, moved too fast for practical mapping. Flying into the shadows, i.e., north to south, allowed more to be seen than did flying with or across the shadows. Some understory species could be recognized but could not be accurately located. As it was rather late in the year (September), shadows were long even at noon, and the north-facing slopes were still difficult to penetrate.

Photo interpretation with supplementary photo height measurements was finally used to produce a map of the understory by five height and three density classes (fig. 1, upper). This was compared with results of a reconnaissance on the ground.

The ground reconnaissance was made by a forester familiar with the vegetation and the study area but not with the aerial photographs. He did not make a map, but classified the understory at intervals along several irregular traverses, using the same categories as for photo interpretation (fig. 1, lower). In all, 89 points were rated and recorded on black-and-white prints in the field (a "point" actually was an area about one-half chain in diameter). However, accidents in handling the photos reduced the record to 68 points with both height and density, 19 with density only and 2 with height only.

Conclusive verification of photo interpretation by means of on-the-ground observations was not possible. Points rated on the ground might be obscured on the photographs or might be considered too small for separate mapping by the photo interpreter. Nevertheless, the mapped area ratings agreed reasonably well with the point ratings (table 1).

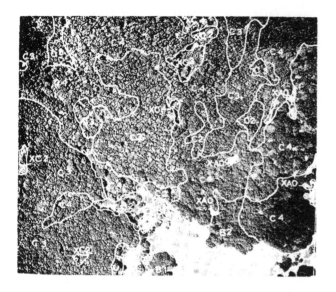

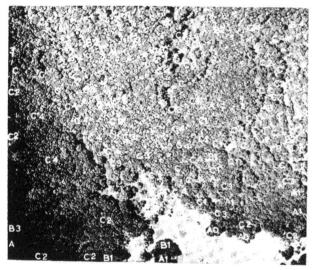

LEGEND

Understory height
(feet):

    0 = 0 to 1
    1 = 1 to 5
    2 = 5 to 10
    3 = 10 to 15
    4 = 15+

Understory density
(percent):

    A = 0 to 33
    B = 33 to 66
    C = 66 to 100
    X = Overstory
        absent

Figure 1.--Comparison of photo interpretation of Muddy Valley
area with ground truth.   *Upper,* type map drawn from photo
interpretation supplemented by understory height measurements.
Lower, independent point determination by observer on ground.
Scale, 1:3,500.

Table 1.--Comparison of photographic and on-the-ground

ratings in aerial photo interpretation of

two Oregon oak stands

Information recorded	Total points	Ratings in agreement	
	Number	Number	Percent
Height and density	68	26	38
Density	87	65	75
Height	70	32	46

The greatest discrepancy resulted from a strong tendency to overestimate height on the aerial photos. Of 38 cases of disagreement, heights were overcalled in 32, undercalled in only 6. However, 61 percent of the discrepant estimates were only one height class above or below that determined on the ground. The tendency was to overestimate density also in comparison with ground observations. Of 22 cases of disagreement, 87 percent were overcalled, 13 percent undercalled, and 82 percent were within one density class.

The results of this exploratory study indicate that understory vegetation can be interpreted from natural-color aerial photography. Density was estimated reasonably well on the first attempt, but more work is needed in determining heights. Crown closure of about 90 percent was the limit; in denser canopies, openings large enough to give a good view of the understory are too scarce. Accuracy and reliability of interpretation should increase as the overstory density decreases. With the K-17 camera, a scale of 1:3,500 is the largest that can be interpreted comfortably and effectively.

A quick trial of 1:20,000 photography on Gray Farm revealed some advantages of the smaller scale for interpreting general understory features. Future research should determine whether a scale smaller than 1:3,500, with its added economies, will be suitable for detailed interpretation. A scale larger than 1:2,000 with either a high-speed camera or one with a smaller format would be needed to identify understory species. Low-altitude, fixed-base-length photography of small areas, using synchronized cameras mounted on a helicopter, may provide a means of double sampling when used in conjunction with small-scale

coverage of the entire area. Film-exposure combinations should be
tested to obtain optimum shadow penetration. Interpretation and
ground truth techniques should be designed to compare the same points
and areas.

* * *

FOREST AND RANGE EXPERIMENT STATION · U.S. DEPARTMENT OF AGRICULTURE · PORTLAND, OREGON

PNW-59   *July 1967*

BOARD-FOOT TREE VOLUME TABLES AND EQUATIONS
FOR WHITE SPRUCE
IN INTERIOR ALASKA

by

Wilbur A. Farr, *Associate Research Mensurationist*
Institute of Northern Forestry

INTRODUCTION

The board-foot volume tables and equations, presented here for white spruce (*Picea glauca* (Moench) Voss), supplement cubic-foot volume tables published earlier.[1] They were made primarily for use in white spruce growth and yield studies,[2] but are suitable for other uses such as timber sales, management plans, and forest inventory. These tables differ from those prepared by Haack (1963)[3] in that volumes are estimated to a fixed top diameter of 6 inches inside bark rather than to a merchantable top. Also, the basic data consist of measurements of nearly twice as many trees.

---

[1] Gregory, Robert A., and Haack, Paul M. Equations and tables for estimating cubic-foot volume of interior Alaska tree species. U.S. Forest Serv. Res. Note NOR-6, 21 pp. 1964.

[2] Farr, Wilbur A. Growth and yield of well-stocked white spruce stands in Alaska. (In preparation for publication. Pacific Northwest Forest & Range Exp. Sta., Inst. North. Forest., U.S. Forest Serv., Juneau, Alaska.)

[3] Haack, Paul M., Jr. Volume tables for trees of interior Alaska. U.S. Forest Serv. Res. Note NOR-5, 11 pp. 1963.

METHODS

The basic data used in constructing these tables and equations were obtained from 309 trees larger than 8.5 inches in diameter at breast height (D), and ranging in height (H) from 40 to 120 feet. Nearly all were from well- or moderately well-stocked stands; few open-grown trees were included in the basic data. The majority were from north of the Alaska Range.

The International 1/4-inch and Scribner rules for 16-foot logs[4] were used to compute board-foot volumes of the sample trees. Volumes were computed from a 1-foot stump to a 6-inch top inside bark.

Predictor equations for V_4 (volume, International 1/4-inch rule) and V_5 (volume, Scribner rule) were determined by stepwise regression analysis.[5] Variables were tested by unweighted and weighted regression, as described by Gregory and Haack.[6] Weighting proved helpful in both board-foot equations. Efficiency of weighted vs. unweighted regression was 1.06 for International 1/4-inch rule volume and 1.13 for Scribner rule volume. Merging did not take place within the range of tabular values.

The weighted equations used and their precision are given in footnote 1 of each volume table.

---

[4] Plus 0.3-foot trim allowance.

[5] Dixon, W. J., ed. Biomedical computer programs. Sch. Med., Dep. Prev. Med. Public Health, 620 pp., illus. Los Angeles: University of California. 1965.

[6] See footnote 1.

Table 1.—Board-foot tree volumes (1-foot stump to 6-inch top), International 1/4-inch rule, for white spruce, interior Alaska[1]

D.b.h.[2] (inches)	Total height (in feet)[3]																				Basis: trees measured[4]
	30	35	40	45	50	55	60	65	70	75	80	85	90	95	100	105	110	115	120	125	
9	42	43	44	45	46	47	48	49	51	52	53	54	55	56	57	58					26
10	48	51	53	56	59	62	64	67	70	73	75	78	81	84	86	89					35
11	53	57	62	67	71	76	81	85	90	94	99	104	108	113	117	122					35
12		64	71	77	84	90	97	104	110	117	124	130	137	144	150	157	163				39
13		70	79	88	97	105	114	123	132	141	150	158	167	176	185	194	203	211			48
14		76	87	98	109	121	132	143	154	165	177	188	199	210	222	233	244	255	266	276	31
15		81	95	109	122	136	150	164	178	191	205	219	233	246	260	274	288	301	315	328	25
16			103	119	136	152	169	185	202	218	235	251	268	284	301	317	334	350	367	382	17
17			111	130	149	169	188	208	227	246	266	285	305	324	343	363	382	402	421	439	18
18				141	163	186	208	231	253	276	298	321	343	366	388	411	433	456	478	499	12
19					177	203	229	254	280	306	332	357	383	409	435	460	486	512	538	562	7
20					191	221	250	279	308	337	367	396	425	454	483	513	542	571	600	628	6
21							272	304	337	370	403	436	469	501	534	567	600	633	665	697	3
22							294	331	367	404	441	477	514	550	587	624	660	697	733	768	2
23									398	439	479	520	561	601	642	682	723	763	804	843	--
24									430	475	520	564	609	654	699	743	788	833	877	921	2
25											561	610	659	708	757	807	856	905	954	1,001	1
26											604	658	711	765	818	872	925	979	1,033	1,085	1
27											649	707	765	823	881	940	998	1,056	1,114	1,171	--
28											694	757	820	883	946	1,010	1,073	1,136	1,199	1,260	--
29											741	809	877	946	1,014	1,082	1,150	1,218	1,286	1,353	--
30											790	863	936	1,009	1,083	1,156	1,229	1,303	1,376	1,448	--
31											839	918	997	1,075	1,154	1,233	1,311	1,390	1,469	1,546	--
32											891	975	1,059	1,143	1,227	1,312	1,396	1,480	1,564	1,647	1

[1] Table volumes obtained from weighted regression equation: $V_4 = 26.211 + 8.4254D - 0.73439D^2 - 1.2126H + 0.017629D^2H - \frac{575.27}{D^2}$, where V_4 = volume, International 1/4-inch rule; D = diameter at breast height; H = height. Standard error or estimate = 20.3 bd. ft. or 11.68 percent of the mean volume.

[2] Midpoint of class (e.g., 12 = 11.6 through 12.5 inches).

[3] Midpoint of class (e.g., 70 = 67.6 through 72.5 feet).

[4] Lines contain basic data for 309 measured trees used for computing regression equation.

Table 2.—Board-foot tree volumes (1-foot stump to 6-inch top), Scribner rule, for white spruce, interior Alaska[1]

D.b.h.[2] (inches)	Total height (in feet)[3]																				Basis: trees measured[4]
	30	35	40	45	50	55	60	65	70	75	80	85	90	95	100	105	110	115	120	125	
9	31	32	32	33	34	34	35	35	36	37	37	38	38	39	40	40					26
10	35	37	39	41	43	46	48	50	52	54	56	58	61	63	65	67					35
11	38	42	46	50	54	58	61	65	69	73	77	81	84	88	92	96					35
12		47	53	59	64	70	76	81	87	93	98	104	110	115	121	127	132	138			39
13		52	60	67	75	83	91	98	106	114	121	129	137	144	152	160	167	175			48
14		57	67	77	86	96	106	116	126	136	146	156	165	175	185	195	205	215	225	234	31
15		62	74	86	98	110	123	135	147	159	171	184	196	208	220	232	245	257	269	280	25
16			81	96	110	125	140	154	169	184	199	213	228	243	257	272	287	301	316	330	17
17			88	106	123	140	158	175	192	210	227	244	262	279	297	314	331	349	366	382	18
18				116	136	156	176	197	217	237	257	277	297	318	338	358	378	398	419	438	12
19					150	173	196	219	242	265	288	312	335	358	381	404	427	451	474	496	7
20					164	190	216	242	269	295	321	348	374	400	427	453	479	506	532	557	6
21							237	267	296	326	356	385	415	445	474	504	533	563	593	621	3
22							259	292	325	358	391	425	458	491	524	557	590	623	656	688	2
23									355	392	429	465	502	539	575	612	649	686	722	758	--
24									386	427	467	508	548	589	629	670	710	751	791	831	2
25											507	552	596	641	685	730	774	818	863	906	1
26											549	598	646	695	743	792	840	889	937	985	1
27											592	645	698	750	803	856	909	962	1,015	1,066	--
28											637	694	751	808	865	923	980	1,037	1,094	1,158	--
29											682	744	806	868	930	992	1,053	1,115	1,177	1,238	--
30											730	796	863	930	996	1,063	1,129	1,196	1,263	1,328	--
31											778	850	922	993	1,065	1,136	1,208	1,279	1,351	1,422	--
32											829	906	982	1,059	1,135	1,212	1,288	1,365	1,442	1,518	1

[1] Table volumes obtained from weighted regression equation: $V_5 = 39.710 + 4.2659D - 0.58865D^2 - 1.1184H + 0.016113D^2H - \dfrac{437.92}{D^2}$, where

V_5 = volume, Scribner rule; D = diameter at breast height; H = height. Standard error of estimate = 17.3 bd. ft. or 11.76 percent of the mean volume.

[2] Midpoint of class (e.g., 12 = 11.6 through 12.5 inches).

[3] Midpoint of class (e.g., 70 = 67.6 through 72.5 feet).

[4] Lines contain basic data for 309 trees used for computing regression equation.

-4-

FROST DEPTH IN FOREST SOILS NEAR JUNEAU, ALASKA

by

J. H. Patric, *Research Hydrologist*
Institute of Northern Forestry

INTRODUCTION

Freezing drastically changes soil-water relations. During freezing, water crystallizes to ice, setting up tension and thermal gradients and pulling water from surrounding moist soil. Other frost effects include changes in soil structure, rupture of plant tissue, and redistribution of soil moisture. Frost-heaved seedlings are a consequence of ice crystal growth well known to foresters. Pierce, Lull, and Storey (1958)[1] recently summarized American literature on forest soil freezing showing, in addition, the generally ameliorating effects of forest litter and canopy on soil freezing in forests of Northeastern United States. Frost penetration has not been measured in old-growth western hemlock-Sitka spruce forests, widespread over southeast Alaska. Although limited in scope, the following frost measurements help fill this gap in the forest literature of southeast Alaska and add to our knowledge of water behavior in local forest soils.

THE STUDY AREA

A small logging operation 5 miles north of Juneau provided a convenient study area. Typical of the region's old-growth forest, the stand was about 80 percent western hemlock, 20 percent Sitka spruce. Trees ranged in height from 75 to 120 feet, in diameter from 18 to 48 inches, with basal area about 250 square feet per acre. The logged

---

[1] Names and dates in parentheses refer to Literature Cited, p. 7.

area was clearcut 3 years ago, leaving much slash scattered about, but the litter-covered forest floor was little disturbed. A primitive logging road (fig. 1) was built on bare soil and maintained more or less snow-free by logging throughout the period of frost observation.

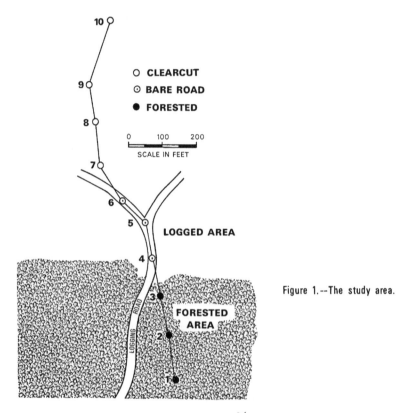

Figure 1.--The study area.

The soil is well-drained Tuxekan[2/] loam gently sloping about 10 percent northwest. A 6- to 8-inch layer of moss and litter covers a bleached, gray A_2 horizon 1 to 2 inches deep. An 18- to 24-inch B horizon is splotchy, reddish brown, and iron stained, overlying loose, water-deposited sand and gravel.

[2/] Tentative name pending final correlation by the U.S. Soil Conservation Service.

METHOD

A plot transect was established as shown in figure 1, permitting frost sampling over a course of similar soil and slope. Starting on November 12, 1965, depth of soil freezing was observed at biweekly intervals during periods of rapid change, at monthly intervals during cold weather. Frost depths were observed by scraping away moss and litter, then digging through the frozen mineral soil with mattock and shovel. Because both the upper and lower frozen soil surfaces were irregularly shaped and the mattock holes much wider on top than bottom, frost depth measurements were approximate although recorded to the apparent nearest inch. Observations ended on May 14, 1966

Mean daily air temperatures were published by the U.S. Environmental Science Services Administration (1965-66) for the climatic station at Juneau Airport, 3 miles west of the study area. These data indicate a colder than normal winter; e.g., mean monthly temperature for January was only 8.6° F. compared with the normal of 25.1° F. for the airport.

RESULTS

Frost measurements are shown in table 1 Despite the probability of sampling error, depths of freezing are consistent among cover types. Measurements of December 3 on the road and of February 2 on the clear-cutting showed the only variation greater than 4 inches within cover types. Temperature at the airport and depths of frost and snow on the study area are shown in figure 2. These sampling sites were selected as representative of data from forest, clearcut, and road stations Note that during November and December soils froze rapidly in the bare road, less rapidly on clearcut plots. The forest plots froze very little, then thawed completely during warm weather in mid-December. During this early winter period, concrete frost (Post and Dreibelbis 1942) formed in the road, honeycomb frost in forested and clearcut soils. Granular frost (Hale 1950) was always found in litter above frozen mineral soil but was not included in these data.

Snow accumulation also influenced frost formation. Concrete frost quickly moved deeply into road plots, most of which were maintained almost snow-free throughout the winter. Maximum frost depth was not measured in the stony, frozen, road soil, but freezing to 18 inches was noted in nearby road construction. Deepest freezing was expected in roads, Kersten (1949) having observed that thermal conductivity of Alaska soils increases with density. Interception losses of snow were evidenced by lesser accumulations on forest plots (fig. 2). Note that heavy snow accumulations terminated frost penetration. Honeycomb frost was noted in forested and litter-covered plots on December 17; concrete frost, in all plots on December 30 and thereafter. Although air temperature increased steadily after mid-January, it remained below freezing until mid-March. During this time, insulation by snow maintained

Table 1.--Thickness of frozen soil near Juneau, Alaska, during the winter of 1965—66

Cover	Station	Nov. 12	Nov. 17	Dec. 3	Dec. 17	Dec. 30	Jan. 10	Feb. 2	Feb. 25	Mar. 26	Apr. 4	Apr. 29	May 9	May 14
								Inches						
Forested	1	0	1/2	0	0	10	12	15	12	5	10	1/5	1/3	0
Forested	2	0	1/2	1-1/2	0	8	11	15	8	6	6	1/9	1/4	0
Forested	3	1/2	1	1/2	0	6	12	11	12	8	8	1/6	0	0
Bare road	4	1	8	11	(2/)	--	--	--	--	--	(3/)	(4/)	0	0
Bare road	5	0	7	6	(2/)	--	--	--	--	--	(3/)	(4/)	(5/)	0
Bare road	6	0	8	1	1	>8	(2/)	--	--	--	(3/)	(4/)	(5/)	0
Clearcut	7	0	2	2	1/2	8	12	16	15	9	8	0	0	0
Clearcut	8	1	4	4	2	8	8	10	12	--	6	0	0	0
Clearcut	9	1	5	5	4	7	12	18	12	10	9	1/5	0	0
Clearcut	10	1	2	5	3	8	12	--	--	--	--	1/1	0	0

1/ Frozen soil thawing on both surfaces.
2/ Road surfaces frozen, partly cleared of snow, used for logging. Frost depths were not measured when roads were in use.
3/ 3 inches of mud overlying soil frozen to unknown depth.
4/ 14 inches of mud overlying soil frozen to unknown depth.
5/ 16 inches of mud overlying soil frozen to unknown depth.

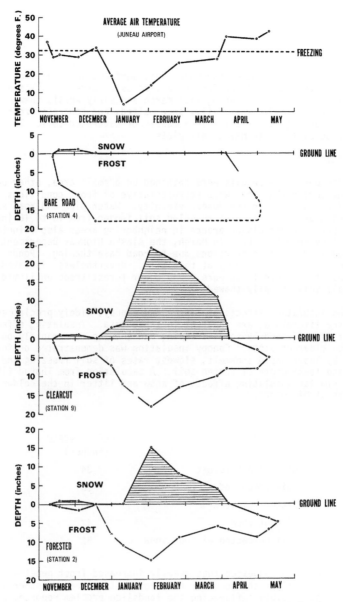

Figure 2.--Air temperature, snow accumulation, and depth of soil freezing under three conditions of soil cover.

subfreezing conditions on the upper soil surface, but heat from within the earth thawed the lower frozen surface as reported from Wisconsin by Bay et al. (1952). During late March and early April, thawing temperatures occurred almost daily, snow melted, and concrete frost became a loose mass of ice crystals in a matrix of saturated soil. This condition persisted into May on all plots.

DISCUSSION

Although these results were obtained on a small area, other observations verify that they were representative of frost conditions in well-drained soils in the Juneau vicinity. Water pipe and road excavations near the study area revealed soil frozen from 16 to 18 inches in January. Frost disappearance in neighboring areas also coincided with study results. Late in March, the Alaska Highway Department imposed load limit restrictions due to road base thawing. Ponds of snowmelt water drained away at this time. Nevertheless, isolated patches of concrete frost were found under forest trees until mid-May when all soils finally thawed.

The insulating effects of litter and canopy, widely proclaimed in forestry literature, are apparent in these data. Insulating effect of litter is evidenced by soils freezing and thawing more rapidly on roads than on clearcut plots. Canopy insulation was demonstrated on forest plots by least rapid snowmelt, slowest rates of soil freezing and thawing, and least depth of frozen soil. A tabulation from Thorud (1965) shows similar insulating effects of snow and litter in the colder winters of Minnesota:

Soil treatment	Freezing depth (inches)
Natural oak forest	34
Soil compacted	36
Litter removed	39
Without snow	47
Soil compacted without snow	52

It has been suggested that greatly increased frost penetration after logging might change water relations, structure, or other soil properties, possibly influencing the landslide problem reported by Bishop and Stevens (1964). It now seems unlikely that clearcut soils can be expected to freeze much deeper than forested soils. In this study, frost penetrated only 4 inches deeper on clearcut than on forested plots. Even less difference seems likely during warmer winters characteristic of the region.

6

LITERATURE CITED

Bay, Clyde E., Wunnecke, George W., and Hays, Orville E.
    1952. Frost penetration into soils as influenced by depth of
        snow, vegetative cover, and air temperatures. Amer.
        Geophys. Union Trans. 33: 541-546.

Bishop, Daniel M., and Stevens, Mervin E.
    1964. Landslides on logged areas in southeast Alaska. U.S. Forest
        Serv. Res. Pap. NOR-1, 18 pp., illus.

Hale, Charles E.
    1950. Some observations on soil freezing in forest and range lands
        of the Pacific Northwest. U.S. Forest Serv. Pacific North-
        west Forest & Range Exp. Sta Res. Note 66, 17 pp.

Kersten, Miles S.
    1949. Laboratory research for the determination of the thermal
        properties of soils. Univ. Minn. Eng. Exp. Sta., 228 pp.,
        illus.

Pierce, Robert S., Lull, Howard W., and Storey, Herbert C.
    1958. Influence of land use and forest condition on soil freezing
        and snow depth. Forest Sci. 4: 246-263, illus.

Post, F. A., and Dreibelbis, F. R.
    1942. Some influences of frost penetration and microclimate on
        the water relationships of woodland, pasture, and cultivated
        soils. Soil Sci. Soc. Amer. Proc. 7: 95-104, illus.

Thorud, David Bruce.
    1965. The effect of snow, litter, and soil compaction on the soil
        frost regime in a Minnesota oak stand. Diss. Abstr.
        26(2): 600.

U.S. Environmental Science Services Administration.
    1965-66. Local climatological data, Juneau, Alaska (Nov.-May).

Lightning Source UK Ltd.
Milton Keynes UK
UKHW05f0243180918
329045UK00028B/848/P